W9-CXQ-018

Programming Games
for Beginners

Christopher A. Howard

Programming Games for Beginners

SAMS
PUBLISHING

To my children,
who show an enthusiasm for playing
computer games that will hopefully one
day extend into programming.

Copyright ©1993 by Sams Publishing

FIRST EDITION

All rights reserved. No part of this book shall be reproduced, stored in a retrieval system, or transmitted by any means, electronic, mechanical, photocopying, recording, or otherwise, without written permission from the publisher. No patent liability is assumed with respect to the use of the information contained herein. Although every precaution has been taken in the preparation of this book, the publisher and author assume no responsibility for errors or omissions. Neither is any liability assumed for damages resulting from the use of the information contained herein. For information, address Sams Publishing, 11711 N. College Ave., Carmel, IN 46032.

International Standard Book Number: 0-672-30313-2

Library of Congress Catalog Card Number: 92-82102

96 95 94 93   4 3 2 1

Interpretation of the printing code: the rightmost double-digit number is the year of the book's printing; the rightmost single-digit, the number of the book's printing. For example, a printing code of 93-1 shows that the first printing of the book occurred in 1993.

Composed in Palatino and MCPdigital by Prentice Hall Computer Publishing

Printed in the United States of America

Trademarks

All terms mentioned in this book that are known to be trademarks or service marks have been appropriately capitalized. Sams Publishing cannot attest to the accuracy of this information. Use of a term in this book should not be regarded as affecting the validity of any trademark or service mark.

IBM is a registered trademark of International Business Machines Corporation.

Microsoft, MS-DOS, Microsoft BASIC, and BASICA are registered trademarks of Microsoft Corporation.

QuickBASIC, Visual Basic, and Windows are trademarks of Microsoft Corporation.

Publisher
Richard K. Swadley

Assistant Publisher
Jordan Gold

Acquisitions Manager
Stacy Hiquet

Development Editor
Scott Palmer

Senior Editor
Tad Ringo

Production Editor
Keith Davenport

Copy Editor
Mary Inderstrodt

Editorial Coordinator
Bill Whitmer

Editorial Assistants
Sharon Cox
Molly Carmody

Technical Reviewer
Bill Hatfield

Marketing Manager
Greg Wiegand

Cover Designer
Dan Armstrong

**Director of Production
and Manufacturing**
Jeff Valler

Imprint Manager
Kelli Widdifield

Book Designer
Michele Laseau

Production Analyst
Mary Beth Wakefield

Proofreading/Indexing Coordinator
Joelynn Gifford

Graphics Image Specialists
Teresa Forrester
Tim Montgomery
Dennis Sheehan
Sue VandeWalle

Production
Lisa Daugherty
Carla Hall
Linda Koopman
Sean Medlock
Mike Mucha
Wendy Ott
Juli Pavey
Linda Quigley
Tonya Simpson
Dennis Wesner
Alyssa Yesh

Indexer
Joy Dean Lee

Overview

Contents

The Basics of Game Programming

Marketing Your Games

Appendixes

Acknowledgments

I would like to thank everyone at Sams Publishing for their help in bringing this book from my computer keyboard into its final form. Although only my name appears on the cover, it takes many people working together to publish a book—thank you.

Thanks also to Scott Murray, for allowing me to interview him about his shareware experience.

Lastly, I would like to thank my wife, Jill, and my five children—Ryan, Lacey, Tyler, Corey and Kyle—who sacrificed some of their time with me while I wrote this book. Thanks for your patience and understanding.

About the Author

Chris Howard is founder and President of Genus Microprogramming, Inc., a developer and publisher of graphics programming toolkits. His background includes mechanical drafting, electrical engineering, and programming in numerous languages. His articles have been featured in many programming magazines, including *Programmer's Journal*, *Microcornucopia*, and *Dr. Dobb's Journal*, and he has appeared several times on local TV computer shows. Although he has written ten programming manuals for software products, this is his first book.

Introduction

BASIC and games have gone hand-in-hand since the very beginning of personal computers. When Microsoft tested its first BASIC interpreter on the Altair (one of the very first computer kits), the program it ran was a version of LANDER—a lunar lander game. Previous versions of BASIC have always been used to write games. Users had easy access to Interpreted BASIC (shipped with every IBM PC), which was simple to learn and had a surprising amount of features necessary for game development: PC speaker sound, joystick support, graphics, events, and more. The first program most people write in BASIC is a game, because it's ultimately more fun than writing a mortgage program! It's my guess that more games have been written in BASIC than any other language (for personal use, anyway).

The early forms of BASIC were great for writing games, and Visual Basic is no exception. Using the power and ease of Visual Basic and the resources of the Microsoft Windows environment, you have the potential to write outstanding games. A good game puts your programming powers to the test. This book is designed to help you sharpen your newly found (or preexisting) skills—and provide you with some fun along the way.

The only thing better than having fun is having fun and getting paid for it, too! This book also provides information to help you market what you write.

Audience

This book can be used by users and programmers of all skill levels:

- If you are a Windows user or game buff, there are a dozen ready-to-play Windows games (no programming required!).

- If you're new to Visual Basic, the information and programming examples help you learn more about Visual Basic in an enjoyable way.

- If you are a game hobbyist, you will learn many valuable tips, tricks, and techniques for writing Windows games—and maybe make some money doing it.

- If you're a game developer, perhaps there are some things in here that you don't already know!

Regardless of your skill level, I believe you will benefit from reading this book.

Requirements

I assume that you have run and used Windows, and that you have Visual Basic 2.0 or above (and have at least played with it some). The standard edition is fine—this book doesn't require any of the professional extensions and won't teach you the basics of using Windows or Visual Basic. If you need more information, you can buy an additional book such as *Do-It-Yourself Visual Basic for Windows* by William J. Orvis, also published by Sams Publishing.

The system requirements for playing this book's games are the same as those for running Windows 3.1 or above—in standard or enhanced mode. However, you will need a mouse (or other cursor-control device). A 386-based computer with a VGA color adapter and display is ideal, but not necessary.

Obviously, you'll need Microsoft Windows 3.1 or above to play the games. You'll also need Visual Basic 2.0 or above to load the game source code.

> You do not need Visual Basic or the game source code in order to play the games included with this book.

That's all the hardware and software you need. You can load and modify images with the Paintbrush program supplied with Windows. You also can create and adjust icons with the example programs (such as IconWorks) provided with Visual Basic. The documentation on Windows API calls is provided in Appendix B.

Oh... you need a desire to learn and have a good time doing it, of course!

Book Overview

This overview will help you get the most out of this book. The book is divided into three sections covering the basics of game programming, game exercises, and game marketing.

Part I: The Basics of Game Programming

Chapter 1 covers programming conventions used throughout the games in this book. This brief chapter is definitely worth reading. It will assist you when reading the programming examples and the game source code.

Chapters 2 through 9 describe programming techniques I use in the book and games. I cover such concepts as input and output, animation, sound, files, and computer "thinking" in detail. To peek into future gaming possibilities, read my discussions about advanced concepts. If you only are interested in playing the games—skip those discussions. For programmers, though, this is where all of the goodies are kept.

Part II: Exercises in Game Programming

Chapters 10 through 18 cover each of this book's specific games: puzzle games, card games, board games, and arcade games. Each game chapter includes game instructions, program listings (unless the listings are on disk), form diagrams, programming techniques used, code descriptions, and suggestions for improvement. To play the games, read the description and game instruction sections.

Part III: Marketing Your Games

Chapters 19 and 20 discuss program protection and distribution. Here, you can learn how to get paid for writing and playing games! These final chapters help you put your program into a final package. Perhaps you will be able to profit from your entertainment.

Appendixes

Appendix A covers the installation of the games and game source code, along with the joystick and PC Speaker drivers. Appendix B provides a complete description of the Windows API functions used in this book.

Source Code Listings

The full source code for each game is listed either in this book and/or on the enclosed disk for your reference. The following information is included for every game:

- ➡ A table listing the files that make up the game.

- ➡ A labeled image of each form. The labels point out the location of the game controls and their names.

- ➡ A listing of the *nondefault* properties of the form and the controls. These are the properties you must change after creating the control.

- ➡ A listing of the menu design of the game (information that appears in the Menu Design window).

- ➡ An alphabetical listing of the game subroutines and functions.

The listings were generated by saving the forms as text. You can type the games in from the book listings, but it's much easier to install the source from the enclosed disk.

If you do type the listings in, make sure you store a 0 for any icons or images (instead of the filename and offset listed). You can load the icons and images after loading the form.

The source listings appear in some chapters and describe individual games. Each chapter also includes instructions for playing the game, hints, techniques, in-depth code descriptions, and suggestions for improvement.

In order to conserve space, some of the source code for the programs in this book is located only on the disk. When you see the following box and icon

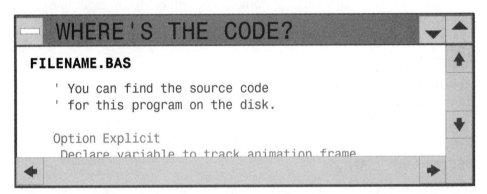

```
WHERE'S THE CODE?

FILENAME.BAS

    ' You can find the source code
    ' for this program on the disk.

    Option Explicit
    Declare variable to track animation frame
```

it means the source code for the file (in this case, FILENAME.BAS) appears on disk only.

If you want to have a printed listing of the file, simply print out the given filename—it's stored as a standard text file. Or, load the appropriate game into Visual Basic and use the Visual Basic Print option.

Conventions Used in This Book

This book uses the following typographic conventions:

➧ Code lines, commands, statements, variables, and any text you see on the screen appear in a computer typeface.

➧ Command output and anything that you type appear in a **bold computer** typeface.

➡ *Italics* highlight technical terms when they first appear in the text, and are sometimes used to emphasize important points.

A monospace font is used for code listings and code examples. The icon (➡) is used to indicate that a line in Visual Basic is too long to fit on the book page and has to be broken. Whenever you see this icon, be sure that you type the broken line of code as one single line. Otherwise, Visual Basic will generate an error message.

Using the Book

For users simply wishing to play the games, read Appendix A, "Installation," which covers game and driver installation. Then, read Part II, "Exercises in Game Programming," which includes descriptions and instructions for the game or games you want to play.

The book has a lot to offer to programmers. If you read the book from front to back, each programming concept and technique will build on the next. This is the preferred method of using the book. But I read a magazine backwards, so what do I know?

You may be anxious to dig right into a particular game—there is nothing wrong with that. Install the games, play each one, and see which ones interest you. You may be interested in the gameplay or in a particular technique used (such as animation). Read the section in Part II concerning that game, and refer to the techniques that the game uses (in Part I).

Whether you read the book forward or backward, or simply skip around, you'll find plenty of tips, tricks, and techniques scattered about. Any way you read it, this book will provide you with plenty of useful information. I hope you have as much fun reading and using this book as I had writing it.

The Basics of Game Programming

Programming Conventions

To write good, readable, and maintainable code, it's necessary to understand some conventions. Although, technically, the formatting of the source code has no effect on the final program, I believe it's important. Sloppy code leads to program inefficiency; six months after writing sloppy code, you might not remember what you were thinking—or know what someone else was thinking. This chapter covers the programming conventions I used when writing the games in this book.

Conventions for Names

What's in a name? Plenty. Specifically, you should be able to differentiate between constants, variables, controls, and files—just by knowing their names. When a name is a variable, you want to know if it is an integer, long integer, or string. This doesn't mean that a variable should have a drawn-out name such as `MyLoopCounterIntegerVariable`—it means you should avoid giving names such as z, zz, and zzz. Filenames also should have naming conventions.

Files

I used a naming scheme for all the source code files in this book. By using a naming scheme for files, you can tell where the file belongs (or what it is) without even loading it. If you have a separate About box form for several different programs, and you name them all ABOUT.FRM, you would have a tough time telling the programs apart.

In this book's games, the makefile names closely match the program names, and the individual forms and files within the makefile begin with a two-letter abbreviation. For example, the name of the makefile for the Puzzler game is PUZZLER.MAK; the name of the File Open form is PZOPEN.FRM.

Constants

Whenever possible, I use a constant instead of a number. I define constants with capital letters so you can distinguish them from variables. There are several advantages to using constants. First, they are more readable. Consider the following code fragment:

```
If ((i% >= 1) And (i% <= 7)) Then ...
```

The significance of 1 and 7 might be clear to you when you write the program, but it might not be clear to you later (or to someone else looking at your code). If you use constants, the statement becomes

```
If ((i% >= MINROW) And (i% <= MAXROW) Then ...
```

which explains exactly what you are doing.

Second, you can easily change a constant. If you use the number 7 in your code to stand for the maximum number of rows, you might use it a dozen or more times. If you suddenly decide to have eight rows in your program, you would get stuck searching thousands of lines of codes for a single-digit number. If you use constants, however, you would just have to make one change and recompile.

Finally, there is no downside to using constants. They don't use any program code or data space, and they don't make your program run any slower.

Variables

In the source code, the `Option Explicit` command is used to prevent automatic variables. This command forces all variables to be declared and acts as a spell checker. Before this command was available, I spent many hours tracking down a bug that turned out to be a typo (such as `GaemOver%` instead of `GameOver%`)!

All variables are declared with the type identifier appended. This convention makes the type of every variable readily apparent and prevents potential programming errors. For instance, `Dim i%` is used instead of `Dim i As Integer`. The common type identifiers are: `%` (integer), `&` (long integer), and `$` (string).

Meaningful variable names are important too. As mentioned, never use variable names like `z`, `zz`, and `z3`. On the other hand, you don't need to get overly descriptive; for example, don't use `ThisVariableCountsLives%`. Following is a list of typical variable names:

➡ `GameOver%`, `Winner%`, `Message$`, `GridColor&` are descriptive

➡ `i%`, `j%`, and `k%` are good for loop counters

➡ `rc%` is good for a return code

Using meaningful variable names improves the readability of your code, just as constants do. A statement like `If (Not GameOver%) Then ...` explains exactly what you are doing.

Controls

Controls are like variables, and you should use the same naming conventions with them. However, I like to distinguish a control from a variable. Control names are prefixed with an abbreviation of the control type. All form names begin with `frm_`, buttons with `btn_`, menus with `mnu_`, images with `img_`, labels with `lbl_`, and so on. This keeps all of the controls of the same type grouped together in the control menu, and it clearly indicates what the control type is. It also shows that the control is not a variable or a constant.

Functions and Subroutines

Function and subroutine names also should be meaningful. I prefer subroutine names like `InitGame` and `MakeMove%` instead of `InGm` or `MkMv`. Functions and procedures also should contain a block of comments above them that explain the purpose of the routine.

Comments

The previous naming conventions go a long way toward producing readable code, but they are no substitute for comments. I believe that you should be able to read the comments and tell what the program is doing every step of the way. This doesn't mean you should use trivial comments such as `Move the value 10 into i%`. Comments such as that are redundant. A better comment is `Begin searching at the tenth row`.

Every line of code does not need a comment, but every block of code does. Just remember that if you change the code, you might have to change the comments too.

Programming

Now that I've covered naming conventions and comments, I need to address code formatting. Even if you have great variable names, it's possible for you to write unreadable code. The following programming conventions help make code easier to read and understand.

Spacing and Indenting

Blank lines are used to separate logical blocks of code and to prevent solid, unending blocks of statements. More importantly, blocks of code are indented two spaces for each code branch. Consider the following two code fragments:

```
For i% = 1 To 10            For i% = 1 To 10
If (i% > 5) Then              If (i% > 5) Then
MyArray%(i%) = 2 * i%           MyArray%(i%) = 2 * i%
Else                           Else
MyArray%(i%) = i%               MyArray%(i%) = i%
End If                         End If
Next i%                     Next i%
```

The fragment on the right is much more readable than the left one, and it clearly indicates which statements are executed by each conditional statement. In a function, statements may be nested many levels deep, so indenting helps keep the code logically organized.

Multiple Lines

Statements are placed one to a line (in keeping with the preceding indentation format). Try reading the following:

```
For i% = 1 To 10: If (i% > 5) Then MyArray%(i%) = 2 * i% Else ...
```

You can see that the line isn't clear.

The only exception to this rule is when you use array initialization (where several array elements are initialized on the same line).

Parentheses

Parentheses should be used to group tests and conditional statements together, specifically in If statements and While loops. To illustrate:

```
If r% >= MINROW And r% <= MAXROW Then ...
```

should be formatted as

```
If ((r% >= MINROW) And (r% <= MAXROW)) Then ...
```

for clarity. This convention becomes even more important when you have more than two conditional statements—should X And Y Or Z be evaluated as ((X And Y) Or Z) or as (X And (Y Or Z))?

Summary

By following the preceding guidelines, you'll not only be able to understand the source code for the games more easily—you'll be able to write better programs. Pick appropriate names for files, constants, variables, and so forth. Comment your code well; and space and indent properly. Write your code as if someone else will read and maintain it. In the end, you'll have a program you can be proud of.

What's Ahead

Now that you have a good programming foundation, I'll show you how to build on it in the upcoming chapters. I'll take you through the steps of handling input, output, animation, sound, and more—all from the perspective of game programming. It's time to get started!

Handling Input

When writing a game, one of the first decisions you need to make is how you'll handle input. Will players use the keyboard for input? Will the game support a mouse? A joystick? All three? Visual Basic takes much of the work out of handling input devices, but you can take advantage of several techniques that I explain in this chapter. I explain keyboard, mouse, and joystick input, and I also discuss useful techniques for handling input from these devices in a game.

The Mouse

The mouse is the primary input device for most Windows applications. As such, it has more flexibility than the other input devices described in this chapter. In this section, I discuss the Visual Basic (VB) mouse procedures, the mouse cursor, and the Windows application program interface (API) mouse functions.

Mouse Procedures

You can detect several mouse events for each form—and for each control you define on that form. However, not all of the following event procedures are present for each control. For instance, a command button only has the `Click` procedure available.

MouseDown, MouseMove, and MouseUp

These procedures are useful when you implement your own "Drag and Drop" method. An object is selected with the MouseDown event, moved during MouseMove events, and finally unselected (placed) in a MouseUp event. Of course, Visual Basic already has Drag and Drop built-in—but more on that in Chapter 4, "Animation." These events are also useful when you are processing at the form level, as the Puzzler game does. See Chapter 15, "Puzzler," for an example of using the MouseDown event.

You can use the MouseMove procedure to update the position of an object (such as a spaceship) and use the MouseDown and MouseUp procedures to, for example, fire lasers.

Click and DblClick

Because the Click procedure handles nearly all the controls, it is the most commonly used mouse event. The DblClick (Double Click) procedure is used occasionally. From a programming perspective, most game objects receive input through the Click method.

The Mouse Pointer

The mouse pointer (or cursor) is one of twelve predefined pointer shapes. Although some of these shapes have limited use in a game environment, I have found several of them handy. Table 2.1 shows the twelve pointer shapes.

Table 2.1. Mouse pointer types.

Value	Description
0	Default
1	Arrow
2	Cross
3	I-Beam
4	Icon
5	Size
6	Size NE SW
7	Size N S

Value	Description
8	Size NW SE
9	Size W E
10	Up Arrow
11	Hourglass
12	No Drop

In Visual Basic, you don't have the liberty of defining any mouse cursor you want. If you call the Windows API (defined later in this chapter), Visual Basic resets the pointer as soon as it crosses a VB control. For now, you're stuck with these standard cursor shapes.

The shapes I use in this book's games include the Cross, the Hourglass, and a couple of sizing arrows. Remember, a shape doesn't have to be used for the purpose suggested by its appearance or name. For instance, the No Drop cursor can be used as a Move Not Allowed cursor.

The mouse pointer shape is very useful for providing instant, effortless feedback to the game player. Use the mouse pointer to instantly identify valid moves or to tell the player to wait (while the game is "thinking," perhaps). Just make sure your user knows what the pointer signifies.

Changing Control Pointers

Changing the mouse pointer for a control is extremely easy. If a button on a game board represents a valid move, I can change the mouse cursor to a cross whenever the cursor is over the button. I do this with the following code:

```
' Change the button mouse pointer to a cross
btn_Board.MousePointer = MPCROSS
```

The control btn_Board is a button on the game board, and the constant MPCROSS has a defined value of 2. I could have used the number 2 directly here—but remember (as stated in Chapter 1, "Programming Conventions"), the code has to be readable.

The beauty of this method is that Visual Basic automatically handles changing and restoring the mouse pointer shape. When the mouse cursor is over the button, it changes to a cross. If the mouse moves off the button, the cursor changes back to an arrow. The previous code is all that's required.

Changing the Screen Pointer

Sometimes, you want the cursor to show that a delay occurs while the program processes something. In a game, this usually happens when files are loaded or saved to and from disk. A delay might also occur when an algorithm is being processed. The accepted method for showing a delay is to change the mouse pointer to an hourglass. However, changing the mouse pointer for every control on the form is a hassle.

Use the Screen object to avoid this hassle. Setting the screen mouse pointer to anything other than the default causes the screen pointer to override all other control pointers—even those from other applications. To use the hourglass, use the following code:

```
' This may take a while, so show an hourglass
Screen.MousePointer = MPHOURGLASS
... Load a file, "think," etc.
' Restore the mouse pointer
Screen.MousePointer = MPDEFAULT
```

In the preceding example, MPHOURGLASS = 11 and MPDEFAULT = 0. When the user moves the mouse over the form and controls, the pointer's shape remains an hourglass while the file is loading.

Mouse API Functions

Even though a lot of support for the mouse is built-in, there isn't enough support for game programming. You might want to control a game object with the mouse, but you don't want the mouse in the way (as in a paddle game). Refer to Chapter 16, "Ping," and Chapter 17, "Bricks," to see how the mouse pointer is hidden during a game. Visual Basic has no direct support for hiding the mouse pointer, but you can solve that problem with the Windows API.

The what? The API is the abbreviation for all the Windows functions available to any Windows program. These functions are built-in, and fortunately, Visual Basic programs can use them.

> For a full explanation of the Windows API, and the API functions and routines used in this book, see Appendix B, "Windows API Functions."

Hide and Show

To hide the pointer, you need the ShowCursor procedure, which is located in the Windows dynamic link library (DLL) USER.DLL. To make this available to your games, use the following declaration in your global module:

```
Declare Sub ShowCursor Lib "User" (ByVal bShow%)
```

Hiding and showing the mouse cursor is easy now, as the following code illustrates:

```
' Hide the mouse cursor
ShowCursor False
... do whatever you want ...
' We need the mouse cursor back
ShowCursor True
```

And that's it. Other API mouse functions are available; I cover those in Chapters 16, "Ping," and 17, "Bricks."

> Be careful with the Hide function! When you use the Visual Basic END menu option or STOP icon, and the cursor is hidden, it remains hidden. In fact, you have to quit Windows to get the cursor back! Mouse Hide and Show commands must be paired together.

The Keyboard

A Windows programmer usually writes a program for the mouse and throws in keyboard support later. It seems that way to me, anyway.

Writing programs for the mouse is probably a pretty safe bet. The majority of Windows users have a mouse, and the ones who don't are at a disadvantage. If you want to support the keyboard, however, I urge you to consider it ahead of time.

I designed most of this book's games to use the mouse. However, you can play many of the games quite adequately with only a keyboard. For instance, you can play BlackJack, Draw Poker, Slider, and Puzzler with a keyboard—partly because Visual Basic handles much of the keyboard for you.

Default Handling

For most controls, you can define a hot key through the Caption property by using the ampersand (&) character. For instance, if you have a button for dealing the cards, set the caption to &Deal, which specifies Alt-D as a hot key. When you press ALT-D, Visual Basic calls the Click procedure—just as if the button were clicked with the mouse.

The Click procedure makes keyboard handling extremely simple. The keyboard cursor keys automatically move from one active control to another.

Another Visual Basic keyboard feature is the TabIndex property. This property defines the order in which control objects are selected when the Tab key is pressed. With the TabStop property, controls can be included and removed from the tabbing order dynamically. The Apples & Oranges game uses TabStop to group the 64 board buttons as a single control. When a player tabs to the board, the individual buttons are selected with the cursor keys.

Keyboard Procedures

Now that I have explained default keyboard handling, take a look at what keyboard procedures are available.

KeyPress

For the KeyPress event procedure, the parameter passed to you is the ASCII code for the key pressed. You normally use this code to assign hot keys to menu options and controls. This is, in fact, what BlackJack and Draw Poker do for the betting buttons:

```
Sub Form_KeyPress (KeyAscii As Integer)

  ' Determine whether this is a key we want
  Select Case KeyAscii
    Case Asc("+")
      ' Bet more
      If (btn_BetMore.Enabled) Then
        btn_BetMore_Click
      End If
    Case Asc("-")
      ' Bet less
      If (btn_BetLess.Enabled) Then
        btn_BetLess_Click
      End If
    Case Asc("="), Asc("*")
      ' Bet last
      If (btn_BetSame.Enabled) Then
        btn_BetSame_Click
      End If
  End Select

End Sub
```

You get notified once for each key press, and as in the preceding example, the appropriate Click procedure is called. In a game, though, you often want to know how long the key is pressed.

KeyUp and KeyDown

The KeyUp and KeyDown event procedures are useful in game scenarios—especially arcade-style games. What if you want to write the Lunar Lander game so it fires the engine continuously when the down arrow cursor key is pressed? When you use the KeyPress procedure, you can turn the engine on—but you need to know when to turn it off. You could use something like the following code:

```
Sub Form_KeyDown (KeyCode As Integer, Shift As Integer)

  ' Is this our engine key?
  If (KeyCode = DOWNARROW) Then
    ' Yes, so fire our engine
    RetroRocket(FIRE)
  End If

End Sub

Sub Form_KeyUp (KeyCode As Integer, Shift As Integer)

  ' Is this our engine key?
  If (KeyCode = DOWNARROW) Then
    ' Yes, so kill our engine
    RetroRocket(KILL)
  End If

End Sub
```

As long as the player pushes the down-arrow key, the lunar lander's retro-rocket engine remains on.

Key States

When you use the KeyUp and KeyDown methods (as explained previously), the keyboard state keys can be monitored. The Ctrl, Alt, and Shift keys will generate up and down events; just look for the values in the Shift function parameter.

An advantage to the state keys is that they won't fill the keyboard buffer when they are held down. They don't generate KeyPress events, because they don't have ASCII values.

KeyPreview

The KeyPreview property enables and disables the global handling of keyboard events. If KeyPreview is True, all keyboard events are sent to the form first. This routine permits you to set up a global keyboard handler for the entire game (instead of setting each control separately).

You might want to enable KeyPreview. You rarely need to handle a key combination based on which control is active.

Keyboard API Functions

The keyboard is well-covered by Visual Basic and Windows. In the course of programming this book's games, I didn't find a reason to dip into the Windows keyboard API.

The Joystick

If you have used BASIC compilers for DOS, you may have used the BASIC joystick functions (like STRIG()). Unfortunately, Visual Basic for Windows doesn't include automatic support for the joystick.

The fact that Visual Basic doesn't automatically support joysticks makes sense, though. The appeal of Windows is that you don't have to worry about what input and output devices are attached—so the joystick has to be supported through Windows. The Windows Control Panel program handles the adding and removing of drivers. But where is the joystick driver?

It's on the disk in the back of this book! After many requests, Microsoft has released the driver to the public domain. To install the driver and make it available for your Windows games and programs (that support joysticks), see Appendix A, "Installation."

Joystick API Functions

Joystick functions are added through the Windows Multimedia (MM) Extensions and shipped separately for Windows 3.0. They are automatically included in Windows 3.1 in the MMSYSTEM.DLL library. There are eight joystick functions, but only two are required in Visual Basic: joyGetPos% and joyGetDevCaps%.

Presence and Position

Actually, joyGetPos% does all the work. The joyGetPos% function returns the (X,Y,Z) position of the joystick with the button status. If there is a problem with the driver or the joystick (the joystick is unplugged, for instance), the function returns an error code. To check the position, call

```
rc% = joyGetPos%(JOYSTICKID, jpos)
```

If the return code is successful (0), a joystick is present and the position information is valid.

The joyGetPos% function is almost all that's needed to handle the input from a joystick. All that's left to do is to poll the joystick position with a timer control. One more piece of information is needed: the ranges of X, Y, and Z.

Joystick Capabilities

The joyGetDevCaps% function gives the range. The function looks like this:

```
rc% = joyGetDevCaps(JOYSTICKID, jcaps, JOYCAPSIZE)
```

You can ignore everything in the JOYCAPS structure except for the maximum position values, Xmax and Ymax. You need to know these values to determine the percentage of joystick movement (left and right, up and down). Suppose you want the joystick to move an object within a 500x400 rectangular area. If you know the joystick driver will report values from 0 to Xmax, and 0 to Ymax, your equation is:

```
X = (jpos.X * 500) / jcaps.Xmax
Y = (jpos.Y * 400) / jcaps.Ymax
```

This is what the joystick example program does—with one exception. In the JOYCAPS structure, the Xmax and Ymax variables are listed as integers. However, these are unsigned integers—which Visual Basic doesn't understand (it sees them as negative numbers).

To get the actual values, convert the values into a long variable:

```
' Get maximum range into a long, for translations
joyMaxX& = (CLng(jcap.Xmax) And &HFFFF&)
joyMaxY& = (CLng(jcap.Ymax) And &HFFFF&)
```

The long variables joyMaxX and joyMaxY can be used in your position percentage calculations.

An Example

The following example illustrates the use of the joystick functions in a test program. The joystick is also utilized in the Space Miner game in Chapter 18.

To test your joystick driver (assuming you have installed it from the instructions in Appendix A), select the Joystick icon from the program group you installed. Joystick is contained in the file JOYSTICK.EXE. When you run the program, you see the About box first. Click OK, and the Joystick test screen appears.

If you don't get an error message, you can move your joystick so that the blue dot moves around the edges of the box. Position information is displayed, and when you press joystick button #1 or #2, the appropriate box is checked. Figure 2.1 illustrates a joystick test in progress.

Figure 2.1. Testing a joystick.

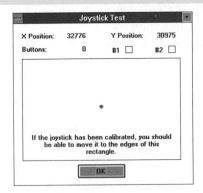

You can run the program from within Visual Basic. The JOYPOS and JOYCAPS structure values are displayed in the Visual Basic Debug window.

See Table 2.2 for the joystick source files.

Table 2.2. Joystick source files.

Filename	Description
JYABOUT.FRM	The About box form
JYMAIN.FRM	The Main Joystick form
JYGLOBAL.BAS	Global constants, variables, and procedures

The source code files listed in Table 2.2 are included on this book's disk. See Appendix A for installation instructions.

Figure 2.2 and Listing 2.1 show the JYMAIN form and source code. This is the main form for the Joystick test program. It contains the calls to the joystick functions `joyGetPos%` and `joyGetDevCaps%` (explained previously).

Figure 2.2. The JYMAIN form.

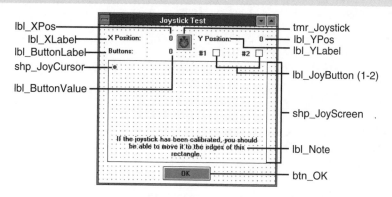

Listing 2.1. A partial listing of the JYMAIN form source code.

```
Option Explicit

Sub btn_OK_Click ()

  ' Unload the form
  Unload Me

End Sub

Sub Form_Load ()

  Dim jcap As JOYCAPS
  Dim jpos As JOYPOS
  Dim i%, rc%

  ' Center on the screen
  Move (Screen.Width - Width) \ 2, (Screen.Height - Height) \ 2

  ' Show about box
  frm_AboutBox.Show 1

  ' Get position information
  rc% = joyGetPos%(JOYSTICKID1, jpos)

  ' Print it out, just to see it
  Debug.Print
```

continues

Listing 2.1. continued

```
Debug.Print "Joystick Information: "
Debug.Print "rc: "; rc%
Debug.Print "X: "; jpos.X
Debug.Print "Y: "; jpos.Y
Debug.Print "Z: "; jpos.Z
Debug.Print "Buttons: "; jpos.Buttons

' Inform the user of any problem
If (rc% <> JOYERR_NOERROR) Then
  MsgBox "Joystick Driver not installed or Joystick unplugged!", MB_OK +
  ➥MB_EXCLAMATION,
        "Joystick Error!"
End If

' Get the joystick capabilities
rc% = joyGetDevCaps%(JOYSTICKID1, jcap, JOYCAPSIZE)

' Print it out, just to see it
Debug.Print
Debug.Print "Joystick #1 Device Capabilities: "
Debug.Print "rc: "; rc%
Debug.Print "Mid: "; jcap.Mid
Debug.Print "Pid: "; jcap.Pid
Debug.Print "Pname: "; jcap.Pname
Debug.Print "Xmin: "; jcap.Xmin
Debug.Print "Xmax: "; jcap.Xmax
Debug.Print "Ymin: "; jcap.Ymin
Debug.Print "Ymax: "; jcap.Ymax
Debug.Print "Zmin: "; jcap.Zmin
Debug.Print "Zmax: "; jcap.Zmax
Debug.Print "NumButtons: "; jcap.NumButtons
Debug.Print "PeriodMin: "; jcap.PeriodMin
Debug.Print "PeriodMax: "; jcap.PeriodMax

' Get maximum range into a long, for translations
joyMaxX& = (CLng(jcap.Xmax) And &HFFFF&)
joyMaxY& = (CLng(jcap.Ymax) And &HFFFF&)

' Set initial position to anything
joyX& = 0
joyY& = 0

' Enable our timer
tmr_Joystick.Enabled = True

End Sub

Sub tmr_Joystick_Timer ()

  Dim jpos As JOYPOS
```

```
    Dim jx&, jy&, mx&, my&
    Dim rc%

    ' Get position information
    rc% = joyGetPos%(JOYSTICKID1, jpos)

    ' Is joystick OK (do we have one, and is it plugged in?)
    If (rc% = 0) Then

      ' Get unsigned 16-bit values into VB longs
      jx& = (CLng(jpos.X) And &HFFFF&)
      jy& = (CLng(jpos.Y) And &HFFFF&)

      ' Display the position and button status
      lbl_XPos.Caption = Str$(jx&)
      lbl_YPos.Caption = Str$(jy&)
      lbl_ButtonValue.Caption = Str$(jpos.Buttons)

      ' Visually display button #1
      If ((jpos.Buttons And JOY_BUTTON1) = JOY_BUTTON1) Then
        chk_JoyButton(1).Value = 1
      Else
        chk_JoyButton(1).Value = 0
      End If

      ' Visually display button #2
      If ((jpos.Buttons And JOY_BUTTON2) = JOY_BUTTON2) Then
        chk_JoyButton(2).Value = 1
      Else
        chk_JoyButton(2).Value = 0
      End If

      ' Update "cursor" position
      If ((jx& <> joyX&) Or (jy& <> joyY&)) Then

        ' Save position
        joyX& = jx&
        joyY& = jy&

        ' Get our own maximum movement area
        mx& = shp_JoyScreen.Width - shp_JoyCursor.Width
        my& = shp_JoyScreen.Height - shp_JoyCursor.Height

        ' Move the "cursor" object
        shp_JoyCursor.Move shp_JoyScreen.Left + ((joyX& * mx&) / joyMaxX&),
    ➡shp_JoyScreen.Top + ((joyY& * my&) / joyMaxY&)

      End If

    End If

End Sub
```

Listing 2.2 shows the JYGLOBAL.BAS source code. This file contains the constant and type declarations for the joystick functions, and the global variables for the test program.

Listing 2.2. The JYGLOBAL.BAS source code.

```
Option Explicit

' Joystick error return values
Global Const JOYERR_NOERROR = 0       ' No error
Global Const JOYERR_PARMS = 165       ' Bad parameters
Global Const JOYERR_NOCANDO = 166     ' Request not completed
Global Const JOYERR_UNPLUGGED = 167   ' Joystick is unplugged


' Constants used with JOYPOS
Global Const JOY_BUTTON1 = &H1
Global Const JOY_BUTTON2 = &H2
Global Const JOY_BUTTON3 = &H4
Global Const JOY_BUTTON4 = &H8


' Joystick ID constants
Global Const JOYSTICKID1 = 0
Global Const JOYSTICKID2 = 1

' Joystick Capabilities
Type JOYCAPS
  Mid As Integer                ' Manufacturer ID
  Pid As Integer                ' Product ID
  Pname As String * 32          ' Product name
  Xmin As Integer               ' Min and max position values
  Xmax As Integer
  Ymin As Integer
  Ymax As Integer
  Zmin As Integer
  Zmax As Integer
  NumButtons As Integer         ' Number of buttons
  PeriodMin As Integer          ' Minimum message period when captured
  PeriodMax As Integer          ' Maximum message period when captured
End Type

' Size of JOYCAP structure (needed for function call)
Global Const JOYCAPSIZE = 54

' Joystick Position Information
Type JOYPOS
  X As Integer                  ' X, Y, and Z position
  Y As Integer
  Z As Integer
  Buttons As Integer            ' Button states
End Type
```

```
' Message Box constants
Global Const MB_OK = 0
Global Const MB_EXCLAMATION = 48

' Windows API Joystick functions
Declare Function joyGetDevCaps% Lib "MMSystem" (ByVal JoyId%, JCaps As
➥JOYCAPS, ByVal
CapSize%)
Declare Function joyGetPos% Lib "MMSystem" (ByVal JoyId%, JPos As JOYPOS)

' Global joystick variables
Global joyX&, joyY&
Global joyMaxX&, joyMaxY&
```

Program Overview

The Joystick test program is provided as a reference for use in games you might develop. I fully discuss use of the joystick functions in Chapter 18, "Space Miner."

Summary

Visual Basic provides comprehensive support for the keyboard and the mouse. Even so, you can use the Windows API to enhance the input device support (especially for the mouse). You also can use the API to add support for input devices that Visual Basic doesn't support—such as the joystick.

What's Ahead

Now that you have input squared away, you can move on to output. If you want to kmow how to handle multiple display resolutions, create images and icons, or adjust for aspect ratios, it's all ahead!

Handling Output

Newton's Law of Computer Gravity states that what goes in must come out. In a game, almost all the output is performed through the display. In this chapter, I cover display resolution issues, icons, image creation, and using images.

Supporting Multiple Resolutions

Device independence is a term that's frequently applied to Windows. It means you can write a Windows program without having to worry about what video card, monitor, and printer the end user has. In effect, the program is written independently from the devices it will run on. While this frees you from a lot of decisions and concerns, you must allow for true device independence in the program of your game.

Selecting a Mode

I believe that in todays' market, the default Windows configuration is the VGA 640x480 16-color display mode. Because the prices of VGA and Super VGA cards are so low, I doubt you will hurt your market potential by requiring at least a VGA adapter. However, Windows provides an EGA driver. If you can support the EGA too, then by all means do so.

But what does "support the EGA" mean? Isn't Windows device-independent? Well, yes it is—but you have to write your game to *be* device-independent. You'll have to consider the aspect ratio, the number of colors available, your window size, and more.

The Aspect Ratio

The aspect ratio of the display mode compares the number of pixels per unit horizontally to the number of pixels per unit vertically. If there are 100 pixels per inch horizontally and 100 pixels per inch vertically, you have a 100 to 100 or 1:1 (pronounced "one-to-one") aspect ratio. For example, the VGA 640x480 display resolution has a 1:1 aspect ratio.

Now, look at the EGA 640x350 resolution. The display area on your monitor hasn't changed from the VGA 640x480 mode, but there are less pixels vertically. This means that each pixel has to stretch a little so that the screen is filled from top to bottom—in effect, you get a rectangular pixel. Because the pixels are stretched, there are fewer pixels per unit vertically (approximately 73 pixels instead of 100). The EGA has an aspect ratio of 1.37:1.

Because there are less pixels vertically, bit-mapped images you create and use in an `Image` or `Picture` control appear slightly stretched vertically in the EGA 640x350 resolution. There are two ways to handle this:

➤ Set the image's `Stretch` property to `False` and leave some room beneath the image. When the aspect ratio is not 1:1, the control resizes, and the image looks stretched. For some images, stretching is not really noticeable.

➤ Set the image's `Stretch` property to `True`. If the aspect ratio is not 1:1, the image inside the control is scaled so that it appears to be the original (1:1) size. This can distort some images slightly.

Keep in mind the converse also can occur. If you run Visual Basic in the EGA resolution mode and create all your images for the EGA, your images will appear compressed vertically in the VGA 640x480 resolution (or any mode with a 1:1 aspect).

Thankfully, the EGA driver resolution is the only non-1:1 aspect resolution for VGA and SVGA Windows drivers.

Twips

Visual Basic supports a unit of measure called a *twip*. Unlike a pixel, a twip is independent of the display resolution. I really haven't found twips useful for game development—although you will have to use them in some cases (such as when you size a window).

Twips are useful for maintaining the sizes of buttons, checkboxes, window sizes, and so on. However, they are not useful when dealing with images. Because games usually deal with a large number of images, it's more convenient to use pixel units (for images) than twips.

Window Size

The window size of your game is also dependent upon the resolution. If you plan to support the EGA, make sure your game window is less than 350 pixels high. Likewise, if you normally use a high-resolution super VGA display mode, remember to make your windows 480 (or less) pixels high. An easy way to test your game is to set up windows using the EGA or VGA drivers. Then, play your game. If your windows don't fit on the display, you'll need to make them smaller.

Graphics Images

Graphics images play a large role in the look and feel of most computer games. Images appear in the form of the game icon, on the About box, as a title or playing piece, as a deck of cards, and so on.

Icons

Visual Basic provides a host of example icons for your use, but you might not find one that adequately represents your game program. Besides, the icons are provided to everyone—so they definitely aren't unique. The icons are mostly for general purpose use (such as for arrows and trashcans). I recommend that you create your own icons for your games.

IconWorks

I used Visual Basic's IconWorks example program for all this book's games. IconWorks is usually installed in the SAMPLES directory (in a directory called ICONWRKS). Just load the project file into Visual Basic and make an executable (using the File Make EXE menu option). I added IconWorks to my Visual Basic group so I could have easy access to it (by double-clicking its icon). Figure 3.1 shows IconWorks in action.

Creating an icon is simple, but creating a good-looking icon can be a challenge. If an idea for an icon does not immediately come to you, wait until you finish programming your game. Then, you can create the icon from some of the other game graphics or draw a miniature version of the game screen. I only created a few of this book's icons from scratch.

Figure 3.1. The IconWorks program.

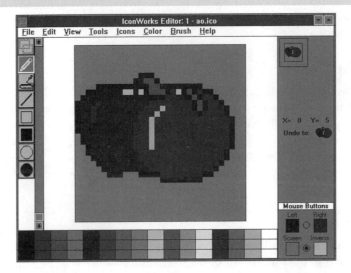

When using existing artwork or images, you can use Paintbrush to scale the image down to icon size. Then, copy the scaled image to the Windows Clipboard and paste it into IconWorks. When you have the image in IconWorks, you can clean it up or enhance it. I used this exact procedure to create the BlackJack game icon.

Using the Icon

The obvious use for an icon is for the main game window's Icon property. This is usually assigned one time during the game design. However, the icon can be changed any time during the game, using

```
frm_MyGame.Icon = img_Icon.Picture
```

One reason for changing the icon during runtime is to animate the icon. See Chapter 4, "Animation," for more information.

Remember to use the icon as part of your About box or for other small images in your game. Use the image or picture controls to display the icon.

Paint Programs

For images larger than an icon, you'll need the assistance of a paint program. You won't have to run out and buy one, because Windows has one already.

Windows Paintbrush

Windows Paintbrush is a simple-to-use image editing program. I used it to create most of the images for the games in this book. Figure 3.2 shows Paintbrush with one such image.

Figure 3.2. The Windows Paintbrush program.

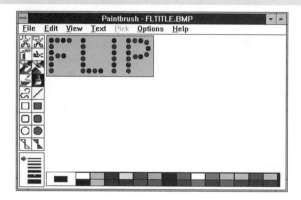

After you draw your image, save it as a BMP file. From a BMP (Windows **BitMaP**), you can load the image into an `Image` or `Picture` control. With Paintbrush, you can cut and paste to the Windows Clipboard.

> To capture graphics from the Windows screen, you can use the PrtScr key. To capture the entire screen, press PrtScr. To capture only the active window, press Alt-PrtScr. This places the image into the Windows Clipboard, from which you can use the Paintbrush Paste command to retrieve the image. Edit the image and save it as a BMP.

You also can use (or at least start with) clip art images. Clip art is usually sold in sets, and all the images match a given theme—such as office, travel, and computers. Most clip art is in the PCX format, which Paintbrush supports. Just read the PCX file into Paintbrush and save it as a BMP file.

DOS Paint Programs

You also can use a DOS-based paint program. Many DOS paint programs have features exceeding those of Windows Paintbrush. If you can generate a PCX file, you can read the image into Windows Paintbrush and save it as a BMP.

Scanning

If you already have artwork for your game, or you want to port a board game to the computer environment, consider getting a scanner. Most scanners come with software that can generate a PCX file, so you'll be set. Just remember to respect the owner of the copyright for whatever you are scanning. You always should ask for the copyright owner's permission.

Using the Images

You can place a BMP file in an Image or Picture control. The decks of cards in BlackJack and Poker each contain an image array of 53 cards (52 card faces plus 1 for the card back). Unless you really need some of the Picture properties, use the Image control. This will save you some speed and a little memory.

Images can be loaded dynamically—just like icons. For a game, you may need most of your images all the time. Only one of the games in this book loads a picture dynamically, and that's the image for the Puzzler game. Puzzler uses the LoadPicture function to do this:

```
' Is there a file name?
If (Len(Filename$) > 0) Then
  ' Yes, so try and load it
  pic_Puzzler.Picture = LoadPicture(Filename$)
End If
```

And voilà! The image appears in the picture control.

Summary

Output for most games includes display manipulation. You must consider the display resolution, game icon, image creation, and window sizes. Planning for these issues in advance can reduce problems later on (such as a game window being too large for the EGA).

What's Ahead

To develop a great game, you must deal with two other forms of output: animation and sound. I cover these topics in Chapter 4, "Animation," and Chapter 5, "Sound Generation." If you want to spin a top, rotate the world, or make a fish swim, follow me to the next chapter.

Animation

Animation and game programming go hand in hand, and when using a graphical environment like Windows, users expect animation in games. In this chapter, I'll discuss various methods for adding animation to your game, and I'll illustrate each of those methods with an animation example program named Anim, which is included at the end of this chapter.

XOR Animation

DrawMode is one of the properties available on a form or picture control. This property determines how drawing operations are rendered. By default, DrawMode = 13 (Copy Pen). However, if you set DrawMode = 7 (XOR Pen), you can yield some animation effects.

XOR, (or Exclusive Or) is the name for a logical operation with a special characteristic: anything you draw using XOR can be erased by redrawing the object with XOR!

If you want to see XOR in action, try moving (with a mouse) a Windows form or window to a new location. An outline of the window appears while you are moving it. This outline is drawn using the XOR drawing operation.

One advantage of using XOR is that you don't need to save any background image data to restore the screen. When the window outline first appears, it is drawn using XOR. When the outline is moved, the outline is removed (and the

screen restored) by simply drawing the outline again using XOR. Then, the outline is drawn with XOR at the new location. The XOR operation also is used when you resize a window.

As the outline is moved over various colors on the screen, you'll notice that the color of the outline changes; this change can be a disadvantage. You might not want your object to change color as it moves against a colored background.

The Animation example program (Anim) at the end of this chapter illustrates the color change of the XOR operation by moving a box over some bands of color. First, the XOR pen is selected by changing the DrawMode property:

```
' Change the drawing mode to XOR
pic_XorBox.DrawMode = 7 'XOR Pen
```

The same command is used to erase the box and draw the box again at the new position (in the tmr_Main_Timer routine):

```
' Draw the box
pic_XorBox.Line (BoxX%, 0)-Step(BoxSize%, BoxSize%), RGB(255, 255, 255),
➡BF
```

The box position BoxX% is changed, of course, between calls to the function.

> The box is drawn initially by the chk_XorBox routine. This lets the timer routine hide the box by drawing it, moving the box, and then drawing it again.

I didn't use the XOR operation in any of the games, but I thought you should be aware of its possible uses. I did illustrate the use of XOR in the Anim example program.

Moving a Control

One of the easiest ways to add animation to your game is by moving a control. There are two ways of moving controls. One way is to change the values of the Left and Top properties or both. If you want to move a button control to the right, use

```
' Move the button to the right
btn_Ok.Left = btn_Ok.Left + 100
```

and the button will move 100 units to the right. Visual Basic also takes care of restoring any underlying graphics (after the button is moved). Unlike XOR, however, the object doesn't change color when moved against a colored background.

The second way to move an object is through the Move method. The Move method updates the Left and Top control properties simultaneously, as well as the Height and Width. If you want to move an image or picture box (for example), use

```
' Move the image diagonally
img_Logo.Move img_Logo.Left + 100, img_Logo.Top + 100
```

and the image is moved diagonally. If you want to change the size of the control, follow the left and top positions with the new width and height.

The Move method is most useful when both the left and top values need changing. You wouldn't want to set the Left property first, and then the Top property, because the control would move horizontally first, and then vertically. The Move method moves the control directly to its new location.

> For more information on the Move method, see Chapter 14, "Slider."

Drag and Drop

The Drag and Drop feature of Visual Basic is another animation technique that you can apply to your games.

Drag and Drop does exactly what its name suggests—it provides an easy method for a control to be dragged to another control and then dropped. If you have a list of filenames, and you use Drag and Drop, you can select a filename with the mouse by pressing the left mouse button. An outline of the filename or an icon appears (instead of the mouse pointer). With the left mouse button down, you can drag the filename outline over to a picture of a trash can. Finally, drop the outline on the trash can by releasing the mouse button. So far, the "drag and drop" of the filename is handled by Visual Basic. The trash can picture control receives a call to its pic_TrashCan_DragDrop function, which deletes the filename you dragged.

I've described a real-world application of Drag and Drop, but you can use it in a game (even though I didn't use this method for a game in this book). The Anim example (listed at the end of this chapter) illustrates the use of Drag and Drop.

The Anim example contains two image controls in an array named, appropriately enough, img_Drag. I've drawn the icons for the image controls so that one looks like a peg in a hole, and the other looks like an empty peg hole. If you select the check box below the images, you can test the Drag and Drop feature.

If you select the image with the peg by pressing the left mouse button, the following code is executed:

```
' Remove the peg by replacing the image
img_Drag(Index).Picture = img_Drag(3).Picture
' Remember where the peg came from
DragIndex% = Index
' Enable dragging
img_Drag(Index).Drag 1
```

First, the image with the peg is replaced with the image without a peg—making it appear as if the peg has disappeared. Next, the index of the image control is recorded so the peg can be returned if the Drag and Drop operation is incomplete. Last, Drag and Drop is enabled with the Drag method.

I didn't want the peg to disappear, though. I wanted it to look like the peg was picked up out of the peg hole. So, I designed a third icon depicting only a peg, and assigned it to the DragIcon property of img_Drag. Visual Basic displays the peg image while the left mouse button remains down (unless you venture outside the form with the mouse, in which case the "No Drop" pointer appears).

NOTE

One limitation of Drag and Drop is that the icon is displayed in black and white only. Because it's an icon, it is limited to 32x32 pixels. Keep these points in mind when you design your drag icon.

Now, the user can take several different directions. The obvious (and planned) direction is for the user to drag the peg icon to the image of the empty peg hole, and drop it. When that happens, the peg icon disappears and the img_Drag_DragDrop routine is called. It resets the drag index and copies the "peg in the hole" image to the image control. This gives the illusion that the peg is dropped into the peg hole.

```
' Reset the drag index, since it is being dropped
DragIndex% = DRAGNONE

' Is this location empty?
If (img_Drag(Index).Picture = img_Drag(DRAGEMPTY).Picture) Then
  ' Yes, so fill it
  img_Drag(Index).Picture = img_Drag(DRAGFULL).Picture
End If
```

Note that the user can drop the peg into the same hole (from which the peg appeared). The Drag and Drop sequence is illustrated in Figure 4.1.

What happens when the peg is dropped onto a different control, or outside the form altogether? Handling this situation is a little less elegant.

Figure 4.1. Dragging and dropping a peg.

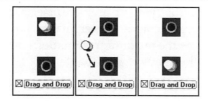

I've kept track of the image control index of the dragged peg (stored in DragIndex%). During a drag operation (while the mouse button is depressed), the form doesn't receive mouse movement messages. After the peg has been dropped, the form receives messages again. So, I check in the Form_MouseMove routine to see whether there are any unresolved drag operations. If there are, I know that the peg was dropped in an inappropriate location. I restore the peg back to its original location and reset the DragIndex% (in the Form_MouseMove routine) as follows:

```
' Are there any unresolved drags?
If (DragIndex% <> DRAGNONE) Then
  ' Yes, so place the peg back into the source
  img_Drag(DragIndex%).Picture = img_Drag(DRAGFULL).Picture
  ' And reset the index
  DragIndex% = DRAGNONE
End If
```

You can try this out for yourself. Drag the peg outside the Anim form and drop it. The peg won't appear back in the hole until you move the mouse pointer back to the Anim form window.

The Drag and Drop method is a quick and easy way of animating a small image according to mouse movement. You can use Drag and Drop for board games (such as Checkers or Chess) or for any game in which you need to pick up a playing piece and move it to another location. If the size and color restrictions get in your way, see the Sprite section (later in this chapter).

Icon Animation

Icons can be animated in several ways. The easiest way is to create several views of an icon and then cycle through them. In the Anim example program, this animation is illustrated by the spinning red top.

```
' Update the icon
img_Icon.Picture = img_Top(IconNum%).Picture
```

With this method, you can animate an icon (and a minimized icon) in an image or picture. When the Anim program is minimized, the icon is animated by cycling through the Earth icons:

```
' We are iconized, so animate the icon
frm_Anim.Icon = pic_Earth(IconNum%).Picture
```

For image and picture controls, you can animate objects larger than the 32x32 icon size by cycling through larger images. Larger images, however, require more program space. They also slow the maximum animation speed. For another example of icon animation using this method, see Chapter 16, "Ping."

The disadvantage to this form of animation is that the images tend to flicker noticeably. This flicker occurs because the image is first erased (and the new image is displayed). One solution is to use the Windows API function BitBlt (pronounced Bit Blit).

Bit Blitting

Bit Block Transfer (BitBlt) is a very fast Windows API routine for copying bitmaps (pictures). The BitBlt function can copy any part of a bitmap to any part of another bitmap—perfect for what you need.

You might not be familiar with the hDC property. This is a read-only Picture control property available at runtime. Because you are dealing directly with the Windows API, you need to have hDC—and Visual Basic puts it nicely into a property. The BitBlt function is declared as follows:

```
Declare Function BitBlt% Lib "GDI" (ByVal hDestDC%, ByVal dx%, ByVal dy%,
➡ByVal nWidth%, ByVal nHeight%, ByVal hSrcDC%, ByVal sx%, ByVal sy%,
➡ByVal dwRop&)
```

Although it's a long function, the parameters are very simple. Specify the destination hDC, the destination location, and the size. Next, specify the source hDC and location. Last, you have the raster operation which specifies how the pixel data is combined with the display. Table 4.1 lists the common raster operations used with BitBlt.

Table 4.1. BitBlt **raster operations.**

dwRop&	Constant	Description
&H00CC0020	SPCCOPY	Destination = Source
&H008800C6	SRCAND	Destination = Source AND Destination
&H00EE0086	SRCPAINT	Destination = Source OR Destination
&H00660046	STCINVERT	Destination = Source XOR Destination

For icon and picture cycling, use the SRCCOPY raster operation. This copies the rectangular region to the destination. I'll show other uses for some of the other raster operations when I discuss sprites later in this chapter.

To animate the earth icon using the BitBlt function, I used the following function call:

```
' Display the icon
rc% = BitBlt%(pic_Icon.hDC, 0, 0, pic_Icon.Width, pic_Icon.Height,
➥pic_Earth(IconNum%).hDC, 0, 0, SRCCOPY)
```

The end result is a flickerless sequence of images. The Slider and Space Miner games (in Chapters 14 and 18) also use BitBlt to animate their icons.

> Make sure the picture boxes have AutoRedraw set to True. This ensures that the bitmaps are available and valid at all times. Without this property set, you will get garbage instead of the image you want.

The BitBlt function can be used to copy any portion of a bitmap to any location in another bitmap. The Puzzler game in Chapter 15 illustrates this use. You also can use the BitBlt function to animate sprites.

Sprites

The term *sprite* is used to refer to an irregularly shaped graphics object that moves across a complex background. Most arcade games use some form of sprite logic to move the game objects around. In Pac-Man, the little yellow circle with an appetite for dots is a sprite (and so are its ghost enemies).

I have covered using the BitBlt function for rectangular bitmap regions. Most of the time, though, objects aren't squares or rectangles. If the background, across which an image will be moved, is a solid color, you can set the area around the image to the same color—and no one will notice. However, if you want to move the image across a multicolored background, you need to do more than just set the same background color. Remember those raster operations I mentioned earlier? Here's where they come in handy.

To display a sprite, you need two images instead of one. The first image contains the actual sprite object, and the second contains the *mask* for the first image. The mask is a black-and-white image representing what part of the sprite image you want to display (the black) and what part you want to mask out (the white). If you want to make part of the sprite transparent (such as the border area around the image), use black pixels in the sprite image and make the same pixels white in the mask image. After the two images are created, the following steps display a sprite:

➡ Save the background. The background image data where the sprite will be placed should be saved—so you can restore it later.

➡ Apply the mask. Place the mask where the sprite will be located, using the SRCAND raster operation. This knocks a "hole" in the background, which you'll fill in with the sprite image.

➡ Display the sprite object. Place the sprite image at the same location as the mask using the SRCPAINT or SRCINVERT raster operation (it doesn't matter which).

The Anim example uses the following code to animate the fish sprite (follow along with each step in Figure 4.2):

Figure 4.2. Displaying a sprite.

```
' Save the background area
rc% = BitBlt%(pic_Save.hDC, 0, 0, pic_Save.Width, pic_Save.Height,
➡pic_Ocean.hDC, SpriteX%, SpriteY%, SRCCOPY)
' Put the sprite up. First the mask ...
rc% = BitBlt%(pic_Ocean.hDC, SpriteX%, SpriteY%, pic_Mask.Width,
➡pic_Mask.Height, pic_Mask.hDC, 0, 0, SRCAND)
' Then the image
rc% = BitBlt%(pic_Ocean.hDC, SpriteX%, SpriteY%, pic_Fish.Width,
➡pic_Fish.Height, pic_Fish.hDC, 0, 0, SRCPAINT)
```

After the sprite is displayed, moving it is quite easy. Restore the background area (using BitBlt and SRCCOPY) and repeat the Save-Mask-Display sequence of calls again at the new sprite location.

This technique works well, but the sprite flickers (as the icon, in the previous examples). Fortunately, you can create a flickerless sprite. Follow the steps in Figure 4.3 after the sprite has been displayed once:

1. Determine overlap. If the new sprite position doesn't overlap the previous position, use the method described previously. Sprites don't flicker when they don't overlap, because the same pixels aren't updated. If the positions overlap, continue with the following steps.

2. Initialize your work area. Your work area is a hidden picture control. Copy the area containing the sprite—including the area to which you are moving the sprite. For instance, if you are moving the sprite 10 units right, copy the width of the sprite plus 10.

3. Restore the sprite background to the work area. Don't restore the background to the display—restore it in the work area. This effectively erases the sprite in the work area.

4. Save the new background from the work area. Again, if you are moving 10 units right, save the area from 10 to `SpriteWidth` plus 10.

5. Apply the mask to the work area. This knocks a hole in the work area for the sprite. Remember to apply the mask at the new sprite location, which is 10 to the right.

6. Display the sprite object in the work area. This fills in the hole, just like before.

7. Copy the work area to the display. In one operation, this removes the previous sprite, and displays it at the new location.

Figure 4.3. Displaying a flickerless sprite.

Actually, there are only two new steps for the flickerless method—copying the work area from and to the display. Saving the sprite background, applying the mask, and displaying the sprite are operations now performed in the work area, rather than directly on the displayed bitmap. There is no flicker, because the display pixels are updated only once instead of twice.

To see the difference between the two sprite methods, select and unselect the Flickerless check box while the sprite animation is running (the swimming fish). You'll see a definite improvement. For more information about sprites, see Chapter 18, "Space Miner."

Collision Detection

In an arcade game, it can be important to detect when two objects (usually sprites) collide. If a missile is shot at an alien spaceship, you need to know when and if the missile hits anything. There are two kinds of collision detection: simple collision detection and complex collision detection.

Simple Collision Detection

The simplest way to detect whether two objects have collided is to use a rectangular overlap test. In Bricks and Space Miner (Chapters 17 and 18), the following function provides this test:

```
Function Overlap% (ax1%, ay1%, aw%, ad%, bx1%, by1%, bw%, bd%)

  Dim ax2%, ay2%, bx2%, by2%, oflag%

  ' Get bottom corners
  ax2% = ax1% + aw% - 1
  ay2% = ay1% + ad% - 1

  bx2% = bx1% + bw% - 1
  by2% = by1% + bd% - 1

  ' Assume overlap
  oflag% = True

  ' Check if overlap is possible
  If ((ax2% < bx1%) Or (ax1% > bx2%) Or (ay2% < by1%) Or (ay1% > by2%))
  ➡Then
    ' No overlap
    oflag% = False
  End If

  ' Return overlap flag
  Overlap% = oflag%

End Function
```

This function actually tests whether the regions do *not* overlap, which is simpler and faster than determining whether any part of region A exists in region B.

In most cases, all you need is detection. The shapes don't have to be rectangular for you to use this method. In Bricks, the ball is round, and the bricks are rectangular. The playability of the game isn't affected by the fact that the ball barely misses a brick or not—the human eye can't tell anyway (at the speed of the game).

In Space Miner, many of the objects aren't rectangular. The main ship certainly isn't. Judge for yourself whether you can tell whether an object should have missed another object.

Complex Collision Detection

If you really want to detect whether two objects truly collide (overlap), one method is to compare the sprite masks. You can copy the first sprite mask to a work area (picture control), and then overlap the second sprite mask in the work area using SRCPAINT (logical OR). Then, scan the work area to determine whether there are any black pixels left. If there are, the objects have collided (see Figure 4.4).

Figure 4.4. Complex collision detection.

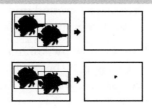

Obviously, complex collision detection consumes more time than the simple collision test performed by the Overlap function. This kind of test could slow down your game considerably, without any significant increase in playability. I haven't needed to use the complex method in any game I've written—although you might. Try using the complex method in Space Miner, and see if it increases the playability. My guess is that the complex collision detection only slows down the game.

If you have an oddly shaped object, you can still use the simple collision detection method. Use a combination of rectangular regions to describe your object (instead of one big rectangle). This is faster than a complex test.

An Animation Example

The following example illustrates the use of the various animation techniques in a test program. Each technique can be observed individually—or all at the same time.

To run the animation example, select the Animation icon from the program group you installed. (See Appendix A for installation instructions.) Animation is contained in the file ANIM.EXE. When you run the program, you'll see the About box first. Click OK, and the Animation test screen appears.

To view a particular animation technique, click the check box below each object. For example, select the Icon Animation check box to begin the animation of the red top. The techniques illustrated are

➤ Icon Animation. The red top is animated when Anim assigns a new icon to the image control for every timer event. Note that this method produces some flickering.

➤ Icon `BitBlt`. The earth is animated by Anim with the Windows API `BitBlt` function. Compare the spinning earth to the spinning top by running both animations simultaneously (select both checkboxes). Notice that the earth animation doesn't flicker like the red top does.

➤ Move Method. A button control is moved both right and left. If you look closely, you can see the screen background updated on the left and right edges of the button, as the button moves.

➤ XOR Drawing. A solid box is drawn by Anim using the XOR draw mode, and then Anim uses XOR to move the box right and left. As the box moves over the colored bands, you can see the box change colors—a side-effect of the XOR animation method.

➤ Drag and Drop. After the checkbox is selected, you can select the peg and move it from one peg hole to the other.

➤ Sprite. A fish appears in the ocean and moves from left to right. The scroll bar controls the speed of the animation. Moving the scroll button to the right increases the animation speed. To see the difference between the sprite animation methods, view the sprite with the Flickerless box checked, and unchecked.

➤ Minimize the Animation form, and the minimized form icon is animated.

Figure 4.5 shows the Animation program in progress. Remember that you can run each test separately, simultaneously, or somewhere in-between—by selecting and unselecting the checkboxes. Table 4.2 shows the animation source files.

Table 4.2. Animation source files.

Filename	Description
ANABOUT.FRM	The About box form
ANMAIN.FRM	The Main Animation form
ANGLOBAL.BAS	Contains global constants, variables, and procedures

Figure 4.5. Animation techniques.

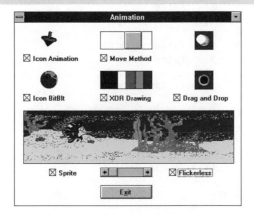

All the files in Table 4.2 are included on this book's disk. See Appendix A
for installation instructions.

Figure 4.6 shows the ANABOUT form, and Listing 4.1 shows this form's source
code. For a full description of the About box form, see Chapter 10, "Apples &
Oranges."

Figure 4.6. The ANABOUT form.

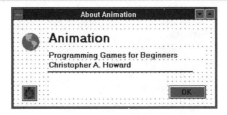

Listing 4.1. The ANABOUT form source code.

```
VERSION 2.00
Begin Form frm_AboutBox
   BorderStyle    =   3  'Fixed Double
   Caption        =   "About Animation"
   ClipControls   =   0   'False
   FontBold       =   -1  'True
```

continues

Listing 4.1. continued

```
FontItalic      =   0    'False
FontName        =   "System"
FontSize        =   9.75
FontStrikethru  =   0    'False
FontUnderline   =   0    'False
Height          =   2775
Icon            =   ANABOUT.FRX:0000
Left            =   1560
MaxButton       =   0    'False
MinButton       =   0    'False
ScaleHeight     =   2370
ScaleWidth      =   5640
Top             =   1335
Width           =   5760
Begin Timer tmr_Icon
   Enabled      =   0    'False
   Interval     =   200
   Left         =   240
   Top          =   1800
End
Begin PictureBox pic_Icon
   AutoSize     =   -1   'True
   BorderStyle  =   0    'None
   Height       =   640
   Left         =   240
   Picture      =   ANABOUT.FRX:0302
   ScaleHeight  =   480
   ScaleWidth   =   480
   TabIndex     =   6
   Top          =   360
   Width        =   480
End
Begin CommandButton btn_OK
   Caption      =   "OK"
   FontBold     =   -1   'True
   FontItalic   =   0    'False
   FontName     =   "System"
   FontSize     =   9.75
   FontStrikethru =  0    'False
   FontUnderline  =  0    'False
   Height       =   360
   Left         =   4350
   TabIndex     =   5
   Top          =   1800
   Width        =   1035
End
Begin Line lin_Divider
   BorderWidth  =   2
   X1           =   975
```

```
   X2              =    5010
   Y1              =    1425
   Y2              =    1425
End
Begin Label lbl_Program
   Caption         =    "Animation"
   FontBold        =    -1   'True
   FontItalic      =    0    'False
   FontName        =    "MS Sans Serif"
   FontSize        =    18
   FontStrikethru  =    0    'False
   FontUnderline   =    0    'False
   Height          =    450
   Left            =    990
   TabIndex        =    1
   Top             =    270
   Width           =    4440
End
Begin Label lbl_Title
   Caption         =    "Programming Games for Beginners"
   FontBold        =    -1   'True
   FontItalic      =    0    'False
   FontName        =    "MS Sans Serif"
   FontSize        =    9.75
   FontStrikethru  =    0    'False
   FontUnderline   =    0    'False
   Height          =    240
   Left            =    990
   TabIndex        =    2
   Top             =    840
   Width           =    4305
End
Begin Label lbl_Author
   Caption         =    "Christopher A. Howard"
   FontBold        =    -1   'True
   FontItalic      =    0    'False
   FontName        =    "MS Sans Serif"
   FontSize        =    9.75
   FontStrikethru  =    0    'False
   FontUnderline   =    0    'False
   Height          =    240
   Left            =    990
   TabIndex        =    3
   Top             =    1110
   Width           =    4365
End
Begin Label lbl_Info
   Height          =    600
   Left            =    1005
   TabIndex        =    4
```

continues

Listing 4.1. continued

```
      Top              =   1545
      Width            =   1875
   End
   Begin Label lbl_InfoValues
      Height           =   600
      Left             =   2880
      TabIndex         =   0
      Top              =   1545
      Width            =   1410
   End
End
Option Explicit

' Windows API functions used
Declare Function GetFreeSpace Lib "Kernel" (ByVal wFlags%) As Long
Declare Function GetWinFlags Lib "Kernel" () As Long

' Windows constants used
Const WF_STANDARD = &H10
Const WF_ENHANCED = &H20
Const WF_80x87 = &H400

Sub btn_OK_Click ()

   ' We are done
   Unload Me

End Sub

Sub Form_Load ()

   Dim WinFlags&
   Dim Mode$, Processor$, CRLF$

   ' Center the AboutBox on the screen
   Move (Screen.Width - Width) \ 2, (Screen.Height - Height) \ 2

   ' Make it easier for strings
   CRLF$ = Chr$(13) + Chr$(10)

   ' Get current Windows configuration
   WinFlags& = GetWinFlags()

   ' Determine mode
   If (WinFlags& And WF_ENHANCED) Then
      Mode$ = "386 Enhanced Mode"
```

```
    Else
      Mode$ = "Standard Mode"
    End If

    ' Free memory
    lbl_Info.Caption = Mode$ + CRLF$ + "Free Memory:" + CRLF$
    ➡+ "Math Co-processor:"

    ' 80x87 math chip
    If (WinFlags& And WF_80x87) Then
      Processor$ = "Present"
    Else
      Processor$ = "None"
    End If

    ' Free space
    lbl_InfoValues.Caption = CRLF$ + Format$(GetFreeSpace(0) \ 1024)
    ➡+ " KB" + CRLF$ + Processor$

    ' Initialize the icon number
    IconNum% = 0

    ' Animate the icon
    tmr_Icon.Enabled = True

End Sub

Sub tmr_Icon_Timer ()

  Dim rc%

    ' Update the icon number
    IconNum% = IconNum% + 1

    ' Check the limits
    If (IconNum% = MAXICON) Then
      IconNum% = 0
    End If

    ' Display it
    rc% = BitBlt%(pic_Icon.hDC, 0, 0, pic_Icon.Width, pic_Icon.Height,
    ➡frm_Anim!pic_Earth(IconNum%).hDC, 0, 0, SRCCOPY)

End Sub
```

Figure 4.7 and Listing 4.2 illustrate the ANMAIN form and source code, respectively. This is the main form for the Animation example program.

Figure 4.7. The ANMAIN form.

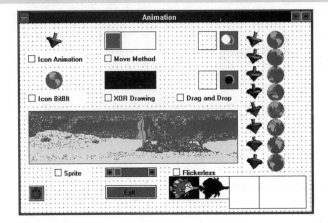

Listing 4.2. The ANMAIN form source code.

```
VERSION 2.00
Begin Form frm_Anim
    BackColor       =   &H00FFFFFF&
    BorderStyle     =   1   'Fixed Single
    Caption         =   "Animation"
    Height          =   5310
    Icon            =   ANMAIN.FRX:0000
    Left            =   1215
    LinkTopic       =   "Form1"
    MaxButton       =   0   'False
    ScaleHeight     =   540
    ScaleWidth      =   540
    Top             =   1170
    Width           =   6360
    Begin HScrollBar hsb_SpriteSpeed
        Height          =   255
        LargeChange     =   5
        Left            =   2400
        Max             =   25
        Min             =   1
        TabIndex        =   24
        Top             =   3960
        Value           =   1
        Width           =   1455
    End
    Begin PictureBox pic_Work
        AutoRedraw      =   -1  'True
        Height          =   900
```

```
      Left            =    6720
      ScaleHeight     =    58
      ScaleMode       =    3    'Pixel
      ScaleWidth      =    87
      TabIndex        =    22
      Top             =    4200
      Visible         =    0    'False
      Width           =    1335
   End
   Begin PictureBox pic_Save
      AutoRedraw      =    -1   'True
      Height          =    900
      Left            =    5880
      ScaleHeight     =    870
      ScaleWidth      =    840
      TabIndex        =    21
      Top             =    4200
      Visible         =    0    'False
      Width           =    870
   End
   Begin PictureBox pic_Ocean
      Height          =    1455
      Left            =    240
      Picture         =    ANMAIN.FRX:0302
      ScaleHeight     =    95
      ScaleMode       =    3    'Pixel
      ScaleWidth      =    391
      TabIndex        =    20
      Top             =    2400
      Width           =    5895
   End
   Begin PictureBox pic_Mask
      AutoRedraw      =    -1   'True
      AutoSize        =    -1   'True
      Height          =    630
      Left            =    5040
      Picture         =    ANMAIN.FRX:4C38
      ScaleHeight     =    40
      ScaleMode       =    3    'Pixel
      ScaleWidth      =    56
      TabIndex        =    19
      Top             =    4200
      Visible         =    0    'False
      Width           =    870
   End
   Begin PictureBox pic_Fish
      AutoRedraw      =    -1   'True
      AutoSize        =    -1   'True
      Height          =    630
      Left            =    4200
      Picture         =    ANMAIN.FRX:5112
      ScaleHeight     =    40
```

continues

Listing 4.2. continued

```
        ScaleMode       =    3   'Pixel
        ScaleWidth      =    56
        TabIndex        =    18
        Top             =    4200
        Visible         =    0    'False
        Width           =    870
    End
    Begin PictureBox pic_XorBox
        AutoRedraw      =    -1   'True
        BackColor       =    &H00000000&
        Height          =    495
        Left            =    2400
        ScaleHeight     =    465
        ScaleWidth      =    1425
        TabIndex        =    17
        Top             =    1320
        Width           =    1455
    End
    Begin CheckBox chk_Drag
        Caption         =    "Drag and Drop"
        Height          =    255
        Left            =    4440
        TabIndex        =    16
        Top             =    1920
        Width           =    1695
    End
    Begin CheckBox chk_Sprite
        Caption         =    "Sprite"
        Height          =    255
        Left            =    960
        TabIndex        =    15
        Top             =    3960
        Width           =    975
    End
    Begin CheckBox chk_XOR
        Caption         =    "XOR Drawing"
        Height          =    255
        Left            =    2400
        TabIndex        =    14
        Top             =    1920
        Width           =    1575
    End
    Begin CheckBox chk_Move
        Caption         =    "Move Method"
        Height          =    255
        Left            =    2400
        TabIndex        =    13
        Top             =    840
        Width           =    1575
    End
```

```
Begin CommandButton btn_Move
   Height           =   495
   Left             =   2400
   TabIndex         =   12
   Top              =   240
   Width            =   495
End
Begin PictureBox pic_Icon
   AutoSize         =   -1  'True
   BorderStyle      =   0   'None
   Height           =   640
   Left             =   720
   Picture          =   ANMAIN.FRX:55EC
   ScaleHeight      =   32
   ScaleMode        =   3   'Pixel
   ScaleWidth       =   32
   TabIndex         =   11
   Top              =   1320
   Width            =   480
End
Begin PictureBox pic_Earth
   AutoRedraw       =   -1  'True
   AutoSize         =   -1  'True
   BorderStyle      =   0   'None
   Height           =   640
   Index            =   7
   Left             =   6960
   Picture          =   ANMAIN.FRX:58EE
   ScaleHeight      =   480
   ScaleWidth       =   480
   TabIndex         =   10
   Top              =   3600
   Visible          =   0   'False
   Width            =   480
End
Begin PictureBox pic_Earth
   AutoRedraw       =   -1  'True
   AutoSize         =   -1  'True
   BorderStyle      =   0   'None
   Height           =   640
   Index            =   6
   Left             =   6960
   Picture          =   ANMAIN.FRX:5BF0
   ScaleHeight      =   480
   ScaleWidth       =   480
   TabIndex         =   9
   Top              =   3120
   Visible          =   0   'False
   Width            =   480
End
```

continues

Listing 4.2. continued

```
Begin PictureBox pic_Earth
    AutoRedraw      =   -1  'True
    AutoSize        =   -1  'True
    BorderStyle     =   0   'None
    Height          =   640
    Index           =   5
    Left            =   6960
    Picture         =   ANMAIN.FRX:5EF2
    ScaleHeight     =   480
    ScaleWidth      =   480
    TabIndex        =   8
    Top             =   2640
    Visible         =   0   'False
    Width           =   480
End
Begin PictureBox pic_Earth
    AutoRedraw      =   -1  'True
    AutoSize        =   -1  'True
    BorderStyle     =   0   'None
    Height          =   640
    Index           =   4
    Left            =   6960
    Picture         =   ANMAIN.FRX:61F4
    ScaleHeight     =   480
    ScaleWidth      =   480
    TabIndex        =   7
    Top             =   2160
    Visible         =   0   'False
    Width           =   480
End
Begin PictureBox pic_Earth
    AutoRedraw      =   -1  'True
    AutoSize        =   -1  'True
    BorderStyle     =   0   'None
    Height          =   640
    Index           =   3
    Left            =   6960
    Picture         =   ANMAIN.FRX:64F6
    ScaleHeight     =   480
    ScaleWidth      =   480
    TabIndex        =   6
    Top             =   1680
    Visible         =   0   'False
    Width           =   480
End
Begin PictureBox pic_Earth
    AutoRedraw      =   -1  'True
    AutoSize        =   -1  'True
    BorderStyle     =   0   'None
    Height          =   640
    Index           =   2
```

```
      Left            =    6960
      Picture         =    ANMAIN.FRX:67F8
      ScaleHeight     =    480
      ScaleWidth      =    480
      TabIndex        =    5
      Top             =    1200
      Visible         =    0    'False
      Width           =    480
   End
   Begin PictureBox pic_Earth
      AutoRedraw      =    -1   'True
      AutoSize        =    -1   'True
      BorderStyle     =    0    'None
      Height          =    640
      Index           =    1
      Left            =    6960
      Picture         =    ANMAIN.FRX:6AFA
      ScaleHeight     =    480
      ScaleWidth      =    480
      TabIndex        =    4
      Top             =    720
      Visible         =    0    'False
      Width           =    480
   End
   Begin PictureBox pic_Earth
      AutoRedraw      =    -1   'True
      AutoSize        =    -1   'True
      BorderStyle     =    0    'None
      Height          =    640
      Index           =    0
      Left            =    6960
      Picture         =    ANMAIN.FRX:6DFC
      ScaleHeight     =    480
      ScaleWidth      =    480
      TabIndex        =    3
      Top             =    240
      Visible         =    0    'False
      Width           =    480
   End
   Begin CheckBox chk_IconBlt
      Caption         =    "Icon BitBlt"
      Height          =    255
      Left            =    240
      TabIndex        =    2
      Top             =    1920
      Width           =    1575
   End
   Begin CheckBox chk_Icon
      Caption         =    "Icon Animation"
      Height          =    255
      Left            =    240
      TabIndex        =    1
```

continues

Listing 4.2. continued

```
    Top             =    840
    Width           =    1575
End
Begin Timer tmr_Main
    Enabled         =    0     'False
    Interval        =    100
    Left            =    240
    Top             =    4440
End
Begin CommandButton btn_Exit
    Caption         =    "E&xit"
    Height          =    375
    Left            =    2400
    TabIndex        =    0
    Top             =    4440
    Width           =    1455
End
Begin CheckBox chk_Flickerless
    Caption         =    "Flickerless"
    Height          =    255
    Left            =    4320
    TabIndex        =    23
    Top             =    3960
    Width           =    1335
End
Begin Image img_Top
    Height          =    480
    Index           =    7
    Left            =    6360
    Picture         =    ANMAIN.FRX:70FE
    Top             =    3600
    Visible         =    0     'False
    Width           =    480
End
Begin Image img_Top
    Height          =    480
    Index           =    6
    Left            =    6360
    Picture         =    ANMAIN.FRX:7400
    Top             =    3120
    Visible         =    0     'False
    Width           =    480
End
Begin Image img_Top
    Height          =    480
    Index           =    5
    Left            =    6360
    Picture         =    ANMAIN.FRX:7702
    Top             =    2640
    Visible         =    0     'False
    Width           =    480
End
```

```
Begin Image img_Top
   Height          =     480
   Index           =     4
   Left            =     6360
   Picture         =     ANMAIN.FRX:7A04
   Top             =     2160
   Visible         =     0    'False
   Width           =     480
End
Begin Image img_Top
   Height          =     480
   Index           =     3
   Left            =     6360
   Picture         =     ANMAIN.FRX:7D06
   Top             =     1680
   Visible         =     0    'False
   Width           =     480
End
Begin Image img_Top
   Height          =     480
   Index           =     2
   Left            =     6360
   Picture         =     ANMAIN.FRX:8008
   Top             =     1200
   Visible         =     0    'False
   Width           =     480
End
Begin Image img_Top
   Height          =     480
   Index           =     1
   Left            =     6360
   Picture         =     ANMAIN.FRX:830A
   Top             =     720
   Visible         =     0    'False
   Width           =     480
End
Begin Image img_Top
   Height          =     480
   Index           =     0
   Left            =     6360
   Picture         =     ANMAIN.FRX:860C
   Top             =     240
   Visible         =     0    'False
   Width           =     480
End
Begin Image img_Drag
   BorderStyle     =     1    'Fixed Single
   DragIcon        =     ANMAIN.FRX:890E
   Height          =     510
   Index           =     3
   Left            =     5640
   Picture         =     ANMAIN.FRX:8C10
```

continues

Listing 4.2. continued

```
        Top             =    1320
        Visible         =    0    'False
        Width           =    510
     End
     Begin Image img_Drag
        BorderStyle     =    1    'Fixed Single
        DragIcon        =    ANMAIN.FRX:8F12
        Height          =    510
        Index           =    2
        Left            =    5640
        Picture         =    ANMAIN.FRX:9214
        Top             =    240
        Visible         =    0    'False
        Width           =    510
     End
     Begin Image img_Drag
        BorderStyle     =    1    'Fixed Single
        DragIcon        =    ANMAIN.FRX:9516
        Height          =    510
        Index           =    1
        Left            =    5040
        Top             =    1320
        Width           =    510
     End
     Begin Image img_Drag
        BorderStyle     =    1    'Fixed Single
        DragIcon        =    ANMAIN.FRX:9818
        Height          =    510
        Index           =    0
        Left            =    5040
        Top             =    240
        Width           =    510
     End
     Begin Shape shp_MoveBox
        BackColor       =    &H00FFFFFF&
        BackStyle       =    1    'Opaque
        Height          =    495
        Left            =    2400
        Top             =    240
        Width           =    1455
     End
     Begin Image img_Icon
        Height          =    480
        Left            =    720
        Picture         =    ANMAIN.FRX:9B1A
        Top             =    240
        Width           =    480
     End
  End
Option Explicit
```

```
Sub btn_Exit_Click ()

  ' Unload the form
  Unload Me

End Sub

Sub chk_Sprite_Click ()

  Dim rc%

  ' Is this the first time?
  If (SpriteFirst%) Then

    ' Yes, so save the new background area
    rc% = BitBlt%(pic_Save.hDC, 0, 0, pic_Save.Width,
    ➡pic_Save.Height, pic_Ocean.hDC, SpriteX%, SpriteY%, SRCCOPY)

    ' Put the sprite up. First the mask ...
    rc% = BitBlt%(pic_Ocean.hDC, SpriteX%, SpriteY%,
    ➡pic_Mask.Width, pic_Mask.Height, pic_Mask.hDC, 0, 0, SRCAND)
    ' Then the image
    rc% = BitBlt%(pic_Ocean.hDC, SpriteX%, SpriteY%,
    ➡pic_Fish.Width, pic_Fish.Height, pic_Fish.hDC, 0, 0, SRCPAINT)

    ' Set the first flag
    SpriteFirst% = False

  End If

End Sub

Sub chk_XOR_Click ()

  Dim i%, clr&

  ' Put the first box up, so we can XOR it later
  If (BoxFirst%) Then
    ' Only draw the box the very first time—after that it's moving
    pic_XorBox.Line (0, 0)-Step(BoxSize%, BoxSize%),
    ➡RGB(255, 255, 255), BF
    ' Draw some colored bands, so we can see the XOR effect
    For i% = 1 To 3
      ' Pick a primary color
      Select Case i%
        Case 1:
          clr& = RGB(255, 0, 0)
        Case 2:
          clr& = RGB(0, 255, 0)
        Case 3:
          clr& = RGB(0, 0, 255)
      End Select
```

continues

Listing 4.2. continued

```
        ' Draw the band (half the size of the box)
        pic_XorBox.Line ((2 + i%) * (BoxSize% / 2) - 50, 0)
        ➡-Step(BoxSize% / 2,
BoxSize%), clr&, BF
    Next i%

    ' Change the drawing mode to XOR
    pic_XorBox.DrawMode = 7 'Xor Pen

    ' Set the flag
    BoxFirst% = False
  End If

End Sub

Sub Form_Load ()

  ' Center on the screen
  Move (Screen.Width - Width) \ 2, (Screen.Height - Height) \ 2

  ' Show about box
  frm_AboutBox.Show 1

  ' Calculate the move animation values
  MoveInc% = (shp_MoveBox.Width - btn_Move.Width) / MAXSTEPS
  MoveStep% = 0
  MoveDir% = 1

  ' Calculate the box animation values (use the move objects as a guide)
  BoxInc% = MoveInc%
  BoxStep% = 0
  BoxDir% = 1
  BoxSize% = btn_Move.Width
  BoxFirst% = True

  ' Disable dragging
  DragIndex% = DRAGNONE

  ' Place the drag images
  img_Drag(0).Picture = img_Drag(DRAGFULL).Picture
  img_Drag(1).Picture = img_Drag(DRAGEMPTY).Picture

  ' Initialize the sprite data
  SpriteX% = 10
  SpriteY% = (pic_Ocean.ScaleHeight - pic_Fish.ScaleHeight) / 3
  SpriteInc% = 10
  SpriteFirst% = True

  ' Kick off the timer
  tmr_Main.Enabled = True
```

```
End Sub

Sub Form_MouseMove (Button As Integer, Shift As Integer,
➥X As Single, Y As
Single)

  ' Is Drag and Drop enabled?
  If (chk_Drag.Value = 1) Then
    ' Yes. Are there any unresolved drags?
    If (DragIndex% <> DRAGNONE) Then
      ' Yes, so place the peg back into the source
      img_Drag(DragIndex%).Picture = img_Drag(DRAGFULL).Picture
      ' And reset the index
      DragIndex% = DRAGNONE
    End If
  End If

End Sub

Sub img_Drag_DragDrop (Index As Integer, Source As Control,
➥X As Single, Y As Single)

  ' Reset the drag index, since it is being dropped
  DragIndex% = DRAGNONE

  ' Is this location empty?
  If (img_Drag(Index).Picture = img_Drag(DRAGEMPTY).Picture) Then
    ' Yes, so fill it
    img_Drag(Index).Picture = img_Drag(DRAGFULL).Picture
  End If

End Sub

Sub img_Drag_MouseDown (Index As Integer, Button As Integer,
➥Shift As Integer, X As Single, Y As Single)

  ' Process Drag and Drop?
  If (chk_Drag.Value = 1) Then
    ' Yes. Does this image have a peg?
    If (img_Drag(Index).Picture = img_Drag(DRAGFULL).Picture) Then
      ' Yes, so remove the peg by replacing the image
      img_Drag(Index).Picture = img_Drag(DRAGEMPTY).Picture
      ' Remember where the peg came from
      DragIndex% = Index
      ' Enable dragging
      img_Drag(Index).Drag 1
    End If
  End If

End Sub
```

continues

Listing 4.2. continued

```
Sub tmr_Main_Timer ()

  Dim rc%

  ' Update the icon number
  IconNum% = IconNum% + 1

  ' Keep it in range
  If (IconNum% = MAXICON) Then
    IconNum% = 0
  End If

  ' Are we not iconized?
  If (WindowState <> 1) Then

    ' Animate the icon?
    If (chk_Icon.Value = 1) Then
      ' Update the icon
      img_Icon.Picture = img_Top(IconNum%).Picture
    End If

    ' Animate the icon, using BitBlt?
    If (chk_IconBlt.Value = 1) Then
      ' Display it
      rc% = BitBlt%(pic_Icon.hDC, 0, 0, pic_Icon.Width,
      ➥pic_Icon.Height, pic_Earth(IconNum%).hDC, 0, 0, SRCCOPY)
    End If

    ' Animate the button?
    If (chk_move.Value = 1) Then
      ' Yes, so move it
      btn_Move.Move btn_Move.Left + (MoveDir% * MoveInc%)
      ' Bump the step
      MoveStep% = MoveStep% + 1
      ' Check the range
      If (MoveStep% = MAXSTEPS) Then
        ' We've reached the end, so go the opposite way
        MoveStep% = 0
        MoveDir% = (-1 * MoveDir%)
      End If
    End If

    ' Animate using XOR?
    If (chk_Xor.Value = 1) Then
      ' Yes, so remove the box by drawing it
      pic_XorBox.Line (BoxX%, 0)-Step(BoxSize%, BoxSize%),
      ➥RGB(255, 255, 255), BF
      ' Update the position and step
      BoxX% = BoxX% + (BoxDir% * BoxInc%)
      BoxStep% = BoxStep% + 1
```

```
' Check the range
If (BoxStep% = MAXSTEPS) Then
  ' We've reached the end, so go the opposite way
  BoxStep% = 0
  BoxDir% = (-1 * BoxDir%)
End If
' Display the box again
pic_XorBox.Line (BoxX%, 0)-Step(BoxSize%, BoxSize%),
➥RGB(255, 255, 255), BF

End If

' Animate the Sprite?
If (chk_Sprite.Value = 1) Then
  ' Yes, so get the sprite increment
  SpriteInc% = hsb_SpriteSpeed.Value
  ' Do we want a flickerless sprite?
  If (chk_Flickerless.Value = 1) Then
    ' Flickerless, so get our work buffer
    rc% = BitBlt%(pic_Work.hDC, 0, 0, pic_Work.Width,
    ➥pic_Work.Height, pic_Ocean.hDC, SpriteX%, SpriteY%, SRCCOPY)
    ' Restore background into work buffer, erasing the fish
    rc% = BitBlt%(pic_Work.hDC, 0, 0, pic_Save.Width,
    ➥pic_Save.Height, pic_Save.hDC, 0, 0, SRCCOPY)
    ' Save the new background from the work buffer
    rc% = BitBlt%(pic_Save.hDC, 0, 0, pic_Save.Width,
    ➥pic_Save.Height, pic_Work.hDC, SpriteInc%, 0, SRCCOPY)
    ' Mask the sprite area in the work buffer
    rc% = BitBlt%(pic_Work.hDC, SpriteInc%, 0, pic_Mask.Width,
    ➥pic_Mask.Height, pic_Mask.hDC, 0, 0, SRCAND)
    ' Place the sprite into the masked area
    rc% = BitBlt%(pic_Work.hDC, SpriteInc%, 0, pic_Fish.Width,
    ➥pic_Fish.Height, pic_Fish.hDC, 0, 0, SRCPAINT)
    ' Now place the sprite
    rc% = BitBlt%(pic_Ocean.hDC, SpriteX%, SpriteY%,
    ➥pic_Work.Width, pic_Work.Height, pic_Work.hDC, 0, 0, SRCCOPY)
    ' Bump the sprite along

    SpriteX% = SpriteX% + SpriteInc%
    ' Check the limits
    If (SpriteX% > pic_Ocean.ScaleWidth) Then
      ' Off the screen, so back it up to the beginning
      SpriteX% = -pic_Fish.ScaleWidth
    End If

  Else
    ' Not flickerless, so restore the saved background
    rc% = BitBlt%(pic_Ocean.hDC, SpriteX%, SpriteY%,
    ➥pic_Save.Width, pic_Save.Height, pic_Save.hDC, 0, 0, SRCCOPY)
    ' Bump the sprite along
    SpriteX% = SpriteX% + SpriteInc%
```

continues

Listing 4.2. continued

```
        ' Check the limits
        If (SpriteX% > pic_Ocean.ScaleWidth) Then
          ' Off the screen, so back it up to the beginning
          SpriteX% = -pic_Fish.ScaleWidth
        End If
        ' Save the new background area
        rc% = BitBlt%(pic_Save.hDC, 0, 0, pic_Save.Width,
        ➥pic_Save.Height, pic_Ocean.hDC, SpriteX%, SpriteY%, SRCCOPY)
        ' Mask the sprite area
        rc% = BitBlt%(pic_Ocean.hDC, SpriteX%, SpriteY%,
        ➥pic_Mask.Width, pic_Mask.Height, pic_Mask.hDC, 0, 0, SRCAND)
        ' Now place the sprite
        rc% = BitBlt%(pic_Ocean.hDC, SpriteX%, SpriteY%,
        ➥pic_Fish.Width, pic_Fish.Height, pic_Fish.hDC, 0, 0, SRCPAINT)


    End If
  End If

Else

  ' We are iconized, so animate the icon
  frm_Anim.Icon = pic_Earth(IconNum%).Picture

End If

End Sub
```

Listing 4.3 shows the ANGLOBAL source code. This file contains all of the global constant and variable definitions for the Anim animation example program.

Listing 4.3. The ANGLOBAL source code.

```
Option Explicit

' Icon Constants
Global Const MAXICON = 8
Global Const ICONINC = 200

' Move Constants
Global Const MAXSTEPS = 10

' Drag and Drop
Global Const DRAGFULL = 2
Global Const DRAGEMPTY = 3
Global Const DRAGNONE = -1
```

```
' Windows API
Global Const SRCAND = &H8800C6
Global Const SRCPAINT = &HEE0086
Global Const SRCCOPY = &HCC0020

' Icon Variables
Global IconNum%

' Move Variables
Global MoveInc%, MoveStep%, MoveDir%

' XOR Box Variables
Global BoxX%, BoxInc%, BoxStep%, BoxDir%, BoxSize%, BoxFirst%

' Drag and Drop
Global DragIndex%

' Sprites
Global SpriteFirst%, SpriteX%, SpriteY%, SpriteInc%

' Windows API functions
Declare Function BitBlt% Lib "GDI" (ByVal hDestDC%, ByVal dx%,
➥ByVal dy%, ByVal nWidth%, ByVal nHeight%, ByVal hSrcDC%,
➥ByVal sx%, ByVal sy%, ByVal dwRop&)
```

Program Overview

The Animation program is a reference for use in other game programs you might develop. The animation techniques are covered in this chapter and are used in the games described in Part II, "Exercises in Game Programming."

Summary

Animation is an important tool and nearly a requirement for any kind of game development. Visual Basic offers several built-in ways to animate a game. Additionally, the Windows API BitBlt% function is an indispensable tool in several animation methods.

What's Ahead

In the next chapter, I cover another important game tool: the power of sound. Without sound, the closest thing you have to a sound effect is a message box with the word "BOOM!". If you're interested in adding background music and sound effects to your game, I'll show you how in the pages ahead.

Sound Generation

Sound is a necessary part of any game program. Unfortunately, Visual Basic provides very little sound support. The Windows Multimedia Extensions (built into Windows 3.1) help solve the sound support problem. In this chapter, I cover the sound capabilities of Visual Basic and explain how to use the extensions to get more sound support.

Beep, Beep!

The only sound output function included in Visual Basic is the Beep statement. This does exactly what you might expect—it beeps the computer's speaker.

The beep function is rather limited, because it lacks the ability to change the tone and duration of the beep. The sound varies from computer to computer, but it's good for simple audio feedback. I used the Beep function in a number of games in this book, such as in Ping and Puzzler.

What we need is something better.

Better Beeps

You can get better beeps with the Windows API MessageBeep function. These beeps aren't the traditional kinds of beeps from the PC speaker—you need a device that can play Windows WAV (pronounced *wave*) files, such as a Sound Blaster. Is there a way to play the wave files through the PC speaker?

Yes, and it's on the disk in the back of this book! After many requests, Microsoft has released a speaker driver to the public domain. To install the driver and make it available to your Windows games and programs (for those users without sound cards), see Appendix A, "Installation."

The MessageBeep function is declared as

```
Declare Sub MessageBeep Lib "User" (ByVal BeepType%)
```

MessageBeep plays a waveform sound corresponding to a given system alert level (BeepType%). The sound for each alert level is identified by an entry in the [sounds] section of the WIN.INI initialization file. The types of sound (alert levels) available are listed in Table 5.1

Table 5.1. MessageBeep **sound types.**

Constant	Description
MB_DEFBEEP	Plays the standard beep sound using the computer speaker.
MB_ICONASTERISK	Plays the sound identified by the SystemAsterisk entry in the [sounds] section of WIN.INI.
MB_ICONEXCLAMATION	Plays the sound identified by the SystemExclamation entry in the [sounds] section of WIN.INI.
MB_ICONHAND	Plays the sound identified by the SystemHand entry in the [sounds] section of WIN.INI.
MB_ICONQUESTION	Plays the sound identified by the SystemQuestion entry in the [sounds] section of WIN.INI.
MB_OK	Plays the sound identified by the SystemDefault entry in the [sounds] section of WIN.INI.

My WIN.INI file contains the following entries under the SOUNDS keyword:

```
[sounds]
SystemAsterisk=CHORD.WAV, Asterisk
SystemHand=DING.WAV, Critical Stop
SystemDefault=DING.WAV, Default Beep
SystemExclamation=CHORD.WAV, Exclamation
SystemQuestion=DING.WAV, Question
SystemExit=CHIMES.WAV, Windows Exit
SystemStart=TADA.WAV, Windows Start
```

To play the SystemExclamation sound, use

```
MessageBeep (MB_ICONEXCLAMATION)
```

and the exclamation sound (CHORD.WAV) is played. The function returns almost immediately, and the sound file is queued to play in the background (asynchronously).

If the specified alert sound can't be played, MessageBeep attempts to play the system default sound. If MessageBeep can't play the system default sound, the function produces a standard beep sound by using the computer speaker. Usually these problems occur when the sound file cannot be located.

> To change the system sounds, use the SOUND utility in the Windows Control Panel or edit the WIN.INI file. If you have a Sound Blaster, remember to configure the Windows driver for it through the DRIVERS utility—also on the Control Panel.

This method is a step in the right direction, but you don't really have control over which specific wave file is played.

Catching a Wave

To play a specific wave file, use the Windows API sndPlaySound function. As with MessageBeep, you need to have a sound card installed in your system in order to hear the enhanced sounds—or you must load the PC Speaker Wave driver. The function is declared as

```
Declare Function sndPlaySound% Lib "MMSystem" (ByVal WaveFile$,
➥ByVal Flags%)
```

The parameter WaveFile$ specifies the name of the sound to play. The function searches the [sounds] section of WIN.INI for an entry with this name and plays the associated waveform file. If no entry by this name exists, WaveFile$ assumes the name is the name of a waveform file. If no filename is given (" "), any currently playing sound is stopped. The Flags% parameter can be a combination of the values shown in Table 5.2.

Table 5.2. sndPlaySound **flags.**

Constant	Description
SND_SYNC	The sound is played synchronously, and the function doesn't return until the sound ends.
SND_ASYNC	The sound is played asynchronously, and the function returns immediately after beginning the sound. To terminate an asynchronously played sound, call sndPlaySound with WaveFile$ = "".
SND_NODEFAULT	If the sound can't be found, the function returns silently without playing the default sound.
SND_LOOP	The sound will continue to play repeatedly until sndPlaySound is called again with WaveFile$ = "". You also must specify the SND_ASYNC flag to loop sounds.
SND_NOSTOP	If a sound is currently playing, the function immediately returns FALSE without playing the requested sound.

The sndPlaySound function returns TRUE if the sound is played; otherwise it returns FALSE.

> The sound must fit in available physical memory and be playable by an installed waveform audio device driver. The directories searched for sound files are, in order: the current directory, the Windows directory, the Windows system directory, the directories listed in the PATH environment variable, and the list of directories mapped in a network.

Windows initially provides four wave files to use with the system sounds (discussed earlier) for the MessageBeep function. To play one of those files directly use the following code:

```
' Play the chord wave file
rc% = sndPlaySound%("CHORD.WAV", SND_NODEFAULT + SND_ASYNC)
```

This plays the CHORD.WAV file asynchronously (in the background). If the file is not found, the PC speaker won't beep because of the SND.NODEFAULT flag.

You also can record your own wave files with the Sound Recorder Windows Accessory program. I created the LASER.WAV and HELLO.WAV files this way. You have everything you need to create your own sounds and sound effects for your games!

Music

Sound effects are nice, but how do you play continuous background music? Using a wave file is impractical, because even a few seconds of sound can create a large file. The answer is in the Multimedia Extensions.

The Media Control Interface (MCI) is a standard method of interfacing with a wide range of devices. Using MCI, you can control many different audio and visual devices. You can even play wave files using the MCI, in lieu of sndPlaySound—but I don't cover that here (sndPlaySound gives everything needed for wave files). What I use MCI for is the MIDI sequencer.

Musical Instrument Digital Interface (MIDI) is a standard format for representing musical instruments. The notes of each instrument are distinctly represented, so MIDI isn't a digitized format. Compared to wave files, MIDI files are smaller and the music is much clearer. But wave files are better for sound effects and speech—so, each format has advantages. An analogy is comparing a WAV file to a bit-mapped image from a paint program and a MID file to a vector drawing (such as those from AutoCAD).

There are many MCI functions, but you need only one: mciSendString. The format of the function looks like this:

```
Declare Function mciSendString& Lib "MMSystem" (ByVal SendString$,
➡ByVal ReturnString$, ByVal ReturnLength%, ByVal Callback%)
```

This function sends a command string to an MCI device (an Adlib, Sound Blaster, or equivalent card). The PC Speaker driver doesn't support MIDI. The device that the command is sent to is specified in the command string SendString$. The ReturnString$ and ReturnLength% parameters specify a buffer for return information. If no return information is needed, set ReturnString$ = "" and ReturnLength% = 0. The Callback% parameter is unusable in Visual Basic and must be set to 0.

All the work is done through the command string. There are many MCI commands, but I'll only deal with four of them: OPEN, PLAY, STOP, and CLOSE.

Opening the Sequencer

To play a MIDI file, you must open the device first. In MCI, the MIDI device is called the Sequencer. To open the CANYON.MID file (which comes with Windows), use the command

```
' Open the MIDI Sequencer
rc& = mciSendString&("OPEN CANYON.MID TYPE SEQUENCER ALIAS SQ", "",
➥0, 0)
```

> You must specify the complete path to the file when opening the file. If the file isn't in the current working directory, use C:\WIN31\CANYON.MID (or whatever your Windows path is).

The OPEN command opens the file, the TYPE keyword specifies the device as the MIDI sequencer, and the ALIAS keyword gives a shorthand way of referring to the opened file and device (SQ). You don't have to worry about the return string— any errors will be returned through the return code.

Playing

If you open the device successfully (rc& = 0), you can play the file. That's done through the PLAY command:

```
rc& = mciSendString&("PLAY SQ FROM 0", "", 0, 0)
```

The file associated with the SQ alias (CANYON.MID) begins playing in the background (from the beginning of the file).

Stopping

To stop the music after it starts, use the STOP command:

```
rc& = mciSendString&("STOP SQ", "", 0, 0)
```

The music stops, but the file is still loaded and ready to play. To restart the music, use the PLAY command again.

Closing the Sequencer

When you are finally done with the file, just close it:

```
rc& = mciSendString&("CLOSE SQ", "", 0, 0)
```

If the music is currently playing, it stops. To play the file again, you must reopen it with the OPEN command.

> Make sure you close the sequencer before your program ends! The music continues in the background, even after your program has ended. Otherwise, when you run your program again, the OPEN command will return an error code—because the device is still open.

Setting Up

If you are not sure whether your Windows configuration is set up for MIDI, look in the Control Panel Drivers program. You should see drivers listed for Adlib, the MIDI Mapper, and the MCI MIDI Sequencer. You also can test your sound output using the Windows Media Player accessory.

An Example

The following test program example illustrates the use of the sound functions. The Space Miner game (Chapter 18, "Space Miner") also utilizes these functions.

To test your sound driver, select the Sounds icon from the program group you installed. (See Appendix A for installation instructions.) Sounds is contained in the file SOUNDS.EXE. When you run the program, you see the About box first. Click OK, and the Sound test screen will appear. Table 5.2 lists the Sounds source files.

Try playing the different MessageBeep and sndPlaySound sounds by pressing the buttons. If you are set up for MIDI, load and play the MIDI file (you can play the beeps and sounds even while the MIDI file is playing). Figure 5.1 illustrates a sound test in progress.

Table 5.2. Sounds source files.

Filename	Description
SDABOUT.FRM	The About box form
SDMAIN.FRM	The Main Sound form
SDGLOBAL.BAS	Contains global constants, variables, and procedures

Figure 5.1. Testing sounds.

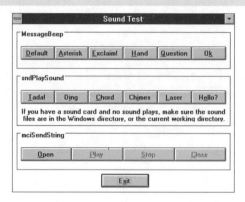

All these files are included on this book's disk. See Appendix A for installation instructions.

Figure 5.2 illustrates SDABOUT.FRM.

Figure 5.2. The SDABOUT form.

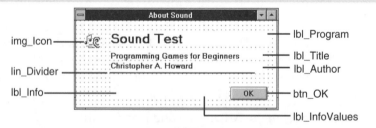

Figure 5.3 illustrates SDMAIN.FRM. This is the main Sounds form that contains all the sound-specific code. A partial listing of this form's code is shown in Listing 5.1.

Figure 5.3. The SDMAIN form.

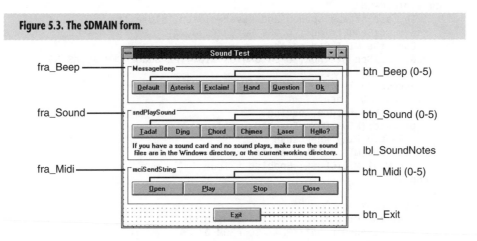

Listing 5.1. A partial listing of the SDMAIN.FRM source code.

```
Option Explicit

Sub btn_Beep_Click (Index As Integer)

  ' Determine the sound to play
  Select Case Index
    Case 0
      MessageBeep (MB_DEFBEEP)
    Case 1
      MessageBeep (MB_ICONASTERISK)
    Case 2
      MessageBeep (MB_ICONEXCLAMATION)
    Case 3
      MessageBeep (MB_ICONHAND)
    Case 4
      MessageBeep (MB_ICONQUESTION)
    Case 5
      MessageBeep (MB_OK)
  End Select

End Sub

Sub btn_Midi_Click (Index As Integer)

  Dim rc&, msg$
```

continues

Listing 5.1 continued

```
' Determine the string to send
Select Case Index
  Case MIDIOPEN
    ' In case it was opened and never closed, close it
    rc& = mciSendString&("CLOSE SQ", "", 0, 0)
    ' Open the MIDI Sequencer
    rc& = mciSendString&("OPEN CANYON.MID TYPE SEQUENCER ALIAS SQ",
    ➥"", 0, 0)
    ' Successful?
    If (rc& = 0) Then
      ' Disable future loading
      btn_Midi(MIDIOPEN).Enabled = False
      ' Enable Play and Close
      btn_Midi(MIDIPLAY).Enabled = True
      btn_Midi(MIDICLOSE).Enabled = True
    End If

  Case MIDIPLAY
    ' Play the MIDI file from the beginning
    rc& = mciSendString&("PLAY SQ FROM 0", "", 0, 0)
    ' Successful?
    If (rc& = 0) Then
      ' Disable playing, since we are now
      btn_Midi(MIDIPLAY).Enabled = False
      ' Enable stopping
      btn_Midi(MIDISTOP).Enabled = True
    End If

  Case MIDISTOP
    ' Stop playing
    rc& = mciSendString&("STOP SQ", "", 0, 0)
    ' Successful?
    If (rc& = 0) Then
      ' Disable stopping
      btn_Midi(MIDISTOP).Enabled = False
      ' Enable playing
      btn_Midi(MIDIPLAY).Enabled = True
    End If

  Case MIDICLOSE
    ' Close the MIDI Sequencer
    rc& = mciSendString&("CLOSE SQ", "", 0, 0)
    ' Successful?
    If (rc& = 0) Then
      ' Enable future opening
      btn_Midi(MIDIOPEN).Enabled = True
      ' Disable other operations
      btn_Midi(MIDIPLAY).Enabled = False
      btn_Midi(MIDISTOP).Enabled = False
      btn_Midi(MIDICLOSE).Enabled = False
    End If
```

```
    End Select

    ' Display any error
    If (rc& <> 0) Then
      msg$ = "Midi Sequencer Error: " + Str$(rc&)
      MsgBox msg$, MB_ICONEXCLAMATION, "MIDI Error!"
    End If

End Sub

Sub btn_OK_Click ()

    ' Unload the form
    Unload Me

End Sub

Sub btn_Sound_Click (Index As Integer)

    Dim sflag%, rc%

    ' Kill any currently playing sound
    rc% = sndPlaySound%("", SND_NODEFAULT)

    ' Set the sound flag to no default (no sound if file not found),
    ' and asynchronous (play in the background)
    sflag% = SND_NODEFAULT + SND_ASYNC

    ' Determine the sound to play
    Select Case Index
      Case 0
        rc% = sndPlaySound%("TADA.WAV", sflag%)
      Case 1
        rc% = sndPlaySound%("DING.WAV", sflag%)
      Case 2
        rc% = sndPlaySound%("CHORD.WAV", sflag%)
      Case 3
        rc% = sndPlaySound%("CHIMES.WAV", sflag%)
      Case 4
        rc% = sndPlaySound%("LASER.WAV", sflag%)
      Case 5
        rc% = sndPlaySound%("HELLO.WAV", sflag%)
    End Select

End Sub

Sub Form_Load ()

    ' Center on the screen
    Move (Screen.Width - Width) \ 2, (Screen.Height - Height) \ 2
```

continues

Listing 5.1 continued

```
' Show about box
frm_AboutBox.Show 1

End Sub

Sub Form_Unload (Cancel As Integer)

  ' Close the Midi Sequencer, if active
  If (btn_Midi(MIDICLOSE).Enabled) Then
    btn_Midi_Click (MIDICLOSE)
  End If

End Sub
```

Listing 5.2 illustrates SDGLOBAL.BAS. This file contains the global constants and variables for the Sounds program.

Listing 5.2. The SDGLOBAL source code.

```
Option Explicit

' Message box beep constants
Global Const MB_DEFBEEP = -1
Global Const MB_ICONASTERISK = 64
Global Const MB_ICONEXCLAMATION = 48
Global Const MB_ICONHAND = 16
Global Const MB_ICONQUESTION = 32
Global Const MB_OK = 0

' sndPlaySound constants
Global Const SND_SYNC = 0
Global Const SND_ASYNC = 1
Global Const SND_NODEFAULT = 2
Global Const SND_LOOP = 8
Global Const SND_NOSTOP = 16

' MCI Buttons
Global Const MIDIOPEN = 0
Global Const MIDIPLAY = 1
Global Const MIDISTOP = 2
Global Const MIDICLOSE = 3

' Windows API Sound functions
Declare Sub MessageBeep Lib "User" (ByVal BeepType%)
Declare Function sndPlaySound% Lib "MMSystem" (ByVal WaveFile$,
➥ByVal Flags%)
Declare Function mciSendString& Lib "MMSystem" (ByVal SendString$,
ÂByVal ReturnString$, ByVal ReturnLength%, ByVal Callback%)
```

Program Overview

The Sound test program is a reference for use in other game programs you may develop. I discuss the use of the sound functions in Chapter 18, "Space Miner."

Summary

Visual Basic provides very limited sound support (one entire function to be exact). With the use of the Windows API and the Multimedia Extensions, you can extend the sound support. This allows virtually any kind of sound output through the use of WAV (wave) and MIDI files on sound cards (such as the Sound Blaster). However, wave files can be played without a sound card, using the PC Speaker wave file driver.

What's Ahead

So far, I've covered general display output, animation, and sound. In the next chapter, I'll look at file input and output and explain how they apply to game programming. If you want an easy place to store game information (such as the last high score), I'll show you how—next.

File I/O

Most programs have some form of file input or output (I/O), and games are no different (although some games don't use any at all). Some specific uses of file I/O in game programs include handling image loading and saving, configuration files, and high scores. In this chapter, I explain file I/O as it applies to game development.

On the Inside

Input and output occurs mostly internal to the game—and the user has no real control over it. Bitmaps, wave (sound) files, and data files, for example, are all read in and used without any user interaction.

Handling files is straightforward—until the user gets into the process. The most common manifestation of this is in the File Open and File Save dialog boxes.

Using Dialog Boxes to Open and Save Files

When programming in C, the construction of a File Open dialog box is a daunting task. Fortunately, Visual Basic includes all the built-in controls you'll need to construct such an animal. The Puzzler game uses one that looks like Figure 6.1.

Figure 6.1. A File Open dialog box.

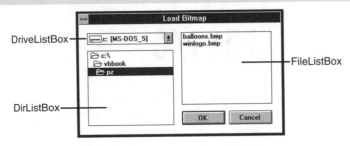

This form has three controls and two buttons. The `DriveListBox` control handles the available drives, the `DirListBox` control handles the directories, and the `FileListBox` control handles the listing of the files on the specified drive, in the specified directory. The two buttons, OK and Cancel, let the user accept or deny the file open request.

Placing the controls on the form is easy enough. To get the controls to work together, use the code shown in Listing 6.1. I'll give you a rough overview of how the form is set up.

First, you have to set the `Pattern` property of the `FileListBox` control to show only the files you are interested in—such as *.BMP. Add to the `flb_Files_DblClick` routine a call to `btn_OK_Click`, so the user can select a filename by double-clicking the mouse.

Second, you have to tell the `FileListBox` when the directory changes. Use this code (while in the `dlb_Dirs_Change` function):

```
' Update the file path
flb_Files.Path = dlb_Dirs.Path
```

This causes the files to be redisplayed when the directory changes. When the drive changes, you need to notify the directory list box in the `vlb_Drives_Change` procedure:

```
' Update the directory drive
dlb_Dirs.Path = vlb_Drives.Drive
```

This updates the directory list, which in turn updates the file list. Now, all three controls are linked together. When the drive changes, the directories and files are updated. When the directory changes, the files are updated. Also, when a file is selected (double-clicked), the OK button routine is called.

Finally, in the `btn_OK_Click` procedure, build the complete filename and path of the selected file.

You can expand on this simple dialog box. Add a combo box to enable the selection of file types (such as BMP and PCX). This addition would update the pattern property of the file list. If you want to get a little more complicated, add an edit control that would allow the user to directly type in a relative or complete pathname, including wildcards.

> If you have Visual Basic 3.0, the Professional Edition of Visual Basic 2.0, you might want to use the File Open common dialog box.

Listing 6.1 shows the source code for the PZLOAD form. This implements the File Open dialog box discussed previously. The form is actually used in the Puzzler game, discussed in Chapter 15.

Listing 6.1. The PZLOAD form source code.

```
VERSION 2.00
Begin Form frm_Load
   BorderStyle    =   3   'Fixed Double
   Caption        =   "Load Bitmap"
   Height         =   3420
   Left           =   2460
   LinkTopic      =   "Form2"
   MaxButton      =   0   'False
   MinButton      =   0   'False
   ScaleHeight    =   3015
   ScaleWidth     =   5685
   Top            =   2220
   Width          =   5805
   Begin CommandButton btn_Cancel
      Caption     =   "Cancel"
      Height      =   375
      Left        =   4200
      TabIndex    =   4
      Top         =   2400
      Width       =   1215
   End
   Begin CommandButton btn_Ok
      Caption     =   "OK"
      Height      =   375
      Left        =   2880
      TabIndex    =   3
      Top         =   2400
      Width       =   1215
   End
```

continues

Listing 6.1. continued

```
    Begin FileListBox flb_Files
        Height      =   1980
        Left        =   2880
        Pattern     =   "*.BMP"
        TabIndex    =   2
        Top         =   255
        Width       =   2535
    End
    Begin DirListBox dlb_Dirs
        Height      =   2055
        Left        =   240
        TabIndex    =   1
        Top         =   720
        Width       =   2415
    End
    Begin DriveListBox vlb_Drives
        Height      =   315
        Left        =   240
        TabIndex    =   0
        Top         =   240
        Width       =   2415
    End
End

Option Explicit

Sub btn_Cancel_Click ()

  ' Unload the form
  Unload Me

End Sub

Sub btn_Ok_Click ()

  ' Do we have a selected file?
  If (flb_Files.FileName <> "") Then

    ' Yes, so start building the complete path
    LoadFilename$ = flb_Files.Path

    ' We may need a backslash, if it's not already there
    If (LoadFilename$ <> "\") Then
      LoadFilename$ = LoadFilename$ + "\"
    End If
```

```
    ' Finally, add the filename
    LoadFilename$ = LoadFilename$ + flb_Files.FileName

  End If

  ' We're done with the form
  Unload Me

End Sub

Sub dlb_Dirs_Change ()

  ' Update the file path
  flb_Files.Path = dlb_Dirs.Path

End Sub

Sub flb_Files_DblClick ()

  ' This is the same as selecting OK
  btn_Ok_Click

End Sub

Sub Form_Load ()

  ' Center on the screen
  Move (Screen.Width - Width) \ 2, (Screen.Height - Height) \ 2

  ' Initialize filename to nothing
  LoadFilename$ = ""

End Sub

Sub vlb_Drives_Change ()

  ' Update the directory drive
  dlb_Dirs.Path = vlb_Drives.Drive

End Sub
```

Loading and Saving a Picture

Just as the File Open dialog box has controls, Visual Basic has built-in functions for loading and saving image bitmaps. These functions are LoadPicture and SavePicture, respectively. To load an image use the following code:

```
' Load a bitmap into the image control MyImage
MyImage.Picture = LoadPicture("MyBitmap.BMP")
```

Talk about easy! Predictably, saving a bitmap is just as easy:

```
' Save an image drawn on a form
SavePicture Image, "MyBitmap.BMP"
```

and voilà, you have a bitmap file! For most games, though, you'll probably be loading images and not saving them. A game typically loads image and sound files and saves files for the game configuration, status, and high scores.

Configuration Files

Speaking of configurations and high scores, just where do you keep track of that stuff? In a DOS game, your only choice is to save such data in a separate file. In Windows, though, you have another choice—the Windows initialization file.

WIN.INI

The file WIN.INI is the **WIN**dows **INI**tialization file. It contains all kinds of goodies for starting up Windows and Windows programs. You can take a look at it with any text editor. You'll see sections with titles in square brackets, such as [spooler]. These sections are for specific applications and their settings.

Other programs use WIN.INI for saving program settings, and you can too. You'll need the help of the Windows API, though. You can store values in WIN.INI by using the WriteProfileString function:

```
Declare Sub WriteProfileString Lib "Kernel" (ByVal AppName$,
➡ByVal KeyName$, ByVal KeyStr$)
```

This writes an entry in the WIN.INI file like so:

```
[AppName$]
KeyName$=KeyStr$
```

The AppName$ entry is usually the application name, and it specifies the title of the section to create and write to. The KeyName$ entry is the name of the key (variable) to store, and KeyStr$ is the string associated with the key (the value).

Say you want to store the high score for a game. Call the function like this:

```
' This is the highest score yet, so save it
WriteProfileString("Space Miner", "HighScore", Str$(Score%))
```

This creates a section in WIN.INI for Space Miner (if there isn't one already). If the high score is 15,600, the section would appear as follows:

```
[Space Miner]
HighScore=15600
```

If you save another high score later, another section won't be created—the current section is updated. Therefore, you can retrieve the high score the next time you play the game.

How do you retrieve the high score? Retrieve it with the help of another API function: GetProfileInt. This function is declared as

```
Declare Function GetProfileInt% Lib "Kernel" (ByVal AppName$,
➥ByVal KeyName$, ByVal DefaultVal%)
```

where AppName$ is the application name, and KeyName$ is the key (variable) name. The DefaultVal% parameter is the default value that gets returned if the key isn't found. Now, retrieve the high score from Space Miner like this

```
'Get the previous high score
HiScore% = GetProfileInt%("Space Miner", "HighScore", 0)
```

which sets HiScore% to 15600.

You can store many key names under a single application name. You can use different key names to save other game configuration information, such as color preferences, difficulty, and game defaults.

> You can retrieve a string instead of an integer by using the API function GetProfileString. Also, you can create and write to your own INI file instead of the WIN.INI file by using the WritePrivateProfileString, GetPrivateProfileInt, and GetPrivateProfileString API functions.

Saving information in the WIN.INI file has more advantages than using a separate file. You know the WIN.INI file is present, so you don't have to worry about finding it (in the path or otherwise). Windows also will handle the opening and closing of the file, reading and writing to it, or searching for it.

Saving a Game

Saving a game is similar to saving a high score. However, the hard part is saving all the necessary game information!

At first glance, saving a game in progress seems like a daunting task. How do you save the state of the entire program? Well, you don't. The value of the game variables is the only information you really need to save—which can be very minimal.

For the games included in this book, the values of the global variables in the *??*GLOBAL.BAS file are a good place to start.

You might have to save more than just game variables, though, depending on the game. If the game difficulty is controlled by what menu option is checked (and not by a variable), you'll have to save that too. One way to restrict the amount of information you have to save is by allowing the player to save a game at specific times only. For instance, have the player save the game at the beginning of a level or between card hands.

> If you have a lot of information and game variables to save, you should create a new .INI file, rather than using WIN.INI.

Summary

Games use file input and output for saving and loading images, and for configuration files. You can create The File Open/Save dialog box by using Visual Basic controls or the Common dialog box control. You can store high scores and other game status and configuration information in the Windows initialization file WIN.INI.

What's Ahead

Programming for file I/O is a straightforward task, but how do you make the computer "think"? In the next chapter, I'll explore ways of teaching a computer to "think," and how to play a game. I'll also discuss ways of making the computer more human. To find out what that entails, read on!

Making the Computer Think

A computer is just a high-speed idiot. It does exactly what you tell it to do and only what you tell it to do—no more, no less. The challenge in many game programs is to make the computer play a game well by "thinking" about its move. In this chapter, I provide some insight into how to make a computer think.

The Computer as Opponent

A computer will make the same mistake millions and millions of times—and never learn from it. A computer won't ever get any worse or better at playing a game. For these reasons, the computer isn't an ideal opponent.

The player doesn't really want to be reminded that the opponent is a computer. Most users want the computer to be as human as possible (slow, unpredictable, and error prone). I'll show how to *humanize* the computer.

Delaying

Timing is an important consideration when designing a game. All of this book's games use a Delay procedure. The delay is used for many things, such as flashing a game piece or allowing enough time for the player to read a message. Delays are used to slow down the computer's responses as well.

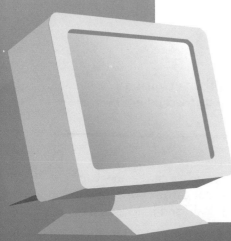

Think about it. Picture yourself playing a game against the computer. Even if the game is as easy as Tic-Tac-Toe, it probably takes you a few seconds to half a minute to make a move. If the computer makes its move instantaneously, you would be depressed! A "real" opponent would take longer.

Something as simple as delaying a response adds to the playability and enjoyment of the game. The player wants to believe the computer is a living, breathing opponent—which means that the computer should take at least a few seconds to make a move. I've increased the delay, depending on the difficulty level—just to give the player the impression the computer is thinking longer!

NOTE

> The Apples & Oranges game uses the delayed response technique. The game also flashes a Thinking... message. This brief delay gives the user time to read the message as well.

Each game includes the Delay procedure in its global module. The procedure is defined as

```
'
' This procedure delays the given number of seconds, which can be
' fractional.
'
Sub Delay (secs!)

  Dim Start!

  ' Get the current seconds since midnight
  Start! = Timer

  ' Wait for seconds to elapse
  While (Timer < (Start! + secs!))
    ' Let other things run while we wait
    DoEvents
  Wend

End Sub
```

The delay can be a fraction of a second. You'd be surprised at what a 1/4- or 1/2-second delay can do to improve a game! To delay a half second use the following:

```
' Delay the move
Delay .5
```

Use delays in your games to enhance the playing experience. In a card game, you wouldn't want the cards dealt instantly—because actual cards take time to deal. This gives the player time to see each card as it is dealt, and it adds to the excitement (Ace, <delay> Eight, <delay> Ace, <delay> ...*I have a pair! Will I get another Ace?...*, King <delay>, ...*Come on Ace!...*, Ace ...*Yes!...*). In the real world, nothing happens instantly—and it shouldn't in your game, either.

Use delays in moderation of course. Nothing is more frustrating than waiting for something to happen. Excessive delays will detract from your game.

Use of Randomness

Computers do the same thing over and over and never get bored. Using the Tic-Tac-Toe example again, what if the computer always took the center square each time it moved first? Not only would this be boring, it would prevent the player from ever winning the game.

The easiest way to vary a computer's moves is with the `GetRandom` function (also included in the global module of the games in this book):

```
'
' This function returns a random number between 0 and range%-1,
' inclusive.
'
Function GetRandom% (range%)

   ' In the Visual Basic manual, the generic formula is:
   ' Int((upperbound-lowerbound+1)*Rnd+lowerbound)
   GetRandom% = Int(range% * Rnd)

End Function
```

Tic-Tac-Toe has nine squares. To randomly pick one, use:

```
' Pick one of the nine squares
sq% = GetRandom%(8)
```

This gives you a number from 0 to 8 which you can use to select a square.

> To generate a different series of random numbers each time your game runs, include the Visual Basic `Randomize` statement in the form load procedure.

Keep in mind that you can use `GetRandom%` for more than just random moves. In the Apples & Oranges game, I used the statement for picking between moves of equal value. For instance, if there are 12 valid moves, and three of those moves captures the same number of pieces, use `GetRandom` to pick between the three moves. That way, the computer doesn't play the game the same way every time (just like a human player).

Difficulty Levels

For the game to be entertaining, it's important to select a good difficulty level. Remember Goldilocks? You have to get the porridge just right.

Too Hot

If the computer always plays a perfect game, it will probably always beat the player. To be repeatedly beaten by the computer is not most users' idea of a good time.

Too Cold

Conversely, a game that's too easy to beat is not any fun. A game has to be challenging, or no one will play it (more than once, anyway).

Just Right

Getting the game just right can be a challenging task. What was perfect for Goldilocks wasn't perfect for Papa Bear! The answer, in many cases, is to let the user set the game difficulty level—but how do you control the difficulty?

Changing the difficulty depends on the game. Following, in the "Algorithms" section, are some hints for varying the difficulty level.

Algorithms

The computer plays the game by using an algorithm that you design. Your algorithm has to account for every possible situation that can happen. The algorithm also controls how smart the computer is at playing the game. Each game has a different algorithm (and might have more than one if you allow for changing the difficulty). Following are some general techniques for controlling the difficulty level, depending on the game type.

Board Games

A board game algorithm can be simple or difficult to implement. Certainly, you can more easily teach a computer to play Checkers than Chess. (Chess algorithms are beyond the scope of this book.)

In a board game, the beginning difficulty can be random moves (which is what I used in A&O and Flip). What's interesting, however, is that the computer does much better at the A&O game using this method than with Flip—see for yourself. The games use different algorithms for increasing the difficulty, such as finding the move that flips the most pieces, or making a move to a position that is more valuable (such as an edge or corner).

Another method of changing the difficulty is for the computer to look ahead to future moves. For instance, for every possible move, the computer could look at the player's best possible response. How would that help? Well, if the algorithm looks for the maximum pieces gained by a move, the algorithm would subtract the pieces gained back by the opponent's next move. If the computer's best move gains four pieces, but the opponent can take six back, the net gain is -2. A better plan is to make a move with a gain of three, with the opponent taking two back, for a net gain of one. If the opponent doesn't see the best comeback, the gain is even higher.

Looking ahead can be time-consuming. If 10 possible moves exist, and the player can make 10 possible responses for each move, 100 moves must be analyzed.

Another method of varying the difficulty level is to handicap the computer. A human opponent won't "see" the best move every time. You can simulate this by only making the best move 33 percent of the time on the easy level, 66 percent on the medium level, and 100 percent on the difficult level.

Card Games

Card game algorithms can be easier than board games. Take BlackJack for instance—the computer dealer draws cards until it has 17 or above, and that's it! A game like Draw Poker, however, can be harder to implement.

This book's Draw Poker algorithm is simple. If the computer already has a hand, it keeps it; if not, it keeps any pairs or more of the same card. This is a conservative way to play poker. What if the computer has four out of five cards of a straight—and a pair? A human opponent might go for the straight and throw away one of the cards in the pair. What about bluffing? You can change the algorithm to bluff when the computer doesn't have a hand.

In multiplayer card games, you can assign a personality to each computer player. "Meek Mike," for instance, always could play conservatively (never throw a pair, never draw to an inside straight, never bluff); "Norm" could play more of a normal game (sometimes split a pair, draw to outside straights, and bluff occasionally); and "Ace" could play aggressively (draw for flushes and straights, bluff, and bet up the pot).

Puzzle Games

Puzzle games don't have a computer opponent (so they don't have computer algorithms). The difficulty level is usually controlled by the number of pieces in the puzzle or the number of necessary moves.

Arcade Games

Arcade games are a little different than board or card games, because the opponent is not usually expected to be human. An arcade game usually isn't a computer version of a familiar board or card game, so it has a totally new environment with different rules.

Many arcade games are shoot-em'-up, blast-the-alien kinds of games (much like the Space Miner game). The computer's role is to make aliens or alien ships or other bad guys appear, and to have them chase you. The bad guys are usually fearless—charging bravely (stupidly?) into your blazing guns. Although this leads to their destruction time and again, there seems to be a never-ending supply of enemies.

The difficulty in arcade games is controlled differently than in board or card games. The difficulty usually progresses through game levels. The first level is easy, perhaps because there are only a few enemies. Successive levels throw more and more enemies at you, so the odds of making it through are less.

Other ways of changing the arcade game difficulty include limiting the resources of the player (ammunition, fuel, crew, air, and so on), increasing the speed of the game, and providing a time limit.

Two Players

Ultimately, another human player is the best opponent. Consider allowing this option in your game. Players can alternate turns, or you can provide simultaneous play by assigning different keys on the keyboard (or different input devices—one player on the keyboard and one on the mouse).

Summary

A computer opponent should be as human as possible—slow, unpredictable, and error prone. This can be accomplished with well-placed delays and random computer moves. You can create difficulty levels by using different algorithms, by looking ahead at future moves, and by ignoring (not seeing) current moves. A human opponent might be the best adversary, but a computer opponent can come very close—while providing both a challenge and a lot of fun.

What's Ahead

Computer games have come a long way in a short time. There seems to be no sign of slowing down. Next, I discuss some of the advanced gaming concepts which are on the horizon—and destined for your desktop.

Advanced Concepts

Many advanced gaming techniques are beyond the scope of this book (the creation of setup programs and Windows help files, flight simulation, texture mapping, 3-D, morphing, and multiplayer routines). Some techniques don't apply to Visual Basic games directly, but they might in the future, so I'll touch on a few of them in this chapter.

Installation and Setup

If you decide to release your game commercially or as shareware, you'll definitely need to provide an installation or setup program. The Visual Basic Professional Edition comes with the Application Setup Wizard (see Figure 8.1), which makes creating a setup program easy. It also provides the source code for the setup program (called SETUP1), which is written in Visual Basic.

Figure 8.1. The Application Setup Wizard.

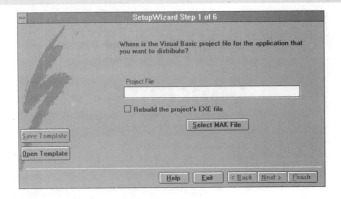

Windows Help

This book's games use normal form windows for displaying the game rules and help. The Professional Edition of Visual Basic provides a Help Compiler used to create professional online help—similar to the kind Visual Basic provides (see Figure 8.2).

Most users expect online help. Unfortunately, writing a good help file can be time-consuming. The Rich Text Format (RTF) and the help macros are like new languages. It will be worth your time learning them, though, because your programs will look more professional.

Use the Help Compiler to generate a help file that includes notes on how to play your game, game options, and strategies. Also, use it to include any registration instructions and information about how the user can contact you or your company.

Flight Simulators

Flight simulators are games which realistically re-create the features and controls of a particular aircraft. The games are very detailed in their cockpit control implementation and flight control. The graphics for the games are usually drawn with lines and polygons, so the detail can be less realistic.

Visual Basic (and Windows in general) isn't well-suited for developing flight simulations because of speed requirements for the graphics computation and display. Games, such as card games and board games, are better suited for Visual Basic, because they adapt well to the form-based architecture. It's possible, however, to write arcade style games—as I'll show in Part II of this book.

Probably the most well-known flight simulators are Microsoft Flight Simulator and Falcon 3.0—both are DOS applications.

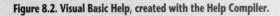

Figure 8.2. Visual Basic Help, created with the Help Compiler.

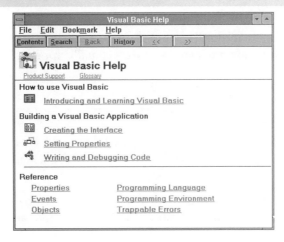

Flic Files

Flic (pronounced *flick*) files are produced by Autodesk Animator. They're bit-mapped frame animations, much like a movie (or "flick").

Some games, like Populous II, use flic files for opening animations and introductions. You'll see flic files used mainly for DOS games, but flic file players, such as AAPLAY, are available for Windows. If you get a chance, download the player and some .FLI files from CompuServe. At the CompuServe "!" prompt, type **GO ADESK** to reach the Autodesk forums.

Texture Mapping

Texture mapping involves mapping (applying) a bitmap to the surface of an object. If you have a cylinder, you might map a marble pattern on it to simulate a marble column. Likewise, you might use a wood pattern on a rectangular surface to simulate a wood floor.

Texture mapping can be time-consuming, but new techniques make the effect fast enough for games. A very successful DOS shareware game, called Wolfenstein 3-D, uses this technique. Patterns are mapped onto walls and floors for brick effects, wood panels, paintings, doors, and so on. All of this is performed at a speed that is fast enough to look like you are really looking around a room.

3-D

Most arcade games are two dimensional—you can move a player or object right, left, up, and down. Three Dimensions (3-D) refers to a game in which the player appears to move into and out of the display. Flight simulators are three-dimensional games, for example.

The term 3-D might change (as it applies to games). It may come to mean the same as 3-D means in a movie, in which the objects actually appear three dimensional and realistic.

Virtual Reality

Virtual reality games are making their way to home game systems, such as Sega and Nintendo. With a 3-D movie, objects project out of the screen. A virtual reality game puts you into the middle of the action.

To play a virtual reality game, you usually have to put on a headset with special glasses. You might also wear a special glove so you can interact with the virtual world. Virtual reality games attach to the player (by goggles and gloves, for instance) and follow the player's movements, making virtual objects seem real at every direction and angle.

Morphing

Morphing is the term used to describe the transformation of one shape or object into another. You can do this with a tool, such as Autodesk Animator, just by specifying the beginning and ending shapes. The in-between shapes are automatically figured for you—a process sometimes called *tweening* (for in-between).

Popular examples of tweening include the Michael Jackson music video for "Black or White," in which various people are smoothly blended from one face to another. Also, in *Terminator 2*, the villain (a liquid metal robot) repeatedly morphs into any shape it chooses.

Multiplayer

Getting back to something closer to home, multiplayer games are emerging in number. They involve more than enabling two players to participate on the same computer and keyboard. A multiplayer game enables you to hook up to another computer through a serial cable or modem and play against a human opponent running the same game.

You can develop a multiplayer game with Visual Basic and the Professional Edition. Use the MSComm custom control for the serial communication interface, and you're job is easy. When you have the communication established between the games, you have to send the player moves back and forth. It might take you a while to get it right (I recommend testing on two computers in the same room!), but the rewards are worth it.

Professional Features

As I've hinted, the controls included with the Professional Edition version of Visual Basic have some uses in games as well. Figure 8.3 shows all of the controls included with the professional edition.

Figure 8.3. The Professional Edition controls.

Other than using the communication control MSComm, you can use controls for 3-D buttons and objects, animated buttons, picture clipping (to display a portion of a picture), spinners, and more. You can purchase controls that offer additional or enhanced controls (such as one that gives you the ability to define your own mouse cursor). Be sure to check out different controls, and see if you can use them in your game.

Other professional features include the Setup Wizard and the Help Compiler. As I mentioned earlier, consider using both these tools if you decide to release your game.

Summary

DOS-based games use many advanced features which might make their way into the Windows and Visual Basic arena in the near future. These features include flight simulation, flic file playback, texture mapping, 3-D, and virtual reality. Additionally, techniques, such as multiplayer options and the use of the Professional Edition, are now used to jazz up games.

What's Ahead

In the next chapter, I'll take a brief look at debugging techniques for games. Debugging your game is important, so don't skip the next chapter! After that, the fun begins as I guide you through the development of the games included with this book.

Debugging

Debugging a game can be different than debugging a normal Visual Basic program. Certain debugging techniques are common to both, of course, but some differences are worth pointing out. When you have a game up and running, you must test the game logic—or how well the computer plays the game. In this chapter, I present a few methods for doing just that.

> Be sure to read the chapter about debugging in your Visual Basic manual. It's an excellent reference and could save you a lot of time and effort.

Normal Debugging

As with any Visual Basic program, you must deal with a host of possible errors. These include:

➡ Syntax Errors

➡ Runtime Errors

➡ Logical Errors

You might commit these errors many times during the development of your game. Make sure you read the Visual Basic documentation about debugging for a complete overview of error types and how to find and correct them.

One Step at a Time

A rule states that you should step through every line of code you write at least once. I believe this makes perfect sense, but I also believe that no one ever does this. Many times, you can tell immediately whether a routine works or not.

Other routines, however, can be very complex. In most games, the nonvisual part of the game involves the routines for determining a move for the computer to make. All you see in the game is a delay or a Thinking message. I definitely recommend stepping through the algorithm functions for the game. Just set a breakpoint on the computer move deduction functions. When the functions get called, step through them.

Using Sound

In some cases, a little audio feedback can make a big difference. Just place a Beep statement to see if the code gets called (or when it gets called). If the function gets called often, however, you probably want to use a different technique.

The Debug Window

The Debug Window is very handy for debugging games. Although you can query variable values interactively, you can print values to the window from the program, as in

```
Debug.Print "The hidden code is: ";code%
```

The value of code% is displayed any time the program runs inside the Visual Basic environment. If you make an EXE out of the game, you don't need to remove the debug statements! They won't appear if you run the program outside of VB. You can add any number of debug print statements to your program. Figure 9.1 shows actual debug output from the Draw Poker game.

Figure 9.1. Printing to the Debug Window.

```
Debug Window [PKWINNER.FRM]
Hands after Counting:
Dealer Hand:   1
Player Hand:   3
```

I used the technique of printing to the debug window quite a bit. That way, I didn't have to add a lot of watch statements to the debug window each time I started a new session. Plus, you have the benefit of adding any description or operation to the data. Being able to leave the code in the final game is an added bonus.

Play, Play, Play

Part of debugging a game is to play, play, play. You have to play the game many times to make sure you have thought of everything. It's a tough job, I know—but somebody has to do it.

Forcing the Issue

However, a Royal Flush comes up only four times out of 2,598,960 hands! You certainly would not want to keep playing Poker until a Royal Flush appears. You have to force a hand to appear (when cheating at cards, this is called "Stacking the Deck"). When thoroughly testing or debugging your game, make sure you test as many possibilities as you can.

Testing the Resolution

Don't forget to try your game using different Windows configurations. Run the game in EGA, VGA, and even SVGA resolutions. Try playing the game in 2-color, 16-color, and 256-color modes. After all, your game will be played on many kinds of system setups.

You may find that you've forgotten to account for the aspect ratio or that your window size is too big. It never hurts to test.

Using Grace

How graceful is your game? Does it display an error message when it can't find a file, or does it just hang the computer? Remember to go back and test such things as low-memory considerations and missing files. Check to see how the game runs off of a floppy, too.

Summary

Use the normal debugging techniques (described in the Visual Basic documenta-tion) for writing your game. In addition, single step through the game algorithms, use the Beep function in key places for audio feedback, use the Debug Window for printing variable information, and play, play, play!

What's Ahead

This chapter concludes Part I: The Basics of Game Programming. In the next sec-tion, Exercises in Game Development, I illustrate the development of nine differ-ent games. So, let's go play some games!

Exercises in Game Programming

PART II

Apples & Oranges

Apples & Orànges is a board game that is similar to Othello and Reversi. In this chapter I describe the game of Apples & Oranges, tell you how it's played, and offer some hints. I also cover the programming of the game, provide the code listings, and give a full description of the techniques used. You'll learn about

- ➤ Hidden controls
- ➤ Mouse pointers
- ➤ Help windows
- ➤ The general purpose About box
- ➤ Control arrays
- ➤ Computer "thinking"
- ➤ Board weighted algorithms
- ➤ Varying game difficulty

Background

You'll probably recognize this game as being similar to Reversi—one of the first games to ship with Microsoft Windows. Before that, it was a board game known as Othello, which was probably based on yet another game. And now we have Apples & Oranges!

Gameplay

Apples & Oranges, or A&O, is a two-player game where each player is represented by an apple or an orange. You also can play against the computer. Each player tries to capture the most pieces on the board by surrounding the other player's pieces. An opponent's pieces are surrounded when a player's piece exists on both ends of a straight line (I'll illustrate this shortly). After a move is made, all surrounded pieces in all directions (including diagonally) are captured (changed) to the moving player's pieces. The game ends when no valid moves can be made, and the winner is the player with the most pieces.

Running A&O

To begin playing A&O, select the A&O icon from the VB Arcade program group you installed. (Appendix A provides installation instructions.) When you run the game, you'll see the About box first. Click OK, and A&O appears.

Playing a Game

From the Options menu, you can select Easy, Medium, or Difficult as the difficulty level for playing against the computer. You also can select the Two Player option to play against yourself or a friend.

The difficulty level can be changed at any time during gameplay.

You can tell whose turn it is by looking at the playing pieces on the right side of the board, and seeing whose piece is surrounded by a thick border. Apple always starts first. Each player's score is indicated under their respective playing piece.

The game begins with two of each player's pieces arranged in the center of the board (See Figure 10.1). From this starting position, you can make four different valid moves. When you move the cursor over a board square, it changes to a cross if the move is valid. A valid move is a move that will capture one or more of your opponent's pieces. Figure 10.2 shows valid moves for Apple—the board squares where a cross appears. Figure 10.3 shows the board after Apple has made the first move.

Figure 10.1. The opening board.

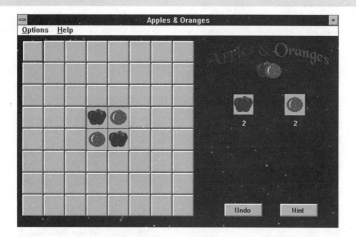

Figure 10.2. Valid moves for Apple.

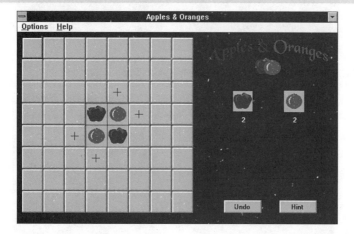

It's important to remember that an opponent's pieces are captured in all directions. Figure 10.4 illustrates a move that Orange can make that will capture Apple's pieces in three directions. This move changes the score from 18-9 to 10-17, putting Orange in the lead.

> Apple may be in the "pits" now, but still has time to put the "squeeze" on Orange!

Figure 10.3. Apple has made a move.

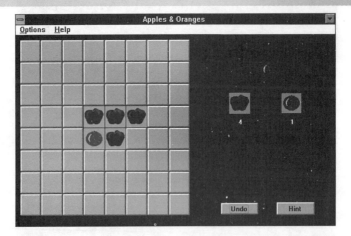

Figure 10.4. An Orange move that captures Apple's pieces in three directions.

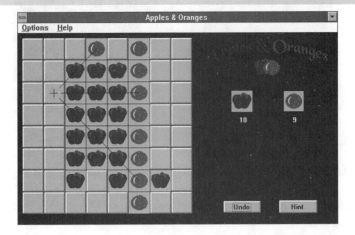

Two other buttons are important during the game: Undo and Hint. The Undo button, as its name suggests, will undo your last move. If you are playing against the computer, it will undo both your move and the computer's. The Hint button provides you with a suggestion of where to move next.

If you select Hint repeatedly—without making a move—you may notice that Hint doesn't always recommend the same move each time. This occurs when several moves have the same relative value.

The game progresses with each player alternating turns until the entire board is filled, or until there are no more valid moves. In either case, the winner is the player with the most pieces on the board. There can be a tie.

> Sometimes a player can't make a valid move. If this occurs, a message such as "Apple Forfeits" appears in the Messages box, and it becomes the other players turn.

Hints

A&O can be a difficult and sometimes frustrating game to play. Just when you think you have the other player backed into a corner, you lose 10 of your pieces. Some simple hints follow:

➡ Try to capture the board edges—especially the corners. It's harder for an opponent to recapture the edges. Edge positions can enable a player to capture entire rows and columns.

➡ Likewise, try not to move to a position that allows your opponent to capture an edge or corner position.

➡ The game is not over until the end. You can be losing miserably at first, but the more opponent pieces there are, the more there are to capture.

➡ Remember that every piece you capture is really worth two points—one point is taken away from your opponent, and one point is added to your score.

➡ Make use of the mouse cursor. Scan the whole board with it to reveal all your valid moves.

Programming

The makefile for A&O contains the files listed in Table 10.1.

Table 10.1. A&O source files.

Filename	Description
AOABOUT.FRM	The About box form
AOMAIN.FRM	The Main A&O form
AORULES.FRM	The A&O Rules form
AOGLOBAL.BAS	Contains global constants, variables, and procedures

TIP

All the files in Table 10.1 are included on this book's disk. See Appendix A for installation instructions.

Figure 10.5 illustrates the AOABOUT form, and Listing 10.1 contains the AOABOUT.FRM source code.

Figure 10.5. The AOABOUT form.

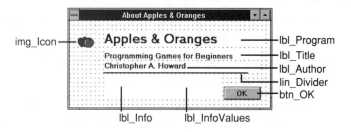

Listing 10.1. The AOABOUT .FRM source code.

```
VERSION 2.00
Begin Form frm_AboutBox
    BorderStyle     =   3   'Fixed Double
    Caption         =   "About Apples & Oranges"
    ClipControls    =   0    'False
    FontBold        =   -1   'True
    FontItalic      =   0    'False
    FontName        =   "System"
    FontSize        =   9.75
    FontStrikethru  =   0    'False
    FontUnderline   =   0    'False
    Height          =   2775
    Icon            =   0
```

```
        Left             =    1575
        MaxButton        =    0     'False
        MinButton        =    0     'False
        ScaleHeight      =    2370
        ScaleWidth       =    5640
        Top              =    1335
        Width            =    5760
        Begin CommandButton btn_OK
            Caption          =    "OK"
            FontBold         =    -1    'True
            FontItalic       =    0     'False
            FontName         =    "System"
            FontSize         =    9.75
            FontStrikethru   =    0     'False
            FontUnderline    =    0     'False
            Height           =    360
            Left             =    4350
            TabIndex         =    5
            Top              =    1800
            Width            =    1035
        End
        Begin Image img_Icon
            Height           =    480
            Left             =    240
            Picture          =    AOABOUT.FRX:0000 'AO.ICO
            Top              =    360
            Width            =    480
        End
        Begin Line lin_Divider
            BorderWidth      =    2
            X1               =    975
            X2               =    5010
            Y1               =    1425
            Y2               =    1425
        End
        Begin Label lbl_Program
            Caption          =    "Apples && Oranges"
            FontBold         =    -1    'True
            FontItalic       =    0     'False
            FontName         =    "MS Sans Serif"
            FontSize         =    18
            FontStrikethru   =    0     'False
            FontUnderline    =    0     'False
            Height           =    450
            Left             =    990
            TabIndex         =    1
            Top              =    270
            Width            =    4440
        End
        Begin Label lbl_Title
            Caption          =    "Programming Games For Beginners"
            FontBold         =    -1    'True
```

continues

Listing 10.1. continued

```
        FontItalic      =    0     'False
        FontName        =    "MS Sans Serif"
        FontSize        =    9.75
        FontStrikethru  =    0     'False
        FontUnderline   =    0     'False
        Height          =    240
        Left            =    990
        TabIndex        =    2
        Top             =    840
        Width           =    4305
    End
    Begin Label lbl_Author
        Caption         =    "Christopher A. Howard"
        FontBold        =    -1    'True
        FontItalic      =    0     'False
        FontName        =    "MS Sans Serif"
        FontSize        =    9.75
        FontStrikethru  =    0     'False
        FontUnderline   =    0     'False
        Height          =    240
        Left            =    990
        TabIndex        =    3
        Top             =    1110
        Width           =    4365
    End
    Begin Label lbl_Info
        Height          =    600
        Left            =    1005
        TabIndex        =    4
        Top             =    1545
        Width           =    1875
    End
    Begin Label lbl_InfoValues
        Height          =    600
        Left            =    2880
        TabIndex        =    0
        Top             =    1545
        Width           =    1410
    End
End
Option Explicit

' Windows API functions used
Declare Function GetFreeSpace Lib "Kernel" (ByVal wFlags%) As Long
Declare Function GetWinFlags Lib "Kernel" () As Long
```

```
' Windows constants used
Const WF_STANDARD = &H10
Const WF_ENHANCED = &H20
Const WF_80x87 = &H400

Sub btn_OK_Click ()

  ' We are done
  Unload Me

End Sub

Sub Form_Load ()

  Dim WinFlags&
  Dim Mode$, Processor$, CRLF$

  ' Center the AboutBox on the screen
  Move (Screen.Width - Width) \ 2, (Screen.Height - Height) \ 2

  ' Make it easier for strings
  CRLF$ = Chr$(13) + Chr$(10)

  ' Get current Windows configuration
  WinFlags& = GetWinFlags()

  ' Determine mode
  If (WinFlags& And WF_ENHANCED) Then
    Mode$ = "386 Enhanced Mode"
  Else
    Mode$ = "Standard Mode"
  End If

  ' Free memory
  lbl_Info.Caption = Mode$ + CRLF$ + "Free Memory:" + CRLF$ + "Math Co-
➥processor:"

  ' 80x87 math chip
  If (WinFlags& And WF_80x87) Then
    Processor$ = "Present"
  Else
    Processor$ = "None"
  End If

  ' Free space
  lbl_InfoValues.Caption = CRLF$ + Format$(GetFreeSpace(0) \ 1024) + " KB"
➥+ CRLF$ + Processor$

End Sub
```

Figure 10.6 shows the AOMAIN form, and Listing 10.2 is the source code for AOMAIN.FRM.

Figure 10.6. The AOMAIN form.

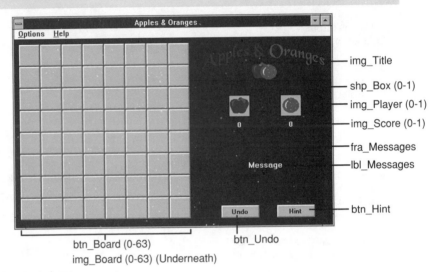

	img_Title
	shp_Box (0-1)
	img_Player (0-1)
	img_Score (0-1)
	fra_Messages
	lbl_Messages
	btn_Hint

btn_Board (0-63)
img_Board (0-63) (Underneath)

btn_Undo

Listing 10.2. The AOMAIN .FRM source code.

```
VERSION 2.00
Begin Form frm_AO
    BackColor       =   &H00800000&
    BorderStyle     =   3   'Fixed Double
    Caption         =   "Apples & Oranges"
    Height          =   5805
    Icon            =   AOMAIN.FRX:0000 'AO.ICO
    KeyPreview      =   -1  'True
    Left            =   1290
    LinkTopic       =   "Form1"
    MaxButton       =   0   'False
    ScaleHeight     =   341
    ScaleMode       =   3   'Pixel
    ScaleWidth      =   592
    Top             =   1110
    Width           =   9000
    Begin Frame fra_Messages
        BackColor       =   &H00800000&
        Caption         =   "Messages"
        ForeColor       =   &H00000000&
        Height          =   1215
        Left            =   5520
        TabIndex        =   68
        Top             =   2760
        Width           =   3015
        Begin Label lbl_Message
```

```
            Alignment       =   2  'Center
            BackColor       =   &H00800000&
            Caption         =   "Message"
            FontBold        =   -1  'True
            FontItalic      =   0   'False
            FontName        =   "MS Sans Serif"
            FontSize        =   9.75
            FontStrikethru  =   0   'False
            FontUnderline   =   0   'False
            ForeColor       =   &H00FFFFFF&
            Height          =   375
            Left            =   120
            TabIndex        =   69
            Top             =   600
            Width           =   2775
        End
    End
    Begin CommandButton btn_Undo
        BackColor       =   &H00800000&
        Caption         =   "Undo"
        Enabled         =   0   'False
        Height          =   375
        Left            =   5760
        TabIndex        =   66
        Top             =   4560
        Width           =   1095
    End
    Begin CommandButton btn_Hint
        BackColor       =   &H00800000&
        Caption         =   "Hint"
        Enabled         =   0   'False
        Height          =   375
        Left            =   7320
        TabIndex        =   67
        Top             =   4560
        Width           =   1095
    End
    Begin CommandButton btn_Board
        BackColor       =   &H00800000&
        Height          =   615
        Index           =   63
        Left            =   4320
        MousePointer    =   2  'Cross
        TabIndex        =   63
        TabStop         =   0   'False
        Top             =   4320
        Width           =   615
    End
    Begin CommandButton btn_Board
        BackColor       =   &H00800000&
        Height          =   615
```

continues

Listing 10.2. continued

```
        Index          =    62
        Left           =    3720
        MousePointer   =    2    'Cross
        TabIndex       =    62
        TabStop        =    0     'False
        Top            =    4320
        Width          =    615
     End
     Begin CommandButton btn_Board
        BackColor      =    &H00800000&
        Height         =    615
        Index          =    61
        Left           =    3120
        MousePointer   =    2    'Cross
        TabIndex       =    61
        TabStop        =    0     'False
        Top            =    4320
        Width          =    615
     End
     Begin CommandButton btn_Board
        BackColor      =    &H00800000&
        Height         =    615
        Index          =    60
        Left           =    2520
        MousePointer   =    2    'Cross
        TabIndex       =    60
        TabStop        =    0     'False
        Top            =    4320
        Width          =    615
     End
     Begin CommandButton btn_Board
        BackColor      =    &H00800000&
        Height         =    615
        Index          =    59
        Left           =    1920
        MousePointer   =    2    'Cross
        TabIndex       =    59
        TabStop        =    0     'False
        Top            =    4320
        Width          =    615
     End
     Begin CommandButton btn_Board
        BackColor      =    &H00800000&
        Height         =    615
        Index          =    58
        Left           =    1320
        MousePointer   =    2    'Cross
        TabIndex       =    58
        TabStop        =    0     'False
        Top            =    4320
        Width          =    615
     End
```

```
Begin CommandButton btn_Board
   BackColor        =    &H00800000&
   Height           =    615
   Index            =    57
   Left             =    720
   MousePointer     =    2   'Cross
   TabIndex         =    57
   TabStop          =    0      'False
   Top              =    4320
   Width            =    615
End
Begin CommandButton btn_Board
   BackColor        =    &H00800000&
   Height           =    615
   Index            =    56
   Left             =    120
   MousePointer     =    2   'Cross
   TabIndex         =    56
   TabStop          =    0      'False
   Top              =    4320
   Width            =    615
End
Begin CommandButton btn_Board
   BackColor        =    &H00800000&
   Height           =    615
   Index            =    55
   Left             =    4320
   MousePointer     =    2   'Cross
   TabIndex         =    55
   TabStop          =    0      'False
   Top              =    3720
   Width            =    615
End
Begin CommandButton btn_Board
   BackColor        =    &H00800000&
   Height           =    615
   Index            =    54
   Left             =    3720
   MousePointer     =    2   'Cross
   TabIndex         =    54
   TabStop          =    0      'False
   Top              =    3720
   Width            =    615
End
Begin CommandButton btn_Board
   BackColor        =    &H00800000&
   Height           =    615
   Index            =    53
   Left             =    3120
   MousePointer     =    2   'Cross
   TabIndex         =    53
   TabStop          =    0      'False
```

continues

Listing 10.2. continued

```
        Top              =    3720
        Width            =    615
    End
    Begin CommandButton btn_Board
        BackColor        =    &H00800000&
        Height           =    615
        Index            =    52
        Left             =    2520 ·
        MousePointer     =    2   'Cross
        TabIndex         =    52
        TabStop          =    0     'False
        Top              =    3720
        Width            =    615
    End
    Begin CommandButton btn_Board
        BackColor        =    &H00800000&
        Height           =    615
        Index            =    51
        Left             =    1920
        MousePointer     =    2   'Cross
        TabIndex         =    51
        TabStop          =    0     'False
        Top              =    3720
        Width            =    615
    End
    Begin CommandButton btn_Board
        BackColor        =    &H00800000&
        Height           =    615
        Index            =    50
        Left             =    1320
        MousePointer     =    2   'Cross
        TabIndex         =    50
        TabStop          =    0     'False
        Top              =    3720
        Width            =    615
    End
    Begin CommandButton btn_Board
        BackColor        =    &H00800000&
        Height           =    615
        Index            =    49
        Left             =    720
        MousePointer     =    2   'Cross
        TabIndex         =    49
        TabStop          =    0     'False
        Top              =    3720
        Width            =    615
    End
    Begin CommandButton btn_Board
        BackColor        =    &H00800000&
        Height           =    615
```

```
      Index           =    48
      Left            =    120
      MousePointer    =    2   'Cross
      TabIndex        =    48
      TabStop         =    0    'False
      Top             =    3720
      Width           =    615
   End
   Begin CommandButton btn_Board
      BackColor       =    &H00800000&
      Height          =    615
      Index           =    47
      Left            =    4320
      MousePointer    =    2   'Cross
      TabIndex        =    47
      TabStop         =    0    'False
      Top             =    3120
      Width           =    615
   End
   Begin CommandButton btn_Board
      BackColor       =    &H00800000&
      Height          =    615
      Index           =    46
      Left            =    3720
      MousePointer    =    2   'Cross
      TabIndex        =    46
      TabStop         =    0    'False
      Top             =    3120
      Width           =    615
   End
   Begin CommandButton btn_Board
      BackColor       =    &H00800000&
      Height          =    615
      Index           =    45
      Left            =    3120
      MousePointer    =    2   'Cross
      TabIndex        =    45
      TabStop         =    0    'False
      Top             =    3120
      Width           =    615
   End
   Begin CommandButton btn_Board
      BackColor       =    &H00800000&
      Height          =    615
      Index           =    44
      Left            =    2520
      MousePointer    =    2   'Cross
      TabIndex        =    44
      TabStop         =    0    'False
      Top             =    3120
      Width           =    615
   End
```

continues

Listing 10.2. continued

```
Begin CommandButton btn_Board
   BackColor      =    &H00800000&
   Height         =    615
   Index          =    43
   Left           =    1920
   MousePointer   =    2  'Cross
   TabIndex       =    43
   TabStop        =    0   'False
   Top            =    3120
   Width          =    615
End
Begin CommandButton btn_Board
   BackColor      =    &H00800000&
   Height         =    615
   Index          =    42
   Left           =    1320
   MousePointer   =    2  'Cross
   TabIndex       =    42
   TabStop        =    0   'False
   Top            =    3120
   Width          =    615
End
Begin CommandButton btn_Board
   BackColor      =    &H00800000&
   Height         =    615
   Index          =    41
   Left           =    720
   MousePointer   =    2  'Cross
   TabIndex       =    41
   TabStop        =    0   'False
   Top            =    3120
   Width          =    615
End
Begin CommandButton btn_Board
   BackColor      =    &H00800000&
   Height         =    615
   Index          =    40
   Left           =    120
   MousePointer   =    2  'Cross
   TabIndex       =    40
   TabStop        =    0   'False
   Top            =    3120
   Width          =    615
End
Begin CommandButton btn_Board
   BackColor      =    &H00800000&
   Height         =    615
   Index          =    39
   Left           =    4320
   MousePointer   =    2  'Cross
```

```
   TabIndex        =    39
   TabStop         =    0    'False
   Top             =    2520
   Width           =    615
End
Begin CommandButton btn_Board
   BackColor       =    &H00800000&
   Height          =    615
   Index           =    38
   Left            =    3720
   MousePointer    =    2    'Cross
   TabIndex        =    38
   TabStop         =    0    'False
   Top             =    2520
   Width           =    615
End
Begin CommandButton btn_Board
   BackColor       =    &H00800000&
   Height          =    615
   Index           =    37
   Left            =    3120
   MousePointer    =    2    'Cross
   TabIndex        =    37
   TabStop         =    0    'False
   Top             =    2520
   Width           =    615
End
Begin CommandButton btn_Board
   BackColor       =    &H00800000&
   Height          =    615
   Index           =    36
   Left            =    2520
   MousePointer    =    2    'Cross
   TabIndex        =    36
   TabStop         =    0    'False
   Top             =    2520
   Width           =    615
End
Begin CommandButton btn_Board
   BackColor       =    &H00800000&
   Height          =    615
   Index           =    35
   Left            =    1920
   MousePointer    =    2    'Cross
   TabIndex        =    35
   TabStop         =    0    'False
   Top             =    2520
   Width           =    615
End
Begin CommandButton btn_Board
   BackColor       =    &H00800000&
   Height          =    615
```

continues

Listing 10.2. continued

```
        Index           =   34
        Left            =   1320
        MousePointer    =   2    'Cross
        TabIndex        =   34
        TabStop         =   0      'False
        Top             =   2520
        Width           =   615
    End
    Begin CommandButton btn_Board
        BackColor       =   &H00800000&
        Height          =   615
        Index           =   33
        Left            =   720
        MousePointer    =   2    'Cross
        TabIndex        =   33
        TabStop         =   0      'False
        Top             =   2520
        Width           =   615
    End
    Begin CommandButton btn_Board
        BackColor       =   &H00800000&
        Height          =   615
        Index           =   32
        Left            =   120
        MousePointer    =   2    'Cross
        TabIndex        =   32
        TabStop         =   0      'False
        Top             =   2520
        Width           =   615
    End
    Begin CommandButton btn_Board
        BackColor       =   &H00800000&
        Height          =   615
        Index           =   31
        Left            =   4320
        MousePointer    =   2    'Cross
        TabIndex        =   31
        TabStop         =   0      'False
        Top             =   1920
        Width           =   615
    End
    Begin CommandButton btn_Board
        BackColor       =   &H00800000&
        Height          =   615
        Index           =   30
        Left            =   3720
        MousePointer    =   2    'Cross
        TabIndex        =   30
        TabStop         =   0      'False
        Top             =   1920
```

```
      Width           =     615
   End
   Begin CommandButton btn_Board
      BackColor       =     &H00800000&
      Height          =     615
      Index           =     29
      Left            =     3120
      MousePointer    =     2    'Cross
      TabIndex        =     29
      TabStop         =     0      'False
      Top             =     1920
      Width           =     615
   End
   Begin CommandButton btn_Board
      BackColor       =     &H00800000&
      Height          =     615
      Index           =     28
      Left            =     2520
      MousePointer    =     2    'Cross
      TabIndex        =     28
      TabStop         =     0      'False
      Top             =     1920
      Width           =     615
   End
   Begin CommandButton btn_Board
      BackColor       =     &H00800000&
      Height          =     615
      Index           =     27
      Left            =     1920
      MousePointer    =     2    'Cross
      TabIndex        =     27
      TabStop         =     0      'False
      Top             =     1920
      Width           =     615
   End
   Begin CommandButton btn_Board
      BackColor       =     &H00800000&
      Height          =     615
      Index           =     26
      Left            =     1320
      MousePointer    =     2    'Cross
      TabIndex        =     26
      TabStop         =     0      'False
      Top             =     1920
      Width           =     615
   End
   Begin CommandButton btn_Board
      BackColor       =     &H00800000&
      Height          =     615
      Index           =     25
      Left            =     720
      MousePointer    =     2    'Cross
```

continues

Listing 10.2. continued

```
        TabIndex        =   25
        TabStop         =   0    'False
        Top             =   1920
        Width           =   615
    End
    Begin CommandButton btn_Board
        BackColor       =   &H00800000&
        Height          =   615
        Index           =   24
        Left            =   120
        MousePointer    =   2    'Cross
        TabIndex        =   24
        TabStop         =   0    'False
        Top             =   1920
        Width           =   615
    End
    Begin CommandButton btn_Board
        BackColor       =   &H00800000&
        Height          =   615
        Index           =   23
        Left            =   4320
        MousePointer    =   2    'Cross
        TabIndex        =   23
        TabStop         =   0    'False
        Top             =   1320
        Width           =   615
    End
    Begin CommandButton btn_Board
        BackColor       =   &H00800000&
        Height          =   615
        Index           =   22
        Left            =   3720
        MousePointer    =   2    'Cross
        TabIndex        =   22
        TabStop         =   0    'False
        Top             =   1320
        Width           =   615
    End
    Begin CommandButton btn_Board
        BackColor       =   &H00800000&
        Height          =   615
        Index           =   21
        Left            =   3120
        MousePointer    =   2    'Cross
        TabIndex        =   21
        TabStop         =   0    'False
        Top             =   1320
        Width           =   615
    End
```

```
Begin CommandButton btn_Board
   BackColor       =    &H00800000&
   Height          =    615
   Index           =    20
   Left            =    2520
   MousePointer    =    2   'Cross
   TabIndex        =    20
   TabStop         =    0    'False
   Top             =    1320
   Width           =    615
End
Begin CommandButton btn_Board
   BackColor       =    &H00800000&
   Height          =    615
   Index           =    19
   Left            =    1920
   MousePointer    =    2   'Cross
   TabIndex        =    19
   TabStop         =    0    'False
   Top             =    1320
   Width           =    615
End
Begin CommandButton btn_Board
   BackColor       =    &H00800000&
   Height          =    615
   Index           =    18
   Left            =    1320
   MousePointer    =    2   'Cross
   TabIndex        =    18
   TabStop         =    0    'False
   Top             =    1320
   Width           =    615
End
Begin CommandButton btn_Board
   BackColor       =    &H00800000&
   Height          =    615
   Index           =    17
   Left            =    720
   MousePointer    =    2   'Cross
   TabIndex        =    17
   TabStop         =    0    'False
   Top             =    1320
   Width           =    615
End
Begin CommandButton btn_Board
   BackColor       =    &H00800000&
   Height          =    615
   Index           =    16
   Left            =    120
   MousePointer    =    2   'Cross
   TabIndex        =    16
   TabStop         =    0    'False
```

continues

Listing 10.2. continued

```
        Top              =    1320
        Width            =    615
    End
    Begin CommandButton btn_Board
        BackColor        =    &H00800000&
        Height           =    615
        Index            =    15
        Left             =    4320
        MousePointer     =    2    'Cross
        TabIndex         =    15
        TabStop          =    0      'False
        Top              =    720
        Width            =    615
    End
    Begin CommandButton btn_Board
        BackColor        =    &H00800000&
        Height           =    615
        Index            =    14
        Left             =    3720
        MousePointer     =    2    'Cross
        TabIndex         =    14
        TabStop          =    0      'False
        Top              =    720
        Width            =    615
    End
    Begin CommandButton btn_Board
        BackColor        =    &H00800000&
        Height           =    615
        Index            =    13
        Left             =    3120
        MousePointer     =    2    'Cross
        TabIndex         =    13
        TabStop          =    0      'False
        Top              =    720
        Width            =    615
    End
    Begin CommandButton btn_Board
        BackColor        =    &H00800000&
        Height           =    615
        Index            =    12
        Left             =    2520
        MousePointer     =    2    'Cross
        TabIndex         =    12
        TabStop          =    0      'False
        Top              =    720
        Width            =    615
    End
    Begin CommandButton btn_Board
        BackColor        =    &H00800000&
        Height           =    615
```

```
    Index           =    11
    Left            =    1920
    MousePointer    =    2   'Cross
    TabIndex        =    11
    TabStop         =    0      'False
    Top             =    720
    Width           =    615
End
Begin CommandButton btn_Board
    BackColor       =    &H00800000&
    Height          =    615
    Index           =    10
    Left            =    1320
    MousePointer    =    2   'Cross
    TabIndex        =    10
    TabStop         =    0      'False
    Top             =    720
    Width           =    615
End
Begin CommandButton btn_Board
    BackColor       =    &H00800000&
    Height          =    615
    Index           =    9
    Left            =    720
    MousePointer    =    2   'Cross
    TabIndex        =    9
    TabStop         =    0      'False
    Top             =    720
    Width           =    615
End
Begin CommandButton btn_Board
    BackColor       =    &H00800000&
    Height          =    615
    Index           =    8
    Left            =    120
    MousePointer    =    2   'Cross
    TabIndex        =    8
    TabStop         =    0      'False
    Top             =    720
    Width           =    615
End
Begin CommandButton btn_Board
    BackColor       =    &H00800000&
    Height          =    615
    Index           =    7
    Left            =    4320
    MousePointer    =    2   'Cross
    TabIndex        =    7
    TabStop         =    0      'False
    Top             =    120
    Width           =    615
End
```

continues

Listing 10.2. continued

```
Begin CommandButton btn_Board
   BackColor        =    &H00800000&
   Height           =    615
   Index            =    6
   Left             =    3720
   MousePointer     =    2   'Cross
   TabIndex         =    6
   TabStop          =    0    'False
   Top              =    120
   Width            =    615
End
Begin CommandButton btn_Board
   BackColor        =    &H00800000&
   Height           =    615
   Index            =    5
   Left             =    3120
   MousePointer     =    2   'Cross
   TabIndex         =    5
   TabStop          =    0    'False
   Top              =    120
   Width            =    615
End
Begin CommandButton btn_Board
   BackColor        =    &H00800000&
   Height           =    615
   Index            =    4
   Left             =    2520
   MousePointer     =    2   'Cross
   TabIndex         =    4
   TabStop          =    0    'False
   Top              =    120
   Width            =    615
End
Begin CommandButton btn_Board
   BackColor        =    &H00800000&
   Height           =    615
   Index            =    3
   Left             =    1920
   MousePointer     =    2   'Cross
   TabIndex         =    3
   TabStop          =    0    'False
   Top              =    120
   Width            =    615
End
Begin CommandButton btn_Board
   BackColor        =    &H00800000&
   Height           =    615
   Index            =    2
   Left             =    1320
   MousePointer     =    2   'Cross
```

```
   TabIndex        =   2
   TabStop         =   0    'False
   Top             =   120
   Width           =   615
End
Begin CommandButton btn_Board
   BackColor       =   &H00800000&
   Height          =   615
   Index           =   1
   Left            =   720
   MousePointer    =   2    'Cross
   TabIndex        =   1
   TabStop         =   0    'False
   Top             =   120
   Width           =   615
End
Begin CommandButton btn_Board
   BackColor       =   &H00800000&
   Height          =   615
   Index           =   0
   Left            =   120
   MousePointer    =   2    'Cross
   TabIndex        =   0
   Top             =   120
   Width           =   615
End
Begin Shape shp_Box
   BorderWidth     =   3
   Height          =   615
   Index           =   1
   Left            =   7440
   Top             =   1560
   Width           =   615
End
Begin Shape shp_Box
   BorderWidth     =   3
   Height          =   615
   Index           =   0
   Left            =   6000
   Top             =   1560
   Width           =   615
End
Begin Label lbl_Score
   Alignment       =   2    'Center
   BackColor       =   &H00800000&
   Caption         =   "0"
   ForeColor       =   &H00FFFFFF&
   Height          =   255
   Index           =   1
   Left            =   7440
   TabIndex        =   65
   Top             =   2280
```

continues

Listing 10.2. continued

```
      Width       =     615
   End
   Begin Label lbl_Score
      Alignment   =     2   'Center
      BackColor   =     &H00800000&
      Caption     =     "0"
      ForeColor   =     &H00FFFFFF&
      Height      =     255
      Index       =     0
      Left        =     6000
      TabIndex    =     64
      Top         =     2280
      Width       =     615
   End
   Begin Image img_Player
      BorderStyle =     1   'Fixed Single
      Height      =     615
      Index       =     1
      Left        =     7440
      Picture     =     AOMAIN.FRX:0302 'AOAPPLE.BMP
      Stretch     =     -1  'True
      Top         =     1560
      Width       =     615
   End
   Begin Image img_Player
      BorderStyle =     1   'Fixed Single
      Height      =     615
      Index       =     0
      Left        =     6000
      Picture     =     AOMAIN.FRX:0688 'AOORANGE.BMP
      Stretch     =     -1  'True
      Top         =     1560
      Width       =     615
   End
   Begin Image img_Board
      BorderStyle =     1   'Fixed Single
      Height      =     615
      Index       =     63
      Left        =     4320
      Stretch     =     -1  'True
      Top         =     4320
      Width       =     615
   End
   Begin Image img_Board
      BorderStyle =     1   'Fixed Single
      Height      =     615
      Index       =     62
      Left        =     3720
      Stretch     =     -1  'True
      Top         =     4320
```

```
   Width          =   615
End
Begin Image img_Board
   BorderStyle    =   1   'Fixed Single
   Height         =   615
   Index          =   61
   Left           =   3120
   Stretch        =   -1  'True
   Top            =   4320
   Width          =   615
End
Begin Image img_Board
   BorderStyle    =   1   'Fixed Single
   Height         =   615
   Index          =   60
   Left           =   2520
   Stretch        =   -1  'True
   Top            =   4320
   Width          =   615
End
Begin Image img_Board
   BorderStyle    =   1   'Fixed Single
   Height         =   615
   Index          =   59
   Left           =   1920
   Stretch        =   -1  'True
   Top            =   4320
   Width          =   615
End
Begin Image img_Board
   BorderStyle    =   1   'Fixed Single
   Height         =   615
   Index          =   58
   Left           =   1320
   Stretch        =   -1  'True
   Top            =   4320
   Width          =   615
End
Begin Image img_Board
   BorderStyle    =   1   'Fixed Single
   Height         =   615
   Index          =   57
   Left           =   720
   Stretch        =   -1  'True
   Top            =   4320
   Width          =   615
End
Begin Image img_Board
   BorderStyle    =   1   'Fixed Single
   Height         =   615
   Index          =   56
   Left           =   120
```

continues

Listing 10.2. continued

```
      Stretch         =    -1  'True
      Top             =    4320
      Width           =    615
   End
   Begin Image img_Board
      BorderStyle     =    1  'Fixed Single
      Height          =    615
      Index           =    55
      Left            =    4320
      Stretch         =    -1  'True
      Top             =    3720
      Width           =    615
   End
   Begin Image img_Board
      BorderStyle     =    1  'Fixed Single
      Height          =    615
      Index           =    54
      Left            =    3720
      Stretch         =    -1  'True
      Top             =    3720
      Width           =    615
   End
   Begin Image img_Board
      BorderStyle     =    1  'Fixed Single
      Height          =    615
      Index           =    53
      Left            =    3120
      Stretch         =    -1  'True
      Top             =    3720
      Width           =    615
   End
   Begin Image img_Board
      BorderStyle     =    1  'Fixed Single
      Height          =    615
      Index           =    52
      Left            =    2520
      Stretch         =    -1  'True
      Top             =    3720
      Width           =    615
   End
   Begin Image img_Board
      BorderStyle     =    1  'Fixed Single
      Height          =    615
      Index           =    51
      Left            =    1920
      Stretch         =    -1  'True
      Top             =    3720
      Width           =    615
   End
   Begin Image img_Board
      BorderStyle     =    1  'Fixed Single
```

```
      Height       =    615
      Index        =    50
      Left         =    1320
      Stretch      =    -1  'True
      Top          =    3720
      Width        =    615
   End
   Begin Image img_Board
      BorderStyle  =    1  'Fixed Single
      Height       =    615
      Index        =    49
      Left         =    720
      Stretch      =    -1  'True
      Top          =    3720
      Width        =    615
   End
   Begin Image img_Board
      BorderStyle  =    1  'Fixed Single
      Height       =    615
      Index        =    48
      Left         =    120
      Stretch      =    -1  'True
      Top          =    3720
      Width        =    615
   End
   Begin Image img_Board
      BorderStyle  =    1  'Fixed Single
      Height       =    615
      Index        =    47
      Left         =    4320
      Stretch      =    -1  'True
      Top          =    3120
      Width        =    615
   End
   Begin Image img_Board
      BorderStyle  =    1  'Fixed Single
      Height       =    615
      Index        =    46
      Left         =    3720
      Stretch      =    -1  'True
      Top          =    3120
      Width        =    615
   End
   Begin Image img_Board
      BorderStyle  =    1  'Fixed Single
      Height       =    615
      Index        =    45
      Left         =    3120
      Stretch      =    -1  'True
      Top          =    3120
      Width        =    615
   End
```

continues

Listing 10.2. continued

```
Begin Image img_Board
    BorderStyle    =    1   'Fixed Single
    Height         =    615
    Index          =    44
    Left           =    2520
    Stretch        =    -1  'True
    Top            =    3120
    Width          =    615
End
Begin Image img_Board
    BorderStyle    =    1   'Fixed Single
    Height         =    615
    Index          =    43
    Left           =    1920
    Stretch        =    -1  'True
    Top            =    3120
    Width          =    615
End
Begin Image img_Board
    BorderStyle    =    1   'Fixed Single
    Height         =    615
    Index          =    42
    Left           =    1320
    Stretch        =    -1  'True
    Top            =    3120
    Width          =    615
End
Begin Image img_Board
    BorderStyle    =    1   'Fixed Single
    Height         =    615
    Index          =    41
    Left           =    720
    Stretch        =    -1  'True
    Top            =    3120
    Width          =    615
End
Begin Image img_Board
    BorderStyle    =    1   'Fixed Single
    Height         =    615
    Index          =    40
    Left           =    120
    Stretch        =    -1  'True
    Top            =    3120
    Width          =    615
End
Begin Image img_Board
    BorderStyle    =    1   'Fixed Single
    Height         =    615
    Index          =    39
    Left           =    4320
```

```
   Stretch        =    -1  'True
   Top            =    2520
   Width          =    615
End
Begin Image img_Board
   BorderStyle    =    1   'Fixed Single
   Height         =    615
   Index          =    38
   Left           =    3720
   Stretch        =    -1  'True
   Top            =    2520
   Width          =    615
End
Begin Image img_Board
   BorderStyle    =    1   'Fixed Single
   Height         =    615
   Index          =    37
   Left           =    3120
   Stretch        =    -1  'True
   Top            =    2520
   Width          =    615
End
Begin Image img_Board
   BorderStyle    =    1   'Fixed Single
   Height         =    615
   Index          =    36
   Left           =    2520
   Stretch        =    -1  'True
   Top            =    2520
   Width          =    615
End
Begin Image img_Board
   BorderStyle    =    1   'Fixed Single
   Height         =    615
   Index          =    35
   Left           =    1920
   Stretch        =    -1  'True
   Top            =    2520
   Width          =    615
End
Begin Image img_Board
   BorderStyle    =    1   'Fixed Single
   Height         =    615
   Index          =    34
   Left           =    1320
   Stretch        =    -1  'True
   Top            =    2520
   Width          =    615
End
Begin Image img_Board
   BorderStyle    =    1   'Fixed Single
   Height         =    615
```

continues

Listing 10.2. continued

```
        Index           =    33
        Left            =    720
        Stretch         =    -1   'True
        Top             =    2520
        Width           =    615
     End
     Begin Image img_Board
        BorderStyle     =    1    'Fixed Single
        Height          =    615
        Index           =    32
        Left            =    120
        Stretch         =    -1   'True
        Top             =    2520
        Width           =    615
     End
     Begin Image img_Board
        BorderStyle     =    1    'Fixed Single
        Height          =    615
        Index           =    31
        Left            =    4320
        Stretch         =    -1   'True
        Top             =    1920
        Width           =    615
     End
     Begin Image img_Board
        BorderStyle     =    1    'Fixed Single
        Height          =    615
        Index           =    30
        Left            =    3720
        Stretch         =    -1   'True
        Top             =    1920
        Width           =    615
     End
     Begin Image img_Board
        BorderStyle     =    1    'Fixed Single
        Height          =    615
        Index           =    29
        Left            =    3120
        Stretch         =    -1   'True
        Top             =    1920
        Width           =    615
     End
     Begin Image img_Board
        BorderStyle     =    1    'Fixed Single
        Height          =    615
        Index           =    28
        Left            =    2520
        Stretch         =    -1   'True
        Top             =    1920
        Width           =    615
```

```
End
Begin Image img_Board
    BorderStyle      =   1   'Fixed Single
    Height           =   615
    Index            =   27
    Left             =   1920
    Stretch          =   -1  'True
    Top              =   1920
    Width            =   615
End
Begin Image img_Board
    BorderStyle      =   1   'Fixed Single
    Height           =   615
    Index            =   26
    Left             =   1320
    Stretch          =   -1  'True
    Top              =   1920
    Width            =   615
End
Begin Image img_Board
    BorderStyle      =   1   'Fixed Single
    Height           =   615
    Index            =   25
    Left             =   720
    Stretch          =   -1  'True
    Top              =   1920
    Width            =   615
End
Begin Image img_Board
    BorderStyle      =   1   'Fixed Single
    Height           =   615
    Index            =   24
    Left             =   120
    Stretch          =   -1  'True
    Top              =   1920
    Width            =   615
End
Begin Image img_Board
    BorderStyle      =   1   'Fixed Single
    Height           =   615
    Index            =   23
    Left             =   4320
    Stretch          =   -1  'True
    Top              =   1320
    Width            =   615
End
Begin Image img_Board
    BorderStyle      =   1   'Fixed Single
    Height           =   615
    Index            =   22
    Left             =   3720
    Stretch          =   -1  'True
```

continues

Listing 10.2. continued

```
        Top             =    1320
        Width           =    615
    End
    Begin Image img_Board
        BorderStyle     =    1   'Fixed Single
        Height          =    615
        Index           =    21
        Left            =    3120
        Stretch         =    -1  'True
        Top             =    1320
        Width           =    615
    End
    Begin Image img_Board
        BorderStyle     =    1   'Fixed Single
        Height          =    615
        Index           =    20
        Left            =    2520
        Stretch         =    -1  'True
        Top             =    1320
        Width           =    615
    End
    Begin Image img_Board
        BorderStyle     =    1   'Fixed Single
        Height          =    615
        Index           =    19
        Left            =    1920
        Stretch         =    -1  'True
        Top             =    1320
        Width           =    615
    End
    Begin Image img_Board
        BorderStyle     =    1   'Fixed Single
        Height          =    615
        Index           =    18
        Left            =    1320
        Stretch         =    -1  'True
        Top             =    1320
        Width           =    615
    End
    Begin Image img_Board
        BorderStyle     =    1   'Fixed Single
        Height          =    615
        Index           =    17
        Left            =    720
        Stretch         =    -1  'True
        Top             =    1320
        Width           =    615
    End
    Begin Image img_Board
        BorderStyle     =    1   'Fixed Single
```

```
      Height       =    615
      Index        =    16
      Left         =    120
      Stretch      =    -1   'True
      Top          =    1320
      Width        =    615
   End
   Begin Image img_Board
      BorderStyle  =    1   'Fixed Single
      Height       =    615
      Index        =    15
      Left         =    4320
      Stretch      =    -1   'True
      Top          =    720
      Width        =    615
   End
   Begin Image img_Board
      BorderStyle  =    1   'Fixed Single
      Height       =    615
      Index        =    14
      Left         =    3720
      Stretch      =    -1   'True
      Top          =    720
      Width        =    615
   End
   Begin Image img_Board
      BorderStyle  =    1   'Fixed Single
      Height       =    615
      Index        =    13
      Left         =    3120
      Stretch      =    -1   'True
      Top          =    720
      Width        =    615
   End
   Begin Image img_Board
      BorderStyle  =    1   'Fixed Single
      Height       =    615
      Index        =    12
      Left         =    2520
      Stretch      =    -1   'True
      Top          =    720
      Width        =    615
   End
   Begin Image img_Board
      BorderStyle  =    1   'Fixed Single
      Height       =    615
      Index        =    11
      Left         =    1920
      Stretch      =    -1   'True
      Top          =    720
      Width        =    615
   End
```

continues

Listing 10.2. continued

```
Begin Image img_Board
   BorderStyle    =    1   'Fixed Single
   Height         =    615
   Index          =    10
   Left           =    1320
   Stretch        =    -1   'True
   Top            =    720
   Width          =    615
End
Begin Image img_Board
   BorderStyle    =    1   'Fixed Single
   Height         =    615
   Index          =    9
   Left           =    720
   Stretch        =    -1   'True
   Top            =    720
   Width          =    615
End
Begin Image img_Board
   BorderStyle    =    1   'Fixed Single
   Height         =    615
   Index          =    8
   Left           =    120
   Stretch        =    -1   'True
   Top            =    720
   Width          =    615
End
Begin Image img_Board
   BorderStyle    =    1   'Fixed Single
   Height         =    615
   Index          =    7
   Left           =    4320
   Stretch        =    -1   'True
   Top            =    120
   Width          =    615
End
Begin Image img_Board
   BorderStyle    =    1   'Fixed Single
   Height         =    615
   Index          =    6
   Left           =    3720
   Stretch        =    -1   'True
   Top            =    120
   Width          =    615
End
Begin Image img_Board
   BorderStyle    =    1   'Fixed Single
   Height         =    615
   Index          =    5
   Left           =    3120
```

```
      Stretch        =    -1   'True
      Top            =    120
      Width          =    615
   End
Begin Image img_Board
      BorderStyle    =    1    'Fixed Single
      Height         =    615
      Index          =    4
      Left           =    2520
      Stretch        =    -1   'True
      Top            =    120
      Width          =    615
   End
Begin Image img_Board
      BorderStyle    =    1    'Fixed Single
      Height         =    615
      Index          =    3
      Left           =    1920
      Stretch        =    -1   'True
      Top            =    120
      Width          =    615
   End
Begin Image img_Board
      BorderStyle    =    1    'Fixed Single
      Height         =    615
      Index          =    2
      Left           =    1320
      Stretch        =    -1   'True
      Top            =    120
      Width          =    615
   End
Begin Image img_Board
      BorderStyle    =    1    'Fixed Single
      Height         =    615
      Index          =    1
      Left           =    720
      Stretch        =    -1   'True
      Top            =    120
      Width          =    615
   End
Begin Image img_Board
      BorderStyle    =    1    'Fixed Single
      Height         =    615
      Index          =    0
      Left           =    120
      Stretch        =    -1   'True
      Top            =    120
      Width          =    615
   End
Begin Image img_Title
      Height         =    1125
      Left           =    5160
```

continues

Listing 10.2. continued

```
        Picture         =    AOMAIN.FRX:0A0E 'AOTITLE.BMP
        Stretch         =    -1  'True
        Top             =    120
        Width           =    3600
    End
    Begin Menu mnu_Options
        Caption         =    "&Options"
        Begin Menu mnu_NewGame
            Caption         =    "&New Game"
        End
        Begin Menu mnu_NewSep
            Caption         =    "-"
        End
        Begin Menu mnu_Easy
            Caption         =    "&Easy"
            Checked         =    -1  'True
        End
        Begin Menu mnu_Medium
            Caption         =    "&Medium"
        End
        Begin Menu mnu_Difficult
            Caption         =    "&Difficult"
        End
        Begin Menu mnu_TwoPlayer
            Caption         =    "&Two Player"
        End
        Begin Menu mnu_ExitSep
            Caption         =    "-"
        End
        Begin Menu mnu_Exit
            Caption         =    "E&xit"
        End
    End
    Begin Menu mnu_Help
        Caption         =    "&Help"
        Begin Menu mnu_Rules
            Caption         =    "&Rules"
        End
        Begin Menu mnu_AboutSep
            Caption         =    "-"
        End
        Begin Menu mnu_About
            Caption         =    "&About A&&O ..."
        End
    End
End
Option Explicit
```

```
'
' This routine determines the best move according to the board algorithm.
' Basically, you try to capture the corners and the edges while staying
' away from positions that allow the opponent to capture them.
'
' NOTE: The valid board positions must already be filled in before this
'       routine is called. The routine returns the position of the move
'       in the array.
'
Function AlgorithmMove% ()

  ' Local variables
  Dim v%, vbest%, vweight%, valgor%

  ' Cycle through all moves, and find best one
  vweight% = -1000
  For v% = 0 To ValTotal% - 1
    ' Get the algorithm weight
    valgor% = Algor%(ValMoves(v%).r, ValMoves(v%).c)
    If (valgor% > vweight%) Then
      ' This is a better move
      vbest% = v%
      vweight% = valgor%
    End If
    ' If weight is equal, randomize (to be less predictable)
    If (valgor% = vweight%) Then
      ' This randomizes TRUE or FALSE (1 or 0)
      If (GetRandom%(2) = 1) Then
        vbest% = v%
        vweight% = valgor%
      End If
    End If
  Next v%

  ' Return best move
  AlgorithmMove% = vbest%

End Function

Sub btn_Board_Click (Index As Integer)

  Dim i%, r%, c%, p%

  ' Is this a valid move?
  If (btn_Board(Index).MousePointer = MPCROSS) Then

    ' Yes, so make it
    Call MakeMove(Index \ MAXCOLS, Index Mod MAXCOLS)
    DisplayBoard

    ' Count pieces, and update score
    CountPieces
```

continues

Listing 10.2. continued

```
    DisplayInfo (MSGNONE)

    ' Check for a winner
    CheckWin

    ' Should computer move? (Use While loop, in case player
    ' has to for feit)
    While ((Not GameOver%) And (Level% <> TWOLEVEL) And (Player% =
    ➡Computer%))
      ' Yes, so make the move
      ComputerMove
      DisplayBoard
      ' Count pieces, and update score
      CountPieces
      DisplayInfo (MSGNONE)
      ' Check for a winner
      CheckWin
    Wend

    ' Change mouse for valid moves
    ValidMouse

    ' Determine a new tabstop
    For i% = 0 To MAXPIECES - 1
      If btn_Board(i%).Visible Then
        btn_Board(i%).TabStop = True
        Exit For
      End If
    Next i%

  End If

End Sub

Sub btn_Hint_Click ()

  ' Local variables
  Dim i%
  Dim vbest%, p%

  ' Build valid move table
  BuildValid

  ' Use the board algorithm
  vbest% = AlgorithmMove%()
  p% = (ValMoves(vbest%).r * MAXCOLS) + ValMoves(vbest%).c

  ' Put the player's piece in that position
  img_Board(p%).Picture = img_Player(Player%).Picture

  ' Now flash that piece
```

```
    For i% = 0 To 1
      ' Remove the button
      btn_Board(p%).Visible = False
      Delay .5
      ' Put it back
      btn_Board(p%).Visible = True
      Delay .5
    Next i%

  End Sub

Sub btn_Undo_Click ()

  Dim r%, c%, u%

  ' Swap logical board and undo board
  For r% = MINROW To MAXROW
    For c% = MINCOL To MAXCOL
      ' Swap piece
      u% = Undo%(r%, c%)
      Undo%(r%, c%) = Board%(r%, c%)
      Board%(r%, c%) = u%
    Next c%
  Next r%

  ' If two players, we need to change player
  If (Level% = TWOLEVEL) Then
    If (Player% = APPLE) Then
      Player% = ORANGE
    Else
      Player% = APPLE
    End If
  End If

  ' Update physical board
  DisplayBoard

  ' Count pieces, and update score
  CountPieces
  DisplayInfo (MSGNONE)

  ' Change mouse for valid moves
  ValidMouse

End Sub

'
' This procedure builds the list of valid moves.
'
Sub BuildValid ()

  ' Local variables
```

continues

Listing 10.2. continued

```
    Dim r%, c%

    ' Get all valid moves (there has to be one, or we would have forfeited)
    ValTotal% = 0
    For r% = MINROW To MAXROW
      For c% = MINCOL To MAXCOL
        ' Is this a blank piece?
        If (Board%(r%, c%) = BLANK) Then
          ' If move is valid, add to board
          If (ValidMove%(r%, c%)) Then
            ValMoves(ValTotal%).r = r%
            ValMoves(ValTotal%).c = c%
            ValTotal% = ValTotal% + 1
          End If
        End If
      Next c%
    Next r%

End Sub


' This function checks whether the current player has any possible
' moves. If not, they have to forfeit.
'
Function CheckForfeit% ()

    ' Local variables
    Dim r%, c%
    Dim vm%
    Dim forfeit%

    ' Assume no valid moves, and no forfeit
    vm% = False
    forfeit% = False

    ' Search until a valid move is found
    For r% = MINROW To MAXROW
      For c% = MINCOL To MAXCOL
        ' If this piece is blank, check for a valid move
        If (Board%(r%, c%) = BLANK) Then
          vm% = ValidMove%(r%, c%)
        End If
        ' Valid move?
        If (vm%) Then
          Exit For
        End If
      Next c%
      ' Valid move?
      If (vm%) Then
        Exit For
```

```
      End If
   Next r%

   ' Does the player have to forfeit?
   If (Not vm%) Then

      ' Yes, because there are no valid moves
      forfeit% = True

      ' Display message
      If (Player% = APPLE) Then
         DisplayInfo (MSGAFOR)
      Else
         DisplayInfo (MSGOFOR)
      End If
      Delay 2

      ' Toggle player
      If (Player% = APPLE) Then
         Player% = ORANGE
      Else
         Player% = APPLE
      End If

      ' Remove message and show player toggle
      DisplayInfo (MSGNONE)

   End If

   ' Return forfeit flag
   CheckForfeit% = forfeit%

End Function

'
' This procedure checks whether a move is valid from a given direction.
' If so, the procedure returns the ending row and column of the player's
' piece found.
'
' NOTE: A move is valid if it surrounds one or more of the opponents
'       pieces. If it is APPLE's turn, a valid move at X is: A O O X.
'
Function CheckMove% (row%, col%, direc%, endrow%, endcol%)

   ' Local variables
   Dim opponent%
   Dim oppfound%, done%
   Dim r%, c%
   Dim vm%

   ' Determine opponent
   If (Player% = APPLE) Then
```

continues

Listing 10.2. continued

```
    opponent% = ORANGE
Else
    opponent% = APPLE
End If

' Assume not valid
vm% = False

' Initialize row and column
r% = row%
c% = col%

' Need to find opponent in between Player% pieces
oppfound% = False

' Search until a square where the opponent is not found
done% = False
While (Not done%)

    ' Adjust row
    Select Case direc%
      Case DUPLEFT, DUP, DUPRIGHT
        If (r% > MINROW) Then
          ' Bump to previous row
          r% = r% - 1
        Else
          ' No more rows, so we are done
          done% = True
        End If
      Case DDOWNLEFT, DDOWN, DDOWNRIGHT
        If (r% < MAXROW) Then
          ' Bump to next row
          r% = r% + 1
        Else
          ' No more rows, so we are done
          done% = True
        End If
    End Select

    ' And column
    Select Case direc%
      Case DDOWNLEFT, DLEFT, DUPLEFT
        If (c% > MINCOL) Then
          ' Bump to previous column
          c% = c% - 1
        Else
          ' No more columns, so we are done
          done% = True
        End If
```

```
      Case DDOWNRIGHT, DRIGHT, DUPRIGHT
        If (c% < MAXCOL) Then
          ' Bump to next column
          c% = c% + 1
        Else
          ' No more columns, so we are done
          done% = True
        End If
    End Select

    ' Is there an opponent here?
    If (Board%(r%, c%) = opponent%) Then
      ' Opponent was found
      oppfound% = True
    Else
      ' No more opponents, so we are done
      done% = True
    End If

  Wend

  ' Is the next square our piece?
  If ((oppfound% = True) And (Board%(r%, c%) = Player%)) Then
    ' Yes, so this move is valid
    vm% = True
  End If

  ' Set ending row and column
  endrow% = r%
  endcol% = c%

  ' Return whether move is valid
  CheckMove% = vm%

End Function

'
' This procedure checks to see if a player has won.
'
Sub CheckWin ()

  ' Local variables
  Dim gameWon%
  Dim p%, px%, py%
  Dim ptotal%
  Dim r%, c%

  ' Game is won if board is filled
  gameWon% = False
  If (Score%(APPLE) + Score%(ORANGE) = MAXPIECES) Then
    gameWon% = True
  End If
```

continues

Listing 10.2. continued

```
' Game is also won if all pieces are gone
If ((Score%(APPLE) = 0) Or (Score%(ORANGE) = 0)) Then
  gameWon% = True
End If

' If game is still not won, handle forfeit
If (Not gameWon%) Then
  ' Check if next player has to forfeit
  If (CheckForfeit%() = True) Then
    ' Yes, so does next player, too?
    ' (player is toggled by forfeit check)

    If (CheckForfeit%() = True) Then
      ' Yes, so no more moves ... game is over
      gameWon% = True
    End If
  End If
End If

' Is the game won?
If (gameWon% = True) Then

  ' Get winner
  If (Score%(APPLE) > Score%(ORANGE)) Then
    ' Apple won
    DisplayInfo MSGAWIN
  Else
    ' Did orange win?
    If (Score%(ORANGE) > Score%(APPLE)) Then
      DisplayInfo MSGOWIN
    Else
      ' They must have tied!
      DisplayInfo MSGTIE
    End If
  End If

  ' Game is now over
  GameOver% = True

  ' Disable buttons
  btn_Undo.Enabled = False
  btn_Hint.Enabled = False

End If

End Sub

'
' This routine controls the computer's move. The algorithms are as
' follows:
```

```
'
'        EASYLEVEL:  Random
'
'     MEDIUMLEVEL:  Most pieces flipped (highest piece gained)
'
'  DIFFICULTLEVEL:  Board algorithm, based on a weighted piece position.
'                   The algorithm pays no attention to pieces flipped.
'
' Other levels would build upon these algorithms. For instance, LEVEL4
' would combine the "weighted piece" algorithm with the "most flipped"
' algorithm. If the best weighted move only flips 1 piece, and the
' second-best weighted move flips 10, which should be selected?
'
Sub ComputerMove ()

  ' Local variables
  Dim mp%, vbest%

  ' Display message
  DisplayInfo (MSGTHINK)

  ' Change cursor
  mp% = Screen.MousePointer
  Screen.MousePointer = MPHOURGLASS

  ' Build the valid move table
  BuildValid

  ' Determine the level%
  Select Case Level%

    Case DIFFICULTLEVEL
      ' Use the weighted board algorithm
      vbest% = AlgorithmMove%()

    Case MEDIUMLEVEL
      ' Maximize pieces flipped
      vbest% = MaximumMove%()

    Case EASYLEVEL
      ' Get a random move
      vbest% = GetRandom%(ValTotal%)

  End Select

  ' Add delay, for effect
  Delay 1

  ' Make the move
  Call MakeMove(ValMoves(vbest%).r%, ValMoves(vbest%).c%)

  ' Change cursor back
```

continues

Listing 10.2. continued

```
  Screen.MousePointer = mp%

End Sub

'
' This procedure counts how many pieces each player has.
'
Sub CountPieces ()

  ' Local variables
  Dim r%, c%

  ' Initialize scores
  Score%(APPLE) = 0
  Score%(ORANGE) = 0

  ' Search the entire board
  For r% = MINROW To MAXROW
    For c% = MINCOL To MAXCOL
      ' Which piece is it?
      If (Board%(r%, c%) <> BLANK) Then
        Score%(Board%(r%, c%)) = Score%(Board%(r%, c%)) + 1
      End If
    Next c%
  Next r%

End Sub

'
' This procedure displays the logical board on the physical board.
'
Sub DisplayBoard ()

  Dim r%, c%, p%

  ' Search the logical board
  For r% = MINROW To MAXROW
    For c% = MINCOL To MAXCOL
      ' Is there a piece here?
      If (Board%(r%, c%) <> BLANK) Then
        ' Yes, so place the piece
        Call PlacePiece(r%, c%, Board%(r%, c%))
      Else
        ' No, so make sure button is visible
        p% = (r% * MAXCOLS) + c%
        btn_Board(p%).Visible = True
      End If
    Next c%
  Next r%
```

```
End Sub

'
' This procedure updates and displays the game information.
'
Sub DisplayInfo (msg$)

  ' Update the score
  lbl_Score(APPLE).Caption = Str$(Score%(APPLE))
  lbl_Score(ORANGE).Caption = Str$(Score%(ORANGE))

  ' And the message
  lbl_Message.Caption = msg$

  ' Add beep if there is a message
  If ((msg$ <> MSGNONE) And (msg$ <> MSGTHINK)) Then
    Beep
  End If

  ' Box the active player
  shp_Box(APPLE).Visible = False
  shp_Box(ORANGE).Visible = False
  shp_Box(Player%).Visible = True

End Sub

Sub Form_Load ()

  ' Center on the screen
  Move (Screen.Width - Width) \ 2, (Screen.Height - Height) \ 2

  ' Show about box
  frm_AboutBox.Show 1

  ' Initialize board algorithm
  Algor%(0, 0) = 15:    Algor%(0, 1) = -7:  Algor%(0, 2) = 6:   Algor%(0,
➡3) = 2

  Algor%(0, 4) = 2:     Algor%(0, 5) = 6:   Algor%(0, 6) = -7:  Algor%(0,
➡7) = 15

  Algor%(1, 0) = -7:    Algor%(1, 1) = -7:  Algor%(1, 2) = -2:  Algor%(1,
➡3) = -2

  Algor%(1, 4) = -2:    Algor%(1, 5) = -2:  Algor%(1, 6) = -7:  Algor%(1,
➡7) = -7

  Algor%(2, 0) = 6:     Algor%(2, 1) = -2:  Algor%(2, 2) = 6:   Algor%(2,
➡3) = 0
  Algor%(2, 4) = 0:     Algor%(2, 5) = 6:   Algor%(2, 6) = -2:  Algor%(2,
➡7) = 6
```

continues

Listing 10.2. continued

```
Algor%(3, 0) = 2:    Algor%(3, 1) = -2:  Algor%(3, 2) = 0:   Algor%(3,
➥3) = 0
Algor%(3, 4) = 0:    Algor%(3, 5) = 0:   Algor%(3, 6) = -2:  Algor%(3,
➥7) = 2
Algor%(4, 0) = 2:    Algor%(4, 1) = -2:  Algor%(4, 2) = 0:   Algor%(4,
➥3) = 0
Algor%(4, 4) = 0:    Algor%(4, 5) = 0:   Algor%(4, 6) = -2:  Algor%(4,
➥7) = 2
Algor%(5, 0) = 6:    Algor%(5, 1) = -2:  Algor%(5, 2) = 6:   Algor%(5,
➥3) = 0
Algor%(5, 4) = 0:    Algor%(5, 5) = 6:   Algor%(5, 6) = -2:  Algor%(5,
➥7) = 6
Algor%(6, 0) = -7:   Algor%(6, 1) = -7:  Algor%(6, 2) = -2:  Algor%(6,
➥3) = -2

Algor%(6, 4) = -2:   Algor%(6, 5) = -2:  Algor%(6, 6) = -7:  Algor%(6,
➥7) = -7
Algor%(7, 0) = 15:   Algor%(7, 1) = -7:  Algor%(7, 2) = 6:   Algor%(7,
➥3) = 2
Algor%(7, 4) = 2:    Algor%(7, 5) = 6:   Algor%(7, 6) = -7:  Algor%(7,
➥7) = 15


    ' Initialize a new game
    InitNewGame

End Sub

'
' This procedure initializes all of the game variables at the beginning
' of a new game.
'
Sub InitNewGame ()

    Dim i%, r%, c%

    ' This takes a little while, so change the cursor
    Screen.MousePointer = MPHOURGLASS

    ' Get a new sequence of numbers
    Randomize

    ' Reset the physical board
    For i% = 0 To MAXPIECES - 1
      btn_Board(i%).Visible = True
      btn_Board(i%).TabStop = False
    Next i%

    ' Reset the logical board
    For r% = MINROW To MAXROW
```

```
         For c% = MINROW To MAXCOL
            Board%(r%, c%) = BLANK
         Next c%
      Next r%

      ' First piece is current tab stop
      btn_Board(0).TabStop = True

      ' Set up the middle of the board
      Board%(3, 3) = APPLE
      Board%(3, 4) = ORANGE
      Board%(4, 3) = ORANGE
      Board%(4, 4) = APPLE

      ' Initialize players
      Player% = APPLE
      Computer% = ORANGE

      ' Set up undo board
      RefreshUndo

      ' Display the board
      DisplayBoard

      ' Count the pieces
      CountPieces

      ' Determine valid mouse moves
      ValidMouse

      ' Display information
      DisplayInfo (MSGNONE)

      ' Game is not over
      GameOver% = False

      ' Enable Undo and Hint buttons
      btn_Undo.Enabled = True
      btn_Hint.Enabled = True

      ' Change cursor back to default
      Screen.MousePointer = MPDEFAULT

End Sub

'
' This procedure actually makes the move, and flips all appropriate
' pieces, on the logical board.
'
Sub MakeMove (row%, col%)

   ' Local variables
```

continues

Listing 10.2. continued

```
Dim d%, p%, r%, c%
Dim erow%, ecol%

' Save board to undo buffer, if it is a Player's turn
If ((Level% = TWOLEVEL) Or (Player% <> Computer%)) Then
  RefreshUndo
End If

' Place a piece at move location
Board%(row%, col%) = Player%

' Search through all potential directions
d% = MINDIR
While (d% <= MAXDIR)

  ' Check for move in this direction
  If (CheckMove%(row%, col%, d%, erow%, ecol%) = True) Then

    ' Determine search direction
    Select Case d%

      Case DUPLEFT
        ' Yes, so flip all pieces between here and move
        c% = ecol%
        For r% = erow% To row% - 1
          Board%(r%, c%) = Player%
          c% = c% + 1
        Next r%

      Case DUP
        ' Yes, so flip all pieces between here and move
        For r% = erow% To row% - 1
          Board%(r%, col%) = Player%
        Next r%

      Case DUPRIGHT
        ' Yes, so flip all pieces between here and move
        c% = ecol%
        For r% = erow% To row% - 1
          Board%(r%, c%) = Player%
          c% = c% - 1
        Next r%

      Case DRIGHT
        ' Yes, so flip all pieces between here and move
        For c% = ecol% To col% + 1 Step -1
          Board%(row%, c%) = Player%
        Next c%

      Case DDOWNRIGHT
        ' Yes, so flip all pieces between here and move
```

```
            c% = ecol%
            For r% = erow% To row% + 1 Step -1
              Board%(r%, c%) = Player%
              c% = c% - 1
            Next r%

        Case DDOWN
          ' Yes, so flip all pieces between here and move
          For r% = erow% To row% + 1 Step -1
            Board%(r%, col%) = Player%
          Next r%

        Case DDOWNLEFT
          ' Yes, so flip all pieces between here and move
          c% = ecol%
          For r% = erow% To row% + 1 Step -1
            Board%(r%, c%) = Player%
            c% = c% + 1
          Next r%

        Case DLEFT
          ' Yes, so flip all pieces between here and move
          For c% = ecol% To col% - 1
            Board%(row%, c%) = Player%
          Next c%

    End Select

    End If

    ' Bump to next direction
    d% = d% + 1

  Wend

  ' Now it is the other Player's turn
  If (Player% = APPLE) Then
    Player% = ORANGE
  Else
    Player% = APPLE
  End If

End Sub

'
' This routine determines the best move by counting the pieces flipped
' by each move. It then selects the move that flips the most pieces
' (maximizing the score).
'
' NOTE: The valid board positions must already be filled in before this
'       routine is called. It returns the position of the move in the
'       array.
```

continues

Listing 10.2. continued

```
'
Function MaximumMove% ()

  ' Local variables
  Dim r%, c%
  Dim v%, vscore%, vbest%
  Static Comp%(MAXROWS, MAXCOLS)

  ' Copy all rows to computer save board
  For r% = MINROW To MAXROW
    ' Copy all columns
    For c% = MINCOL To MAXCOL
      Comp%(r%, c%) = Board%(r%, c%)
    Next c%
  Next r%

  ' Cycle through all moves, and find best one
  vscore% = Score%(Computer%)
  For v% = 0 To ValTotal% - 1

    ' Make the move
    Call MakeMove(ValMoves(v%).r%, ValMoves(v%).c%)

    ' Is this better than last best move?
    CountPieces
    If (Score%(Computer%) > vscore%) Then
      ' Yes, so record it
      vbest% = v%
      vscore% = Score%(Computer%)
    End If

    ' If score is equal, randomize (for less predictability)
    If (Score%(Computer%) = vscore%) Then
      ' This randomizes TRUE or FALSE (1 or 0)
      If (GetRandom%(2) = 1) Then
        vbest% = v%
        vscore% = Score(Computer%)
      End If
    End If

    ' Reset board
    For r% = MINROW To MAXROW
      ' Copy all columns
      For c% = MINCOL To MAXCOL
        Board%(r%, c%) = Comp%(r%, c%)
      Next c%
    Next r%

    ' And Player (since reset by MakeMove)
    Player% = Computer%
```

```
    Next v%

    ' Return the move
    MaximumMove% = vbest%

End Function

Sub mnu_About_Click ()

    ' Show the about box
    frm_AboutBox.Show 1

End Sub

Sub mnu_Difficult_Click ()

    ' Check Difficult, and uncheck the others
    mnu_Easy.Checked = False
    mnu_Medium.Checked = False
    mnu_Difficult.Checked = True
    mnu_TwoPlayer.Checked = False

    ' Set the flag
    Level% = DIFFICULTLEVEL

End Sub

Sub mnu_Easy_Click ()

    ' Check Easy, and uncheck the others
    mnu_Easy.Checked = True
    mnu_Medium.Checked = False
    mnu_Difficult.Checked = False
    mnu_TwoPlayer.Checked = False

    ' Set the flag
    Level% = EASYLEVEL

End Sub

Sub mnu_Exit_Click ()

    ' Exit, so just unload the form
    Unload Me

End Sub

Sub mnu_Medium_Click ()

    ' Check Medium, and uncheck the others
    mnu_Easy.Checked = False
```

continues

Listing 10.2. continued

```
    mnu_Medium.Checked = True
    mnu_Difficult.Checked = False
    mnu_TwoPlayer.Checked = False

    ' Set the flag
    Level% = MEDIUMLEVEL

End Sub

Sub mnu_NewGame_Click ()

    ' Start a new game
    InitNewGame

End Sub

Sub mnu_Rules_Click ()

    ' Show the rules
    frm_Rules.Show 1

End Sub

Sub mnu_TwoPlayer_Click ()

    ' Check Two Player, and uncheck the others
    mnu_Easy.Checked = False
    mnu_Medium.Checked = False
    mnu_Difficult.Checked = False
    mnu_TwoPlayer.Checked = True

    ' Set the flag
    Level% = TWOLEVEL

End Sub

'
' This procedure places a player's piece at a given location.
'
Sub PlacePiece (row%, col%, piece%)

    Dim p%

    ' Determine actual piece location
    p% = (row% * MAXCOLS) + col%

    ' Place the image
    img_Board(p%).Picture = img_Player(piece%).Picture

    ' Remove button, to show image
```

```
     btn_Board(p%).Visible = False

End Sub

'
' This procedure copies the current logical game board into an undo
' buffer in order to "undo" a previous move.
'
Sub RefreshUndo ()

  Dim r%, c%

  ' Copy the whole board
  For r% = MINROW To MAXROW
    For c% = MINCOL To MAXCOL
      ' Copy this piece
      Undo%(r%, c%) = Board%(r%, c%)
    Next c%
  Next r%

End Sub

'
' This procedure validates moves for blank pieces, and updates the
' button mouse pointer.
'
Sub ValidMouse ()

  Dim r%, c%, p%

  For r% = MINROW To MAXROW
    For c% = MINCOL To MAXCOL
      ' Is there a piece here?
      If (Board%(r%, c%) = BLANK) Then
        ' Blank piece, so is it valid?
        p% = (r% * MAXCOLS) + c%
        If (ValidMove%(r%, c%)) Then
          ' Yes, so set cursor to cross
          btn_Board(p%).MousePointer = MPCROSS
        Else
          ' No, so leave as default
          btn_Board(p%).MousePointer = MPDEFAULT
        End If
      End If
    Next c%
  Next r%

End Sub

Function ValidMove% (row%, col%)
```

continues

Listing 10.2. continued

```
' Local variables
Dim d%
Dim vm%
Dim erow%, ecol%

' Assume not valid
vm% = False

' Search through all potential directions
d% = MINDIR
While ((d% <= MAXDIR) And (Not vm%))

   ' Check the move in this direction
   vm% = CheckMove%(row%, col%, d%, erow%, ecol%)

   ' Bump to next direction
   d% = d% + 1

Wend

' Return whether move is valid
ValidMove% = vm%

End Function
```

Figure 10.7 shows the AORULES form, and Listing 10.3 is the AORULES.FRM source. As the name suggests, this form displays the A&O rules when Help is selected in the main game menu.

Figure 10.7. The AORULES form.

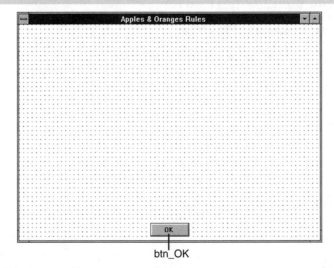

btn_OK

Listing 10.3. The AORULES .FRM source code.

```
VERSION 2.00
Begin Form frm_Rules
   BackColor       =   &H00FFFFFF&
   BorderStyle     =   1   'Fixed Single
   Caption         =   "Apples & Oranges Rules"
   FontBold        =   -1  'True
   FontItalic      =   0   'False
   FontName        =   "System"
   FontSize        =   9.75
   FontStrikethru  =   0   'False
   FontUnderline   =   0   'False
   ForeColor       =   &H00000000&
   Height          =   6285
   Icon            =   0
   Left            =   990
   LinkTopic       =   "Form1"
   MaxButton       =   0   'False
   MinButton       =   0   'False
   ScaleHeight     =   5880
   ScaleWidth      =   8490
   Top             =   1500
   Width           =   8610
   Begin CommandButton btn_OK
      BackColor       =   &H00800000&
      Caption         =   "OK"
      Height          =   375
      Left            =   3720
      TabIndex        =   0
      Top             =   5400
      Width           =   1095
   End
End
Option Explicit

Function AlgorithmMove% ()

  ' Local variables
  Dim v%
  Dim vbest%
  Dim vweight%
  Dim valgor%

  ' Cycle through all moves, and find best one
  vweight% = -1000
  For v% = 0 To ValTotal% - 1
    ' Get the algorithm weight
    valgor% = Algor%(ValMoves(v%).r%, ValMoves(v%).c%)
    If (valgor% > vweight%) Then
      ' This is a better move
      vbest% = v%
```

continues

Listing 10.3. continued

```
      vweight% = valgor%
   End If
   ' If weight is equal, randomize (to be less predictable)
   If (valgor% = vweight%) Then
      ' This randomizes TRUE or FALSE (1 or 0)
     If (GetRandom%(2) = 1) Then
        vbest% = v%
        vweight% = valgor%
     End If
   End If
 Next v%

 ' Return best move
 AlgorithmMove% = vbest%

End Function ' end of AlgorithmMove

Sub btn_OK_Click ()

 ' Unload the form
 Unload Me

End Sub

Sub Form_Load ()

 ' Center on the screen
 Move (Screen.Width - Width) \ 2, (Screen.Height - Height) \ 2

End Sub

Sub Form_Paint ()

 ' Position rule text
 CurrentX = 0
 CurrentY = 0

 ' Display them
 Print
 Print "  This is the classic battle of the opposites. The object of the
 ➥game is to finish"
 Print "  with more pieces than your opponent. You take pieces by flank-
 ➥ing (surrounding on"
 Print "  two sides) an opponents pieces in any direction, which includes
 ➥diagonally. You"
 Print "  may only make a move when you can take an opposing piece. If no
 ➥moves are"
 Print "  possible, the computer will forfeit your turn. "
 Print
 Print "  The Easy, Medium, and Difficult Levels pit you (pun intended)
 ➥against the computer."
```

```
Print "  The first level should be fairly easy — the moves are totally
➥random. On Medium,"
Print "  the moves that flip the most number of pieces are made. The
➥final level (Difficult)"
Print "  uses a board weighted algorithm to determine the best possible
➥moves."
Print
Print "  The game can be changed to a '2 Player' level, which involves
➥no computer"
Print "  interaction. At this level, you can play both the APPLE and
➥ORANGE turns, or"
Print "  compete with someone else."
Print
Print "  The cursor will change to a cross whenever it is over a valid
➥move. The Hint button"
Print "  can also be used to determine the current player's best move.
➥The hint square will"
Print "  flash on the board."
Print
Print "  The game ends when all of an opponent's pieces are taken, there
➥are no more valid"
Print "  moves, or all of the squares are filled."

End Sub
```

Listing 10.4 lists the AOGLOBAL.BAS source code. The file contains global constants and variables, and any global function routines.

Listing 10.4. The AOGLOBAL.BAS source code.

```
Option Explicit

' Pieces
Global Const MINROW =
Global Const MINCOL = 0
Global Const MAXROW = 7
Global Const MAXCOL = 7
Global Const MAXROWS = (MAXROW - MINROW + 1)
Global Const MAXCOLS = (MAXCOL - MINCOL + 1)
Global Const MAXPIECES = (MAXROWS * MAXCOLS)

' Levels
Global Const EASYLEVEL = 0
Global Const MEDIUMLEVEL = 1
Global Const DIFFICULTLEVEL = 2
Global Const TWOLEVEL = 3

' Players
```

continues

Listing 10.4. continued

```
Global Const MAXPLAYERS = 2

' Piece types
Global Const BLANK = -1
Global Const APPLE = 0
Global Const ORANGE = 1

' Tie
Global Const TIE = -1

' Directions
Global Const MINDIR = 1            ' Minimum direction
Global Const DUPLEFT = 1           '
Global Const DUP = 2               '    1  2  3
Global Const DUPRIGHT = 3          '
Global Const DRIGHT = 4            '    8  *  4
Global Const DDOWNRIGHT = 5        '
Global Const DDOWN = 6             '    7  6  5
Global Const DDOWNLEFT = 7         '
Global Const DLEFT = 8             '
Global Const MAXDIR = 8            ' Maximum direction

' Messages
Global Const MSGNONE = "                "
Global Const MSGAFOR = "Apple Forfeits"
Global Const MSGOFOR = "Orange Forfeits"
Global Const MSGTHINK = "Thinking ..."
Global Const MSGAWIN = "Apple Wins!"
Global Const MSGOWIN = "Orange Wins!"
Global Const MSGTIE = "You Tied!"

' Mouse Pointers
Global Const MPDEFAULT = 0
Global Const MPCROSS = 2
Global Const MPHOURGLASS = 11

' Position
Type ROWCOL
  r As Integer
  c As Integer
End Type

' Game board
Global Board%(MAXROWS, MAXCOLS)

' Game board algorithm
Global Algor%(MAXROWS, MAXCOLS)

' Game board undo
```

```
Global Undo%(MAXROWS, MAXCOLS)

' Valid moves
Global ValTotal%
Global ValMoves(MAXPIECES) As ROWCOL

' Players
Global Player%
Global Computer%

' Level
Global Level%

' Score
Global Score%(MAXPLAYERS)

' Game over flag
Global GameOver%

'
' This procedure delays the given number of seconds,
' which can be fractional.
'
Sub Delay (secs!)

    Dim Start!

    ' Get the current seconds since midnight
    Start! = Timer

    ' Wait for seconds to elapse
    While (Timer < (Start! + secs!))
        ' Let other things run while we wait
        DoEvents
    Wend

End Sub

'
' This function returns a random number between 0 and range%-1, inclusive.

Function GetRandom% (range%)

    ' In the Visual Basic manual, the generic formula is:
    ' Int((upperbound-lowerbound+1)*Rnd+lowerbound)
    GetRandom% = Int(range% * Rnd)

End Function
```

Form Overview

Several forms make up the game of A&O. The following sections provide a brief discussion of the forms and their controls. Consult the previous figures and listings for additional information.

About Box

The AOABOUT form is the standard About box form for all the games in this book. Because I didn't want to reinvent the wheel, I took the form from the IconWorks example program (included with Visual Basic). The form was predesigned and had code to show the Windows mode, the amount of free memory, and whether a math co-processor was present. Figure 10.8 shows you what the About box form looks like when the form is actually running.

Figure 10.8. The About box when running.

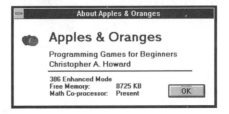

I reformatted the code and changed the form and control names to match my naming conventions. I set the lbl_Program label to Apples & Oranges, and the img_Icon image to AO.ICO. These are the only two changes you'll have to make when using the About box for other games in this book.

Rules

The AORULES form displays the A&O rules when you select Rules from the Help menu. The form itself consists of a lot of blank space for the rule text and a single OK button (which unloads the form). The form is centered when it is loaded, and the rule text is displayed when the window is painted.

Global

The AOGLOBAL basic file contains the global variable and constant definitions. It also contains the global procedures Delay and GetRandom.

The Main Form

The AOMAIN form is the main form for the game, and as such it contains the most controls and functions. The img_Title control contains an image for the Apples & Oranges game title.

To simplify the programming of the game, many of the controls on the main form have control arrays. The main game board consists of two control arrays: img_Board() and btn_Board(). These buttons are placed directly on top of the images.

Whenever you have this many controls in an array, it's always best to get the control properties the way you want them before duplicating the control. I first created the image control, set the properties, and copied it into a row of eight. Then, to form the 8x8 board, I copied the entire row seven times. I performed the same steps while creating the button array.

This all sounds fine and well, but rarely do you think of everything. I had to go back to the images two or three times during the development of the game. This was a difficult process, because the images are completely hidden by the buttons. I selected each button in a row using the Shift-Click selection method and moved the row up. (You can't select them as a group because you'll also select the images underneath.) Then, I selected the images in that row as a group and changed the properties.

There are three other control arrays: img_Player(), which holds the image for each player; shp_Box(), which draws a box around the player images to indicate the active player; and lbl_Score(), which holds the player score value.

There are only two buttons in this game. The btn_Hint button, which gives the player a hint about which move to make, and the btn_Undo button, which enables the player to undo his last move. Lastly, the fra_Messages frame and lbl_Message label handle the game messages.

Programming Overview

The A&O program is a board game, and as such it adapts to the fixed-control nature of Visual Basic very well. None of the controls change their position during the course of the game, although some are hidden, redisplayed, and changed.

Creating the Images

For this game, I needed three images: the apple, the orange, and a title image. I created all three images using Windows Paintbrush, and saved them as BMP files.

I loaded the images into the picture properties of img_Title and img_Player(). I used part of the title image to create the icon AO.ICO, which I created with the IconWorks program supplied with Visual Basic.

Program Flow

When you run the game, the program flows as follows:

➡ When the main form is loaded, it is centered, and the About box is displayed. The board-level algorithm array is initialized, and a new game is set with the InitNewGame procedure.

➡ The InitNewGame procedure initializes the physical (the button array), logical (internal position array), and undo game boards. It goes on to display the board with DisplayBoard, count the pieces with CountPieces, set valid mouse positions with ValidMouse, display score and information with DisplayInfo, and finally enables the Hint and Undo buttons.

➡ At this point, the game depends on the player. The player can set the difficulty level, look at the rules, or get a hint. When ready to play, he or she must click a button that represents a valid move.

➡ The btn_Board_Click routine handles the move selection. If the move is valid (which depends on the mouse pointer set up by the ValidMouse function), the MakeMove procedure makes the move. MakeMove places the piece at the selected location, and then captures any opponent pieces by scanning in all directions. The btn_Board_Click routine goes on to display and count the board, and check for a winner. If the computer needs to move next, it calls ComputerMove.

➡ The game continues until CheckWin determines the game is over. The message box displays the winner and sets the GameOver% flag. The Hint and Undo buttons are also disabled. To begin a new game, the player must select the New Game option from the Options menu.

Menu options show the game rules and the About box; they also display frm_AboutBox and frm_Rules, respectively.

Techniques Used

The Apples & Oranges game illustrates several game programming techniques, such as hiding controls, using mouse pointers, and using control arrays. I give the details of these techniques in the following sections.

Hiding Controls

The board consists of buttons that you can hide in order to reveal the images underneath. To hide a control, use the `Visible` property. This is probably the method used by the Minesweeper game included with Windows 3.1.

Mouse Pointers

The mouse pointer can be changed dynamically at runtime. The `ValidMouse` function changes the `MousePointer` property to indicate all valid moves for the appropriate button controls. Visual Basic frees you from having to constantly query the mouse position and manually change it—it knows what control the mouse is over and sets the pointer shape automatically.

The mouse pointer (usually referred to as a cursor) can be changed dynamically at runtime—a capability that is used by the `ValidMouse` function.

> You can change the mouse pointer for the screen by setting the `MousePointer` property of the `Screen` object. This is usually used to show a "waiting" or "busy" cursor, such as an hourglass.

Control Arrays

Control arrays are important because they simplify the amount of programming you have to do. For instance, all the buttons on the board can be handled by the same function, because their actions are the same.

While the board may be an obvious use for an array, some less obvious uses are the `img_Player()`, `lbl_Score()`, and `shp_Box()` control arrays. By defining `APPLE=0` and `ORANGE=1`, each control can be identified by the current player. This also makes the code more readable.

Bitmaps, Scaling, and Driver Resolution

I drew the image bitmaps at a 1:1 aspect ratio (standard VGA 16-color). I also loaded a player piece into one of the `img_Player()` image controls, so the image frame would snap to the correct size. I then set the `Stretch` property to `True`.

If you always ran A&O on a VGA in 640x480x16 or 800x600x16 color mode (or any other mode with a 1:1 aspect ratio), the value of the `Stretch` property would not matter. On an EGA, however, the resolution is 640x350x16, and it does not have a

1:1 aspect. With Stretch=False, Visual Basic resizes the image frame; the board images overlap and are truncated—which would not impress your customer. With Stretch=True, the image frame remains a relative size and the image is stretched (scaled) within it.

Data Organization

The global variables consist of the game board Board%(), the algorithm board Algor%(), and the undo board Undo%(). All three boards have indexes of (MAXROWS, MAXCOLS). For each position on the board, a value indicates whether the position is blank or occupied by orange or apple.

Another array, called ValMoves(), maintains a list of valid moves. This list is used for selecting computer moves and for marking valid moves for the mouse pointer.

Other global variables include those for defining the player and computer (Player% and Computer%), the current difficulty level (Level%), the score for each player (Score%()), and the game over flag (GameOver%).

Constants are used liberally to define maximum columns and rows, levels, players, directions, messages, and mouse pointers.

Global Functions

Two global functions are defined in the AOGLOBAL module. The first is the Delay function, which allows delays from fractional seconds on up. While the delay is being performed, the Visual Basic function DoEvents is called to allow other programs and pending events to complete. The other global function is GetRandom, which returns a random number between 0 and (range%-1).

Although these functions are neither long nor complicated, they allow you to be consistent. These functions are used repeatedly in the games in this book.

Checking for a Valid Move

Determining a valid move is central to the A&O game, and the CheckMove function performs this task. This function searches from a given move location and direction, and looks to see if any of the opponent's pieces are between the move and another player's piece.

The ValidMove function (which simply cycles through all the possible directions for a given move) calls CheckMove. The ValidMouse routine calls ValidMove to set all the mouse pointers after each turn; and CheckForfeit calls ValidMove to make sure that valid moves exist for the current player. Finally, MakeMove calls the CheckMove function, when actually making a move, so that it can find all of the pieces to capture.

Forfeiting a Turn

The computer moves after the player makes a move, which is usually fine and dandy. However, what if the player has to forfeit his turn? The computer must move again. And what if the player must forfeit yet again? Yes, it looks like a while loop will do the trick:

```
' Should computer move? (Use While loop, in case player must forfeit)
While ((Not GameOver%) And (Level% <> TWOLEVEL) And (Player% = Computer%))
   ' Yes, so make the move
   ComputerMove
   DisplayBoard
   ' Count pieces, and update score
   CountPieces
   DisplayInfo (MSGNONE)
   ' Check for a winner
   CheckWin
Wend
```

The computer continues to take its turn until the game is over or the player has a valid move. The MakeMove routine (called by ComputerMove) always swaps the current player. Then, Checkwin calls CheckForfeit, which swaps the current player back (if necessary).

Determining the Game Is Over

When I first wrote the game, I coded the CheckWin function so that it just checked if Score%(APPLE)+Score%(ORANGE) = MAXPIECES. I assumed that the game was over when all of the squares had been filled. I later determined that this wasn't enough. The game also is over when a player captures all the other player's pieces, or when no more valid moves exist for either player (in which case, both players must forfeit their turn).

Without those two final conditions, the game could loop indefinitely—with each player forfeiting his turn to the next player!

The Computer as Opponent

The computer play logic uses several algorithms to vary the difficulty. The ComputerMove function handles the computer move selection.

On the easiest level, a random move is selected from the currently valid moves. It's interesting to note that this doesn't mean the game is always easy to win for an inexperienced player. Perhaps a really easy level would look for poor moves.

On the medium level, the MaximumMove function selects the move that captures the greatest number of pieces. On the surface this would seem to be the best algorithm.

(In a moment I'll show you why it might not be.) First, the routine copies the current board to a save buffer, and makes the first valid move. It counts the pieces to get the total score, and then restores the board. It does this for every valid move on the board, and then returns the one with the highest ending score.

On the difficult level, the `AlgorithmMove` function uses a board weighted algorithm. This algorithm assigns a weight to every position on the board, and then tries to make the move that results in the highest weight—regardless of the number of pieces captured! Basically, the algorithm tries to capture the edge and corner positions. It also tries to avoid positions that allow the opponent to capture the edges and corners. The algorithm "knows" that by capturing those favorable positions, it will have the upper hand in the end.

NOTE

In order to make the game less predictable, the `GetRandom` function is used when two or more moves have equal weight. When using the `MaximumMove` function, two moves can capture the same number of pieces. The board algorithm also can assign the same value to several different moves. By randomizing the selection, the first move is not picked each time.

Summary

The following important programming points have been covered:

- I used the A&O `AboutBox` form as a model for all `AboutBox` game forms.

- Two global functions, called `Delay` and `GetRandom`, are used in all future games.

- Controls can be hidden and made visible again—as a tool for revealing other controls.

- Mouse pointers are handled automatically by Visual Basic for each control. You can change the mouse pointer at runtime, which enables you to use it as a tool for valid move selections. If you set the `MousePointer` property of the `Screen` object, it overrides all other pointer shapes. A common use for the screen pointer is the displaying of an hourglass.

- You can use control arrays for simplifying code.

➤ You can automatically scale Bitmaps by using the `Stretch` property. This allows the game to run correctly when you use video drivers of various resolutions.

➤ If you use different algorithms, you can vary game difficulty.

Suggestions for Improvement

The following suggestions are ideas for enhancing A&O.

➤ Add a `DisplayWinner` routine. You could display a large image of the Apple or Orange piece over the game board. Consider randomly revealing buttons to display the large image (which could be scaled using the `Stretch` property). What would you do for a tie—display a banana?

➤ When an apple captures an orange, or vice versa, use an animation sequence. One idea is to make the pieces look like they are being flipped. Speaking of flipping, check out the next game for an idea of how this can be done.

➤ Add new levels. How would you code an algorithm that would look at both the board algorithm and how many pieces you could capture? For an even higher level, consider looking ahead several moves. For every move you make, determine what the best move your opponent would make to determine your total gain. It doesn't make sense to make a move to capture four pieces if your opponent can turn around and capture eight of yours!

➤ Add a new button, like Hint, that would place the total pieces captured on the button of every valid move. Most of the work is already completed in the `MaximumMove` routine—you just use the button caption to display the total.

➤ Disable buttons that are invalid moves so they can't be pushed. A good place to do that would be in the `ValidMouse` routine.

➤ Let the player to save the game. You could write the logical board array and undo array to a file.

What's Ahead

The Apples & Oranges game illustrates the development of a board type of game. It can be used as a model or starting point from which to develop other board games. I do just that in Chapter 11, "Flip," so read on.

Flip

Flip is a board game that is similar to Spot and Attaxx. In this chapter, I describe the game of Flip, explain how the game is played, and offer you some hints. I also cover the programming of the game and give a full description of the techniques used. You will learn about

➡ Modifying an existing game into a new game

➡ Hidden controls

➡ Mouse pointers

➡ Control arrays

➡ Computer "thinking"

➡ Animation (flipping a piece)

➡ Varying game difficulty

Background

This game has appeared in various forms—most notably the Spot game (licensed from 7-Up). It also appeared in an arcade game called Attaxx. Now, we can add Flip to the list.

Gameplay

Flip is a two-player game; each player is represented by a colored playing piece. You also can play against the computer. Each player tries to flip the most pieces on the board by getting near the other player's pieces. After a player makes a move, all surrounding opponent pieces within one square in all directions (including diagonally) are flipped to the moving player's piece. The game ends when all valid moves have been made. The winner is the player with the most pieces.

Running Flip

To begin playing Flip, select the Flip icon from the program group (which you installed in the introduction). The file FLIP.EXE contains the game. When you run the game, you'll see the About box first. Click OK, and Flip appears.

Playing a Game

From the Options menu, you can select an Easy, Medium, or Difficult level for playing against the computer. Or, select the Two Player option to play against yourself or a friend.

> The difficulty level can be changed at any time during game play.

The current player is indicated by a thick border around the playing pieces to the right of the board. Red usually starts first. Each player's score is indicated under their respective playing piece.

The game begins with two of each player's pieces arranged at opposite corners of the board (see Figure 11.1). From this starting position, you can make 16 different valid moves. When you move the cursor over a board square, the cursor changes to a cross if the move is valid. Figure 11.2 indicates the board squares where a cross can appear.

To make a move, you must select one of your pieces by placing the mouse pointer over the piece and pressing the left mouse button. When a piece is selected, it begins to flash. If you want to choose a different piece, unselect the flashing piece by selecting it again. Once a piece is selected, the cursor will show you valid moves for that piece only (Figure 11.3).

Figure 11.1. The opening board.

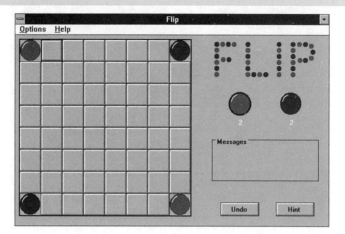

Figure 11.2. Valid moves for Red.

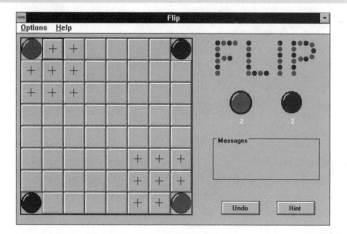

Valid moves for Flip are more complicated than in the game in the last chapter, Apples & Oranges (A&O). There are essentially three types of moves: Step, Skip, and Jump (see Figure 11.4). When you make a Step move (one square away), you retain your original piece, and it replicates itself. If you make a Skip or Jump move, you move your piece, but don't replicate it. This leaves the square you came from empty (which could be an opportunity for your opponent!). Skips and Jumps can be made over empty or occupied squares.

Figure 11.3. Valid moves for selected piece.

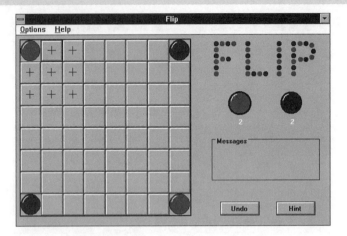

Figure 11.4. Valid move types.

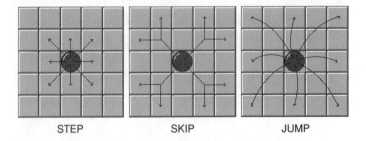

| STEP | SKIP | JUMP |

It's important to remember that an opponent's pieces are flipped in all directions. Figure 11.5 illustrates a move that Blue makes that captures Red's pieces in seven directions. This move changes the score from 17-14 to 10-21, putting Blue in the lead.

Two other buttons are important during the game: Undo and Hint. The Undo button, as its name suggests, will undo your last move. If you are playing against the computer, it will undo both your move and the computer's. The Hint button provides you with a hint of where to move next.

If you select Hint repeatedly with no intervening moves, you might notice that it doesn't always recommend the same move every time. This occurs when several moves have the same weighted score.

The game progresses with each player taking turns until the entire board is filled. In either case, the winner is the player with the most pieces on the board. There can be a tie.

Figure 11.5. A Blue move that captures Red's pieces in seven directions.

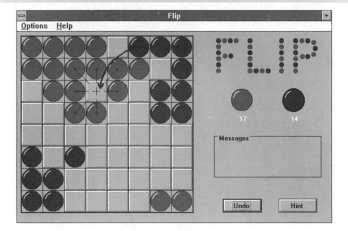

Sometimes a player has no valid moves. When this happens, a message such as "Red Forfeits" appears in the message box, and the other player can take a turn.

Hints

Like A&O, Flip can be a difficult and frustrating game to play. Just when you think you have the other player backed into a corner, he or she captures eight of your pieces. The game strategy is different than A&O, however, so some simple hints to follow are

➡ Be on the defense. Make a step move to adjacent squares instead of skipping or jumping. This replicates your piece without leaving blank squares behind that your opponent can take advantage of.

➡ Likewise, look for empty squares left behind by your opponent, and move in to flip their pieces.

➡ Try to build up a base of squares at the beginning of the game. Squares of two by two or more are easier to protect.

➡ If you plan on making a Skip or Jump move, look at what you leave behind. It's best to move a piece that is surrounded mostly by your opponent's pieces.

➤ The game is not over until the end. You can be losing miserably at first, but the more opponent pieces there are, the more there are to flip. If you are winning, avoid Skip or Jump moves—but if you are losing, go for what you can get!

➤ Remember that every piece you flip is really worth two points—one point is taken away from your opponent, and one point is added to your score.

➤ Make use of the mouse pointer. Scan the whole board with it to reveal all your valid moves (indicated by a cross pointer).

Programming

The makefile for Flip contains the files listed in Table 11.1.

Table 11.1. Flip source files.

Filename	Description
FLABOUT.FRM	The About box form
FLMAIN.FRM	The Main Flip form
FLRULES.FRM	The Flip Rules form
FLGLOBAL.BAS	Contains global constants, variables, and procedures

All of the files in Table 11.1 are included on the disk in the back of this book. See Appendix A for installation instructions.

Figure 11.6 illustrates the FLABOUT form. This is the standard About box I'll continue to use throughout the book.

Figure 11.7 shows the FLMAIN form. The main form contains the game board and the main controls for the game.

Figure 11.6. The FLABOUT form.

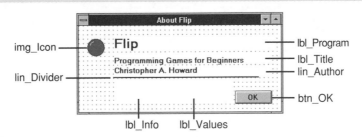

img_Icon — lbl_Program

lin_Divider — lbl_Title
— lin_Author

— btn_OK

lbl_Info   lbl_Values

WHERE'S THE CODE?

FLABOUT.FRM

```
' You can find the source code
' for this program on the disk.

Option Explicit
  Declare variable to track animation frame
```

Figure 11.7. The FLMAIN form.

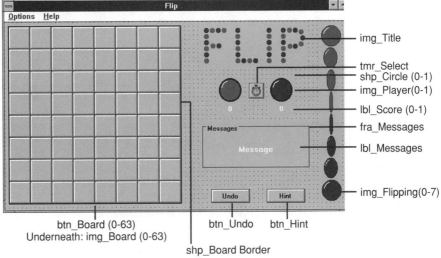

— img_Title

tmr_Select
shp_Circle (0-1)
— img_Player(0-1)

— lbl_Score (0-1)

— fra_Messages

— lbl_Messages

— img_Flipping(0-7)

btn_Board (0-63)
Underneath: img_Board (0-63)

shp_Board Border

btn_Undo   btn_Hint

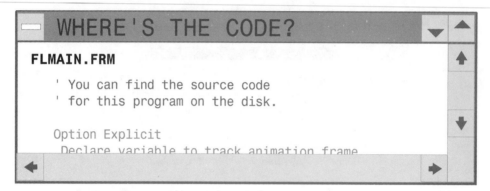

Figure 11.8 shows the FLRULES form. It is blank now, but it will contain the rules for the game when displayed.

Figure 11.8. The FLRULES form.

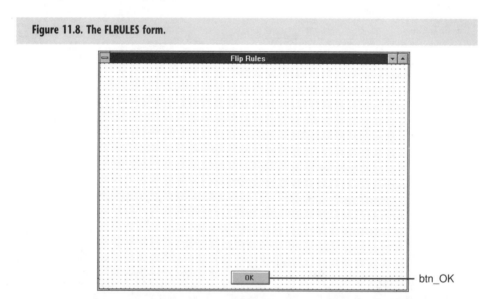

btn_OK

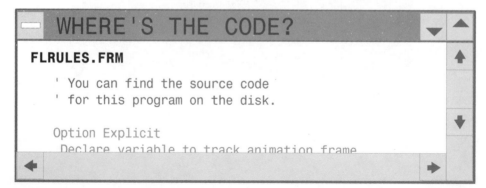

Although the global file, FLGLOBAL.BAS doesn't have a form, it's one of the most important files. Be sure to look it over to get an understanding of the constants, variables, and API functions used.

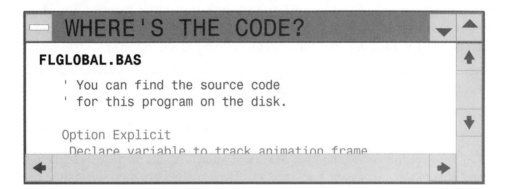

```
WHERE'S THE CODE?

FLGLOBAL.BAS

' You can find the source code
' for this program on the disk.

Option Explicit
  Declare variable to track animation frame
```

Form Overview

The game of Flip consists of several forms. Following is a brief discussion of these forms and their controls. Many of these forms closely match the Apples & Oranges forms, so if you studied those you may wish to skip this overview. Consult the preceding form figures for additional information.

About Box

The FLABOUT form is the standard About box form. The label lbl_Program has been set to Flip, and the image img_Icon has been set to FL.ICO. For a full description of the form, see Chapter 10, "Apples & Oranges."

Rules

When you select the Rules selection from the Help menu, the FLRULES form displays the Flip rules. The form itself consists of blank space for the rule text and a single OK button (which unloads the form). The form is centered when loaded, and the rule text is displayed when the window is painted.

Global

The FLGLOBAL basic file contains the global variable and constant definitions. It also contains the global procedures Delay and GetRandom.

The Main Form

The FLMAIN form is the main form for the game, and it contains the most controls and functions. The img_Title control contains an image for the Flip game title.

To simplify the programming of the game, you can use any of control arrays on the controls on the main form. The main game board consists of two control arrays: img_Board() and btn_Board(). These buttons are placed directly on top of the images.

> See the A&O Main Form description for a discussion about overlaying
> controls (Chapter 10, "Apples & Oranges").

I added a control array called img_Flipping() that contains the images of the red and blue pieces as they are being flipped. These images are used during the flip animation sequence. The images are located outside the form border, so they can't be seen.

There are three other control arrays. img_Player() holds the image for each player; shp_Circle() draws a circle around the player images to indicate the active player; and lbl_Score() holds the player's score values.

There are only two buttons in this game. The btn_Hint button gives the player a hint about which move to make; the btn_Undo button allows the player to undo his or her last move. The fra_Messages frame and lbl_Message label handle the game messages.

Finally, a shp_BoardBorder object puts a border around the game board. Without this shape, the edge of the board disappears when the game piece is flashed. The img_Board() border is turned off when the object is not visible. See the following discussion about Blinking for more information.

Programming Overview

The Flip program is a board game, and like A&O, it adapts to the fixed-control nature of Visual Basic very well. None of the controls change their position during the course of the game, although some are hidden, redisplayed, and changed.

Creating the Images

For this game, three images are needed: the red pieces, blue pieces, and the title image. I created all three images with Paintbrush, and saved them as BMP files. Then, I loaded the images into the picture properties of img_Title and img_Player(). I created the game icon in IconWorks to look like a playing piece.

After I created the red and blue pieces, I narrowed them to give the illusion of the pieces flipping. These images are stored in the img_Flipping() controls.

> I used Paintbrush to create these images. I used the Shrink and Grow option from the Pick menu to narrow the images; then I zoomed in to touch up the edges.

NOTE

Program Flow

When the game runs, the program flows as follows:

➡️ When you load the main form, it is centered and the About box is displayed. A new game starts with the InitNewGame procedure.

➡️ The InitNewGame procedure initializes the physical (the button array), logical (internal position array), and undo game boards. Then, it displays the board with DisplayBoard, counts the pieces with CountPieces, sets valid mouse positions with ValidMouse, and displays scores and information with DisplayInfo. The InitNewGame procedure finally enables the Hint and Undo buttons.

➡️ After the game has been initialized, the direction of the game depends on the player. The player can set the difficulty level, look at the rules, or get a hint. When ready to play, he or she must select a piece currently on the board.

➡️ The img_Board_Click routine handles the piece selection. If the current player's piece is there, it is selected (or unselected if already selected). The piece is recorded both in the SourceMove variable and in the selection state stored in SourceSel%. The valid moves and mouse positions are then recalculated with the BuildValid and ValidMouse routines.

➡️ If the game is not over, and a source piece has been selected, the piece is flashed by the tmr_Select_Timer function.

➡️ The btn_Board_Click routine handles the move selection. If a source piece is selected and the move is valid (the mouse pointer set up by the ValidMouse function relates whether it is or not), the MakeMove procedure places the piece at the selected location. Then, any opponent pieces are flipped by scanning in all directions. If a piece needs to be flipped, the FlipPiece routine is called to perform the animation. The btn_Board_Click routine goes on to display and count the pieces and check for a winner. If the computer needs to move next, ComputerMove is called.

➡ The game continues until `CheckWin` determines the game is over. If it is, the winner is displayed in the Message box, and the `GameOver%` flag is set. The Hint and Undo buttons are also disabled. To begin a new game, the player must select the New Game option from the Options menu.

You can view the game rules and the About box through menu options; the options display `frm_AboutBox` and `frm_Rules`, respectively.

Techniques Used

The Flip game illustrates several of the same techniques as A&O, because the game forms and programming were derived from it. The following is a summary of those techniques, and some important new ones.

Starting at 50 Percent Completed

I was able to base much of the Flip game on A&O. This allowed me to start with almost all of the forms designed: the controls, the functions, the artwork, the code, and the logic. There were still many changes to make—but I didn't have to start from scratch.

After changing the title image and the images for the playing pieces, the game looked almost done! But the underlying game logic was different, so I still had plenty of coding to do.

I had to rename the Apple and Orange references and constants to Red and Blue. I also changed the Current Player highlight from a square to a circle. The valid move and move making logic required a rewrite, although the main flow of the game remained the same.

Hiding Controls

The board consists of buttons that are hidden to reveal the images underneath. To hide a control, use the `Visible` property. This is probably the method used by the Minesweeper game included with Windows 3.1, and is definitely the same method as A&O.

The images for the flipping piece are stored on the main form, outside the right edge of the window. There isn't any room to place the images within the window.

Timer Blinking

The timer is used to flash the currently selected source piece. Every 500 ms (1/2 second), the `SourceMove` piece is hidden or shown using the `Visible` property (explained previously). When changing selections or making a move, though, you have to remember to show the previous selection—otherwise it remains hidden.

One problem with hiding the image was that I also hid the image's border. Because the individual image borders overlap, the hidden border was only noticeable on the outside edges of the board. I added the shp_BoardBorder object to fix this.

Mouse Pointers

The Mouse Pointer can be changed dynamically at runtime. The ValidMouse function uses this method. I indicate valid moves by changing the MousePointer property for the appropriate button controls. This action changes the pointer to a cross. Visual Basic frees you from having to constantly query the mouse position and manually change the pointer—it knows what control the mouse is over and sets the pointer shape automatically.

> You can change the mouse pointer for the screen by setting the
> MousePointer property of the Screen object. This is usually used to
> show a waiting or busy pointer—such as an hourglass.

In Flip, the valid mouse positions have to be changed quite often. When no piece has been selected, the ValidMouse routine indicates all valid moves for all pieces. When a piece is selected, only the valid moves for that chosen piece are displayed. A piece can then be unselected, and another piece selected, and so on. The BuildValid function handles this logic.

Control Arrays

Control arrays are important, because they simplify the amount of programming you have to do. For instance, all of the buttons on the board can be handled by the same function, because their action is the same.

While the board may be an obvious use for an array, some other uses are the img_Player(), lbl_Score(), and shp_Circle() control arrays. By defining CHIPRED=0 and CHIPBLUE=1, the current player can be used to index into each control, and the code is more readable.

Bitmaps, Scaling, and Driver Resolution

I drew the image bitmaps at a 1:1 aspect ratio (standard VGA 16-color). Also, I loaded a player piece into one of the img_Player() image controls so that the image frame would snap to the correct size. Then, I set the Stretch property to True.

NOTE

See the programming techniques (in Chapter 10, "Apples & Oranges.") for a full description of aspects and stretching.

Data Organization

The global variables consist of the game board Board%() and the undo board Undo%(). There is no algorithm board in Flip. Both boards have indexes of (MAXROWS, MAXCOLS), and for each position on the board, a value indicates whether the position is blank or occupied by Red or Blue.

Another array maintains a list of valid moves—ValMoves(). This list is used for selecting computer moves and for marking valid moves for the mouse pointer.

Some new variables (since A&O) are the SourceSel% and SourceMove% variables. These help you know what the currently selected piece to move is.

Other global variables include those for defining the following: the player and computer (Player% and Computer%), the current difficulty level (Level%), the score for each player (Score%()), and the game over flag (GameOver%).

I use constants liberally to define maximum columns and rows, levels, players, directions, messages, and mouse pointers.

Checking for a Valid Move

Making a valid move is central to the Flip game, and the BuildValid and ValidMove functions perform this task. These functions search the entire board and mark all valid moves.

The valid move logic is simpler than that in A&O. Basically, you have to search all squares within a two square range of a blank square. When any of the current player's pieces are found within that search area, the square is a valid move. The only tricky part to this search is determining the valid search range so that you don't go off the board. The FindRange routine handles the search range.

Forfeiting a Turn

As in A&O, you must handle forfeiting a turn—and not just one turn. The computer has to keep moving until the player has a valid move. The btn_Board_Click performs the logic for this routine.

> For further explanation of forfeiting a turn, see Chapter 10, "Apples & Oranges."

Flipping a Piece

The game is called Flip, so it is only right that the pieces are flipped when they are captured. As I noted previously, I created the images in Paintbrush and stored them in the img_Flipping() control array. The routine FlipPiece, as its name implies, handles the actual flip animation.

When flipping from Red to Blue, the array is traversed from front to back (0 to 7); when flipping from Blue to Red, the array goes back to front (7 to 0). Each image in the array is copied to the appropriate board position, one after the other, and the effect is a flipping piece!

> Although the delay between each frame is very small, the Delay function calls DoEvents—which processes all pending events. This is important, because without it, you would not see all of the frames. In fact, it would appear that all of the pieces are flipped instantaneously! Comment out DoEvents, and see for yourself.

Determining the Game Is Over

It would be easy to assume that the game is over when there are no more blank squares left. But the game also is over when a player captures all of the other player's pieces.

The Computer as Opponent

The computer play logic uses several algorithms to vary the game difficulty. The ComputerMove function handles the computer move selection.

At the easiest level, a random move is selected from the currently valid moves. Unlike A&O, however, this causes the computer to be fairly brain dead. Why? Well, in A&O, a valid move is defined as one that will, at least, capture some of the opponent's pieces. In Flip, a move can be a Skip or Jump move—which may net you zero additional pieces! Besides, one lone piece out in the middle of the board is pretty indefensible. This illustrates the difference in performance the same algorithm can have in two similar but different games.

For the medium level of difficulty, I improved the random algorithm slightly. When possible, you should select a move that is only one square away (a Step). This always results in a gain of at least one piece and causes the computer to build up its corners before the opponent can attack.

There are times when a Skip or Jump move is necessary, and you need to allow for it. The RandomMove function tries three different pieces for three moves each; if it can't find a valid move one step away, it increases the distance to include Skip or Jump moves. This usually occurs near the end of the game when more pieces get blocked in.

At the difficult level, the MaximumMove function selects the move that flips the greatest number of pieces. First, the routine copies the current board to a save buffer; then it makes the first valid move. The routine counts the pieces to get the total score, and then it restores the board. It does this for every valid move on the board, and then returns the move with the highest ending score.

This is different than in the A&O game, where a board level algorithm is used for the most difficult level. The corners and sides of the board do offer some advantage (you can't be attacked as easily), but you start the game from those positions and work your way toward the middle.

> To make the game less predictable, the GetRandom function is used when two or more moves have equal weight. When you use the MaximumMove function, two moves may capture the same number of pieces. Because the selection is random, the first move is not picked each time.

Summary

I have covered the following important programming points:

➡ You can program one game to be used as a starting point for another. This maximizes previous artwork and development (a theme we will carry throughout this book).

➡ You can hide controls and make them visible again as a tool for revealing other controls. You also can hide controls by placing them outside the edges of the form.

➡ Like A&O, Flip uses the mouse pointer to indicate valid moves (with a cross). Valid moves change frequently in Flip because of varying source selection, so this is important. You can use the Screen object for setting the hourglass cursor during long waits.

➧ Use control arrays for simplifying code (another technique we will tout often).

➧ You can scale Bitmaps automatically by using the Stretch property. This allows the game to run correctly when you use video drivers of various resolutions.

➧ You can perform animation by cycling through an array of images. The DoEvents function enables you to see each frame.

➧ You can vary game difficulty by using different algorithms. What works in some games, however, may not work so well in others (such as random moves or board algorithms).

Suggestions for Improvement

The following suggestions are ideas for enhancing Flip.

➧ Add a DisplayWinner routine. You can flip all of the remaining pieces to the winning color. Don't do anything for a tie (or flip the pieces to green!).

➧ Place barricades on the board (squares that a player can't move to). Generate the barricades randomly, and keep them symmetric. This might also affect the difficulty level.

➧ Add the option for three or four players to play. Each player could have a single chip in an opposite corner, using a different color. Use the option of specifying human or computer opponent for each player. Computer opponents can be given varying difficulty levels.

➧ Add new levels. Look ahead a move or two, and see if a move you make actually gives the next player an even better move. Or, have the computer favor completing a square of pieces rather than jumping out to flip some pieces. Is it better to make a Jump move to flip two pieces when you can make a Step move for two pieces instead? Probably.

➧ Add a new button like Hint that would place the total pieces captured on the button of every valid move. Most of the work is already in the MaximumMove routine—you could just use the button caption to display the total.

➧ Allow the player to save his or her game. You could write the logical board array and undo array to a file.

➧ Add a different animation technique for the piece flipping, similar to Spot and Attaxx.

What's Ahead

Flip is the last board game I'll cover in this book. Other board games you might want to implement include Checkers, Chess, or your own made-up game. In the next chapter, I'll start exploring the world of card games with a popular gambling game: BlackJack. Grab your money and read on.

BlackJack

Blackjack is one of the world's most popular card games for gambling. Just walk into any Las Vegas casino, and you'll see table after table of Blackjack—each with five or more players. In this chapter, I describe my game of BlackJack, explain how the game is played, and offer some hints. I also cover the programming of the game, provide the code listings, and give a full description of the techniques I used. You will learn about

➡ Card deck logic

➡ Guiding the user with button enabling

➡ Bitmaps and scaling

➡ Hidden forms

➡ The advantage of control arrays

➡ Simple computer thinking

Background

Blackjack, also known as *Twenty-One,* can be traced back to Italian, Spanish, or French card games of similar nature. By its French name, *Vingt-et-un* (21), it was a popular parlor game in the eighteenth century. Various forms of the game include *Van John* in England and *Pontoon* in Australia.

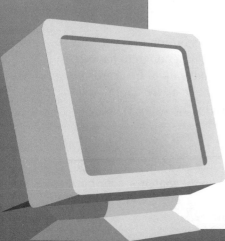

Blackjack gained considerable popularity in the first half of this century, mostly because of the United States Armed Services. Since then, it has become a big betting game—and because the House has a 5.8 percent advantage, it's a favorite of the Las Vegas Casinos!

Gameplay

This is a one-player game; the computer plays as dealer. The object of the game is to get as close to 21 as possible, without *busting* (going over 21). You must also beat the dealer's hand. Face cards count as 10, Aces as 1 or 11 (your choice), and all other cards at face value. The ultimate object of the game is to *Break the House* (win all of its money). The game is usually over when you have lost all of your money—just like in Vegas!

To begin playing BlackJack, select the BlackJack icon from the program group you installed. (See Appendix A for installation instructions.) BlackJack is contained in the file BLAKJAK.EXE. When you run the game, you see the About box first. Click OK, and BlackJack appears.

Playing a Hand

The House extends you a $2,500 line of credit and has $25,000 more for you to win. Before the dealer deals the cards, you must bet. Select the Bet More button (+) to place your bet (in increments of $25). You can place a maximum bet of $250 if you feel lucky! If you aren't so sure of yourself, use the Bet Less button (-) to decrease your bet. If you want to bet the same amount each time, use the Bet Same button (=) for future bets.

After you place your bet, you'll notice that the Deal button is available. Select Deal when your bet is ready, and the computer will deal you your first two cards. The dealer has one Hole Card which you cannot see.

If you have 21, you have a Blackjack! Definitely select the Stay button, and you will be paid 3:2 for your bet (one and one-half). If you aren't lucky enough to have 21 already, select the Hit button (for another card). You can have up to five cards in your hand. If you draw five cards without busting, you have a *Five-Card Charlie* which wins you the hand (this does not count in Vegas, by the way). When you have all of the cards you want, select Stay.

When you stay, the dealer flips over his hole (down) card. The dealer must draw to 17, even if he has a hand that will beat you. He will stay on 17 or above. If he busts, or ends up with less than you have, you win. Then, he matches your bet. Otherwise, he takes your money. A *Push* (tie) keeps everyone even, and your bet rides to the next hand. A typical hand is shown in Figure 12.1.

Figure 12.1. Playing a hand of BlackJack.

Counting and Messages

If you prefer not to count your cards, you can have the game add them for you. Select Add Cards from the Options menu at any time, and you are all set. This will not help you prepare for Vegas, however.

You can turn off the messages that appear after each hand if they start to get annoying. Select Hand Messages from the Options menu.

Hints

There are many strategies for playing BlackJack, and it may help to get a book about the game. Some simple hints to follow are

➡️ Always assume the dealer's hole card is 10, and play your hand accordingly.

➡️ If the dealer's up card shows a 6, always stay—no matter what you have. If the dealer has 16, he has the highest odds of busting.

➡️ Always count aces as 1—until you finish counting your hand. Then, add 10 if you can. This makes your hand easier to count (and helps when you have more than one ace).

Here is a simple card counting strategy: count 2's through 6's as +1, and 10's and Aces as -1. At zero, the deck doesn't favor the player or the dealer. When you get a high plus count, more low cards have been dealt and the deck favors the player—so increase your bet. For minus counts, the deck favors the dealer, so you should bet smaller. This strategy is based on the fact that smaller cards favor the dealer, because they help him get to 17. Higher cards would bust his hand.

Programming

The makefile for BlackJack contains the files listed in Table 12.1.

Table 12.1. BlackJack source files.

Filename	Description
BJABOUT.FRM	The About box form
BJBROKE.FRM	The player or dealer is broke form
BJCARDS.FRM	Contains all of the card images
BJMAIN.FRM	The main BlackJack form
BJRULES.FRM	The BlackJack Rules form
BJSHUFFL.FRM	The Shuffling Deck Message form
BJGLOBAL.BAS	Contains global constants, variables, and procedures

All of these files are included on the disk in the back of this book. See Appendix A for installation instructions.

Figure 12.2 and Listing 12.1 illustrate the BJABOUT form and source code. This form should start to look familiar to you!

Figure 12.2. The BJABOUT form.

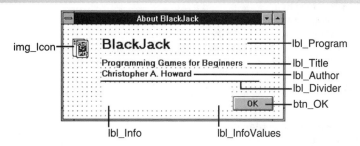

img_Icon
lbl_Program
lbl_Title
lbl_Author
lbl_Divider
btn_OK
lbl_Info
lbl_InfoValues

Listing 12.1. The BJABOUT form source code.

```
VERSION 2.00

Begin Form frm_AboutBox
    BorderStyle     =   3   'Fixed Double
    Caption         =   "About BlackJack"
    ClipControls    =   0   'False
    FontBold        =   -1  'True
    FontItalic      =   0   'False
    FontName        =   "System"
    FontSize        =   9.75
    FontStrikethru  =   0   'False
    FontUnderline   =   0   'False
    Height          =   2775
    Icon            =   0
    Left            =   1305
    MaxButton       =   0   'False
    MinButton       =   0   'False
    ScaleHeight     =   2370
    ScaleWidth      =   5640
    Top             =   1080
    Width           =   5760

    Begin Image img_Icon
        Height      =       480
        Left        =       240
        Picture     =       BJABOUT.FRX:0000
        Top         =       360
        Width       =       480
    End

    Begin CommandButton btn_OK
        Caption     =       "OK"
        FontBold    =       -1  'True
        FontItalic  =       0   'False
        FontName    =       "System"
        FontSize    =       9.75
```

continues

Listing 12.1. continued

```
        FontStrikethru  =    0     'False
        FontUnderline   =    0     'False
        Height          =    360
        Left            =    4350
        TabIndex        =    6
        Top             =    1800
        Width           =    1035
     End

     Begin Line lin_Divider
        BorderWidth     =    2
        X1              =    975
        X2              =    5010
        Y1              =    1425
        Y2              =    1425
     End

     Begin Label lbl_Program
        Caption         =    "BlackJack"
        FontBold        =    -1    'True
        FontItalic      =    0     'False
        FontName        =    "MS Sans Serif"
        FontSize        =    18
        FontStrikethru  =    0     'False
        FontUnderline   =    0     'False
        Height          =    450
        Left            =    990
        TabIndex        =    1
        Top             =    270
        Width           =    1920
     End

     Begin Label lbl_Title
        Caption         =    "Programming Games for Beginners"
        FontBold        =    -1    'True
        FontItalic      =    0     'False
        FontName        =    "MS Sans Serif"
        FontSize        =    9.75
        FontStrikethru  =    0     'False
        FontUnderline   =    0     'False
        Height          =    240
        Left            =    990
        TabIndex        =    2
        Top             =    840
        Width           =    4305
     End

     Begin Label lbl_Author
        Caption         =    "Christopher A. Howard"
        FontBold        =    -1    'True
```

```
              FontItalic      =   0    'False
              FontName        =   "MS Sans Serif"
              FontSize        =   9.75
              FontStrikethru  =   0    'False
              FontUnderline   =   0    'False
              Height          =   240
              Left            =   990
              TabIndex        =   3
              Top             =   1110
              Width           =   4365
          End

          Begin Label lbl_Info
              Height          =   600
              Left            =   1005
              TabIndex        =   5
              Top             =   1545
              Width           =   1875
          End

          Begin Label lbl_InfoValues
              Height          =   600
              Left            =   2880
              TabIndex        =   0
              Top             =   1545
              Width           =   1410
          End

      End

  Option Explicit

  ' Windows API functions used
  Declare Function GetFreeSpace Lib "Kernel" (ByVal wFlags%) As Long
  Declare Function GetWinFlags Lib "Kernel" () As Long

  ' Windows constants used
  Const WF_STANDARD = &H10
  Const WF_ENHANCED = &H20
  Const WF_80x87 = &H400

  Sub btn_OK_Click ()

    ' We are done
    Unload Me

  End Sub

  Sub Form_Load ()

    Dim WinFlags&
    Dim Mode$, Processor$, CRLF$
```

continues

Listing 12.1. continued

```
' Center the About box on the screen
Move (Screen.Width - Width) \ 2, (Screen.Height - Height) \ 2

' Make it easier for strings
CRLF$ = Chr$(13) + Chr$(10)

' Get current Windows configuration
WinFlags& = GetWinFlags()

' Determine mode
If (WinFlags& And WF_ENHANCED) Then
  Mode$ = "386 Enhanced Mode"
Else
  Mode$ = "Standard Mode"
End If

' Free memory
lbl_Info.Caption = Mode$ + CRLF$ + "Free Memory:" + CRLF$ + "Math Co-
➥processor:"

' 80x87 math chip
If (WinFlags& And WF_80x87) Then
  Processor$ = "Present"
Else
  Processor$ = "None"
End If

' Free space
lbl_InfoValues.Caption = CRLF$ + Format$(GetFreeSpace(0) \ 1024) + " KB"
➥+ CRLF$ + Processor$

End Sub
```

Figure 12.3 and Listing 12.2 show the BJBROKE form and source code. This form is displayed whenever the dealer or player goes broke.

Figure 12.3. The BJBROKE form.

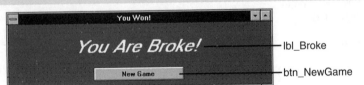

Listing 12.2. The BJBROKE form source code.

```
VERSION 2.00

Begin Form frm_Broke
    BackColor       =   &H00008000&
    BorderStyle     =   1   'Fixed Single
    Caption         =   "You Won!"
    Height          =   2115
    Icon            =   0
    Left            =   1890
    LinkTopic       =   "Form1"
    MaxButton       =   0   'False
    MinButton       =   0   'False
    ScaleHeight     =   1710
    ScaleWidth      =   7365
    Top             =   2970
    Width           =   7485

    Begin CommandButton btn_NewGame
        BackColor       =   &H00008000&
        Caption         =   "New Game"
        Height          =   375
        Left            =   2400
        TabIndex        =   1
        Top             =   1200
        Width           =   2535
    End

    Begin Label lbl_Broke
        Alignment       =   2   'Center
        BackColor       =   &H00008000&
        Caption         =   "You Are Broke!"
        FontBold        =   -1  'True
        FontItalic      =   -1  'True
        FontName        =   "MS Sans Serif"
        FontSize        =   24
        FontStrikethru  =   0   'False
        FontUnderline   =   0   'False
        ForeColor       =   &H00FFFFFF&
        Height          =   615
        Left            =   120
        TabIndex        =   0
        Top             =   360
        Width           =   7095
    End

End

Option Explicit

Sub btn_NewGame_Click ()
```

continues

Listing 12.2. continued

```
' Just unload the form
Unload Me

End Sub

Sub Form_Load ()

  ' Center the form on the screen
  Move (Screen.Width - Width) \ 2, (Screen.Height - Height) \ 2

  ' Change message, depending upon who is broke
  If (PInfo(DEALER).Pot% <= 0) Then
    frm_Broke.Caption = "You Won!"
    lbl_Broke.Caption = "You Broke the House!"
  Else
    frm_Broke.Caption = "You Lost!"
    lbl_Broke.Caption = "You Are Broke!"
  End If

End Sub
```

Figure 12.4 and Listing 12.3 show the BJCARDS form and a partial listing of the source code. This form contains the images for each card—forming an electronic deck of cards.

Figure 12.4. The BJCARDS form.

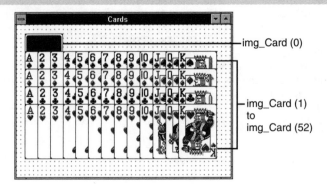

Listing 12.3. The BJCARDS form source code.

For brevity, the image listings for img_card structures 1 through 50 are omitted from the printed book listing. For a complete listing, see the BJCARDS.FRM file.

```
VERSION 2.00

Begin Form frm_Cards
    Caption         =   "Cards"
    ClipControls    =   0    'False
    Height          =   4560
    Icon            =   0
    Left            =   5040
    ScaleHeight     =   4155
    ScaleWidth      =   6030
    Top             =   1170
    Width           =   6150

    Begin Image img_Card
        Height      =   1500
        Index       =   52
        Left        =   4560
        Picture     =   BJCARDS.FRX:0000 'KHCARD.BMP
        Top         =   2160
        Visible     =   0    'False
        Width       =   1080
    End

    Begin Image img_Card
        Height      =   1500
        Index       =   0
        Left        =   240
        Picture     =   BJCARDS.FRX:305D8 'XXCARD.BMP
        Top         =   240
        Visible     =   0    'False
        Width       =   1080
    End

End

Option Explicit
```

Figure 12.5 and Listing 12.4 show the BJMAIN form and source code. This is the main form for the game, which represents the BlackJack table top.

Figure 12.5. The BJMAIN form.

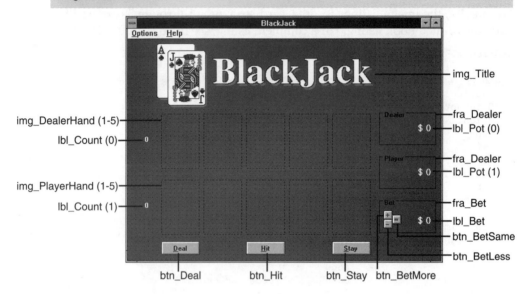

Listing 12.4. The BJMAIN form source code.

```
VERSION 2.00

Begin Form frm_BlackJack
    BackColor      =   &H00008000&
    BorderStyle    =   3   'Fixed Double
    Caption        =   "BlackJack"
    FontBold       =   -1  'True
    FontItalic     =   0   'False
    FontName       =   "MS Sans Serif"
    FontSize       =   9.75
    FontStrikethru =   0   'False
    FontUnderline  =   0   'False
    Height         =   6735
    Icon           =   BJMAIN.FRX:0000 'BJ.ICO
    KeyPreview     =   -1  'True
    Left           =   1635
    MaxButton      =   0   'False
    ScaleHeight    =   403
    ScaleMode      =   3   'Pixel
    ScaleWidth     =   586
    Top            =   1170
    Width          =   8910

    Begin Frame fra_Bet
        BackColor      =   &H00008000&
        Caption        =   "Bet"
        Height         =   975
```

```
Left              =    7080
TabIndex          =    7
Top               =    4320
Width             =    1575

Begin CommandButton btn_BetSame
    BackColor        =    &H00008000&
    Caption          =    "="
    FontBold         =    -1   'True
    FontItalic       =    0    'False
    FontName         =    "Times New Roman"
    FontSize         =    9
    FontStrikethru   =    0    'False
    FontUnderline    =    0    'False
    Height           =    255
    Left             =    360
    TabIndex         =    13
    Top              =    480
    Width            =    255
End

Begin CommandButton btn_BetLess
    BackColor        =    &H00008000&
    Caption          =    "-"
    FontBold         =    -1   'True
    FontItalic       =    0    'False
    FontName         =    "Courier New"
    FontSize         =    9.75
    FontStrikethru   =    0    'False
    FontUnderline    =    0    'False
    Height           =    255
    Left             =    120
    TabIndex         =    10
    Top              =    600
    Width            =    255
End

Begin CommandButton btn_BetMore
    BackColor        =    &H00008000&
    Caption          =    "+"
    FontBold         =    -1   'True
    FontItalic       =    0    'False
    FontName         =    "Times New Roman"
    FontSize         =    9.75
    FontStrikethru   =    0    'False
    FontUnderline    =    0    'False
    Height           =    255
    Left             =    120
    TabIndex         =    9
    Top              =    360
    Width            =    255
End
```

continues

Listing 12.4. continued

```
    Begin Label lbl_Bet
        Alignment       =    1    'Right Justify
        BackColor       =    &H00008000&
        Caption         =    "$ 0"
        FontBold        =    -1   'True
        FontItalic      =    0    'False
        FontName        =    "MS Sans Serif"
        FontSize        =    12
        FontStrikethru  =    0    'False
        FontUnderline   =    0    'False
        ForeColor       =    &H00FFFFFF&
        Height          =    375
        Index           =    1
        Left            =    480
        TabIndex        =    8
        Top             =    480
        Width           =    975
    End

End

Begin Frame fra_Player
    BackColor           =    &H00008000&
    Caption             =    "Player"
    Height              =    975
    Left                =    7080
    TabIndex            =    4
    Top                 =    3120
    Width               =    1575

    Begin Label lbl_Pot
        Alignment       =    1    'Right Justify
        BackColor       =    &H00008000&
        Caption         =    "$ 0"
        FontBold        =    -1   'True
        FontItalic      =    0    'False
        FontName        =    "MS Sans Serif"
        FontSize        =    12
        FontStrikethru  =    0    'False
        FontUnderline   =    0    'False
        ForeColor       =    &H00FFFFFF&
        Height          =    375
        Index           =    1
        Left            =    120
        TabIndex        =    6
        Top             =    360
        Width           =    1335
    End

End
```

```
Begin Frame fra_Dealer
   BackColor      =    &H00008000&
   Caption        =    "Dealer"
   Height         =    975
   Left           =    7080
   TabIndex       =    3
   Top            =    1920
   Width          =    1575

   Begin Label lbl_Pot
      Alignment      =    1   'Right Justify
      BackColor      =    &H00008000&
      Caption        =    "$ 0"
      FontBold       =    -1   'True
      FontItalic     =    0    'False
      FontName       =    "MS Sans Serif"
      FontSize       =    12
      FontStrikethru =    0    'False
      FontUnderline  =    0    'False
      ForeColor      =    &H00FFFFFF&
      Height         =    375
      Index          =    0
      Left           =    120
      TabIndex       =    5
      Top            =    360
      Width          =    1335
   End

End

Begin CommandButton btn_Stay
   BackColor      =    &H0000C000&
   Caption        =    "&Stay"
   Height         =    375
   Left           =    5760
   TabIndex       =    2
   Top            =    5520
   Width          =    1095
End

Begin CommandButton btn_Hit
   BackColor      =    &H00008000&
   Cancel         =    -1   'True
   Caption        =    "&Hit"
   Height         =    375
   Left           =    3360
   TabIndex       =    1
   Top            =    5520
   Width          =    1095
End
```

continues

Listing 12.4. continued

```
Begin CommandButton btn_Deal
    BackColor       =   &H00008000&
    Caption         =   "&Deal"
    Height          =   375
    Left            =   960
    TabIndex        =   0
    Top             =   5520
    Width           =   1095
End

Begin Label lbl_Count
    Alignment       =   1   'Right Justify
    BackColor       =   &H00008000&
    Caption         =   "0"
    ForeColor       =   &H00FFFFFF&
    Height          =   255
    Index           =   1
    Left            =   240
    TabIndex        =   12
    Top             =   4440
    Width           =   375
End

Begin Label lbl_Count
    Alignment       =   1   'Right Justify
    BackColor       =   &H00008000&
    Caption         =   "0"
    ForeColor       =   &H00FFFFFF&
    Height          =   255
    Index           =   0
    Left            =   240
    TabIndex        =   11
    Top             =   2640
    Width           =   375
End

Begin Image img_PlayerHand
    Height          =   1500
    Index           =   5
    Left            =   5760
    Stretch         =   -1  'True
    Top             =   3840
    Width           =   1080
End

Begin Image img_PlayerHand
    Height          =   1500
    Index           =   4
    Left            =   4560
    Stretch         =   -1  'True
```

```
      Top              =    3840
      Width            =    1080
   End

   Begin Image  img_PlayerHand
      Height           =    1500
      Index            =    3
      Left             =    3360
      Stretch          =    -1   'True
      Top              =    3840
      Width            =    1080
   End

   Begin Image  img_PlayerHand
      Height           =    1500
      Index            =    2
      Left             =    2160
      Stretch          =    -1   'True
      Top              =    3840
      Width            =    1080
   End

   Begin Image  img_PlayerHand
      Height           =    1500
      Index            =    1
      Left             =    960
      Stretch          =    -1   'True
      Top              =    3840
      Width            =    1080
   End

   Begin Image  img_DealerHand
      Height           =    1500
      Index            =    5
      Left             =    5760
      Stretch          =    -1   'True
      Top              =    2040
      Width            =    1080
   End

   Begin Image  img_DealerHand
      Height           =    1500
      Index            =    4
      Left             =    4560
      Stretch          =    -1   'True
      Top              =    2040
      Width            =    1080
   End

   Begin Image  img_DealerHand
      Height           =    1500
      Index            =    3
```

continues

Listing 12.4. continued

```
        Left            =    3360
        Stretch         =    -1   'True
        Top             =    2040
        Width           =    1080
    End

    Begin Image img_DealerHand
        Height          =    1500
        Index           =    2
        Left            =    2160
        Stretch         =    -1   'True
        Top             =    2040
        Width           =    1080
    End

    Begin Image img_DealerHand
        Height          =    1500
        Index           =    1
        Left            =    960
        Stretch         =    -1   'True
        Top             =    2040
        Width           =    1080
    End

    Begin Image img_Title
        Height          =    1740
        Left            =    840
        Picture         =    BJMAIN.FRX:0302  'BJTITLE.BMP
        Stretch         =    -1   'True
        Top             =    120
        Width           =    6075
    End

    Begin Menu mnu_Options
        Caption         =    "&Options"
        Begin Menu mnu_NewGame
            Caption         =    "&New Game"
        End
        Begin Menu mnu_Add
            Caption         =    "&Add Cards"
        End
        Begin Menu mnu_HandMessages
            Caption         =    "&Hand Messages"
            Checked         =    -1   'True
        End
        Begin Menu mnu_ExitSep
            Caption         =    "-"
        End
        Begin Menu mnu_Exit
            Caption         =    "E&xit"
```

```
        End
     End

     Begin Menu mnu_Help
        Caption           =    "&Help"
        Begin Menu mnu_Rules
           Caption         =    "&Rules"
        End
        Begin Menu mnu_AboutSep
           Caption         =    "-"
        End
        Begin Menu mnu_About
           Caption         =    "&About BlackJack ..."
        End
     End

End

Option Explicit

Sub btn_BetLess_Click ()

  Dim Bet%

  ' Is the bet above zero?
  If (PInfo(PLAYER).Bet% > 0) Then

     ' Yes, so determine bet
     If (PInfo(PLAYER).Bet% >= MINBET) Then
       Bet% = MINBET
     Else
       Bet% = PInfo(PLAYER).Bet%
     End If

     ' Add to the player cash, and take away from the bet
     PInfo(PLAYER).Pot% = PInfo(PLAYER).Pot% + Bet%
     PInfo(PLAYER).Bet% = PInfo(PLAYER).Bet% - Bet%

     ' Update values
     DisplayStatus

     ' If we are at zero now, don't allow dealing
     If (PInfo(PLAYER).Bet% = 0) Then
       btn_Deal.Enabled = False
     End If

  End If

End Sub

Sub btn_BetMore_Click ()
```

continues

Listing 12.4. continued

```
Dim Bet%

' Does the player have any more cash? And is the bet less then the
' maximum?
If ((PInfo(PLAYER).Pot% > 0) And (PInfo(PLAYER).Bet% < MAXBET)) Then

  ' Yes, so determine bet
  If (PInfo(PLAYER).Pot% >= MINBET) Then
    Bet% = MINBET
  Else
    Bet% = PInfo(PLAYER).Pot%
  End If

  ' Keep it below the maximum
  If PInfo(PLAYER).Bet% + Bet% > MAXBET Then
    Bet% = MAXBET - PInfo(PLAYER).Bet%
  End If

  ' Add to the bet cash, and take the cash from the player
  PInfo(PLAYER).Bet% = PInfo(PLAYER).Bet% + Bet%
  PInfo(PLAYER).Pot% = PInfo(PLAYER).Pot% - Bet%

  ' Update values
  DisplayStatus

  ' If player bet is above zero now, allow dealing
  If (PInfo(PLAYER).Bet% > 0) Then
    btn_Deal.Enabled = True
  End If

End If

End Sub

Sub btn_BetSame_Click ()

  Dim Bet%

  ' Put current bet back into the pot
  PInfo(PLAYER).Pot% = PInfo(PLAYER).Pot% + PInfo(PLAYER).Bet%
  PInfo(PLAYER).Bet% = 0

  ' Yes, so determine bet
  If (PInfo(PLAYER).Pot% >= PInfo(PLAYER).LastBet%) Then
    Bet% = PInfo(PLAYER).LastBet%
  Else
    Bet% = PInfo(PLAYER).Pot%
  End If

  ' Add to the bet cash, and take the cash from the player
```

```
    PInfo(PLAYER).Bet% = Bet%
    PInfo(PLAYER).Pot% = PInfo(PLAYER).Pot% - Bet%

    ' Update values
    DisplayStatus

    ' If player bet is above zero now, allow dealing
    If (PInfo(PLAYER).Bet% > 0) Then
      btn_Deal.Enabled = True
    Else
      ' Remember the last bet could have been zero!
      btn_Deal.Enabled = False
    End If

End Sub

Sub btn_Deal_Click ()

    Dim i%

    ' Deal two cards each to the dealer and player
    For i% = 1 To 2
      ' First, the dealer
      DealHit (DEALER)
      ' Then the player
      DealHit (PLAYER)
    Next i%

    ' Count what we have
    CountCards

    ' We have dealt the cards, so disable dealing and betting
    btn_Deal.Enabled = False
    btn_BetMore.Enabled = False
    btn_BetLess.Enabled = False
    btn_BetSame.Enabled = False

    ' and enable hitting and staying
    btn_Hit.Enabled = True
    btn_Stay.Enabled = True

    ' Display card counts
    DisplayStatus

End Sub

Sub btn_Hit_Click ()

    ' Hit the player
    DealHit (PLAYER)

    ' Did the player bust, or have a 5-card Charlie?
```

continues

Listing 12.4. continued

```
  If ((PInfo(PLAYER).CardSum% > BLACKJACK) Or (PInfo(PLAYER).CardNum% =
➥5)) Then
    ' Force a stay
    btn_Stay_Click
  End If

End Sub

Sub btn_Stay_Click ()

  Dim Winner%, Bet%
  Dim MsgStr$

  ' We are staying, so disable hitting or staying buttons
  btn_Hit.Enabled = False
  btn_Stay.Enabled = False

  ' Show dealer "Hole" card
  img_DealerHand(1).Picture =
frm_Cards!img_Card(PInfo(DEALER).Card%(1)).Picture

  ' Display count
  DisplayStatus

  ' Wait, for effect
  Delay (1)

  ' Assume dealer won
  Winner% = DEALER

  ' Did the player bust?
  If (PInfo(PLAYER).CardSum% <= BLACKJACK) Then
    ' No. Does the player have a BlackJack or a "5-Card Charlie"?
    If (((PInfo(PLAYER).CardSum% = BLACKJACK) And (PInfo(PLAYER).CardNum%
➥= 2))

Or (PInfo(PLAYER).CardNum% = 5)) Then
      ' Player wins if dealer does not have a BlackJack
      If (PInfo(DEALER).CardSum% < BLACKJACK) Then
        Winner% = PLAYER
      End If
    Else
      ' Draw until we have 17 or more, or we have 5 cards
      While ((PInfo(DEALER).CardSum% < DEALERSTAY) And
➥(PInfo(DEALER).CardNum% < 5))
        ' Hit the dealer
        DealHit (DEALER)
        ' Pause for effect
        Delay (1)
      Wend
```

```
    ' Did we bust?
    If (PInfo(DEALER).CardSum% <= BLACKJACK) Then
      ' No, so did the player beat us?
      If (PInfo(DEALER).CardSum% < PInfo(PLAYER).CardSum%) Then
        ' Yes
        Winner% = PLAYER
      Else
        ' A Tie?
        If (PInfo(DEALER).CardSum% = PInfo(PLAYER).CardSum%) Then
          ' Yes
          Winner% = -1
        End If
      End If
    Else
      ' Dealer busted, so player wins
      Winner% = PLAYER
    End If
  End If
End If

' Wait, for effect
Delay (1)

' Credit winner and debit loser
Select Case Winner%

  Case DEALER
    ' Take the player's money
    PInfo(DEALER).Pot% = PInfo(DEALER).Pot% + PInfo(PLAYER).Bet%
    MsgStr$ = "Dealer Wins ..."
  Case PLAYER
    ' Get the player's bet
    Bet% = PInfo(PLAYER).Bet%
    ' Did the player get BlackJack?
    If ((PInfo(PLAYER).CardSum% = 21) And (PInfo(PLAYER).CardNum% = 2))
    ➡Then

      ' Yes, so give the player 1.5*bet
      Bet% = Bet% + (Bet% \ 2)
      MsgStr$ = "BlackJack! You Won!"
    Else
      ' Player won, but check for 5 cards (Dealer or Player gives win to
      ' Player)

      If (((PInfo(DEALER).CardSum% < DEALERSTAY) And
      ➡(PInfo(DEALER).CardNum% = 5)) Or (PInfo(PLAYER).CardNum% = 5))
      ➡Then
        MsgStr$ = "5-Card Charlie! You Won!"
      Else
        MsgStr$ = "You Won!"
      End If
```

continues

Listing 12.4. continued

```
      End If
      ' Adjust the pots
      PInfo(PLAYER).Pot% = PInfo(PLAYER).Pot% + PInfo(PLAYER).Bet% + Bet%

      PInfo(DEALER).Pot% = PInfo(DEALER).Pot% - Bet%
    Case Else
      ' Must be a tie
      MsgStr$ = "Push (Tie) ..."
  End Select

  ' Display Message
  If (mnu_HandMessages.Checked) Then
    MsgBox MsgStr$, MB_OK + MB_ICONINFORMATION, "Hand Results"
  End If

  ' Record last bet, for later betting
  PInfo(PLAYER).LastBet% = PInfo(PLAYER).Bet%

  ' Reset the bet, if not a tie
  If (Winner% <> -1) Then
    PInfo(PLAYER).Bet% = 0
  End If

  ' Get ready for a new hand
  InitNewHand

  ' Check if either player or dealer went broke
  If ((PInfo(PLAYER).Pot% <= 0) Or (PInfo(DEALER).Pot% <= 0)) Then
    ' Player or dealer is broke
    frm_Broke.Show 1
    ' Go ahead and start a new game
    InitNewGame
  End If

End Sub

'
' This procedure clears the cards from the table.
'
Sub ClearTable ()

  Dim i%

  ' Clear the dealer and player hands
  For i% = 1 To 5
    img_DealerHand(i%).Picture = LoadPicture()
    img_PlayerHand(i%).Picture = LoadPicture()
  Next i%

End Sub
```

```
'
' This procedure counts the cards in both the Dealer and Player hands.
'
Sub CountCards ()

  Dim i%, j%, CardVal%, AceVal%

  ' Count both hands
  For i% = DEALER To PLAYER

    ' Count the cards in the hand
    PInfo(i%).CardSum% = 0
    AceVal% = 0
    For j% = 1 To PInfo(i%).CardNum%

      ' Determine card value
      CardVal% = PInfo(i%).Card(j%) Mod 13

      ' Kings and other face cards count as ten
      If ((CardVal% = 0) Or (CardVal% > 10)) Then
        CardVal% = 10
      End If

      ' Aces can count as 1 or 11, so determine value later
      If (CardVal% = 1) Then
        AceVal% = 10
      End If

      ' Add card to total
      PInfo(i%).CardSum% = PInfo(i%).CardSum% + CardVal%

    Next j%

    ' If we have an ace, can we count it as 11?
    If ((AceVal% > 0) And (PInfo(i%).CardSum% + AceVal% <= 21)) Then
      ' The Ace counts as 11
      PInfo(i%).CardSum% = PInfo(i%).CardSum% + AceVal%
    End If

  Next i%

End Sub

'
' This procedure deals a hit (card) to the player or dealer.
'
Sub DealHit (p%)

  Dim i%

  ' Get a card
  i% = PInfo(p%).CardNum% + 1
```

continues

Listing 12.4. continued

```
  PInfo(p%).Card%(i%) = GetCard%()

  ' Update picture
  If (p% = DEALER) Then
    ' Hide the dealer's "Hole" card
    If (i% = 1) Then
      img_DealerHand(i%).Picture =
frm_Cards!img_Card(PInfo(p%).Card%(0)).Picture
    Else
      img_DealerHand(i%).Picture =
frm_Cards!img_Card(PInfo(p%).Card%(i%)).Picture
    End If
  Else
    img_PlayerHand(i%).Picture =
frm_Cards!img_Card(PInfo(p%).Card%(i%)).Picture

  End If

  ' Count it
  PInfo(p%).CardNum% = i%

  ' Count the cards and display the total
  CountCards
  DisplayStatus

End Sub

'
' This procedure updates the Dealer and Player status information.
'
Sub DisplayStatus ()

  ' Display the Dealer status information
  lbl_Pot(DEALER).Caption = "$" + Str$(PInfo(DEALER).Pot%)

  ' Display the Player status information
  lbl_Pot(PLAYER).Caption = "$" + Str$(PInfo(PLAYER).Pot%)
  lbl_Bet(PLAYER).Caption = "$" + Str$(PInfo(PLAYER).Bet%)

  ' Display the count values, if requested (default to nothing)
  lbl_Count(DEALER).Caption = ""
  lbl_Count(PLAYER).Caption = ""
  If (mnu_Add.Checked And (PInfo(PLAYER).CardNum% > 0)) Then
    ' Make sure we don't reveal the dealer total! (Show if player has
    ' stayed)

    If (btn_Stay.Enabled = False) Then
      lbl_Count(DEALER).Caption = Str$(PInfo(DEALER).CardSum%)
    End If
    ' Always show the player total, if requested
```

```
      lbl_Count(PLAYER).Caption = Str$(PInfo(PLAYER).CardSum%)
    End If

End Sub

Sub Form_KeyPress (KeyAscii As Integer)

  ' Determine whether this is a key we want
  Select Case KeyAscii
    Case Asc("+")
      ' Bet more
      If (btn_BetMore.Enabled) Then
        btn_BetMore_Click
      End If
    Case Asc("-")
      ' Bet less
      If (btn_BetLess.Enabled) Then
        btn_BetLess_Click
      End If
    Case Asc("="), Asc("*")
      ' Bet last
      If (btn_BetSame.Enabled) Then
        btn_BetSame_Click
      End If
  End Select

End Sub

Sub Form_Load ()

  ' Center on the screen
  Move (Screen.Width - Width) \ 2, (Screen.Height - Height) \ 2

  ' Show About box
  frm_AboutBox.Show 1

  ' Initialize a new game
  InitNewGame

End Sub

'
' This procedure gets a card from the shuffled deck.
'
Function GetCard% ()

  ' Get the next card from the deck
  GetCard% = CardDeck%(CardNum%)

  ' Bump to the next card
  CardNum% = CardNum% + 1
```

continues

Listing 12.4. continued

```
End Function

'
' This procedure initializes all of the game variables at the beginning
' of a new game.
'
Sub InitNewGame ()

   ' Reset the dealer and player cash values
   PInfo(DEALER).Pot% = 25000
   PInfo(PLAYER).Pot% = 2500

   ' Reset other player information
   PInfo(PLAYER).Bet% = 0
   PInfo(PLAYER).LastBet% = 0

   ' Shuffle the card deck
   frm_Shuffle.Show 1

   ' Get ready for a new hand
   InitNewHand

End Sub

'
' This procedure initializes all of the game variables at the beginning
' of a new hand.
'
Sub InitNewHand ()

   ' Initialize the card numbers
   PInfo(DEALER).CardNum% = 0
   PInfo(PLAYER).CardNum% = 0

   ' Reset the card sums
   PInfo(DEALER).CardSum% = 0
   PInfo(PLAYER).CardSum% = 0

   ' Enable betting buttons
   btn_BetMore.Enabled = True
   btn_BetLess.Enabled = True
   btn_BetSame.Enabled = True

   ' Disable other buttons, since there is no bet value
   btn_Deal.Enabled = False
   btn_Hit.Enabled = False
   btn_Stay.Enabled = False

   ' Clear the cards from the table
   ClearTable
```

```
  ' If there are not enough cards left, shuffle the deck
  If (CardNum% >= MAXCARDS - 10) Then
    frm_Shuffle.Show 1
  End If

  ' Display the status
  DisplayStatus

End Sub

Sub mnu_About_Click ()

  ' Show the About box
  frm_AboutBox.Show 1

End Sub

Sub mnu_Add_Click ()

  ' Enable or disable the display of the card count
  If (mnu_Add.Checked = True) Then
    mnu_Add.Checked = False
  Else
    mnu_Add.Checked = True
  End If

  ' Update fields
  DisplayStatus

End Sub

Sub mnu_Exit_Click ()

  ' Exit, so just unload the form
  Unload Me

End Sub

Sub mnu_HandMessages_Click ()

  ' Enable or disable the display of hand messages
  If (mnu_HandMessages.Checked = True) Then
    mnu_HandMessages.Checked = False
  Else
    mnu_HandMessages.Checked = True
  End If

End Sub

Sub mnu_NewGame_Click ()
```

continues

Listing 12.4. continued

```
  ' Start a new game
  InitNewGame

End Sub

Sub mnu_Rules_Click ()

  ' Show the rules
  frm_Rules.Show 1

End Sub
```

Figure 12.6 and Listing 12.5 show the BJRULES form and source code. The rules form is blank now, but when the game runs, the Rules text is displayed.

Figure 12.6. The BJRULES form.

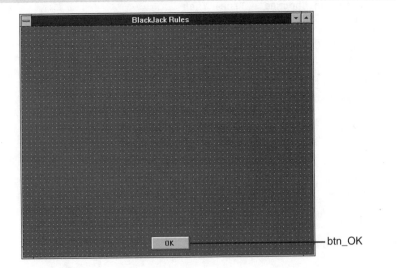

btn_OK

Listing 12.5. The BJRULES form source code.

```
VERSION 2.00

Begin Form frm_Rules
    BackColor       =   &H00008000&
    BorderStyle     =   1   'Fixed Single
    Caption         =   "BlackJack Rules"
    FontBold        =   -1  'True
    FontItalic      =   0   'False
    FontName        =   "System"
```

```
FontSize        =    9.75
FontStrikethru  =    0    'False
FontUnderline   =    0    'False
ForeColor       =    &H00FFFFFF&
Height          =    6690
Icon            =    0
Left            =    2700
LinkTopic       =    "Form1"
MaxButton       =    0    'False
MinButton       =    0    'False
ScaleHeight     =    6285
ScaleWidth      =    8145
Top             =    1515
Width           =    8265

Begin CommandButton btn_OK
   BackColor    =    &H00008000&
   Caption      =    "OK"
   Height       =    375
   Left         =    3600
   TabIndex     =    0
   Top          =    5760
   Width        =    1095
End

End

Option Explicit

Sub btn_OK_Click ()

  ' Unload the form
  Unload Me

End Sub

Sub Form_Load ()

  ' Center on the screen
  Move (Screen.Width - Width) \ 2, (Screen.Height - Height) \ 2

End Sub

Sub Form_Paint ()

  ' Position rule text
  CurrentX = 0
  CurrentY = 0

  ' Display them
  Print
  Print "  This is Single Deck BlackJack. The cards are shuffled when
```

continues

Listing 12.5. continued

```
➥there are 10 or less"
Print "  cards left in the deck. The object is to obtain a higher card
➥count than the dealer"
Print "  by reaching 21, or as close as possible. A count over 21 is a
➥'bust', and the bet"
Print "  is lost."
Print
Print "  Aces count either 1 or 11 at the discretion of the player.
➥Kings, Queens, and Jacks"
Print "  each have a count of 10. All other cards are counted at face
➥value."
Print
Print "  Before the deal begins, the player places his bet. The minimum
➥bet is $25, with a"
Print "  maximum of $250, in increments of $25. After the deal, the
➥player can take a 'hit'"
Print "  (card) to increase his card count. Once he 'stays', the dealer
➥MUST draw until he"
Print "  has 17 or more. The dealer stays on soft 17. "
Print
Print "  A player with 'BlackJack' (21 with 2 cards) gets paid 3:2 on
➥his bet, unless the"
Print "  dealer also has BlackJack (a tie). If the player ties the
➥dealer, they 'push' (no one"
Print "  loses). Otherwise, the dealer takes the bet when the player
➥loses, or matches it"
Print "  when the player wins. The player also wins with a '5-Card
➥Charlie'. This occurs"
Print "  when the player draws 5 cards without busting, or the dealer
➥draws 5 cards and"
Print "  does not beat the player."
Print
Print "  The game ends when the player leaves the table, is broke, or
➥the player 'Breaks"
Print "  the House' (wins all of the money)."


End Sub
```

Figure 12.7 and Listing 12.6 show the BJSHUFFL form and source code. The shuffle form is displayed each time the card deck is shuffled.

Figure 12.7. The BJSHUFFL form.

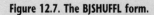 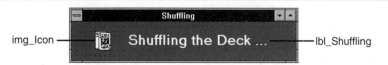

Listing 12.6. The BJSHUFFL form source code.

```
VERSION 2.00

Begin Form frm_Shuffle
    BackColor       =   &H00008000&
    BorderStyle     =   1  'Fixed Single
    Caption         =   "Shuffling"
    Height          =   1380
    Icon            =   0
    Left            =   2835
    LinkTopic       =   "Form1"
    MaxButton       =   0    'False
    MinButton       =   0    'False
    ScaleHeight     =   975
    ScaleWidth      =   5760
    Top             =   2730
    Width           =   5880

    Begin Image img_Icon
        Height      =   480
        Left        =   600
        Picture     =   BJSHUFFL.FRX:0000 'BJ.ICO
        Top         =   240
        Width       =   480
    End

    Begin Label lbl_Shuffling
        BackColor       =   &H00008000&
        Caption         =   "Shuffling the Deck ..."
        FontBold        =   -1  'True
        FontItalic      =   0    'False
        FontName        =   "MS Sans Serif"
        FontSize        =   18
        FontStrikethru  =   0    'False
        FontUnderline   =   0    'False
        ForeColor       =   &H00FFFFFF&
        Height          =   615
        Left            =   1440
        TabIndex        =   0
        Top             =   240
        Width           =   3855
    End
```

continues

Listing 12.6. continued

```
End

Option Explicit

Sub Form_GotFocus ()

  ' Shuffle the cards
  ShuffleDeck

  ' Delay for awhile
  Delay (3)

  ' Now unload the form
  Unload Me

End Sub

Sub Form_Load ()

  ' Center on the screen
  Move (Screen.Width - Width) \ 2, (Screen.Height - Height) \ 2

End Sub
```

Listing 12.7 shows the BJGLOBAL.BAS source code. The global file contains global constants, variables, and functions for the BlackJack game.

Listing 12.7. The BJGLOBAL.BAS source code.

```
Option Explicit

' Number of cards in the deck
Global Const MAXCARDS = 52

' Bet limits
Global Const MINBET = 25
Global Const MAXBET = 250

' Special card counts
Global Const DEALERSTAY = 17
Global Const BLACKJACK = 21

' Player structure
Type PLAYERINFO
  Pot As Integer
  Bet As Integer
  LastBet As Integer
```

```
      CardNum As Integer
      CardSum As Integer
      Card(5) As Integer
End Type

' Player values
Global Const DEALER = 0
Global Const PLAYER = 1

' MessageBox
Global Const MB_OK = 0
Global Const MB_ICONINFORMATION = 64

' Card Information
Global CardNum%
Global CardDeck%(MAXCARDS)

' Player Information
Global PInfo(2) As PLAYERINFO

'
' This procedure delays the given number of seconds.
'
' Note: This will fail if timing across midnight ...
'
Sub Delay (secs%)

  Dim Start

  ' Get the current seconds since midnight
  Start = Timer

  ' Wait for seconds to elapse
  While (Timer - Start < secs%)
    ' Let other things run while we wait
    DoEvents
  Wend

End Sub

'
' This function returns a random number between 0 and range%-1, inclusive.
'
Function GetRandom (range%)

  ' In the Visual Basic manual, the generic formula is:
  ' Int((upperbound-lowerbound+1)*Rnd+lowerbound)
  GetRandom = Int((range% + 1) * Rnd)

End Function

'
```

continues

Listing 12.7. continued

```
' This procedure "shuffles" the cards by randomizing an array of card
' numbers.

'
Sub ShuffleDeck ()

  Dim i%, j%, r%

  ' Initialize the card array to no entries
  For i% = 1 To MAXCARDS
    CardDeck%(i%) = -1
  Next i%

  ' Randomize the cards
  Randomize
  For i% = 1 To MAXCARDS
    ' Get a random number, between cards left
    r% = GetRandom(MAXCARDS - i%) + 1
    ' Now search for that slot
    j% = 1
    While (r% > 0)
      ' Position filled?
      If (CardDeck%(j%) = -1) Then
        ' No, so count it
        r% = r% - 1
      End If
      ' Bump to next card slot
      If (r% > 0) Then
        j% = j% + 1
      End If
    Wend
    ' Store card in this slot
    CardDeck(j%) = i%
  Next i%

  ' Deal from the first card
  CardNum% = 1

End Sub
```

Form Overview

The game of BlackJack consists of several forms. The following is a brief discussion of these forms and their controls. Consult the previous form figures for additional information.

About Box

The BJABOUT form is the standard About box form. I set the label lbl_Program to BlackJack and the image img_Icon to BJ.ICO. For a full description of the form, see Chapter 10, "Apples & Oranges."

You're Broke!

The BJBROKE form only appears when the player or dealer is broke (has no more money). Both the caption and the label lbl_Broke are set appropriately before the form is shown (note that the default caption and label are opposites!). The button, btn_NewGame, doesn't actually begin a new game—it simply unloads the form. The form is centered when loaded.

The Cards

The BJCARDS form contains all the card images. This form never actually appears, nor does it contain code. The card images are contained in an array of images named img_Card (with the first position 0 used as the card back). The other cards are loaded in the array so that their values closely match the array index. The Two of Spades is at position two, the Three of Spades at position three, and so on. For easy decoding with the modulus operator, I have loaded each suit in the same sequential sequence.

When I first created the BJCARDS form, I placed the cards side by side—and soon ran out of room. Visual Basic wouldn't let me increase the form size past the resolution of the screen. The solution to my dilemma soon became obvious. The cards can be overlapped, because nobody sees the form; therefore, overlapping the cards has no effect on the images.

You can select a group of controls by clicking and dragging the pointer around them. Or, select your first object, and use Shift-click to select additional objects. In the img_Card array, I copied and pasted the first 13 image controls, and then copied all 13 controls three times. This was a lot faster than individually copying and pasting all 52 controls. Visual Basic automatically increments the index appropriately.

Rules

When you select Rules from the Help menu, the BJRULES form appears. The form consists of blank space for the rule text and a single OK button (which unloads the form). The form is centered when it is loaded, and the rule text is displayed when the window is painted.

Shuffle

The BJSHUFFL form is displayed whenever the card deck needs reshuffling. This form consists of a single icon and label (which never change). When the form gets the program focus, it shuffles the deck and then unloads itself. The form is centered when it is loaded.

Global

The BJGLOBAL basic file contains the global variable and constant definitions. It also contains the global procedures Delay, GetRandom, and ShuffleDeck.

The Main Form

The BJMAIN form is the main form for the game, and it contains the most controls and functions. The img_Title control contains an image for the BlackJack game title.

To simplify the programming of the game, I use control arrays for many of the controls on the main form. The img_DealerHand and img_PlayerHand image arrays (which are filled by the appropriate card face during play) define the dealer and player hands. The lbl_Count array holds the count of the cards (hand total) for the dealer and player. This array also keeps count for the Add Cards menu option (when enabled). The label lbl_Pot is also an array; it holds the current pot for each player. The array index 0 always represents the dealer, and 1 represents the player. These constants are defined in BJGLOBAL.BAS.

Five buttons are used for dealing, hitting, staying, and betting (btn_Deal, btn_Hit, btn_Stay, btn_BetMore, btn_BetLess, and btn_BetSame). Finally, three frames are used to group the dealer, player, and betting statistics (fra_Dealer, fra_Player, and fra_Bet).

Programming Overview

The BlackJack program is similar to the previous two games (Apples & Oranges, and Flip), because the controls and images remain fixed in their locations. What is different, however, is that now you are playing with a full deck of cards (pun intended!).

Creating the Images

The card images were created and saved as individual BMP files. Using the naming scheme philosophy of Chapter 1, "Programming Conventions," I named the card files AHCARD.BMP (for Ace of Hearts), 8SCARD.BMP (for Eight of Spades), and so on. Getting the cards in the right order is crucial to the logic of the game. As I stated previously, the BJCARDS form contains the image array for the card images. The order of the card faces facilitates the easy decoding of the card value. After I created the image array, I loaded each image into position using the Picture property.

> I wish I could say that I created the card images myself, but I didn't. One of the problems with writing graphical games is that the game is only as good as its artwork. If you are thinking of creating a commercial game, consider hiring an artist.

I created the game title image by using two of the card images; I also used the font capabilities in Paintbrush (including outlining and shadowing). For the game icon, I scaled the title card pair down and pulled it into IconWorks for some touch-up.

After you've paid for artwork (or invested your own time in creating it), use it in as many places as possible. I used the card images in both the title and the game icon. I used the icon for the form, the About box, and the shuffling message. Maximize your investment, but don't overdo it! Graphics certainly make the game more appealing.

Program Flow

When the game runs, the program flows as follows:

▶ When the main form is loaded, it's centered, and the About box is displayed. Then, the InitNewGame procedure initializes a new game.

▶ The InitNewGame procedure initializes the dealer, player, pots, and the bet. It also shuffles the card deck by showing the frm_Shuffle form. After the cards are shuffled, the InitNewHand routine initializes a new hand.

▶ InitNewHand resets both the number of cards in each hand and the card count sum. It enables the betting buttons and disables the Deal, Hit, and Stay buttons (because a player hasn't placed a bet). This routine clears any previous cards from the table, and checks to make sure the deck has enough cards. It also displays the game status to the player.

➡ Now, the direction of the game depends on the player. The player must place a bet using the betting buttons. These buttons are controlled by the btn_BetMore_Click, btn_BetLess_Click, and btn_BetSame_Click procedures. If the bet is not zero, the Deal button btn_Deal is enabled.

➡ After a player selects btn_Deal_Click, the player and dealer receive two cards apiece (which the DealHit procedure handles). DealHit gets a card from the deck, updates the img_DealerHand or img_PlayerHand image arrays, and increments the total card count. Then, the btn_Deal_Click procedure counts the card values, disables dealing and betting, and enables hitting and staying.

➡ Now, the player can hit or stay. If the player chooses hit, the btn_Hit_Click procedure deals another card using the DealHit routine; then, if the player busts, the routine forces a stay by calling btn_Stay_Click.

➡ The central routine in BlackJack is the btn_Stay_Click procedure. After the player stays, the Hit and Stay buttons are disabled, and the dealer's hole card flips over. If the player doesn't bust or have a blackjack, the dealer draws cards using DealHit until reaching 17 or above. Next, the program compares the card totals and decides who is the winner. The appropriate message appears, and the bet is paid out accordingly. Then, the InitNewHand is called to get ready for the next hand. Finally, the pots are checked to see if the dealer or player went broke. If so, the frm_Broke form is displayed, and InitNewGame initializes a new game.

The game repeats this sequence (beginning at InitNewHand) until the player ends the game. The menu options enable the player to initialize a new game at any time by selecting New Game. The player also can determine whether the hand result messages are displayed. The menu options also show game rules and the About box (frm_AboutBox and frm_Rules) when the player selects Rules or Help.

Techniques Used

The BlackJack game illustrates several important programming techniques (discussed in the following section).

Card Deck Logic

This is the first game in this book to use a card deck (Chapter 13, "Draw Poker," describes Poker, which also uses the card deck). Remember that the order of the cards is important and that the cards have been placed so their values closely match their index positions.

So how are the cards shuffled? They aren't physically shuffled in the array, because that would destroy the index-to-value correlation I have worked so hard to maintain. The ShuffleDeck routine actually shuffles a separate array of 52 values called CardDeck. First, ShuffleDeck gets a number between 1 and 52. Then, it stores the first card (the Ace of Diamonds) at that number's array position. Next, from the remaining cards, it gets a number between 1 and 51. ShuffleDeck skips that many empty positions in the CardDeck array and stores the next card—the Two of Diamonds—in its array position. It continues in this manner until all cards are placed into the CardDeck array—resulting in a shuffled deck.

To make it possible to retrieve the next card, the GetCard function maintains an index in the CardDeck array called CardNum%. A particular card value can be determined by

```
' Get the card value (1 to 10) from the index (1 to 52)
CardVal% = CardIndex% Mod 13
' Kings and other face cards count as ten
If ((CardVal% = 0) Or (CardVal% > 10)) Then
  CardVal% = 10
End If
```

which is essentially what the CountCards routine does. In BlackJack, though, you have to count Aces as 1 or 11—so you need some extra logic. Look at the CountCards routine to see how this is handled in Listing 12.4.

> Notice that in BlackJack, it doesn't really matter what the suit is. The suit can be decoded in a similar manner to the card value decoding, though, which you'll see in Chapter 13, "Draw Poker."

Button Enabling

It's always important to let the player know when a button selection is valid. The BlackJack game guides the user from the betting buttons to the action buttons by enabling and disabling the buttons accordingly. Because the Bet-Deal-Hit-Stay button sequence appears on-screen, the player sees visual prompts (so he or she understands what to do when playing the game).

Enabling and disabling the buttons also makes the game easier to program. The btn_Stay_Click routine does not get called unless the Deal button is enabled (which only occurs when a player places a bet). If a player bets, the routine doesn't have to check for a bet. Likewise, the routine doesn't have to check to see if the cards have been dealt.

Bitmaps, Scaling, and Driver Resolution

I drew the card bitmaps at a 1:1 aspect ratio (standard VGA 16-color). I loaded a card into one of the img_DealerHand image controls so the image frame would snap to the correct size. I then set the Stretch property to True.

If you always run BlackJack on a VGA in 640x480x16 or 800x600x16 color mode (or any other mode with a 1:1 aspect ratio), the value of the Stretch property would not matter. On an EGA, however, the resolution is 640x350x16, and it does not have a 1:1 aspect. With Stretch=False, Visual Basic resizes the image frame, and the cards overlap—which would not impress your customer. With Stretch=True, the image frame remains a relative size, and the card is stretched (scaled) within.

Hidden Forms

You may not realize that all the forms in your project don't have to be displayed. The BJCARDS.FRM is an example of a hidden form. You could have placed the card images on the main form, but it is more convenient to have the entire deck on a separate form (in case you want to write a different card game, hint-hint).

Data Organization

BlackJack uses very few global variables. There are three to be exact: the current card deck number CardNum%, the shuffled card deck array CardDeck%(MAXCARDS), and the player information structure array, PInfo(2) AS PLAYERINFO. The player information is used for the dealer (who is just a player too, right?) and the player. The structure contains the current player pot, bet, last bet, number of cards in hand, card sum, and the card hand.

I used several constants to define bet limits, stay and bust values, and so on. The two most important constants are DEALER=0 and PLAYER=1. The program uses these constants throughout, and the code is much more readable. I took care when creating the form, so that the dealer controls are always index 0, and the player controls are index 1. I use these values for indexing into the PInfo array, as well as passing them to procedures like DealHit.

The Computer as Opponent

BlackJack is one of the simplest games to program for computer opponent play. Basically, the computer (dealer) must draw until the hand totals 17 or until it busts. There are no logic branches, strategies, or anything else to consider. The dealer algorithm is

```
' Draw until we have 17 or more, or we have 5 cards
While ((PInfo(DEALER.CardSum% < DEALERSTAY) And (PInfo(DEALER).CardNum% <
➡5))
  DealHit (DEALER)
Wend
```

Think of this the next time you are up against a Blackjack dealer; the strategy and house percentage are built right into the game—the dealer doesn't require any card playing skill.

Summary

I have covered the following important programming points:

➤ The arrangement of cards in the array simplifies the card deck decoding logic. The card deck is placed on a hidden form; this placement provides ease of use and portability to other card games. When the computer shuffles the deck, it doesn't actually physically shuffle the cards.

➤ A user can be (and should be) guided by the enabling and disabling of valid controls—in this case buttons. Button enabling makes the game easier to learn and play. It also simplifies the programming.

➤ You must consider the scaling of bitmaps when you play the game on other target machines of various resolution. The Stretch property can help.

➤ Artwork plays an important role in the overall look and feel of the game. Consider hiring an artist, and make good use of the art.

➤ By organizing controls into arrays and using meaningful constants, you can simplify programming.

➤ BlackJack doesn't involve real thinking on the part of the dealer.

Suggestions for Improvement

The following suggestions are ideas for enhancing BlackJack.

➤ Add a Double Down button. A player can double down (double his bet) after he sees his first two cards. The price for this is that he gets only one more card (which he must take). Why would you want to double down? If the computer deals you two cards totalling 11, your chances of getting a face card are relatively high—a six or above does not hurt, either. But if you get anything less, you better hope the dealer busts!

➡ Add a Split button. A player can split when his first two cards are the same. The best pair to split is a pair of aces. Obviously, the player would hope a couple of face cards were coming his way. If the player chooses to split, the bet is basically doubled, because you play each hand separately. The player has to play the first hand to completion before playing the next one. A player can win both hands, lose one and win one, or lose both.

➡ Add an option to increase the deck size. The current game uses a single deck. You could add an option to play two, four, or six deck BlackJack (like the card shoes at Vegas). Hint: don't double the number of card images— just double the size of the CardDeck() array.

➡ Add sound. Use the routines (found in later chapters) to add background music, or even a voice for the dealer. You could have the dealer say "BlackJack!", "Nice Hand", or "Hurry up, place your bet."

➡ The current board allows for only one player and the dealer. Add more players by scaling the cards down, or overlap the cards dealt so just the left edge can be seen.

➡ Add an automated Card Counting scheme (as described earlier in Gameplay Hints). You could easily implement this as a number somewhere on the board.

➡ The $25,000 house limit may be hard to break or play up to. Consider dropping the amount to $5,000 or $10,000. You can use this to set a difficulty level.

➡ Remove the Hand Messages box and replace it with a status bar on the main game form. This may be less annoying than popping a message for every hand.

➡ Keep track of statistics. Display the number of times a player has won and lost, and display it on request. You could even keep track of the odds of drawing to a 16, 17, 18, 19, 20, or 21. You could base these numbers on the player's past hands, or by the number of available cards left in the deck.

What's Ahead

This ends the discussion about the first card game. Next, I'll take the framework of the BlackJack game and turn it into another popular gambling card game —Poker. It's a simple matter to teach the computer to play BlackJack, but teaching it which cards to throw is another matter! Take your BlackJack winnings, bring them to the poker table for a few hands of Five Card Draw, and join me in the next chapter.

Draw Poker

Draw Poker is a variation of Straight Poker, and is one of the most popular gambling games (after Blackjack). The Draw Poker game builds on the programming of BlackJack—found in Chapter 12, "BlackJack"—and illustrates how one game can be modified into a new variation. In this chapter, I describe the game of Draw Poker, explain how the game is played, and offer some hints. I also cover the programming of the game and provide a full description of the techniques I used. You will learn about

- ➡️ Modifying an existing game into a new game

- ➡️ Advanced card deck logic

- ➡️ Guiding the user with button enabling

- ➡️ Bitmaps and scaling

- ➡️ Hidden forms

- ➡️ The advantage of control arrays

- ➡️ Hiding and showing images

- ➡️ Advanced computer thinking

Background

In the original straight version of Poker, the player receives five cards face down and doesn't show any of them until the end. He or she doesn't have a chance to improve his or her hand either. Draw Poker is the first of many innovations designed to speed up the game and allow for more betting. Now, a player can discard any number of cards and receive new cards to replace them.

Gameplay

This is a one-player game; the computer acts as dealer. The object of the game is to hold a better poker hand than the dealer. A poker hand consists of exactly five cards. To play Draw Poker, you need to understand the different kinds of poker hands.

Poker Hands

There are several types of poker hands, and each hand has a ranking based on the probability of drawing each one. In the following definitions, cards are represented by the following: A = Ace, K = King, Q = Queen, J = Jack, and 2 through 10 represent numbers. For suits, C = Clubs, D = Diamonds, H = Hearts, and S = Spades. For example, the card KH is the King of Hearts, and 8D is the Eight of Diamonds. The probability of getting each hand is listed in Table 13.1.

A *Straight Flush* ranks highest and consists of five cards in suit and sequence. Examples of a Straight Flush are 8H 7H 6H 5H 4H and JC 10C 9C 8C 7C. The highest possible Straight Flush is the highest poker hand—a *Royal Flush*. An example of a Royal Flush is AD KD QD JD 10D.

Four of a Kind is the next highest hand, consisting of four cards of any one rank together—with any fifth card. The hand 9C 9D 9H 9S 3C is four nines, or Four of a Kind (with 3 being the extra fifth card).

A *Full House* is next down in rank. This hand consists of three of one kind and a pair of any other kind, as in: JC JD JH 7D 7S.

A *Flush* is any five cards of the same suit, but not in sequence (if they are in sequence, you have a *Straight Flush*—see preceding explanation). An example of a flush is: QH 7H 5H 3H 2H.

A *Straight* is any five cards of two or more suits in sequence (again, if they are all in the same suit, it's a *Straight Flush*—see above). The hand 7D 6C 5D 4D 3H is a straight.

Three of a Kind consists of any three cards of the same kind plus two other cards (that are not a pair or do not include the fourth card of the same kind). 7H 7D 7C QH 3S is an example of Three of a Kind (with three sevens).

Two Pairs is next down in rank, with two cards of one kind, two cards of another kind, and any fifth card which is neither of those ranks. An example of two pairs is AH AS 8C 8S 2D.

> When Wild Bill Hickock was shot in the back while playing poker, he held two pairs: Aces and Eights. To this day, two pairs of Aces and Eights are referred to as the *Dead Man's Hand.*

A *Pair* is any two cards of the same kind, with three other cards which do not combine with the other two to form one of the hands above. The hand JC JS 9C 8H 3H contains a pair of jacks—therefore, it's a Pair.

No Pair is the lowest ranking hand, and consists of five cards not meeting any of the previous requirements. It's usually rated by the highest card, so a hand like JD 10C 7D 6H 2S would be referred to as *Jack High.*

Table 13.1. Probability of poker hands.

Poker Hand	Probability
Straight Flush	40
Four of a Kind	624
Full House	3,744
Flush	5,108
Straight	10,200
Three of a Kind	54,912
Two Pairs	123,552
One Pair (84,480 of each)	1,098,240
No Pair	1,302,540
Total	2,598,960

Running Draw Poker

To begin playing Draw Poker, select the Poker icon from the program group you installed. See Appendix A for installation instructions. Draw Poker is contained in the file POKER.EXE. When you run the game, you'll see the About box first. Click OK, and Draw Poker appears.

Playing a Hand

The House extends you a $2,500 line of credit, and it has $25,000 more for you to win. Before the dealer deals the cards, you must ante (bet). Select the Bet More button (+) to place your ante (in increments of $25). You can place a maximum ante of $250 if you feel lucky! Use the Bet Less button (-) to decrease your ante. If you want to bet the same amount each time, use the Bet Same button (=).

> Normally, you would ante the minimum possible—$25—because you don't know your cards yet. You can increase your bet later.

After you place your ante, you'll notice that the Deal button is available. Select Deal when your ante is ready, and you will be dealt your first five cards. The dealer's hand is also dealt, face down. Your game should look similar to the game shown in Figure 13.1.

Figure 13.1. An initial hand in Draw Poker.

Now, you have a hand to look at. You may already have a good poker hand—or the potential for one. Click the cards you want to *throw* (discard), and the cards disappear. If you change your mind, you can click the card location again to make the card reappear. Increase your bet using the betting buttons (you won't be able to decrease your bet after your original ante). When you are ready, select the Throw button to throw your cards. See Figure 13.2 for throwing cards for a better poker hand.

> Watch to see how many cards the dealer throws. This will give you a clue to the strength of his hand.
>
> **TIP**

Figure 13.2. Throwing some cards for a better poker hand.

The computer deals you a new card for each one you discard—which might be all five if you have a poor starting hand! These are your final cards, so read 'em and weep. If you think you can beat the dealer, increase your bet. Select the Stay button for the final showdown.

The dealer's hand is shown, and both hands are evaluated. If you beat the dealer, you win the pot (twice what you bet, because the dealer has to match your bet). Figures 13.1 through 13.3 illustrate the sequence of a typical hand.

Figure 13.3. The final showdown.

Hand Messages

You can turn off the messages that appear after each hand if they start to get annoying. Select Hand Messages from the the Options menu.

Hints

Most poker strategies apply to a group of people playing, including those who use an occasional bluff. You can't bluff the dealer in this version of the game, however, so follow these simple hints:

➡ Bet the minimum amount for the ante.

➡ If you don't have a good initial hand, don't raise the bet until you see your final cards.

➡ If you don't have a good final hand, just Stay. You'll only be out your original ante.

➡ Watch to see what the dealer throws. If a lot of cards are thrown, you know the dealer doesn't have much and you can raise more (if you have a good hand, of course).

➡ If you feel lucky, make a $250 ante, and raise $250 each time. This gives you a total pot of $750.

Programming

The makefile for Draw Poker contains the files listed in Table 13.2.

Table 13.2. Poker source files.

Filename	Description
PKABOUT.FRM	The About box form
PKBROKE.FRM	The player or dealer is broke form
PKCARDS.FRM	The card images form
PKMAIN.FRM	The main Poker form
PKRULES.FRM	The Poker Rules form
PKSHUFFL.FRM	The Shuffling Deck message form
PKWINNER.FRM	The Winner message form
PKGLOBAL.BAS	Contains global constants, variables, and procedures

All these files are included on the disk in the back of this book. See Appendix A, "Installation," for installation instructions.

Figures 13.4 through 13.10 show the forms for the source code files. Figure 13.4 is my standard About box, with a new name and icon.

Figure 13.4 shows the PKABOUT form.

WHERE'S THE CODE?

```
PKABOUT.FRM

    ' You can find the source code
    ' for this program on the disk.

    Option Explicit
    Declare variable to track animation frame
```

Figure 13.4. The PKABOUT form.

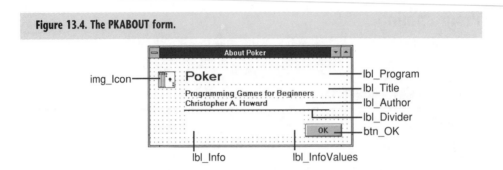

Figure 13.5 shows the PKBROKE form. This form is displayed whenever the player goes broke.

Figure 13.5. The PKBROKE form.

Figure 13.6 shows the PKCARDS form which contains the images for all the cards.

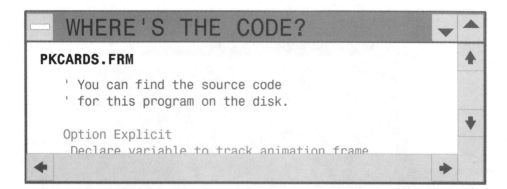

Figure 13.6. The PKCARDS form.

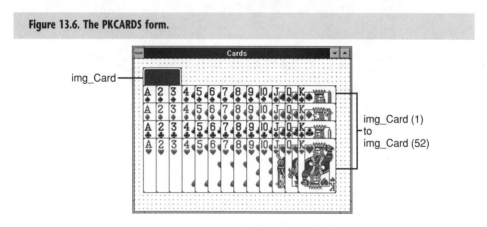

Figure 13.7 shows the PKMAIN form which handles most of the poker gameplay.

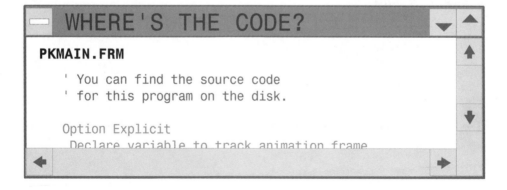

Figure 13.7. The PKMAIN form.

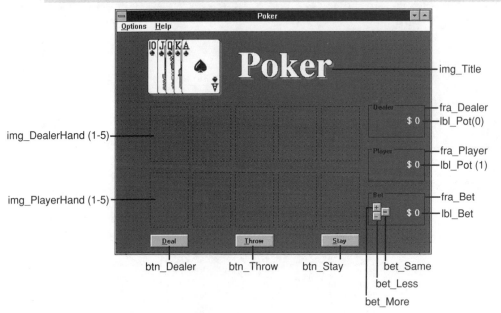

Figure 13.8 shows the PKRULES form. The rules are printed on the form at runtime—so the form appears blank now.

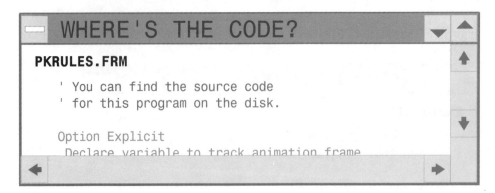

Figure 13.8. The PKRULES form.

btn_OK

Figure 13.9 shows the PKSHUFFL form, which is displayed before every hand (while the deck is shuffled).

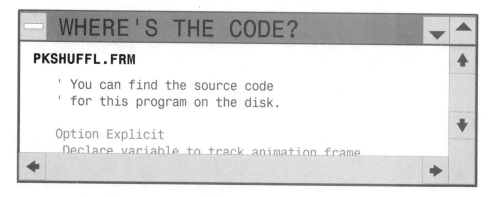

WHERE'S THE CODE?

PKSHUFFL.FRM

```
' You can find the source code
' for this program on the disk.

Option Explicit
  Declare variable to track animation frame
```

Figure 13.9. The PKSHUFFL form.

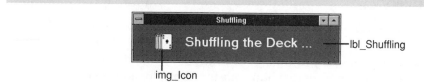

img_Icon

Figure 13.10 shows the PKWINNER form, which displays the winner of the poker hand.

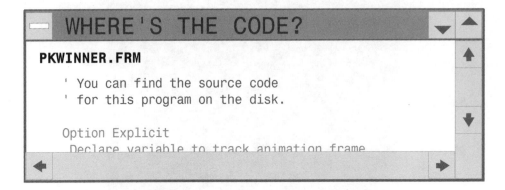

```
PKWINNER.FRM

    ' You can find the source code
    ' for this program on the disk.

    Option Explicit
    Declare variable to track animation frame
```

Figure 13.10. The PKWINNER form.

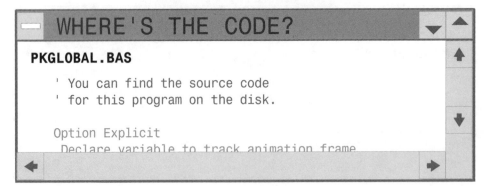

```
PKGLOBAL.BAS

    ' You can find the source code
    ' for this program on the disk.

    Option Explicit
    Declare variable to track animation frame
```

Form Overview

The game of Draw Poker consists of several forms. The following is a brief discussion of the Draw Poker forms and their controls. Many of these forms closely match the BlackJack forms, so if you studied those you may want to skip this overview. Consult the previous figures (that illustrate the forms) for additional information.

About Box

The PKABOUT form is our standard About box form. The label lbl_Program has been set to Poker, and the image img_Icon has been set to PK.ICO. For a full description of the form, see Chapter 10, "Apples & Oranges."

You're Broke!

The PKBROKE form only appears when the player or dealer is broke (has no more money). Both the caption and the label lbl_Broke are appropriately set before the form is shown. (Note that the default caption and label are opposites!) The button btn_NewGame doesn't actually begin a new game—it simply unloads the form. The form is centered when loaded.

The Cards

The PKCARDS form contains all of the card images. This form never actually appears, and it contains no code. The card images are contained in an array of images named img_Card, with the first position 0 used as the card back. The other cards are loaded in the array so that their values closely match the array index. The Two of Spades is at position 2, the Three of Spades at position 3, and so on. The following suits are loaded in the same sequential sequence (for easy decoding with the modulus operator).

Rules

When you select Rules from the Help menu, the PKRULES form displays the Draw Poker rules. The form itself consists of blank space for the rule text and a single OK button (which unloads the form). The form is centered when loaded, and the rule text is displayed when the window is painted.

Shuffle

When the deck is shuffled, the PKSHUFFL form appears before every hand. The form consists of a single icon and label that never changes. When the form gets the program focus, it shuffles the deck and unloads itself. The form is centered when loaded.

Winner

The PKWINNER form is displayed at the end of every hand. The form shows what poker hands the dealer and player have and who wins the pot.

Global

The PKGLOBAL basic file contains the global variable and constant definitions. It also contains the global procedures `Delay`, `GetRandom`, and `ShuffleDeck`.

The Main Form

The PKMAIN form is the main form for the game, and it contains the most controls and functions. The `img_Title` control contains an image for the Draw Poker game title.

Control arrays—which simplify the programming of the game—are used for many of the controls on the main form. The dealer and player hands (defined by the `img_DealerHand` and `img_PlayerHand` image arrays) are filled by the appropriate card face during play. The label `lbl_Pot` is an array that holds the current pot for each player. The dealer is always represented by array index 0, and the player by 1 (these constants are defined in PKGLOBAL.BAS).

Buttons are also used for dealing, throwing, staying, and betting (`btn_Deal`, `btn_Throw`, `btn_Stay`, `btn_BetMore`, `btn_BetLess`, and `btn_BetSame`). Finally, three frames are used to group the dealer, player, and betting statistics (`fra_Dealer`, `fra_Player`, and `fra_Bet`).

Programming Overview

The Draw Poker program was derived from the BlackJack game. I copied all the forms from BlackJack and added the PKWINNER form. This illustrates how you can design one game from another completely different game—just by changing some of the underlying logic.

Creating the Images

I previously created the card images for the BlackJack game with Paintbrush. The only new image is the Draw Poker title image which I created using some of the card faces and a Paintbrush font. I created the icon in IconWorks.

> Remember what I said about maximizing your artwork? Now you have used the same art for two games (BlackJack and Draw Poker). These card images can actually be used for any number of card games that you might create.

Program Flow

When the game runs, the program flows as follows:

➡️ When the main form is loaded, it is centered and the About box is displayed. The InitNewGame procedure initializes a new game.

➡️ The InitNewGame procedure initializes the dealer, player pots, and the bet. It also shuffles the card deck by showing the frm_Shuffle form (which in turn shuffles the cards). After the cards are shuffled, the InitNewHand routine initializes a new hand.

➡️ InitNewHand resets the number of cards in each hand. The betting buttons are enabled, and the Deal, Throw, and Stay buttons are disabled (because a player hasn't placed a bet). Any previous cards are cleared from the table, and the game status appears on-screen for the user.

➡️ Now, the game's direction depends on the player. The player must place a bet (ante) using the betting buttons (which are controlled by the btn_BetMore_Click, btn_BetLess_Click, and btn_BetSame_Click procedures). If the bet is not zero, the Deal button btn_Deal is enabled.

➡️ After btn_Deal_Click is called, five cards are dealt both to the player and the dealer using the DealHit procedure. DealHit gets a card from the deck and updates the img_DealerHand or img_PlayerHand image arrays. The btn_Deal_Click procedure then disables dealing and betting, and it enables throwing.

➡️ Now, the player can increase his or her bet by using the betting buttons. The player also can throw any unwanted cards by clicking the card images. The img_PlayerHand_Click routine flips the card over (or back again). When the player has selected all desired cards, he or she must select the Throw button.

➡️ The btn_Throw_Click procedure disables future throwing, and it clears the pictures of the "thrown" cards. The DealHit routine enables the dealing of new cards. The dealer discards with DealerThrow, and new cards are dealt again using DealHit. The Stay button is finally enabled.

➡️ Now, the player can adjust his or her final bet and select Stay. The btn_Stay_Click procedure disables staying and betting and turns over the dealer's cards. Now, the hard part is determining who wins. The EvaluateCards function handles this determination. The winner is credited, and the bet is reset. InitNewHand is called to get ready for the next hand. Finally, the pots are checked to see if the dealer or player went broke (from the previous game). If so, the frm_Broke form is displayed, and InitNewGame initializes a new game.

The game repeats this sequence (beginning with `InitNewHand`) until the player ends the game. The menu options enable the player to initialize a new game at any time (with `InitNewGame`). The options also display the hand result. You can view the game rules and the About box if you select the Help menu options (which show `frm_AboutBox` and `frm_Rules`).

Techniques Used

The Draw Poker game illustrates several of the same techniques as BlackJack, because the forms and programming were derived from BlackJack. The following is a summary of those techniques, as well as some important new ones.

Starting at 50 Percent Completed

As I've said, I based much of the Draw Poker game on BlackJack. This allowed me to start with almost all of the forms already designed: the controls, functions, artwork, code, and logic. There still were many changes, but I didn't have to start from scratch.

Card Deck Logic

This is the second game in this book to use a card deck (BlackJack also uses it). I have covered the fact that the order of the cards is important; also, I placed the cards so their values closely match their index positions. I also have described how the cards are shuffled. See Chapter 12, "BlackJack," for more information.

The card decoding is a little different in Draw Poker, because the suit is important. To decode the card suit, use:

```
' Get the card suit (0 to 3) from the index (1 to 52)
CardVal% = CardIndex% \ 13
```

The suit changes every thirteen cards, so I just divide the index by thirteen. Again, the ordering of the cards helps to determine the card value (`Mod 13`) and the card suit (`Div 13`).

Button Enabling

It's always important to let the user know when a button selection is valid. Draw Poker, like BlackJack, guides the user from the betting buttons to the action buttons by enabling and disabling the buttons accordingly. When the screen visually illustrates the Bet-Deal-Throw-Stay button sequence, the player immediately knows what can or can't be done.

Button enabling and disabling also makes the game easier to program. The btn_Deal_Click routine doesn't get called unless the Deal button is enabled—this only occurs when a bet is placed. This frees the deal routine from checking if there is a bet. Likewise, the btn_Stay_Click routine does not have to check if the cards have been dealt.

Bitmaps, Scaling, and Driver Resolution

As in the BlackJack game, I sized the image control arrays appropriately for a 1:1 aspect ratio. If the current screen resolution is not 1:1, the Stretch property rescales the images automatically.

Hidden Forms

Once again, I have hidden the cards on a form I never display. With the cards on a separate form, I just copied the form from the BlackJack game to use in the Draw Poker program.

Data Organization

There are very few global variables used in Draw Poker. Three are used in BlackJack: the current card deck number CardNum%, the shuffled card deck array CardDeck%(MAXCARDS), and the player information structure array, PInfo(2) AS PLAYERINFO. The player information is used for both the dealer (who is just a player too, right?) and the player. For Draw Poker, I added CardHand (to indicate what poker hand is held) and CardKind() (to hold the number of card kinds in the hand—in numbers of twos, threes, and so on). The CardSum variable is not necessary in Draw Poker.

The same BlackJack constants are used to define bet limits, stay and bust values, and player and dealer data. I also added constants to define all of the various poker hand types.

The Computer as Opponent

Draw Poker was more difficult to program for computer opponent play than BlackJack. Instead of just drawing to 17 and busting or staying, the computer must analyze the poker hand and discard unwanted cards. It also must know how to recognize each kind of poker hand (as well as knowing which hands are more valuable).

I must admit that, at first, I thought it was going to be easy to program the computer logic. How hard could it be to look at five cards and determine what to throw? Or to figure out who has the winning hand? During my first implementation, I looked at the dealer and player hands and just figured out whose poker hand was higher. This method was only partially correct. The hard part is determining the winner when both the poker hands are the same: a pair, a straight, and so on.

No problem—just keep track of the high card, right? Wrong. In the worst case, both players can have the exact same cards in their hands (except for suit, of course). Even the fifth card can determine the winner, as in QD 9S 7D 5H 4H over QS 9C 7C 5D 3H. To complicate things further, a tie can occur in more than just High Card hands. The only poker hands that can't tie are a Full House, Four of a Kind, and Three of a Kind.

> The odds of two hands tying are pretty slim, but because it's even possible to tie a Royal Flush, you have to consider how to handle it. For instance, if only 10,000 people buy this book, and each person plays 100 hands of poker, that's one million poker games and two million poker hands!

The final algorithm for determining poker hands is fairly simple. The CountCards function (a naming holdover from BlackJack) has only 120 lines of code. The tricky part is analyzing the cards in the order that you test for poker hands. You can have just a Straight, just a Flush, or both for a Straight Flush. You don't want to look for a Pair before Three of a Kind— a Pair could be Two Pair or a Full House.

After determining a good hand, I needed an algorithm for deciding what cards to throw. I developed the DealerThrow routine to handle this decision. It first checks to see whether the dealer has a better hand than Three of a Kind. If not, it throws away any cards that aren't a pair or more. It also keeps an Ace if the dealer has no pairs at all.

> This may seem like an over-simplified algorithm, but it's pretty close to the way most people play Poker. How many times have you actually drawn cards to get a Straight or a Flush? The other five poker hands require two or more of the same card, so the DealerThrow logic is optimized with that in mind.

The second half of the algorithm, performed by the EvaluateCard procedure, compares the two poker hands. If one poker hand ranks above the other, it easily determines the winner. In the case of a tie, the routine has to look for the highest card in Straights and Flushes, or it looks for who has the highest pair. Once I complete this algorithm, the computer has all it needs to play Draw Poker.

Debugging

It takes many, many games of Poker for some of the poker hands to appear. I played my share of hands during the development of the game, but there are still hands I haven't seen. Just take a look at Table 13.1 again, and you'll understand why. To test the algorithms, you have to force the hands to appear.

I forced the hands to appear (for example, a Royal Flush) by altering the code in the EvaluateCards function. I commented out the lines of code I used to force the hands (so you can test the hands too). The function overwrites whatever cards you actually have. You won't actually see the card pictures, but after you select the Stay button, the hands will be set and evaluated. You can set a breakpoint on EvaluateCards, and then step through the logic of both CountCards and EvaluateCards.

Remember to add a multiple of thirteen to some of the forced card values. The first 13 cards in the deck are all one suit, followed by the next 13 cards, and so on. By adding thirteen, you can avoid detecting the hand as a Flush (unless you are testing for a Flush).

Another debugging technique is to print to the Visual Basic Debug window. The EvaluateCards procedure uses the following:

```
' Debug
  Debug.Print "Hands after Counting:"
  Debug.Print "Dealer Hand: "; PInfo(DEALER).CardHand%
  Debug.Print "Player Hand: "; PInfo(PLAYER).CardHand%
' Debug
```

The relative poker hand values are printed out when you run the game in Visual Basic (VB). Printing to the debug window lets you see program variables, without your having to query repeatedly. These statements can be left in the program, because they are valid only in VB. They have no affect on the final executable program.

Summary

I have covered the following important programming points:

➡ One game can be used as a starting point for programming another. This maximizes previous artwork and development.

➡ As in BlackJack, the arrangement of cards simplifies the card deck logic. Placing the card deck on a hidden form enables you to use it in Draw Poker (and other card games) with no modifications. I borrowed other techniques from BlackJack such as guiding the user with buttons, scaling bitmaps with the Stretch property, and reusing artwork.

➡ Poker logic can be complicated, but can be easily coded if well thought-out.

➡ All possible combinations (in this case, poker hands) should be tested. This can be done by forcing the combinations to appear. You can use the Visual Basic Debug window for adding feedback.

Suggestions for Improvement

The following suggestions are ideas for enhancing Draw Poker.

➡ Add sound. Use the routines (found in later chapters) to add background music or even a voice for the dealer. You could have the dealer say "Royal Flush!," "Nice Hand," or "Hurry up, place your bet."

➡ The current board allows for only one player and the dealer. Add more players by scaling the cards down. Or, overlap the cards dealt so just the left edge can be seen. Give each player a personality (aggressive, timid, and so on).

➡ Add a Fold button. A player can fold either on the first deal or after throwing his or her cards. The money would automatically go to the dealer. Consider whether you should show them what the dealer had. (Some people say you have to pay to see the cards!)

➡ Improve the DealerThrow logic. What if the hand is one card short of a Straight or a Flush? Should you draw to an Inside Straight where the missing card is in the middle of the series (instead of at either end)? What if the card you need to throw gives you a pair, as in 5C 5D 6S 7D 8H? You might make this decision based on the computer's personality (agressive or timid).

➡ Take the computer's hand away, and pay on the player's hand, as in the Las Vegas video poker machines. If they have a pair, pay the players back their bets. If they have a Royal Flush—jackpot!

➡ Animate the cards so they appear to flip over, as in the Flip game.

➡ Add logic to recognize Ace as Low straights, as in AH 2C 3C 4D 5S.

➡ Improve the PKWINNER form with a bigger "You Won!" message.

What's Ahead

Draw Poker is the last card game I'll cover. Besides, you're probably out of money, anyway! Up ahead, I'll discuss puzzle games. Remember those sliding number puzzles? In the next chapter, you'll learn how to create such a game.

Slider

Slider is a replica of a popular children's sliding puzzle game. In this chapter, I describe the game of Slider, offer some hints, and explain the programming of the game. I also cover the code listings and the programming techniques. The items covered are

- ➤ Using twips instead of pixels

- ➤ Dynamic mouse pointers

- ➤ Animation using the Move method

- ➤ Effects of `Delay` and `DoEvents`

- ➤ Icon animation

- ➤ Calling the Windows API (`BitBlt`)

- ➤ A game without bitmaps!

Background

Slider is my computer version of the numbered, sliding puzzle game my daughter likes. This game uses the traditional numbered squares, but some games have pictures instead of numbers—at the end of this chapter, I suggest using pictures to enhance this game!

Gameplay

Slider is a one-player game. The pieces are scrambled, and your object is to move them into numerical sequence by sliding the pieces around. It's harder than it looks—especially toward the end.

Running Slider

To begin playing Slider, select the Slider icon from the program group you installed. (See Appendix A for installation instructions.) The file SLIDER.EXE contains the game Slider. When you run the game, you'll see the About box first. Click OK, and Slider appears.

Playing a Game

From the Options menu, select New Game. The pieces of the puzzle are scrambled as you watch. After the pieces stop moving, you can begin playing. To slide a square, click it (or use the Tab key to select it, and press Enter). The selected square then slides into the blank square position, leaving a new blank location behind. Figure 14.1 shows a game in progress.

Figure 14.1. Playing a game of Slider.

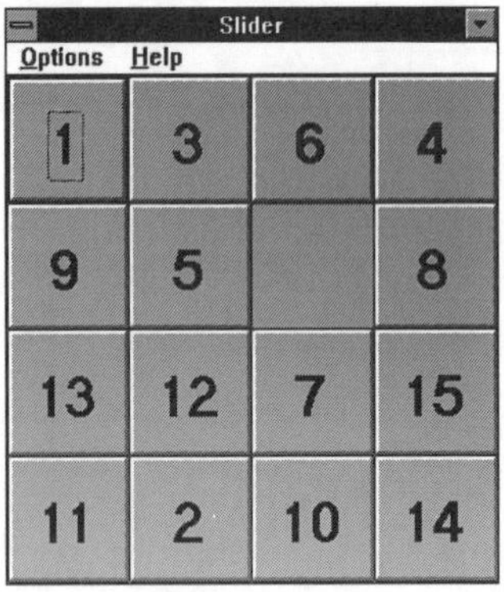

1	3	6	4
9	5		8
13	12	7	15
11	2	10	14

You only can move the pieces immediately adjacent to the blank square. The mouse pointer changes to a horizontal or vertical arrow when it's over a piece that can be moved.

There are no points or time limits in this game. From the Options menu, you can change the difficulty level by selecting the number of scramble moves you want made. Then, select New Game again. You can rescramble the puzzle at any time. For faster scrambles, you can hide the moves by unselecting Show Moves.

The game continues until you solve the puzzle or exit the game.

To get help, select Rules from the Help menu. The help form appears and displays the game help (see Figure 14.2).

Figure 14.2. Getting help.

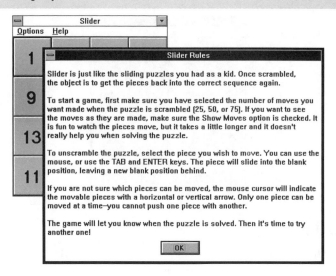

Hints

This is a pretty basic game, but here are some hints:

➤ Start with the #1 square, and move it up into position. Always work the game in numerical sequence—from top to bottom.

➤ It's okay to move a square or squares out of position, but keep them together. For instance, while working #4 into place, you may have to move #1, #2, and #3. Do this by moving #1 down one square, follow with #2 left, and then #3 left—this keeps them in order. Now you can rotate the four squares in the upper-right corner until #4 is in position. Then, slide #3 back to the right, follow with #2, and slide #1 up.

➤ Solving the bottom of the puzzle is difficult, because there isn't a "spare" row to work with. Essentially, you have to follow the preceding advice about keeping the rows together and moving them left and down when necessary. In fact, you'll probably end up with #9-#10-#11-#12 in a square at the left, so you can move #13-#14-#15 in order on the right. The trick is that you want the numbers in reverse order (#15-#14-#13). So, when you cycle everything left, they end up in the correct sequence (see Figure 14.3 for a puzzle that is almost solved).

Figure 14.3. The puzzle is almost solved.

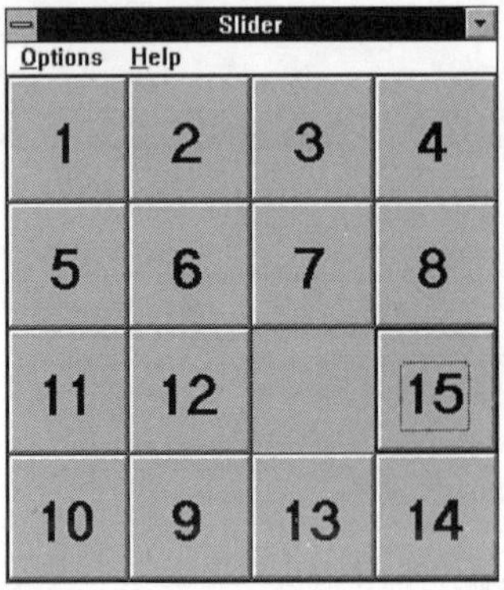

Slider			
1	2	3	4
5	6	7	8
11	12		15
10	9	13	14

Programming

The makefile for Slider contains the files listed in Table 14.1.

Table 14.1. Slider source files.

Filename	Description
SLABOUT.FRM	The About box form
SLMAIN.FRM	The Main Slider form
SLRULES.FRM	The Rules form
SLGLOBAL.BAS	Contains global constants, variables, and procedures

All these files are included in this book's disk. See Appendix A for installation instructions.

Figures 14.4 through 14.6 and Listings 14.1 through 14.4 contain all of the information needed to re-create the above source code files.

Figure 14.4 and Listing 14.1 show the SLABOUT form and source code. Again, this is the standard About box.

Figure 14.4. The SLABOUT form.

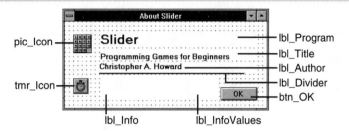

Listing 14.1. The SLABOUT form source code.

```
VERSION 2.00
Begin Form frm_AboutBox
    BorderStyle     =   3   'Fixed Double
    Caption         =   "About Slider"
    ClipControls    =   0   'False
    FontBold        =   -1  'True
    FontItalic      =   0   'False
    FontName        =   "System"
    FontSize        =   10
    FontStrikethru  =   0   'False
    FontUnderline   =   0   'False
    Height          =   2780
    Icon            =   0
    Left            =   1590
    MaxButton       =   0   'False
    MinButton       =   0   'False
    ScaleHeight     =   2280
    ScaleWidth      =   5640
    Top             =   1260
    Width           =   5760
    Begin PictureBox pic_Icon
        AutoSize        =   -1  'True
        Height          =   680
        Left            =   240
        Picture         =   SLABOUT.FRX:0000 'SL,ICO
        ScaleHeight     =   640
        ScaleWidth      =   480
        TabIndex        =   6
        Top             =   360
        Width           =   510
    End
    Begin Timer tmr_Icon
        Left            =   240
        Top             =   1560
    End
```

continues

Listing 14.1. continued

```
Begin CommandButton btn_OK
    Caption          =   "OK"
    FontBold         =   -1   'True
    FontItalic       =   0    'False
    FontName         =   "System"
    FontSize         =   10
    FontStrikethru   =   0    'False
    FontUnderline    =   0    'False
    Height           =   360
    Left             =   4350
    TabIndex         =   5
    Top              =   1800
    Width            =   1035
End
Begin Line lin_Divider
    BorderWidth      =   2
    X1               =   975
    X2               =   5010
    Y1               =   1425
    Y2               =   1425
End
Begin Label lbl_Program
    Caption          =   "Slider"
    FontBold         =   -1   'True
    FontItalic       =   0    'False
    FontName         =   "MS Sans Serif"
    FontSize         =   18
    FontStrikethru   =   0    'False
    FontUnderline    =   0    'False
    Height           =   450
    Left             =   990
    TabIndex         =   1
    Top              =   270
    Width            =   4305
End
Begin Label lbl_Title
    Caption          =   "Programming Games for Beginners"
    Height           =   240
    Left             =   990
    TabIndex         =   2
    Top              =   840
    Width            =   4305
End
Begin Label lbl_Author
    Caption          =   "Christopher A. Howard"
    Height           =   240
    Left             =   990
    TabIndex         =   3
    Top              =   1110
    Width            =   4365
End
```

```
  Begin Label lbl_Info
     Height        =    600
     Left          =    1005
     TabIndex      =    4
     Top           =    1545
     Width         =    1875
  End
  Begin Label lbl_InfoValues
     Height        =    600
     Left          =    2880
     TabIndex      =    0
     Top           =    1545
     Width         =    1410
  End
End
Option Explicit

' Windows API functions used
Declare Function GetFreeSpace Lib "Kernel" (ByVal wFlags%) As Long
Declare Function GetWinFlags Lib "Kernel" () As Long

' Windows constants used
Const WF_STANDARD = &H10
Const WF_ENHANCED = &H20
Const WF_80x87 = &H400

Sub btn_OK_Click ()

  ' We are done
  Unload Me

End Sub

Sub Form_Load ()

  Dim WinFlags&
  Dim Mode$, Processor$, CRLF$

  ' Center the About box on the screen
  Move (Screen.Width - Width) \ 2, (Screen.Height - Height) \ 2

  ' Make it easier for strings
  CRLF$ = Chr$(13) + Chr$(10)

  ' Get current Windows configuration
  WinFlags& = GetWinFlags()

  ' Determine mode
  If (WinFlags& And WF_ENHANCED) Then
    Mode$ = "386 Enhanced Mode"
  Else
    Mode$ = "Standard Mode"
  End If
```

continues

Listing 14.1. continued

```
' Free memory
lbl_Info.Caption = Mode$ + CRLF$ + "Free Memory:" + CRLF$ + "Math
➥Co-processor:"

' 80x87 math chip
If (WinFlags& And WF_80x87) Then
  Processor$ = "Present"
Else
  Processor$ = "None"
End If

' Free space
lbl_InfoValues.Caption = CRLF$ + Format$(GetFreeSpace(0) \ 1024) + " KB"
➥+ CRLF$ + Processor$

' Set up the icon
IconNum% = 0
IconDir% = 1
' Begin changing the icon
tmr_Icon.Interval = ICONINC

End Sub

Sub tmr_Icon_Timer ()

  Dim rc%

  ' Update the icon number
  IconNum% = IconNum% + IconDir%

  ' Check the limits
  If (IconNum% < 0) Then
    IconNum% = 0
    IconDir% = -IconDir%
  ElseIf (IconNum% > MAXICON) Then
    IconNum% = MAXICON
    IconDir% = -IconDir%
  End If

  ' Display it
  rc% = BitBlt%(pic_Icon.hDC, 0, 0, pic_Icon.Width, pic_Icon.Height,
  ➥frm_Slider!pic_Icon(IconNum%).hDC, 0, 0, SRCCOPY)

End Sub
```

Figure 14.5 and Listing 14.2 show the SLMAIN form and source code.

Figure 14.5. The SLMAIN form.

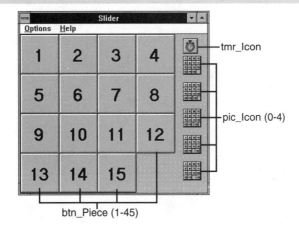

Listing 14.2. The SLMAIN form source code.

```
VERSION 2.00
Begin Form frm_Slider
   BackColor       =   &H00C0C0C0&
   BorderStyle     =   1   'Fixed Single
   Caption         =   "Slider"
   FillColor       =   &H00FFFFFF&
   FillStyle       =   0   'Solid
   FontBold        =   -1  'True
   FontItalic      =   0   'False
   FontName        =   "Terminal"
   FontSize        =   6
   FontStrikethru  =   0   'False
   FontUnderline   =   0   'False
   ForeColor       =   &H00FFFFFF&
   Height          =   5025
   Icon            =   SLMAIN.FRX:0000 'SL.ICO
   KeyPreview      =   -1  'True
   Left            =   2280
   LinkTopic       =   "Form1"
   MaxButton       =   0   'False
   ScaleHeight     =   4335
   ScaleWidth      =   4320
   Top             =   1200
   Width           =   4440
   Begin PictureBox pic_Icon
      AutoRedraw   =   -1  'True
      AutoSize     =   -1  'True
      Height       =   680
      Index        =   4
      Left         =   4560
      Picture      =   SLMAIN.FRX:0302 'SL4.ICO
      ScaleHeight  =   480
```

continues

Listing 14.2. continued

```
          ScaleWidth      =      480
          TabIndex        =      19
          Top             =      3480
          Width           =      510
       End
       Begin PictureBox pic_Icon
          AutoRedraw      =      -1      'True
          AutoSize        =      -1      'True
          Height          =      680
          Index           =      3
          Left            =      4560
          Picture         =      SLMAIN.FRX:0604  'SL3.ICO
          ScaleHeight     =      480
          ScaleWidth      =      480
          TabIndex        =      18
          Top             =      2760
          Width           =      510
       End
       Begin PictureBox pic_Icon
          AutoRedraw      =      -1      'True
          AutoSize        =      -1      'True
          Height          =      680
          Index           =      2
          Left            =      4560
          Picture         =      SLMAIN.FRX:0906  'SL2.ICO
          ScaleHeight     =      480
          ScaleWidth      =      480
          TabIndex        =      17
          Top             =      2040
          Width           =      510
       End
       Begin PictureBox pic_Icon
          AutoRedraw      =      -1      'True
          AutoSize        =      -1      'True
          Height          =      680
          Index           =      1
          Left            =      4560
          Picture         =      SLMAIN.FRX:0C08  'SL1.ICO
          ScaleHeight     =      480
          ScaleWidth      =      480
          TabIndex        =      16
          Top             =      1320
          Width           =      510
       End
       Begin PictureBox pic_Icon
          AutoRedraw      =      -1      'True
          AutoSize        =      -1      'True
          Height          =      680
          Index           =      0
          Left            =      4560
          Picture         =      SLMAIN.FRX:0F0A  'SL.ICO
```

```
      ScaleHeight    =    480
      ScaleWidth     =    480
      TabIndex       =    15
      Top            =    600
      Width          =    510
   End
   Begin Timer tmr_Icon
      Left           =    4560
      Top            =    120
   End
   Begin CommandButton btn_Piece
      BackColor      =    &H00C0C0C0&
      Caption        =    "15"
      FontBold       =    -1    'True
      FontItalic     =    0     'False
      FontName       =    "MS Sans Serif"
      FontSize       =    24
      FontStrikethru =    0     'False
      FontUnderline  =    0     'False
      Height         =    1095
      Index          =    15
      Left           =    2160
      TabIndex       =    14
      Top            =    3240
      Width          =    1095
   End
   Begin CommandButton btn_Piece
      BackColor      =    &H00C0C0C0&
      Caption        =    "14"
      FontBold       =    -1    'True
      FontItalic     =    0     'False
      FontName       =    "MS Sans Serif"
      FontSize       =    24
      FontStrikethru =    0     'False
      FontUnderline  =    0     'False
      Height         =    1095
      Index          =    14
      Left           =    1080
      TabIndex       =    13
      Top            =    3240
      Width          =    1095
   End
   Begin CommandButton btn_Piece
      BackColor      =    &H00C0C0C0&
      Caption        =    "13"
      FontBold       =    -1    'True
      FontItalic     =    0     'False
      FontName       =    "MS Sans Serif"
      FontSize       =    24
      FontStrikethru =    0     'False
      FontUnderline  =    0     'False
      Height         =    1095
```

continues

Listing 14.2. continued

```
        Index          =    13
        Left           =    0
        TabIndex       =    12
        Top            =    3240
        Width          =    1095
     End
     Begin CommandButton btn_Piece
        BackColor      =    &H00C0C0C0&
        Caption        =    "12"
        FontBold       =    -1    'True
        FontItalic     =    0     'False
        FontName       =    "MS Sans Serif"
        FontSize       =    24
        FontStrikethru =    0     'False
        FontUnderline  =    0     'False
        Height         =    1095
        Index          =    12
        Left           =    3240
        TabIndex       =    11
        Top            =    2160
        Width          =    1095
     End
     Begin CommandButton btn_Piece
        BackColor      =    &H00C0C0C0&
        Caption        =    "11"
        FontBold       =    -1    'True
        FontItalic     =    0     'False
        FontName       =    "MS Sans Serif"
        FontSize       =    24
        FontStrikethru =    0     'False
        FontUnderline  =    0     'False
        Height         =    1095
        Index          =    11
        Left           =    2160
        TabIndex       =    10
        Top            =    2160
        Width          =    1095
     End
     Begin CommandButton btn_Piece
        BackColor      =    &H00C0C0C0&
        Caption        =    "10"
        FontBold       =    -1    'True
        FontItalic     =    0     'False
        FontName       =    "MS Sans Serif"
        FontSize       =    24
        FontStrikethru =    0     'False
        FontUnderline  =    0     'False
        Height         =    1095
        Index          =    10
        Left           =    1080
        TabIndex       =    9
```

```
      Top             =    2160
      Width           =    1095
   End
   Begin CommandButton btn_Piece
      BackColor       =    &H00C0C0C0&
      Caption         =    "9"
      FontBold        =    -1   'True
      FontItalic      =    0    'False
      FontName        =    "MS Sans Serif"
      FontSize        =    24
      FontStrikethru  =    0    'False
      FontUnderline   =    0    'False
      Height          =    1095
      Index           =    9
      Left            =    0
      TabIndex        =    8
      Top             =    2160
      Width           =    1095
   End
   Begin CommandButton btn_Piece
      BackColor       =    &H00C0C0C0&
      Caption         =    "8"
      FontBold        =    -1   'True
      FontItalic      =    0    'False
      FontName        =    "MS Sans Serif"
      FontSize        =    24
      FontStrikethru  =    0    'False
      FontUnderline   =    0    'False
      Height          =    1095
      Index           =    8
      Left            =    3240
      TabIndex        =    7
      Top             =    1080
      Width           =    1095
   End
   Begin CommandButton btn_Piece
      BackColor       =    &H00C0C0C0&
      Caption         =    "7"
      FontBold        =    -1   'True
      FontItalic      =    0    'False
      FontName        =    "MS Sans Serif"
      FontSize        =    24
      FontStrikethru  =    0    'False
      FontUnderline   =    0    'False
      Height          =    1095
      Index           =    7
      Left            =    2160
      TabIndex        =    6
      Top             =    1080
      Width           =    1095
   End
```

continues

Listing 14.2. continued

```
Begin CommandButton btn_Piece
    BackColor       =   &H00C0C0C0&
    Caption         =   "6"
    FontBold        =   -1   'True
    FontItalic      =   0    'False
    FontName        =   "MS Sans Serif"
    FontSize        =   24
    FontStrikethru  =   0    'False
    FontUnderline   =   0    'False
    Height          =   1095
    Index           =   6
    Left            =   1080
    TabIndex        =   5
    Top             =   1080
    Width           =   1095
End
Begin CommandButton btn_Piece
    BackColor       =   &H00C0C0C0&
    Caption         =   "5"
    FontBold        =   -1   'True
    FontItalic      =   0    'False
    FontName        =   "MS Sans Serif"
    FontSize        =   24
    FontStrikethru  =   0    'False
    FontUnderline   =   0    'False
    Height          =   1095
    Index           =   5
    Left            =   0
    TabIndex        =   4
    Top             =   1080
    Width           =   1095
End
Begin CommandButton btn_Piece
    BackColor       =   &H00C0C0C0&
    Caption         =   "4"
    FontBold        =   -1   'True
    FontItalic      =   0    'False
    FontName        =   "MS Sans Serif"
    FontSize        =   24
    FontStrikethru  =   0    'False
    FontUnderline   =   0    'False
    Height          =   1095
    Index           =   4
    Left            =   3240
    TabIndex        =   3
    Top             =   0
    Width           =   1095
End
Begin CommandButton btn_Piece
    BackColor       =   &H00C0C0C0&
    Caption         =   "3"
```

```
    FontBold        =   -1   'True
    FontItalic      =   0    'False
    FontName        =   "MS Sans Serif"
    FontSize        =   24
    FontStrikethru  =   0    'False
    FontUnderline   =   0    'False
    Height          =   1095
    Index           =   3
    Left            =   2160
    TabIndex        =   2
    Top             =   0
    Width           =   1095
End
Begin CommandButton btn_Piece
    BackColor       =   &H00C0C0C0&
    Caption         =   "2"
    FontBold        =   -1   'True
    FontItalic      =   0    'False
    FontName        =   "MS Sans Serif"
    FontSize        =   24
    FontStrikethru  =   0    'False
    FontUnderline   =   0    'False
    Height          =   1095
    Index           =   2
    Left            =   1080
    TabIndex        =   1
    Top             =   0
    Width           =   1095
End
Begin CommandButton btn_Piece
    BackColor       =   &H00C0C0C0&
    Caption         =   "1"
    FontBold        =   -1   'True
    FontItalic      =   0    'False
    FontName        =   "MS Sans Serif"
    FontSize        =   24
    FontStrikethru  =   0    'False
    FontUnderline   =   0    'False
    Height          =   1095
    Index           =   1
    Left            =   0
    TabIndex        =   0
    Top             =   0
    Width           =   1095
End
Begin Menu mnu_Options
    Caption         =   "&Options"
    Begin Menu mnu_NewGame
        Caption     =   "&New Game"
    End
```

continues

Listing 14.2. continued

```
        Begin Menu mnu_ScrambleSep
            Caption         =   "-"
        End
        Begin Menu mnu_Moves
            Caption         =   "&25 Moves"
            Checked         =   -1  'True
            Index           =   0
        End
        Begin Menu mnu_Moves
            Caption         =   "&50 Moves"
            Index           =   1
        End
        Begin Menu mnu_Moves
            Caption         =   "&75 Moves"
            Index           =   2
        End
        Begin Menu mnu_ShowMoves
            Caption         =   "&Show Moves"
            Checked         =   -1  'True
        End
        Begin Menu mnu_ExitSep
            Caption         =   "-"
        End
        Begin Menu mnu_Exit
            Caption         =   "E&xit"
        End
    End
    Begin Menu mnu_Help
        Caption         =   "&Help"
        Begin Menu mnu_Rules
            Caption         =   "&Rules ..."
        End
        Begin Menu mnu_AboutSep
            Caption         =   "-"
        End
        Begin Menu mnu_About
            Caption         =   "&About Slider ..."
        End
    End
End
Option Explicit

Sub btn_Piece_Click (Index As Integer)

    Dim p%, pr%, pc%
    Dim valmove%

    ' Make sure game is not already over
    If (Not GameOver%) Then
```

```
    ' We need to find this piece in the piece position array
    For p% = 1 To MAXPIECES
      If (Pieces%(p%) = Index) Then
        ' We found it, so exit
        Exit For
      End If
    Next p%

    ' Decode the piece row and column
    pr% = (p% - 1) \ MAXCOLS
    pc% = (p% - 1) Mod MAXCOLS

    ' Assume move is invalid
    valmove% = False

    ' Can this piece move into the blank position along a row?
    If (pr% = BlankRow%) Then
      If (((pc% - 1) = BlankCol%) Or ((pc% + 1) = BlankCol%)) Then
        valmove% = True
      End If
    End If

    ' Can this piece move into the blank position along a col?
    If (pc% = BlankCol%) Then
      If (((pr% - 1) = BlankRow%) Or ((pr% + 1) = BlankRow%)) Then
        valmove% = True
      End If
    End If

    ' Do we have a valid move?
    If (valmove%) Then
      ' Yes, so make it
      Call MakeMove(pr%, pc%)
      ' Check if we won
      CheckWin
    End If

  End If

End Sub

'
' This routine checks to see of all of the pieces are back in the
' right position.
'
Sub CheckWin ()

  Dim i%, j%, gamewon%

  ' Assume they are
  gamewon% = True
```

continues

Listing 14.2. continued

```
' Search the position array
For i% = 1 To MAXPIECES - 1
   ' Is this piece in the right position?
   If (Pieces%(i%) <> i%) Then
      ' No, so game isn't won yet
      gamewon% = False
      Exit For
   End If
Next i%

' Is the game won?
If (gamewon%) Then
   ' Yes! So end the game
   GameOver% = True
   ' Show some pizazz!
   For j% = 1 To 3
      ' Set all of the pieces to a small font
      For i% = 1 To MAXPIECES - 1
         btn_Piece(i%).FontSize = 12
      Next i%
      Delay .5
      ' And back to a large font
      For i% = 1 To MAXPIECES - 1
         btn_Piece(i%).FontSize = 24
      Next i%
      ' Add some sound
      Beep
      Delay .5
   Next j%
End If

End Sub

Sub Form_Load ()

   ' Center on the screen
   Move (screen.Width - Width) \ 2, (screen.Height - Height) \ 2

   ' Start with game over
   GameOver% = True

   ' Get the piece "sizes"
   PWidth% = btn_Piece(2).Left
   PDepth% = btn_Piece(5).Top

   ' Set scramble moves
   ScrambleMoves% = MINMOVES

   ' Show about box
   frm_AboutBox.Show 1

End Sub
```

```
Sub Form_Resize ()

  ' Are we minimizing?
  If (WindowState = 1) Then
    ' Set up the icon
    IconNum% = 0
    IconDir% = 1
    ' Begin changing the icon
    tmr_Icon.Interval = ICONINC
  Else
    ' Maximizing or Normal, so stop the icon timer
    tmr_Icon.Interval = 0
  End If

End Sub


' This procedure initializes all of the game variables at the beginning
' of a new game.

Sub InitNewGame ()

  ' Get a new sequence of numbers
  Randomize

  ' Scramble the pieces
  ScramblePieces

  ' Game is no longer over
  GameOver% = False

End Sub


' This routine actually moves one of the pieces on the board
' into the blank piece position.

' NOTE: This procedure does NOT check whether the given move
'       is valid.

Sub MakeMove (r%, c%)

  Dim p%, mp%
  Dim i%, rinc%, cinc%

  ' Decode the piece we are moving
  mp% = (r% * MAXCOLS) + c% + 1
  p% = Pieces%(mp%)

  ' Are we showing the move?
  If (ShowMove%) Then
```

continues

Listing 14.2. continued

```
    ' Are we moving along a row, or a column?
    If (r% = BlankRow%) Then
      ' Column, so set increments appropriately
      rinc% = 0
      cinc% = PWidth% \ MOVESTEP
    Else
      ' Row, so set increments appropriately
      rinc% = PDepth% \ MOVESTEP
      cinc% = 0
    End If

    ' Do we need to change the increment direction?
    If ((r% > BlankRow%) Or (c% > BlankCol%)) Then
      ' Move up or left
      rinc% = -rinc%
      cinc% = -cinc%
    End If

    ' Now move the piece a little each step
    For i% = 1 To MOVESTEP
      ' Move
      btn_Piece(p%).Move btn_Piece(p%).Left + cinc%, btn_Piece(p%).Top +
      ➡rinc%
      ' Delay
      Delay .05
    Next i%

  End If

  ' Take care of any remainder
  btn_Piece(p%).Move BlankCol% * PWidth%, BlankRow% * PDepth%

  ' Update the piece locations
  Pieces%(mp%) = BLANK
  Pieces%(BlankPiece%) = p%

  ' Keep track of the blank piece
  BlankPiece% = mp%
  BlankRow% = (BlankPiece% - 1) \ MAXCOLS
  BlankCol% = (BlankPiece% - 1) Mod MAXCOLS

  ' Set up the mouse pointers
  SetupMouse

End Sub

Sub mnu_About_Click ()

  ' Show the about box
  frm_AboutBox.Show 1

End Sub
```

```
Sub mnu_Exit_Click ()

  ' Exit, so just unload the form
  Unload Me

End Sub

Sub mnu_Moves_Click (Index As Integer)

  Dim i%

  ' Clear all options
  For i% = 0 To MAXMENUMOVES - 1
    mnu_Moves(i%).Checked = False
  Next i%

  ' Check this one
  mnu_Moves(Index).Checked = True

  ' Determine the scramble moves
  ScrambleMoves% = (Index + 1) * MINMOVES

End Sub

Sub mnu_NewGame_Click ()

  ' Start a new game
  InitNewGame

End Sub

Sub mnu_Rules_Click ()

  ' Show the Rules form
  frm_Rules.Show 1

End Sub

Sub mnu_ShowMoves_Click ()

  ' Toggle the flag
  mnu_ShowMoves.Checked = Not mnu_ShowMoves.Checked

End Sub

'
' This routine places all of the pieces into their initial
' positions. From here, they can be scrambled.
'
Sub ResetPieces ()

  Dim r%, c%, i%
```

continues

Listing 14.2. continued

```
' Set the button positions
For r% = 0 To MAXROWS - 1
  For c% = 0 To MAXCOLS - 1
    ' Get the index
    i% = c% + (r% * MAXCOLS) + 1
    ' Skip the last corner piece
    If (i% <> (MAXPIECES)) Then
      btn_Piece(i%).Left = c% * PWidth%
      btn_Piece(i%).Top = r% * PDepth%
    End If
  Next c%
Next r%

' Initialize the piece position array
For i% = 1 To (MAXPIECES - 1)
  Pieces%(i%) = i%
Next i%

' The last piece position is blank
Pieces%(MAXPIECES) = BLANK
BlankPiece% = MAXPIECES

' Get current blank row and column
BlankRow% = (BlankPiece% - 1) \ MAXCOLS
BlankCol% = (BlankPiece% - 1) Mod MAXCOLS

End Sub

'
' This routine scrambles the playing pieces so that they can
' be unscrambled again. Note that you have to physically move
' the pieces to insure the puzzle can be solved.
'
Sub ScramblePieces ()

  Dim om%, m%, mr%, mc%
  Static odir%(MAXDIR)
  Dim i%

  ' First, reset the board
  ResetPieces

  ' Build 'opposite direction' array
  odir%(DUP) = DDOWN
  odir%(DDOWN) = DUP
  odir%(DLEFT) = DRIGHT
  odir%(DRIGHT) = DLEFT

  ' Set last opposite move to anything (for first time through)
  om% = DUP
```

```
' Set the "show move" flag
ShowMove% = mnu_ShowMoves.Checked

' Make the required number of scramble moves
For i% = 1 To ScrambleMoves%

  ' Loop, until we get a move that isn't the opposite of our
  ' last move (to prevent the piece from shuffling back and
  ' forth...)
  Do

    ' Randomly select a move (up,down,right,left)
    m% = GetRandom%(MAXDIR)

    ' Start row and col move off at zero
    mr% = 0
    mc% = 0

    ' Translate into row and col movement
    Select Case (m%)
      Case DUP
        mr% = -1
      Case DDOWN
        mr% = 1
      Case DRIGHT
        mc% = 1
      Case DLEFT
        mc% = -1
    End Select

    ' Check row range
    If ((BlankRow% + mr% < 0) Or (BlankRow% + mr% = MAXROWS)) Then
      ' Off the board, so move other way
      mr% = -mr%
      m% = odir%(m%)
    End If

    ' Check col range
    If ((BlankCol% + mc% < 0) Or (BlankCol% + mc% = MAXCOLS)) Then
      ' Off the board, so move other way
      mc% = -mc%
      m% = odir%(m%)
    End If

  Loop While (m% = om%)

  ' Record opposite move
  om% = odir%(m%)

  ' Make the move
  Call MakeMove(BlankRow% + mr%, BlankCol% + mc%)
```

continues

Listing 14.2. continued

```
    Next i%

    ' Reset the move flag, so all user moves are shown
    ShowMove% = True

End Sub


' This routine sets up the mouse pointers so that they show
' the appropriate moves.
'
Sub SetupMouse ()

    Dim p%, pr%, pc%, bp%

    ' Set the mouse pointer for all of the pieces
    For p% = 1 To MAXPIECES

        ' Get the button index
        bp% = Pieces%(p%)

        ' Make sure this position is not blank
        If (bp% <> BLANK) Then

            ' Decode the piece row and column
            pr% = (p% - 1) \ MAXCOLS
            pc% = (p% - 1) Mod MAXCOLS

            ' Assume piece cannot be moved
            btn_Piece(bp%).MousePointer = MOUSEDEFAULT

            ' Can this piece move into the blank position along a row?
            If (pr% = BlankRow%) Then
              If (((pc% - 1) = BlankCol%) Or ((pc% + 1) = BlankCol%)) Then
                btn_Piece(bp%).MousePointer = MOUSEARROWWE
              End If
            End If

            ' Can this piece move into the blank position along a col?
            If (pc% = BlankCol%) Then
              If (((pr% - 1) = BlankRow%) Or ((pr% + 1) = BlankRow%)) Then
                btn_Piece(bp%).MousePointer = MOUSEARROWNS
              End If
            End If

        End If

    Next p%

End Sub
```

```
Sub tmr_Icon_Timer ()

  Dim rc%

  ' Update the icon number
  IconNum% = IconNum% + IconDir%

  ' Check the limits
  If (IconNum% < 0) Then
    IconNum% = 0
    IconDir% = -IconDir%
  ElseIf (IconNum% > MAXICON) Then
    IconNum% = MAXICON
    IconDir% = -IconDir%
  End If

  ' Display it
  rc% = BitBlt%(frm_Slider.hDC, 2, 2, pic_Icon(0).Width,
pic_Icon(0).Height, pic_Icon(IconNum%).hDC, 0, 0, SRCCOPY)

End Sub
```

Figure 14.6 and Listing 14.3 show the SLRULES form and source code.

Figure 14.6. The SLRULES form.

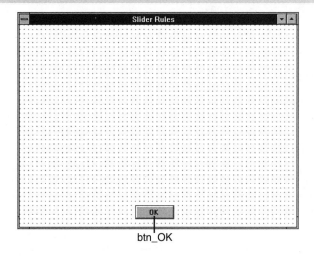

btn_OK

Listing 14.3 The SLRULES form source code.

```
VERSION 2.00
Begin Form frm_Rules
   BackColor       =    &H00FFFFFF&
```

continues

Listing 14.3 continued

```
    BorderStyle     =   3   'Fixed Double
    Caption         =   "Slider Rules"
    FontBold        =   -1  'True
    FontItalic      =   0   'False
    FontName        =   "System"
    FontSize        =   9.75
    FontStrikethru  =   0   'False
    FontUnderline   =   0   'False
    ForeColor       =   &H00000000&
    Height          =   5910
    Icon            =   0
    Left            =   990
    LinkTopic       =   "Form1"
    MaxButton       =   0   'False
    MinButton       =   0   'False
    ScaleHeight     =   5505
    ScaleWidth      =   7785
    Top             =   1500
    Width           =   7905
    Begin CommandButton btn_OK
        BackColor       =   &H00800000&
        Caption         =   "OK"
        Height          =   375
        Left            =   3240
        TabIndex        =   0
        Top             =   4920
        Width           =   1095
    End
End
Option Explicit

Sub btn_OK_Click ()

  ' Unload the form
  Unload Me

End Sub

Sub Form_Load ()

  ' Center on the screen
  Move (Screen.Width - Width) \ 2, (Screen.Height - Height) \ 2

End Sub

Sub Form_Paint ()

  ' Position rule text
  CurrentX = 0
  CurrentY = 0
```

```
' Display them
Print
Print " Slider is just like the sliding puzzles you had as a kid. Once
➥scrambled,"
Print " the object is to get the pieces back into the correct sequence
➥again."
Print
Print " To start a game, first make sure you have selected the number of
➥moves you"
Print " want made when the puzzle is scrambled (25, 50, or 75). If you
➥want to see"
Print " the moves as they are made, make sure the Show Moves option is
➥checked. It"
Print " is fun to watch the pieces move, but it takes a little longer
➥and it doesn't "
Print " really help you when solving the puzzle."
Print
Print " To unscramble the puzzle, select the piece you wish to move. You
➥can use the"
Print " mouse, or use the TAB and ENTER keys. The piece will slide into
➥the blank"
Print " position, leaving a new blank position behind."
Print
Print " If you are not sure which pieces can be moved, the mouse cursor
➥will indicate"
Print " the movable pieces with a horizontal or vertical arrow. Only one
➥piece can be"
Print " moved at a time--you cannot push one piece with another."
Print
Print " The game will let you know when the puzzle is solved. Then it's
➥time to try "
Print " another one!"

End Sub
```

Listing 14.4 shows the SLGLOBAL.BAS source code. This file contains all the Slider global constants and variables.

Listing 14.4. The SLGLOBAL.BAS source code.

```
Option Explicit

' Board size
Global Const MAXROWS = 4
Global Const MAXCOLS = 4
Global Const MAXPIECES = (MAXROWS * MAXCOLS)

' Moving and scrambling
Global Const MOVESTEP = 5
```

continues

Listing 14.4. continued

```
Global Const MINMOVES = 25
Global Const MAXMENUMOVES = 3

' Directions
Global Const DUP = 0
Global Const DDOWN = 1
Global Const DLEFT = 2
Global Const DRIGHT = 3
Global Const MAXDIR = 4

' A blank piece
Global Const BLANK = -1

' Icon timer
Global Const ICONINC = 250
Global Const MAXICON = 4

' Mouse pointers
Global Const MOUSENODROP = 12
Global Const MOUSEARROWWE = 9
Global Const MOUSEARROWNS = 7
Global Const MOUSEDEFAULT = 0

' Windows API
Global Const SRCCOPY = &HCC0020

' Keep track of the blank piece
Global BlankPiece%
Global BlankRow%, BlankCol%

' Icon
Global IconNum%, IconDir%

' Number of scramble moves
Global ScrambleMoves%

' Whether we should show the moves
Global ShowMove%

' Piece width and depth
Global PWidth%, PDepth%

' Game over flag
Global GameOver%

' Piece array
Global Pieces%(16)

' Windows API Functions
Declare Function BitBlt% Lib "GDI" (ByVal hDestDC%, ByVal dx%, ByVal dy%,
➡ByVal nWidth%, ByVal nHeight%, ByVal hSrcDC%, ByVal sx%, ByVal sy%,
➡ByVal dwRop&)
```

```
'
' This procedure delays the given number of seconds, which can be
 ➡fractional.
'
Sub Delay (secs!)

  Dim Start!

  ' Get the current seconds since midnight
  Start! = Timer

  ' Wait for seconds to elapse
  While (Timer < (Start! + secs!))
    ' Let other things run while we wait
    DoEvents
  Wend

End Sub


'
' This function returns a random number between 0 and range%-1, inclusive.
'
Function GetRandom% (range%)

  ' In the Visual Basic manual, the generic formula is:
  ' Int((upperbound-lowerbound+1)*Rnd+lowerbound)
  GetRandom% = Int(range% * Rnd)

End Function
```

Form Overview

The following is a brief discussion of the Slider forms and their controls. Consult the form figures for additional information.

About Box

The SLABOUT form is my standard About box form. I have set the label to Slider and the image to SL.ICO. For a full description of the form, see Chapter 10, "Apples and Oranges."

I made a change to this form (unlike in the other games). I animated the icon in the same manner as the minimized game icon (which I describe later in this chapter). I had to change the control from an image to a picture control (so that the hDC property was available). I also needed a timer to perform the animation. For a description of the animation, see the following Programming Overview section (under "Icon Animation").

Rules

The SLRULES form displays the Slider rules when you select Rules from the Help menu. The form itself consists of blank space for the rule text and a single OK button (which unloads the form). The form is centered when loaded, and the rule text is displayed when the window is painted.

Global

The SLGLOBAL basic file contains the global variable and constant definitions. It also has the global procedures `Delay` and `GetRandom`.

The Main Form

The SLMAIN form is the main form for the game. It consists of fifteen buttons in the control array (`btn_Piece()`). This is really all that is necessary to program the game.

The picture array (`pic_Icon()`) has four icons and a timer (`tmr_Icon`). These are used to animate the icon when it's minimized. These objects are located off the normally visible form area.

Programming Overview

The Slider game, like most puzzle games, is very simple to program. It requires no artwork, but it still looks good and it's fun to play. Also, in this game, you can actually move the control positions.

Program Flow

When the game runs, the program flows as follows:

➡️ When the main form is loaded, it is centered, and the About box is displayed. The piece sizes are recorded (so that you can move them later), the scrambling moves are set to the minimum (to match the menu), and the `GameOver%` flag declares that the game is over.

➡️ The player begins a new game by selecting New Game from the Options menu. The `mnu_NewGame_Click` routine initializes a new game by calling `InitNewGame`.

➡️ The `InitNewGame` procedure randomizes the number generator and scrambles the game pieces by calling `ScramblePieces`. It starts a new game by resetting the `GameOver%` flag.

➤ ScramblePieces resets the game pieces by calling ResetPieces, and proceeds to make random moves with MakeMove until the requested number has been made. The Piece%() array keeps track of the piece positions.

➤ The btn_Piece_Click routine handles the game interaction. If the selected piece can be moved, MakeMove makes the move.

➤ The MakeMove routine finds the corresponding piece position in the Piece%() array. Once found, the piece is moved incrementally by the Move method. The Piece%() array is updated, and SetupMouse is called to set up the mouse pointers for each piece. Lastly, CheckWin is called to see if the player has won the game.

➤ CheckWin checks to see if all pieces are in their correct positions. If they are, the button font is cycled up and down to signal a win—with some beeps. The GameOver% flag declares that the game is over.

You can view the game rules and the About box by selecting the Help menu options. These options display the frm_AboutBox and call the mnu_Rules function.

Techniques Used

The Slider game includes several game concepts that are outlined in the following sections.

Twips

This game uses twips instead of pixels for the ScaleMode. As you might know (from your Visual Basic manual), a *twip* is 1/1440 of an inch. Using twips ensures that a form or control is the same size on the display—no matter the resolution of the video adapter or monitor.

However, twips can be harder than pixels to use. Bitmaps are device-dependent, because they contain a fixed number of pixels. Most games use bitmaps, which is why I usually stick to the pixel coordinate system. Slider uses no bitmaps—so I used twips instead. To learn more about twips, refer to your VB documentation or see Chapter 15, "Puzzler."

Dynamic Mouse Pointer

Like Apples & Oranges and Flip, Slider uses the mouse pointer to indicate valid moves. SetupMouse handles this routine.

Object Animation

Slider uses the Visual Basic Move method to move the buttons around the form. The Move method enables you to change the left, top, width, and height of a control—all at the same time. I could have just changed the Left or Top properties, because the pieces are only moved horizontally or vertically. However, if you need to change both the top and left positions, use Move, because it updates both values simultaneously.

The sliding of the pieces makes this game interesting. If the pieces appeared instantly in their new positions, I wouldn't play the game as much. The scrambling of the pieces also is fun to watch.

> Speaking of scrambling, it's important to actually move the pieces instead of randomly placing them on the board. If you randomly select a position for each piece, the puzzle might be unsolvable! You have to make valid moves when scrambling the puzzle. This ensures a possible solution.

If you look at the MakeMove code closely, you'll notice that extra effort is made so that the opposite move of the previous move isn't made. When I first wrote the game, I watched as the pieces were scrambled, and at several points, the same piece shuffled back and forth two or three times (wasting six or more moves). This happened even though the moves were selected randomly.

Delay and DoEvents

When the user doesn't want to see the moves, the MakeMove function jumps right to the final move. When the board is being scrambled, you don't actually see all of the pieces all the time—some are hidden. I left it that way on purpose, but what's happening? Take a look at it.

The "hidden" pieces don't appear hidden when sliding the pieces because of the Delay function. Delay calls the Visual Basic DoEvents function which enables all processing (calculating, drawing, painting, and so on). When you skip to the final move, there is no delay and consequently no DoEvents. The buttons move so fast that Windows doesn't have time to update everything. Therefore, the buttons are hidden. When the buttons finish moving, Windows catches up, and all of the buttons appear.

The hidden effect plays right into our purpose—to hide the moves from the user. To change this, add a short Delay or a call to DoEvents after the final Move call in MakeMove.

Icon Animation

This game was a good candidate for a little pizazz. I decided to add some by animating the About box and program icons. I animated the main program icon and created the icon images in IconWorks. Then, I put the images on the form outside the border (where they can't be seen). I added a timer and assigned a new icon to frm_Slider.Icon every timer interval.

Animating the icon in this way works fine, and is in fact one of the methods I explained in Chapter 4, "Animation." I went a little further and animated the About box icon as well. The flicker (occasional flashes of color) though, is quite noticeable.

So, I decided to use the Windows BitBlt (pronounced "Bit-Blit") function. This is the second method of icon animation, also discussed in Chapter 4. For this game, I used Picture boxes instead of Image boxes for the icons.

> Make sure the icon picture boxes have AutoRedraw set to True. This ensures that the bitmaps are available and valid at all times. Without this property set, you'll get garbage instead of the icon you want.

I won't go into BitBlt just yet; I just wanted to show you the advantages of using it. Compare the Slider minimized animated icon with Ping's, and you'll see what I mean. For a full description, see Chapter 4, "Animation," and Chapter 15, "Puzzler."

Sound

There isn't a lot of sound in this game. As in some of the other games, the only function I use is the Beep function.

Data Organization

This game's global variables include the blank square information: BlankPiece%, BlankRow%, and BlankCol%. The ScrambleMoves% variable records how many moves to make when scrambling the puzzle. The ShowMove% flag indicates whether the moves are shown.

The Pieces%(16) array keeps track of the piece positions. The piece (button) width and depth are recorded in PWidth% and PDepth%.

In the icon animation, `IconNum%` holds the current icon frame number; `IconDir%` handles the direction of cycling through the images (+1 or -1). Finally, the game is over when `GameOver%` is set.

Summary

I have covered the following important programming points:

➡ Twips are device-independent and can easily be used instead of pixels—especially when there are no bitmaps to deal with. Because Visual Basic uses twips as its default coordinate system, I recommend you read your VB's manual (and the chapter about coordinate systems).

➡ Mouse pointers are handy for giving the user important feedback quickly and easily.

➡ You can perform animation by using the Visual Basic `Move` method. Controls can be moved and sized with a single function call.

➡ The `DoEvents` function lets Windows catch up with the program. Use `DoEvents` to make sure Windows displays every action. If you don't, some moves might be hidden.

➡ Icon animation spices up a program—especially a game. As discussed in Chapter 4, "Animation," icon animation can be performed using two methods. Of these two, the `BitBlt` method has the best results.

Suggestions for Improvement

The following are ideas for enhancing Slider:

➡ Modify the game so that it uses more pieces. Do you think this will make the game easier or harder?

➡ Add a menu option that lets the computer solve the puzzle. Coming up with the algorithm might be a little tricky though.

➡ Hide the buttons before the piece scrambling, and redisplay them when done. This gets rid of the jumping, flickering effect when `ShowMoves` is selected.

➡ Change the main window border so that it can be sized. Add the code necessary that will size the buttons along with it (so that the game can be played at different sizes). How would you keep the pieces square? Would the font size have to change, too?

➤ Use graphics to clearly indicate some order, instead of numbers. You might
have to use picture controls instead of buttons.

➤ Keep track of elapsed time and the number of moves the player makes to
solve the puzzle. Report the information, on a new form, when the puzzle
is solved. For an example, see Chapter 15, "Puzzler."

➤ Allow the player to slide two or more pieces at a time.

What's Ahead

If you like puzzle games, another one is coming up. In the next chapter, I'll explain
how to program a jigsaw puzzle game with square pieces. You'll also be able to
load your own images and use them for puzzles. Can you solve the puzzle without peeking? Turn to the next chapter to find out.

Puzzler

Puzzler is a puzzle game with square pieces. In this chapter, I describe the game of Puzzler and offer some hints. I also cover the programming of the game, provide the code listings, and give a full description of the techniques used. The items covered are

➡ Converting between twips and pixels

➡ Designing a file open form

➡ Getting parameters at runtime

➡ Launching a game from a filename

➡ Loading the bitmap file

➡ Handling the keyboard

➡ Displaying Help text differently

➡ Calling the Windows API (BitBlt)

Background

Puzzler is a simplified version of the old, familiar jigsaw puzzles. I say simplified, because all of the pieces are square (which makes the game easy to program). The square pieces, however, can be challenging to play.

Gameplay

Puzzler is a one-player game. After the puzzle pieces are scrambled, your object is to re-create the original picture.

Running Puzzler

To begin playing Puzzler, select the Puzzler icon from the program group you installed. (See Appendix A for installation instructions.) The file PUZZLER.EXE contains the game. When you run the game, you'll see the About box first. Click OK, and Puzzler appears.

Playing a Game

From the Options menu, select Scramble. The pieces of the puzzle are scrambled, and a blinking box appears. The box surrounds the currently selected puzzle piece. To select a different piece, click it with the left mouse button. To place the selected piece into a new location, click the right mouse button. Figure 15.1 shows a game in progress.

> The selected piece is placed at the new position, and the piece already at that position is placed at the old piece's location. Basically, the pieces are swapped.

Figure 15.1. Playing a game of Puzzler.

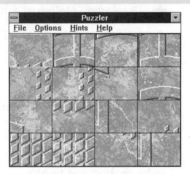

You also can use the keyboard to move the pieces. If you press one of the arrow keys, another blinking box appears. This blinking box is the piece selector, whereas the first box indicates your source piece. To make the selected piece the source piece, press the Spacebar. To place the source piece at a new location (which swaps the pieces between the boxes), press the Enter key.

After the puzzle is scrambled, the program keeps track of your number of moves and elapsed time. These statistics are displayed after you solve the puzzle.

You can change the difficulty level (by selecting the number of puzzle pieces you want) from the Options menu. The puzzle is automatically rescrambled for you. If you want to play an extra difficult level, disable the "correct move" beep by unselecting Beep from the Options menu. You can rescramble the puzzle any time by selecting Scramble from the Options menu.

If you want to change the puzzle image, use the Load option from the File menu. You can load any standard Windows Bitmap BMP file.

> Some images are better for puzzles than others. If the image has a lot of open area with similar colors or patterns, you might not be able to distinguish one puzzle piece from another.

You can get some tips from the hints menu: Peek shows the completed puzzle, Locate shows where the currently selected puzzle piece goes, and Correct displays all of the puzzle pieces that are currently in the correct positions. Figure 15.2 illustrates pieces currently in the correct positions. To view the current puzzle again, select Display Puzzle or click the mouse in the puzzle area.

Figure 15.2. Getting a hint on correct pieces.

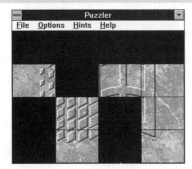

There are penalties for hints, however. Peeking costs you five moves, locating a piece costs you two moves, and viewing the correct pieces costs three moves. Penalty moves are totalled at the end of the game.

To get help, select Rules from the Help menu. The game continues until you solve the puzzle or exit the game. Figure 15.3 shows the winning form.

Figure 15.3. Solving the puzzle.

Hints

Like Slider, this is a pretty basic game. But here are some hints:

➡ Look for a landmark on the image—something unique or recognizable. Trademarks and copyrights are always handy, because they're usually at the bottom. When you place your landmark piece correctly, work outward from there.

➡ Work the game just like a real puzzle, and look for edge pieces. Is there a border around the image?

➡ Look for text. It's easy to place several pieces in a row when they contain words. This is also why trademark and copyright notices are helpful.

➡ If you're trying to work the puzzle in as few moves as possible, look for opportunities to place two pieces with one move. Remember that the source and destination pieces swap.

➡ If a piece really stumps you, use the Locate hint. It only costs two moves. This costs less than hunting around for the correct position until you hear the beep.

Programming

The makefile for Puzzler contains the files listed in Table 15.1.

Table 15.1. Puzzler source files.

Filename	Description
PZABOUT.FRM	The About box form
PZLOAD.FRM	The Bitmap Load form

Filename	Description
PZMAIN.FRM	The Main Puzzler form
PZRULES.FRM	The Rules form
PZWINNER.FRM	The Winner form
PZGLOBAL.BAS	Global constants, variables, and procedures

All these files are included in this book's disk. See Appendix A for installation instructions.

See Figure 15.4 and Listing 15.1 for the PZABOUT form and source code. PZABOUT is the About box for the Puzzler game.

Figure 15.4. The PZABOUT form.

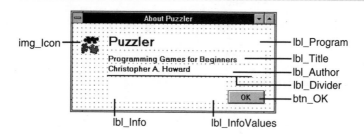

Listing 15.1. The PZABOUT form source code.

```
VERSION 2.00
Begin Form frm_AboutBox
   BorderStyle    =   3   'Fixed Double
   Caption        =   "About Puzzler"
   ClipControls   =   0   'False
   FontBold       =   -1  'True
   FontItalic     =   0   'False
   FontName       =   "System"
   FontSize       =   9.75
   FontStrikethru =   0   'False
   FontUnderline  =   0   'False
   Height         =   2775
   Icon           =   0
```

continues

Listing 15.1. continued

```
Left             =    2190
MaxButton        =    0    'False
MinButton        =    0    'False
ScaleHeight      =    2370
ScaleWidth       =    5640
Top              =    1710
Width            =    5760
Begin CommandButton btn_OK
    Caption          =    "OK"
    FontBold         =    -1   'True
    FontItalic       =    0    'False
    FontName         =    "System"
    FontSize         =    9.75
    FontStrikethru   =    0    'False
    FontUnderline    =    0    'False
    Height           =    375
    Left             =    4350
    TabIndex         =    5
    Top              =    1800
    Width            =    1035
End
Begin Image img_Icon
    Height           =    480
    Left             =    240
    Picture          =    PZABOUT.FRX:0000 'PZ.ICO
    Top              =    360
    Width            =    480
End
Begin Line lin_Divider
    BorderWidth      =    2
    X1               =    975
    X2               =    5010
    Y1               =    1425
    Y2               =    1425
End
Begin Label lbl_Program
    Caption          =    "Puzzler"
    FontBold         =    -1   'True
    FontItalic       =    0    'False
    FontName         =    "MS Sans Serif"
    FontSize         =    18
    FontStrikethru   =    0    'False
    FontUnderline    =    0    'False
    Height           =    450
    Left             =    990
    TabIndex         =    1
    Top              =    270
    Width            =    4440
End
```

```
Begin Label lbl_Title
   Caption        =    "Programming Games for Beginners"
   FontBold       =    -1   'True
   FontItalic     =    0    'False
   FontName       =    "MS Sans Serif"
   FontSize       =    9.75
   FontStrikethru =    0    'False
   FontUnderline  =    0    'False
   Height         =    240
   Left           =    990
   TabIndex       =    2
   Top            =    840
   Width          =    4305
End
Begin Label lbl_Author
   Caption        =    "Christopher A. Howard"
   FontBold       =    -1   'True
   FontItalic     =    0    'False
   FontName       =    "MS Sans Serif"
   FontSize       =    9.75
   FontStrikethru =    0    'False
   FontUnderline  =    0    'False
   Height         =    240
   Left           =    990
   TabIndex       =    3
   Top            =    1110
   Width          =    4365
End
Begin Label lbl_Info
   Height         =    600
   Left           =    1005
   TabIndex       =    4
   Top            =    1545
   Width          =    1875
End
Begin Label lbl_InfoValues
   Height         =    600
   Left           =    2880
   TabIndex       =    0
   Top            =    1545
   Width          =    1410
End
End
Option Explicit

' Windows API functions used
Declare Function GetFreeSpace Lib "Kernel" (ByVal wFlags%) As Long
Declare Function GetWinFlags Lib "Kernel" () As Long

' Windows constants used
Const WF_STANDARD = &H10
```

continues

Listing 15.1. continued

```
Const WF_ENHANCED = &H20
Const WF_80x87 = &H400

Sub btn_OK_Click ()

  ' We are done
  Unload frm_AboutBox

End Sub

Sub Form_Load ()

  Dim WinFlags&
  Dim Mode$, Processor$, CRLF$

  ' Center the AboutBox on the screen
  Move (Screen.Width - Width) \ 2, (Screen.Height - Height) \ 2

  ' Make it easier for strings
  CRLF$ = Chr$(13) + Chr$(10)

  ' Get current Windows configuration
  WinFlags& = GetWinFlags()

  ' Determine mode
  If (WinFlags& And WF_ENHANCED) Then
    Mode$ = "386 Enhanced Mode"
  Else
    Mode$ = "Standard Mode"
  End If

  ' Free memory
  lbl_Info.Caption = Mode$ + CRLF$ + "Free Memory:" + CRLF$ + "Math Co-
➥processor:"

  ' 80x87 math chip
  If (WinFlags& And WF_80x87) Then
    Processor$ = "Present"
  Else
    Processor$ = "None"
  End If

  ' Free space
  lbl_InfoValues.Caption = CRLF$ + Format$(GetFreeSpace(0) \ 1024) + " KB"
➥+ CRLF$ + Processor$

End Sub
```

Figure 15.5 and Listing 15.2 show the PZLOAD form and source code. This form is used to obtain a filename from the user.

Figure 15.5. The PZLOAD form.

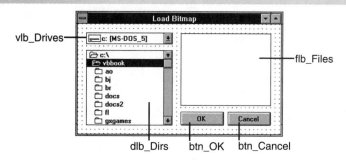

Listing 15.2. The PZLOAD form source code.

```
VERSION 2.00
Begin Form frm_Load
   BorderStyle      =    3   'Fixed Double
   Caption          =    "Load Bitmap"
   Height           =    3420
   Left             =    2460
   LinkTopic        =    "Form2"
   MaxButton        =    0    'False
   MinButton        =    0    'False
   ScaleHeight      =    3015
   ScaleWidth       =    5685
   Top              =    2220
   Width            =    5805
   Begin CommandButton btn_Cancel
      Caption          =    "Cancel"
      Height           =    375
      Left             =    4200
      TabIndex         =    4
      Top              =    2400
      Width            =    1215
   End
   Begin CommandButton btn_Ok
      Caption          =    "OK"
      Height           =    375
      Left             =    2880
      TabIndex         =    3
      Top              =    2400
      Width            =    1215
   End
   Begin FileListBox flb_Files
      Height           =    1980
      Left             =    2880
```

continues

Listing 15.2. continued

```
      Pattern         =    "*.BMP"
      TabIndex        =    2
      Top             =    255
      Width           =    2535
   End
   Begin DirListBox dlb_Dirs
      Height          =    2055
      Left            =    240
      TabIndex        =    1
      Top             =    720
      Width           =    2415
   End
   Begin DriveListBox vlb_Drives
      Height          =    315
      Left            =    240
      TabIndex        =    0
      Top             =    240
      Width           =    2415
   End
End
Option Explicit

Sub btn_Cancel_Click ()

  ' Unload the form
  Unload Me

End Sub

Sub btn_Ok_Click ()

  ' Do we have a selected file?
  If (flb_Files.FileName <> "") Then

    ' Yes, so start building the complete path
    LoadFilename$ = flb_Files.Path

    ' We may need a backslash, if it's not already there
    If (LoadFilename$ <> "\") Then
      LoadFilename$ = LoadFilename$ + "\"
    End If

    ' Finally, add the filename
    LoadFilename$ = LoadFilename$ + flb_Files.FileName

  End If

  ' We're done with the form
  Unload Me

End Sub
```

```
Sub dlb_Dirs_Change ()

  ' Update the file path
  flb_Files.Path = dlb_Dirs.Path

End Sub

Sub flb_Files_DblClick ()

  ' This is the same as selecting OK
  btn_Ok_Click

End Sub

Sub Form_Load ()

  ' Center on the screen
  Move (Screen.Width - Width) \ 2, (Screen.Height - Height) \ 2

  ' Initialize filename to nothing
  LoadFilename$ = ""

End Sub

Sub vlb_Drives_Change ()

  ' Update the directory drive
  dlb_Dirs.Path = vlb_Drives.Drive

End Sub
```

Figure 15.6 and Listing 15.3 show the PZMAIN form and source code. This form contains the main Puzzler code.

Figure 15.6. The PZMAIN form.

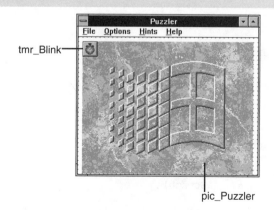

tmr_Blink

pic_Puzzler

Listing 15.3. The PZMAIN form source code.

```
VERSION 2.00
Begin Form frm_Puzzler
   BorderStyle       =   1  'Fixed Single
   Caption           =   "Puzzler"
   Height            =   4420
   Icon              =   PZMAIN.FRX:0000 'PZ.ICO
   Left              =   1020
   LinkMode          =   1  'Source
   LinkTopic         =   "Form1"
   MaxButton         =   0  'False
   ScaleHeight       =   179
   ScaleMode         =   3  'Pixel
   ScaleWidth        =   337
   Top               =   780
   Width             =   5175
   Begin Timer tmr_Blink
      Left           =   8
      Top            =   8
   End
   Begin PictureBox pic_Puzzler
      AutoRedraw     =   -1  'True
      AutoSize       =   -1  'True
      BorderStyle    =   0  'None
      Height         =   3600
      Left           =   120
      Picture        =   PZMAIN.FRX:0302 'WINLOGO.BMP
      ScaleHeight    =   240
      ScaleMode      =   3  'Pixel
      ScaleWidth     =   320
      TabIndex       =   0
      Top            =   120
      Visible        =   0    'False
      Width          =   4800
   End
   Begin Menu mnu_File
      Caption        =   "&File"
      Begin Menu mnu_Load
         Caption     =   "&Load..."
      End
      Begin Menu mnu_ExitSep
         Caption      =   "-"
      End
      Begin Menu mnu_Exit
         Caption     =   "E&xit"
      End
   End
   Begin Menu mnu_Options
      Caption        =   "&Options"
      Begin Menu mnu_Scramble
         Caption     =   "&Scramble"
      End
```

```
      Begin Menu mnu_ScrambleSep
         Caption          =    "-"
      End
      Begin Menu mnu_16
         Caption          =    "&16"
         Checked          =    -1   'True
      End
      Begin Menu mnu_36
         Caption          =    "&36"
      End
      Begin Menu mnu_64
         Caption          =    "&64"
      End
      Begin Menu mnu_BeepSep
         Caption          =    "-"
      End
      Begin Menu mnu_Beep
         Caption          =    "&Beep"
         Checked          =    -1   'True
      End
   End
   Begin Menu mnu_Hints
      Caption          =    "&Hints"
      Begin Menu mnu_Peek
         Caption          =    "&Peek"
         Enabled          =    0    'False
      End
      Begin Menu mnu_Locate
         Caption          =    "&Locate"
         Enabled          =    0    'False
      End
      Begin Menu mnu_Correct
         Caption          =    "&Correct"
         Enabled          =    0    'False
      End
      Begin Menu mnu_DisplaySep
         Caption          =    "-"
      End
      Begin Menu mnu_Display
         Caption          =    "&Display Puzzle"
         Enabled          =    0    'False
      End
   End
   Begin Menu mnu_Help
      Caption          =    "&Help"
      Begin Menu mnu_Rules
         Caption          =    "&Rules..."
      End
      Begin Menu mnu_RulesSep
         Caption          =    "-"
      End
```

continues

Listing 15.3. continued

```
        Begin Menu mnu_About
            Caption          =   "&About Puzzler..."
        End
    End
End
Option Explicit

'
' This routine checks to see if the puzzle has been solved.
'
Sub CheckWin ()

  Dim i%

  ' Count the number of correct pieces
  CountCorrect

  ' Are all of the pieces correct
  If (Correct% = NumPieces%) Then

    ' Yes, mark time puzzle was solved
    StopTime# = Now

    ' Set puzzle status
    SetPuzzlerStatus (PUZWIN)

    ' Force a refresh
    Form_Paint

    ' Give some fanfare
    For i% = 1 To 3
      Delay .5
      Beep
    Next i%

    ' Display the Winner form
    frm_Winner.Show 1

  End If

End Sub

'
' This function counts the number of pieces that are placed correctly.
'
Sub CountCorrect ()

  Dim i%

  ' Assume that no pieces are correct
  Correct% = 0
```

```
  ' Loop through all pieces
  For i% = 0 To (NumPieces% - 1)
    ' Is this piece in its correct place?
    If (Grid%(i%) = i%) Then
      ' Yes, then increment correct count
      Correct% = Correct% + 1
    End If
  Next

End Sub


' This function displays the current correct puzzle pieces.

Sub DisplayCorrect ()

  Dim i%

  ' Display all puzzle pieces
  For i% = 0 To (NumPieces% - 1)
    ' Display piece if in correct place, or clear it if not
    Call DisplayPiece(i%, (Grid%(i%) = i%))
  Next i%

End Sub


' This function displays the puzzle grid.

Sub DisplayGrid ()

  Dim r%, c%

  ' Draw the vertical lines in grid
  For c% = 0 To Cols%
    Line ((c% * PWidth%), 0)-((c% * PWidth%), IDepth%), RGB(0, 0, 0)
  Next c%

  ' Draw the horizontal lines in grid
  For r% = 0 To Rows%
    Line (0, (r% * PDepth%))-(IWidth%, (r% * PDepth%)), RGB(0, 0, 0)
  Next r%

End Sub


' This function displays the location for a given piece.

Sub DisplayLocation (ByVal p%)
```

continues

Listing 15.3. continued

```
  ' Is piece in its correct place?
  If (p% <> Grid%(p%)) Then
    ' No, then clear the piece
    Call DisplayPiece(Grid%(p%), False)
  End If

End Sub

'
' This function displays the original image.
'
Sub DisplayOriginal ()

  Dim rc%

  ' Display the entire image
  rc% = BitBlt%(frm_Puzzler.hDC, 0, 0, pic_Puzzler.ScaleWidth,
  ➡pic_Puzzler.ScaleHeight, pic_Puzzler.hDC, 0, 0, SRCCOPY)

End Sub

'
' This function displays a puzzle piece.
'
Sub DisplayPiece (ByVal iPiece%, ByVal pflag%)

  Dim vx%, vy%
  Dim r%, c%
  Dim rc%

  ' Get the column and row for this piece
  c% = iPiece% Mod Cols%
  r% = iPiece% \ Cols%

  ' Should we show or clear the piece?
  If (pflag%) Then

    ' Showing piece, calculate coordinates
    vx% = (Grid%(iPiece%) Mod Cols%) * PWidth%
    vy% = (Grid%(iPiece%) \ Cols%) * PDepth%

    ' Fit in grid, so grid is not erased (no flicker)
    rc% = BitBlt%(frm_Puzzler.hDC, (c% * PWidth%), (r% * PDepth%),
    ➡PWidth%, PDepth%, pic_Puzzler.hDC, vx%, vy%, SRCCOPY)

  Else

    ' Clearing piece, draw a black rectangle
    Line ((c% * PWidth%), (r% * PDepth%))-(((c% + 1) * PWidth%), ((r% + 1)
    ➡* PDepth%)), RGB(0, 0, 0), BF

  End If
```

```
End Sub

'
' This function displays the puzzle.
'
Sub DisplayPuzzle ()

  Dim i%

  ' Display all puzzle pieces
  For i% = 0 To (NumPieces% - 1)
    Call DisplayPiece(i%, True)
  Next

  ' Display the grid
  DisplayGrid

End Sub

Sub Form_KeyDown (KeyCode As Integer, Shift As Integer)

  Dim r%, c%
  Dim od%

  ' Were they getting a hint?
  If ((Status% <> PUZWIN) And (Status% <> PUZPLAYING)) Then
    ' Yes, so force a puzzle display
    mnu_Display_Click
  End If

  ' Save the old destination
  od% = DPiece%

  ' Find the current row and column
  c% = DPiece% Mod Cols%
  r% = DPiece% \ Cols%

  ' Determine which key was pressed
  Select Case (KeyCode)
    Case KEY_UP
      ' Up a row
      r% = r% - 1
    Case KEY_DOWN
      ' Down a row
      r% = r% + 1
    Case KEY_LEFT
      ' Left a column
      c% = c% - 1
    Case KEY_RIGHT
      ' Right a column
      c% = c% + 1
```

continues

Listing 15.3. continued

```
    Case KEY_HOME
      ' Go to the upper-left corner
      c% = 0
      r% = 0
    Case KEY_END
      ' Got to the lower-right corner
      c% = Cols% - 1
      r% = Rows% - 1
    Case KEY_SPACE
      ' Select piece as the source (like a left click)
      KeyCode = KEY_LBUTTON
    Case KEY_RETURN
      ' Select piece as the destination (like a right click)
      KeyCode = KEY_RBUTTON
  End Select

  ' Make sure we stay within the limits
  c% = Min(c%, Cols% - 1)
  c% = Max(c%, 0)
  r% = Min(r%, Rows% - 1)
  r% = Max(r%, 0)

  ' Find new piece
  DPiece% = (r% * Cols%) + c%

  ' If this is a new location, clear the grid
  If (DPiece% <> od%) Then
    DisplayGrid
  End If

  ' Pass this on to the mouse handler
  If ((KeyCode = KEY_LBUTTON) Or (KeyCode = KEY_RBUTTON)) Then
    Call Form_MouseDown(KeyCode, Shift, (c% * PWidth%) + 1, (r% * PDepth%)
    ➥+ 1)
  End If

End Sub

Sub Form_Load ()

  ' Center on the screen
  Move (Screen.Width - Width) \ 2, (Screen.Height - Height) \ 2

  ' Show about box
  frm_AboutBox.Show 1

  ' Initialize variables
  Status% = PUZWIN
  FlipFlop% = 0
```

```
' Currently we have 16 pieces (a 4 by 4 puzzle)
Cols% = 4
Rows% = 4

' Load the file from the command line (if given)
LoadFile (Command$)

End Sub

Sub Form_MouseDown (Button As Integer, Shift As Integer, X As Single, Y As
➡Single)

Dim r%, c%, p%

' Were they getting a hint?
If ((Status% <> PUZWIN) And (Status% <> PUZPLAYING)) Then
  ' Yes, so force a puzzle display
  mnu_Display_Click
End If

' Determine what piece was selected
c% = (X - 1) \ PWidth%
r% = (Y - 1) \ PDepth%
p% = (Cols% * r%) + c%

' Was the left button pressed?
If (Button And KEY_LBUTTON) Then

  ' Yes, so make this piece the source piece
  SPiece% = p%

  ' Clear any destination piece
  DPiece% = SPiece%

  ' Display grid to move source location
  DisplayGrid

' Was the right button pressed?
ElseIf (Button And KEY_RBUTTON) Then

  ' Yes, so make this piece the destination piece
  DPiece% = p%

  ' Are source and destination pieces different?
  If (SPiece% <> DPiece%) Then
    ' Swap the pieces
    Call SwapPieces(SPiece%, DPiece%)
    ' Is this piece correct?
    If ((Grid%(DPiece%) = DPiece%) And (mnu_Beep.Checked)) Then
      ' Yes, then beep
      Beep
    End If
```

continues

Listing 15.3. continued

```
    End If

    ' Count this as a move
    Moves% = Moves% + 1

    ' Update grid and force a refresh
    DisplayGrid

    ' Is the puzzle solved?
    CheckWin

  End If

End Sub

Sub Form_Paint ()

  ' Determine status and display puzzle accordingly
  Select Case (Status%)
    Case PUZPLAYING
      ' Display puzzle
      DisplayPuzzle
    Case PUZPEEKING
      ' Display unscrambled image
      DisplayOriginal
      ' Display the grid
      DisplayGrid
    Case PUZLOCATE
      ' Display the puzzle
      DisplayPuzzle
      ' Display location of current piece
      DisplayLocation (SPiece%)
    Case PUZCORRECT
      ' Display pieces that are correctly placed
      DisplayCorrect
      ' Display the grid
      DisplayGrid
    Case PUZWIN
      ' Display unscrambled image
      DisplayOriginal
  End Select

End Sub

'
' This function displays the source piece with a white outline.
'
Sub HighlightPiece (ByVal FlipFlop%, ByVal iPiece%)

  Dim r%, c%
  Dim RectColor&
```

```
' Get the piece's column and row
c% = iPiece% Mod Cols%
r% = iPiece% \ Cols%

' Erase piece by drawing a black rectangle
Line ((c% * PWidth%), (r% * PDepth%))-(((c% + 1) * PWidth%), ((r% + 1) *
➡PDepth%)), RGB(0, 0, 0), B

' Are we flashing piece?
If (FlipFlop%) Then
  ' Yes, then draw rectangle in white
  RectColor& = RGB(255, 255, 255)
Else
  RectColor& = RGB(0, 0, 0)
End If

' Outline the piece
Line ((c% * PWidth%), (r% * PDepth%))-(((c% + 1) * PWidth%), ((r% + 1) *
➡PDepth%)), RectColor&, B

End Sub

'
' This function initializes the puzzle.
'
Sub InitPuzzle ()

  Dim i%, j%, r%

  ' Get a new sequence of numbers
  Randomize

  ' Initialize the grid
  For i% = 0 To (MAXPIECES - 1)
    Grid%(i%) = -1
  Next

  ' Determine number of pieces
  NumPieces% = Cols% * Rows%

  ' Randomize the pieces
  For i% = 0 To (NumPieces% - 1)
    ' Get a random number, between pieces left
    r% = GetRandom%(NumPieces% - i%) + 1
    ' Search for a slot
    j% = 0
    While (r% > 0)
      ' Position filled?
      If (Grid%(j%) = -1) Then
        ' No, so count it
        r% = r% - 1
      End If
```

continues

Listing 15.3. continued

```
      ' Bump to next slot
      If (r% > 0) Then
        j% = j% + 1
      End If
    Wend
    ' Place the piece in the grid
    Grid%(j%) = i%
  Next

  ' Display the piece grid
  DisplayGrid

  ' Start the timer
  tmr_Blink.Interval = BLINKINC

  ' Set window size
  SetWindowSize

End Sub

'
' This functions loads in a BMP file.
'
Sub LoadFile (ByVal Filename$)

  ' Is there a file name?
  If (Len(Filename$) > 0) Then
    ' Yes, so try and load it
    pic_Puzzler.Picture = LoadPicture(Filename$)
  End If

  ' Set it up
  SetupImage (Filename$)

End Sub

'
' This function returns the larger value of two integers.
'
Function Max% (ByVal a%, ByVal b%)

  ' Is A larger than B?
  If (a% >= b%) Then
    Max% = a%
  Else
    Max% = b%
  End If

End Function
```

```
'
' This function returns the smaller value of two integers.
'
Function Min% (ByVal a%, ByVal b%)

  ' Is A smaller than B?
  If (a% <= b%) Then
    Min% = a%
  Else
    Min% = b%
  End If

End Function

Sub mnu_16_Click ()

  ' Check appropriate menu item and uncheck the rest
  mnu_16.Checked = True
  mnu_36.Checked = False
  mnu_64.Checked = False

  ' Set number of columns and rows
  Cols% = 4
  Rows% = 4

  ' Force a rescramble
  mnu_Scramble_Click

End Sub

Sub mnu_36_Click ()

  ' Check appropriate menu item and uncheck the rest
  mnu_16.Checked = False
  mnu_36.Checked = True
  mnu_64.Checked = False

  ' Set number of columns and rows
  Cols% = 6
  Rows% = 6

  ' Force a rescramble
  mnu_Scramble_Click

End Sub

Sub mnu_64_Click ()

  ' Check appropriate menu item and uncheck the rest
  mnu_16.Checked = False
```

continues

Listing 15.3. continued

```
mnu_36.Checked = False
mnu_64.Checked = True

' Set number of columns and rows
Cols% = 8
Rows% = 8

' Force a rescramble
mnu_Scramble_Click

End Sub

Sub mnu_About_Click ()

' Load the About form
frm_AboutBox.Show 1

End Sub

Sub mnu_Beep_Click ()

' Toggle the beep flag
mnu_Beep.Checked = Not mnu_Beep.Checked

End Sub

Sub mnu_Correct_Click ()

' Are we currently playing a puzzle?
If (Status% = PUZPLAYING) Then

' Yes, so penalize for viewing correct pieces.
Penalties% = Penalties% + PENCORRECT

' Set puzzle status
SetPuzzlerStatus (PUZCORRECT)

' Force a refresh
Form_Paint

End If

End Sub

Sub mnu_Display_Click ()

' Set puzzle status
SetPuzzlerStatus (PUZPLAYING)
```

```
  ' Force a refresh
  Form_Paint

End Sub

Sub mnu_Exit_Click ()

  ' End the program
  Unload Me

End Sub

Sub mnu_Load_Click ()

  ' Load the 'Load Bitmap' dialog box
  frm_Load.Show 1

  ' If we got a name back, load it
  If (LoadFilename$ <> "") Then
    LoadFile (LoadFilename$)
  End If

End Sub

Sub mnu_Locate_Click ()

  ' Are we currently playing a puzzle?
  If (Status% = PUZPLAYING) Then

    ' Yes, so penalize for asking location of piece
    Penalties% = Penalties% + PENLOCATE

    ' Set puzzler status
    SetPuzzlerStatus (PUZLOCATE)

    ' Force a refresh
    Form_Paint

  End If

End Sub

Sub mnu_Peek_Click ()

  ' Are we currently playing a puzzle?
  If (Status% = PUZPLAYING) Then

    ' Yes, so penalize for peeking
    Penalties% = Penalties% + PENPEEKING
```

continues

Listing 15.3. continued

```
    ' Set puzzle status
    SetPuzzlerStatus (PUZPEEKING)

    ' Force a refresh
    Form_Paint

  End If

End Sub

Sub mnu_Rules_Click ()

  ' Load the Rules form
  frm_Rules.Show 1

End Sub

Sub mnu_Scramble_Click ()

  ' Initialize fields
  Penalties% = 0
  Moves% = 0
  Correct% = 0
  SPiece% = 0
  DPiece% = 0

  ' Mark time puzzle was started
  StartTime# = Now

  ' Initialize puzzle
  InitPuzzle

  ' Set puzzle status
  SetPuzzlerStatus (PUZPLAYING)

  ' Force a refresh
  Form_Paint

End Sub

'
' This function sets the window caption text.
'
Sub SetCaption ()

  Dim TempStr$
```

```
' Format the caption
If (Len(CurFilename$) > 0) Then
  TempStr$ = "Puzzler [" + CurFilename$ + "]"
Else
  TempStr$ = "Puzzler"
End If

' Set it
frm_Puzzler.Caption = TempStr$

End Sub

'
' This function sets menu items according to the puzzle status.
'
Sub SetPuzzlerStatus (ByVal iStat%)

  ' Update puzzle status
  Status% = iStat%
  Select Case (Status%)
    Case PUZPLAYING
      ' We are playing, so enable all penalties
      mnu_Peek.Enabled = True
      mnu_Locate.Enabled = True
      mnu_Correct.Enabled = True
      ' and disable going back to playing
      mnu_Display.Enabled = False
    Case PUZPEEKING, PUZCORRECT, PUZLOCATE
      ' We are being penalized, so disable all penalties
      mnu_Peek.Enabled = False
      mnu_Locate.Enabled = False
      mnu_Correct.Enabled = False
      ' and enable going back to playing
      mnu_Display.Enabled = True
    Case PUZWIN
      ' We have won or image is not scrambled, so disable everything
      mnu_Peek.Enabled = False
      mnu_Locate.Enabled = False
      mnu_Correct.Enabled = False
      mnu_Display.Enabled = False
  End Select

End Sub

'
'  This function sets up the new image, caption and menu items.
'
Sub SetupImage (ByVal ImageName$)
```

continues

Listing 15.3. continued

```
    ' Make sure our status is correct
    SetPuzzlerStatus (PUZWIN)

    ' Set up file name
    CurFilename$ = ImageName$

    ' Set the window size
    SetWindowSize

    ' Set the new title
    SetCaption

End Sub

'
' This function sets up the window size.
'
Sub SetWindowSize ()

    Dim ww%, wd%
    Dim md%, cd%

    ' Get the minimum window size
    ww% = Min%(pic_Puzzler.ScaleWidth, (Screen.Width \
    ➥Screen.TwipsPerPixelX))
    wd% = Min%(pic_Puzzler.ScaleHeight, (Screen.Height \
    ➥Screen.TwipsPerPixelY))

    ' Make sure image dimensions are evenly divisible by number of columns
    ' and rows
    IWidth% = (ww% \ Cols%) * Cols%
    IDepth% = (wd% \ Rows%) * Rows%

    ' Get width and depth of squares
    PWidth% = IWidth% \ Cols%
    PDepth% = IDepth% \ Rows%

    ' Get depth of the menu and caption bars
    md% = GetSystemMetrics%(SM_CYMENU)
    cd% = GetSystemMetrics%(SM_CYCAPTION)

    ' Adjust window size
    frm_Puzzler.Width = (IWidth% + 3) * Screen.TwipsPerPixelX
    frm_Puzzler.Height = (IDepth% + md% + cd% + 3) * Screen.TwipsPerPixelY

    ' Center on the screen
    Move (Screen.Width - Width) \ 2, (Screen.Height - Height) \ 2

End Sub
```

```
'
' This function swaps the source and destination pieces.
'
Sub SwapPieces (ByVal s%, ByVal d%)

  Dim temp%

  ' Swap the pieces
  temp% = Grid%(d%)
  Grid%(d%) = Grid%(s%)
  Grid%(s%) = temp%

  ' Display source and destination pieces
  Call DisplayPiece(s%, True)
  Call DisplayPiece(d%, True)

  ' Move source location
  SPiece% = DPiece%

End Sub

Sub tmr_Blink_Timer ()

  ' Make sure window is not minimized
  If (frm_Puzzler.WindowState = 0) Then

    ' Flip the flip-flop
    FlipFlop% = Not FlipFlop%

    ' What are we currently doing?
    Select Case (Status%)
      Case PUZLOCATE
        ' Highlight the source piece
        Call HighlightPiece(FlipFlop%, SPiece%)
        ' Highlight the destination piece
        Call HighlightPiece(Not FlipFlop%, Grid%(SPiece%))
      Case PUZPLAYING
        ' Highlight the source piece
        Call HighlightPiece(FlipFlop%, SPiece%)
        ' And the destination piece, if different (for keyboard use)
        If (SPiece% <> DPiece%) Then
          Call HighlightPiece(Not FlipFlop%, DPiece%)
        End If
    End Select

  End If

End Sub
```

Figure 15.7 and Listing 15.4 show the PZRULES form and source code.

Figure 15.7. The PZRULES form.

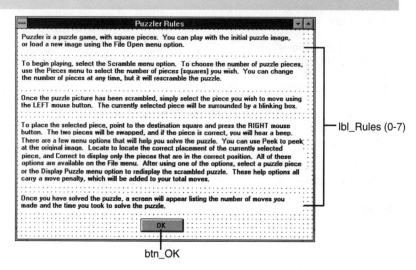

btn_OK

Listing 15.4. The PZRULES form source code.

```
VERSION 2.00
Begin Form frm_Rules
    BorderStyle     =   3   'Fixed Double
    Caption         =   "Puzzler Rules"
    Height          =   6140
    Left            =   540
    LinkMode        =   1   'Source
    LinkTopic       =   "Form2"
    MaxButton       =   0       'False
    MinButton       =   0       'False
    ScaleHeight     =   5640
    ScaleWidth      =   8310
    Top             =   340
    Width           =   8430
    Begin CommandButton btn_Ok
        Caption         =   "OK"
        Height          =   375
        Left            =   3480
        TabIndex        =   8
        Top             =   5160
        Width           =   1215
    End
    Begin Label lbl_Rules
        Caption         =   "Once you have solved the puzzle, a screen will
appear listing the number of moves you made and the time you took to solve
the puzzle."
```

```
        Height        =   435
        Index         =   7
        Left          =   105
        TabIndex      =   7
        Top           =   4515
        Width         =   7890
     End
     Begin Label lbl_Rules
        Caption       =   "or the Display Puzzle menu option to redisplay
the scrambled puzzle.  These help options all carry a move penalty, which
will be added to your total moves."
        Height        =   495
        Index         =   6
        Left          =   105
        TabIndex      =   6
        Top           =   3780
        Width         =   8175
     End
     Begin Label lbl_Rules
        Caption       =   "piece, and Correct to display only the pieces
that are in the correct position.  All of these options are available on
the File menu.  After using one of the options, select a puzzle piece."

        Height        =   495
        Index         =   5
        Left          =   120
        TabIndex      =   5
        Top           =   3360
        Width         =   7935
     End
     Begin Label lbl_Rules
        Caption       =   "There are a few menu options that will help you
solve the puzzle.  You can use Peek to peek at the original image. Use
Locate to locate the correct placement of the currently selected piece."

        Height        =   375
        Index         =   4
        Left          =   105
        TabIndex      =   4
        Top           =   2940
        Width         =   7935
     End
     Begin Label lbl_Rules
        Caption       =   "To place the selected piece, point to the
destination square and press the RIGHT mouse button.  The two pieces will
be swapped, and if the piece is correct, you will hear a beep."

        Height        =   375
        Index         =   3
        Left          =   105
```

continues

Listing 15.4. The PZRULES form source code.

```
        TabIndex        =    3
        Top             =    2520
        Width           =    8175
    End
    Begin Label lbl_Rules
        Caption         =    "Once the puzzle picture has been scrambled,
simply select the piece you wish to move using the LEFT mouse button.  The
currently selected piece will be surrounded by a blinking box."

        Height          =    495
        Index           =    2
        Left            =    105
        TabIndex        =    2
        Top             =    1785
        Width           =    8055
    End
    Begin Label lbl_Rules
        Caption         =    "To begin playing, select the Scramble menu
option.  To choose the number of puzzle pieces, use the Pieces menu to
select the number of pieces (squares) you wish.  You can change the number
of pieces at any time, but it will rescramble the puzzle."

        Height          =    735
        Index           =    1
        Left            =    120
        TabIndex        =    1
        Top             =    840
        Width           =    7935
    End
    Begin Label lbl_Rules
        Caption         =    "Puzzler is a puzzle game, with square pieces.
You can play with the initial puzzle image, or load a new image using the
File Open menu option."

        Height          =    495
        Index           =    0
        Left            =    120
        TabIndex        =    0
        Top             =    120
        Width           =    7815
    End
End
Option Explicit

Sub btn_Ok_Click ()

    ' Unload the form
    Unload Me

End Sub
```

```
Sub Form_Load ()

  ' Center on the screen
  Move (screen.Width - Width) \ 2, (screen.Height - Height) \ 2

End Sub
```

Figure 15.8 and Listing 15.5 show the PZWINNER form and source code. The Winner form is displayed when the Puzzle is solved.

Figure 15.8. The PZWINNER form.

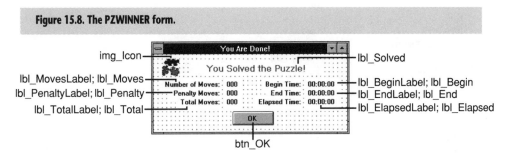

Listing 15.5. The PZWINNER form source code.

```
VERSION 2.00
Begin Form frm_Winner
   BorderStyle      =   3  'Fixed Double
   Caption          =      "You Are Done!"
   ControlBox       =   0   'False
   Height           =   2520
   Left             =   2355
   LinkMode         =   1   'Source
   LinkTopic        =      "Form1"
   MaxButton        =   0   'False
   MinButton        =   0   'False
   ScaleHeight      =   2020
   ScaleWidth       =   5430
   Top              =   2100
   Width            =   5550
   Begin CommandButton btn_OK
      Caption       =      "OK"
      Height        =   375
      Left          =   2220
      TabIndex      =   4
      Top           =   1560
      Width         =   1155
   End
```

continues

Listing 15.5. continued

```
Begin Image img_Icon
   Height           =    640
   Left             =    240
   Picture          =    PZWINNER.FRX:0000 'PZ.ICO
   Top              =    120
   Width            =    480
End
Begin Label lbl_Elapsed
   Caption          =    "00:00:00"
   Height           =    255
   Left             =    4320
   TabIndex         =    13
   Top              =    1200
   Width            =    855
End
Begin Label lbl_ElapsedLabel
   Alignment        =    1    'Right Justify
   Caption          =    "Elapsed Time:"
   Height           =    255
   Left             =    2880
   TabIndex         =    7
   Top              =    1200
   Width            =    1275
End
Begin Label lbl_Total
   Caption          =    "000"
   Height           =    255
   Left             =    2040
   TabIndex         =    10
   Top              =    1200
   Width            =    375
End
Begin Label lbl_TotalLabel
   Alignment        =    1    'Right Justify
   Caption          =    "Total Moves:"
   Height           =    255
   Left             =    720
   TabIndex         =    3
   Top              =    1200
   Width            =    1155
End
Begin Label lbl_End
   Caption          =    "00:00:00"
   Height           =    255
   Left             =    4320
   TabIndex         =    12
   Top              =    960
   Width            =    855
End
Begin Label lbl_EndLabel
   Alignment        =    1    'Right Justify
   Caption          =    "End Time:"
```

```
       Height          =    255
       Left            =    3240
       TabIndex        =    6
       Top             =    960
       Width           =    915
    End
    Begin Label lbl_Penalty
       Caption         =    "000"
       Height          =    255
       Left            =    2040
       TabIndex        =    9
       Top             =    960
       Width           =    375
    End
    Begin Label lbl_PenaltyLabel
       Alignment       =    1    'Right Justify
       Caption         =    "Penalty Moves:"
       Height          =    255
       Left            =    480
       TabIndex        =    2
       Top             =    960
       Width           =    1395
    End
    Begin Label lbl_Begin
       Caption         =    "00:00:00"
       Height          =    255
       Left            =    4320
       TabIndex        =    11
       Top             =    720
       Width           =    855
    End
    Begin Label lbl_BeginLabel
       Alignment       =    1    'Right Justify
       Caption         =    "Begin Time:"
       Height          =    255
       Left            =    3120
       TabIndex        =    5
       Top             =    720
       Width           =    1035
    End
    Begin Label lbl_Moves
       Caption         =    "000"
       Height          =    255
       Left            =    2040
       TabIndex        =    8
       Top             =    720
       Width           =    435
    End
    Begin Label lbl_MovesLabel
       Alignment       =    1    'Right Justify
       Caption         =    "Number of Moves:"
       Height          =    255
```

continues

Listing 15.5. continued

```
        Left            =    240
        TabIndex        =    1
        Top             =    720
        Width           =    1635
    End
    Begin Label lbl_Solved
        Alignment       =    2    'Center
        Caption         =    "You Solved the Puzzle!"
        FontBold        =    -1   'True
        FontItalic      =    0    'False
        FontName        =    "MS Sans Serif"
        FontSize        =    12
        FontStrikethru  =    0    'False
        FontUnderline   =    0    'False
        ForeColor       =    &H000000FF&
        Height          =    255
        Left            =    1080
        TabIndex        =    0
        Top             =    240
        Width           =    3615
    End
End
Option Explicit

'
' This function handles the OK button.
'
Sub btn_Ok_Click ()

    ' Unload the form
    Unload Me

End Sub

Sub Form_Load ()

    ' Center the form on the screen
    Move (Screen.Width - Width) \ 2, (Screen.Height - Height) \ 2

    ' Initialize frm_Winner form strings
    lbl_Moves.Caption = Format$(Moves%, "##0")
    lbl_Penalty.Caption = Format$(Penalties%, "##0")
    lbl_Total.Caption = Format$((Moves% + Penalties%), "##0")
    lbl_Begin.Caption = Format$(StartTime#, "hh:mm:ss")
    lbl_End.Caption = Format$(StopTime#, "hh:mm:ss")
    lbl_Elapsed.Caption = Format$((StopTime# - StartTime#), "hh:mm:ss")

End Sub
```

Listing 15.6 shows the PZGLOBAL.BAS source code. This file contains the global constants and variable definitions for the Puzzler game.

Listing 15.6. The PZGLOBAL.BAS source code.

```
Option Explicit

' KeyCode (KeyDown, KeyUp)
Global Const KEY_LBUTTON = &H1
Global Const KEY_RBUTTON = &H2
Global Const KEY_RETURN = &HD
Global Const KEY_SPACE = &H20
Global Const KEY_END = &H23
Global Const KEY_HOME = &H24
Global Const KEY_LEFT = &H25
Global Const KEY_UP = &H26
Global Const KEY_RIGHT = &H27
Global Const KEY_DOWN = &H28

' System metric constants
Global Const SM_CYCAPTION = 4
Global Const SM_CYMENU = 15

' Minimum window size
Global Const MINWIDTH = 225
Global Const MINDEPTH = 100

' Penalties
Global Const PENPEEKING = 5
Global Const PENCORRECT = 3
Global Const PENLOCATE = 2

' Puzzler Status
Global Const PUZPLAYING = 0
Global Const PUZPEEKING = 1
Global Const PUZCORRECT = 2
Global Const PUZLOCATE = 3
Global Const PUZWIN = 4

' Maximum number of pieces
Global Const MAXPIECES = 64

' Blinking
Global Const BLINKINC = 250

' Windows API
Global Const SRCCOPY = &HCC0020
```

continues

```
' Global variables
Global LoadFilename$
Global CurFilename$

' Puzzle grid
Global Grid%(MAXPIECES)

' Columns and rows
Global Cols%, Rows%

' Image width and depth
Global IWidth%, IDepth%

' Piece information
Global PWidth%, PDepth%
Global SPiece%, DPiece%
Global NumPieces%

' Puzzle status
Global Correct%, Moves%, Penalties%

' Start and end time
Global StartTime#
Global StopTime#

' Status flag
Global Status%
Global FlipFlop%

' Windows API
Declare Function GetSystemMetrics% Lib "USER" (ByVal nIndex%)
Declare Function BitBlt% Lib "GDI" (ByVal hDestDC%, ByVal dx%, ByVal dy%,
➥ByVal nWidth%, ByVal nHeight%, ByVal hSrcDC%, ByVal sx%, ByVal sy%,
➥ByVal dwRop&)

'
' This procedure delays the given number of seconds, which can be
' fractional.
'
Sub Delay (secs!)

  Dim Start!

  ' Get the current seconds since midnight
  Start! = Timer

  ' Wait for seconds to elapse
  While (Timer < (Start! + secs!))
    ' Let other things run while we wait
    DoEvents
  Wend
```

```
End Sub

'
' This function returns a random number between 0 and range%-1, inclusive.
'
Function GetRandom% (range%)

  ' In the Visual Basic manual, the generic formula is:
  ' Int((upperbound-lowerbound+1)*Rnd+lowerbound)
  GetRandom% = Int(range% * Rnd)

End Function
```

Form Overview

The following is a brief discussion of the Puzzler forms and their controls. Consult the form figures for additional information.

About Box

The PZABOUT form is my standard About box form. I set the label to `Puzzler` and the image to `PZ.ICO`. For a full description of this form, see Chapter 10, "Apples & Oranges."

Loading Bitmaps

The PZLOAD form is a basic File Open dialog box. The drive list box (`vlb_Drives`), directory list box (`dlb_Dirs`), and file list box (`flb_Files`) find the files. The OK button (`btn_Ok`) puts the drive, directory, and filename together. The cancel button (`btn_Cancel`) unloads the form.

If you use this form in your own games, you can add a textbox so the user can type in a path and filename directly. Currently, the `flb_Files.Pattern` property is set to "*.BMP," so only BMP files are displayed.

Rules

The PZRULES form displays the Puzzler rules when you select Rules from the Help menu. This form is a little different than the rule forms for the games described previously in this book. Instead of the form's paint routine printing the text, an array of text labels contains the text.

Using an array of text labels enables you to view and position the text on the form without having to run the program over and over. Having to use several text boxes makes it a little less convenient than printing the text at runtime. Visual Basic doesn't let you use strings that are much longer than a couple sentences, so you need to use more than one text label control.

Winning

When you solve the puzzle, the PZWINNER form displays all the statistics (such as number of moves and time elapsed). It also contains the Puzzler icon, labels, and the obligatory OK button. Note that the colorful icon and the red text jazz up what could be a pretty boring form.

Global

The PZGLOBAL basic file contains the global variable and constant definitions. It also contains the global procedures `Delay` and `GetRandom`.

The Main Form

The PZMAIN form is the main form for the game, and it contains two controls. The timer (`tmr_Blink`) handles the blinking piece selector box, and (`pic_Puzzler`) holds the puzzle image.

The `pic_Puzzler` picture has several important properties. First, it's invisible (`Visible=False`). Second, it gets copied to the window by the `DisplayPiece` routine that uses the Windows API function `BitBlt` (discussed in Chapter 4, "Animation"). Finally, it needs to be persistent, so it uses `AutoRedraw=True`—ensuring that the picture data is available when needed. The PZMAIN might be our simplest main form!

Programming Overview

The Puzzler program is a little more complicated than Slider. This game has more general routines, but most of them are similar (`DisplayLocate`, `DisplayCorrect`, and so on). The routines also are brief.

Program Flow

When the game runs, the program flows as follows:

➡ When the main form is loaded, it is centered and the About box is displayed. The piece row and columns are set, and the puzzle is declared solved when the `Status%` flag is set to `PUZWIN`.

➤ The player must scramble the puzzle by selecting Scramble from the Options menu. The mnu_Scramble_Click routine initializes a new game by resetting the move and time counts and by calling InitPuzzle. The puzzle is displayed when a form paint is forced.

➤ The InitPuzzle procedure randomizes the number generator and scrambles the puzzle pieces. Then, it starts a new game by setting the Status% flag and kicking off the blink timer.

➤ The form_Paint routine calls DisplayPuzzle to display the scrambled puzzle. DisplayPuzzle calls DisplayPiece to display each puzzle piece from the scrambled grid.

➤ DisplayPiece uses the Windows API BitBlt function to copy a section of the hidden image (pic_Puzzler) into a section of the main form. The array (Grid%()) controls where each puzzle piece is located.

➤ The form_MouseDown and form_KeyDown routines handle the game interaction. There aren't any controls to select. The form_KeyDown procedure processes the cursor keys and passes control to the form_MouseDown routine.

➤ The form_MouseDown routine checks to see if the user currently has a hint, and if so, forces a redisplay of the puzzle. If the left or right mouse button is clicked, the routine either moves the source location or swaps the puzzle pieces. After each move, the puzzle may have been solved—so CheckWin is called.

➤ CheckWin checks to see if all the pieces are in their correct positions. If so, the frm_Winner form is displayed with the final statistics.

➤ At any time, the player can load a new image through the File Load menu option. The mnu_Load_Click routine brings up the Load Bitmap form (frm_Load). Then, frm_Load gets a filename. If a filename is selected, it is loaded into the pic_Puzzler picture and displayed.

The player can view game rules and the About box in the Help menu options. These options display frm_AboutBox or call the mnu_Rules function.

Techniques Used

The Puzzler game includes several game concepts that are outlined in the following sections.

Converting Twips

Twips are device-independent, but bitmaps are not. You need to be able to size the Puzzler form so that it matches the size of the loaded bitmap. This means that pixels are converted to twips (and sometimes vice versa). In Visual Basic, you must specify the form height and width in twips—even though the picture units are pixels.

At one time, programmers had to calculate the conversion between pixels and twips. In Visual Basic 2.0 and up, however, there are two read-only properties for the Screen object: TwipsPerPixelX and TwipsPerPixelY (can you guess what each property contains?). These properties allow the SetWindowSize routine to work properly by providing the conversion factors needed to convert twips to pixels (and vice versa).

File Open Form

Puzzler is this book's first game that has file access. The frm_Load form is a fairly basic file loading form. The Visual Basic drive, directory, and file list box controls make the form extremely easy to create. I've created it in C before, and it wasn't any fun. I remember muttering something like "Why doesn't Windows provide this automatically?"

> If you have the Professional Edition of Visual Basic, check out the Common Dialog box control. The Common Dialog box control simplifies file access.

In Puzzler, I used the file open form I discussed in Chapter 6, "File I/O." The Visual Basic file, directory, and drive ListBox controls make designing a file open form very easy.

Runtime Parameters and Launching

Visual Basic provides the command-line parameters in the string COMMAND$. When running DOS, it's easy for the user to provide extra information to the program. The user must type the filename anyway. In Windows, COMMAND$ is usually empty, because the user double-clicks the icon.

The Puzzler program looks for a bitmap filename in COMMAND$ in Form_Load. There are three ways that a filename can appear in COMMAND$. The first is when the user uses the Program Manager File Run menu option. The user types, for example, **Puzzler** *MYBITMAP.BMP*, where *MYBITMAP.BMP* is the name of the bitmap the user wants to use. The game then loads with the image the user provided.

The second way to associate BMP files to Puzzler is for the user to add the following line under the [Extensions] key:

```
BMP=PUZZLER.EXE ^.BMP
```

If a line already exists for BMP (usually for PBRUSH.EXE), comment it out with a semicolon. If Puzzler is not in the system path, add the entire path to the preceding line. Now when the user double-clicks a file with a .BMP extension, Puzzler automatically loads with that file. This is sometimes referred to as *launching*.

Third, the user can set up a group with several Puzzler icons in it. Each icon can be configured to run Puzzler with a different bitmap by adding the bitmap filename to the command-line parameter.

Handling the Keyboard

This is one of the few games in this book that can be played without a mouse. I can't imagine anyone running Windows without a mouse, but it's possible.

The Form_KeyDown procedure processes the keyboard events. It looks for the cursor keys and adjusts the DPiece% value accordingly. For the Spacebar and Enter key, though, the procedure changes the keycode.

The interesting point of this routine is that it passes keyboard handling on to the Form_MouseDown procedure. Why? Because it's simpler. All of the movement logic is kept in one place. If the code is duplicated in both routines, the chance for error increases. I could have made another function for both routines to call, but that was unnecessary. By changing the Spacebar into a left mouse click, and the Enter key into a right click, all that's left is to call Form_MouseDown. Keep this technique in mind when designing programs with multiple input methods.

Bit Blitting

The Slider game briefly introduced the Windows API function BitBlt (in a game context). See Chapter 4, "Animation," for more information. BitBlt is short for Bit Block Transfer. It's a fast routine for copying bitmaps. You might recall that I used it to animate the Slider icon. BitBlt is the workhorse function for Puzzler—without it, there wouldn't be much of a game.

The Visual Basic Image and Picture controls don't offer the capability to display a particular portion of a bitmap. If you want to scramble an image, you definitely need BitBlt. The Windows BitBlt function can copy any part of a bitmap to any part of another bitmap—perfect for this game.

You may not be familiar with the hDC property. This is a read-only property available at runtime. Because you are dealing with the Windows API, you need to have it. Visual Basic nicely puts it into a property for us. The BitBlt function is declared in PZGLOBAL as follows:

```
Declare Function BitBlt% Lib "GDI" (ByVal hDestDC%, ByVal dx%, ByVal dy%,
➥ByVal nWidth%, ByVal nHeight%, ByVal hSrcDC%, ByVal sx%, ByVal sy%,
➥ByVal dwRop&)
```

Although it's a long function, the parameters are very simple. First, you specify the destination hDC, followed by its location and size. Next, specify the source hDC and location. Finally, Windows defines numerous raster operations (ways of combining source and destination pixel values), but in this case you only need one: copy. This is defined by the SRCCOPY constant, because the raster operations are long, meaningless numbers.

> To ensure that bitmaps are available and valid at all times, make sure the picture boxes have AutoRedraw set to True. Without this property set, you'll get garbage instead of the part of the image you want.

In Puzzler, I copy the bitmap data for the puzzle piece (from the hidden control picture pic_Puzzler) into the main form picture. You'll see the BitBlt function used again quite a bit in the upcoming Space Miner game.

Sound

There isn't a lot of sound in this game. As in some of this book's other games, the Beep function is used.

Data Organization

The global variables include the puzzle grid array Grid%(), puzzle columns (Cols%), and rows (Rows%). The image width and depth are recorded in IWidth% and IDepth% and the piece size in PWidth%, PDepth%. The source, destination, and number of pieces are kept in SPiece%, DPiece%, and NumPieces%.

The puzzle status includes the number of correct pieces (Correct%), the number of moves (Moves%), and the number of penalties (Penalties%). Puzzle time is kept in StartTime# and StopTime#. Finally, the puzzle display status is maintained in Status%.

Summary

I have covered the following important programming points:

→ Twips and pixels can be converted back and forth by using the Screen property TwipsPerPixelX and TwipsPerPixelY. These properties come in handy when mixing bitmaps with twips.

→ A File Open form is easy to make using the Visual Basic controls. Loading a bitmap is just as easy with LoadPicture.

→ Runtime parameters are stored in the COMMAND$ variable. This variable is set from the Program Manager's File Run menu option, from launching a file (if the file is set up in WIN.INI) or from the icon's command-line parameters.

→ One method for handling the keyboard is to modify the information and pass it to the mouse handling function.

→ The Windows API function BitBlt is a fast bitmap copy routine. It can copy any portion of a bitmap to any position in another bitmap. It also can perform raster operations (which you'll see more of in Chapter 18, "Space Miner").

Suggestions for Improvement

The following suggestions are ideas for enhancing Puzzler:

→ Display the number of moves, the pieces correct, and the time elapsed on the Puzzler form. Make these statistics visible at all times.

→ Add a Pause feature so the elapsed time is not recorded when the user isn't playing.

→ Make the puzzle like Slider, where the pieces slide into position. Leave a blank square, and make the scrambling algorithm like Slider's.

→ Add an option to play music in the background. See Chapter 5, "Sound Generation," for an example of how this is done.

→ Keep track of the High Scores for each difficulty level (16, 36, and 64 pieces). Add a bonus for completing the puzzle without the Beep.

→ Change the main window border so it can be sized. Add the code necessary to size the image and pieces with it—so the game can be played at different sizes. Hint: you'll have to use the Windows API function StretchBlt instead of BitBlt.

➡ Make the image loading more robust. What happens if the image is too small? Too large? What happens if the user tries to load a file that is not a valid BMP file? Right now, Puzzler doesn't do any error checking, so these conditions will cause an error.

What's Ahead

Puzzles are great fun, and so are arcade games. In the next chapter, I'll explain how to re-create one of the very first video games (hint: it has a ball and a paddle). Grab your quarters and meet me in the next chapter.

Ping

Ping is a computer game similar to the arcade game, Pong. In this chapter, I describe how Ping is played, offer some hints, and cover the programming of the game. I also provide the code listings and a full description of the techniques used. You will learn about

➡ Using the Visual Basic drawing functions

➡ Animation (moving objects)

➡ Icon animation

➡ Calling the Windows API

➡ Hiding, showing, and restricting the mouse cursor

➡ Coordinate scaling

➡ Basic Collision Detection

Background

Ping is my variation of Pong (which was the first video arcade game ever). Pong was created by Nolan Bushnell, who founded a company called Atari. You may have heard of it!

Gameplay

Ping is a one-player game. The object is to keep hitting a moving ball with your paddle. The ball bounces off walls until you miss it. The game is a lot like racquetball and handball.

Running Ping

To begin playing Ping, select the Ping icon from the program group you installed. See Appendix A for installation instructions. The file, PING.EXE, contains Ping. When you run the game, you'll see the About box first. Click OK, and Ping appears.

Playing a Game

From the Options menu, select New Game. A GET READY message flashes on the screen, and the first ball is served. Move the mouse right and left to move the game paddle. You get 10 points every time you hit the ball. Figure 16.1 shows a game in progress.

Figure 16.1. Playing a game of Ping.

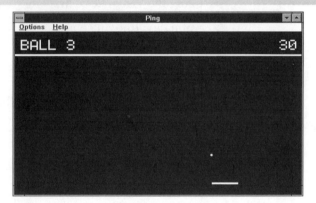

You get three balls, so the game continues until you miss three times. To pause the game, click the left mouse button. The ball freezes in position, and the mouse cursor appears—along with a PAUSED message.

You can change the size of the playing area by sizing the Ping window. For instance, you might want to play the game on a full screen, so click and drag the corner of the form to maximize the window. It's best that you size the window before you begin a new game. However, you can adjust the size during a pause.

Minimize the game and look at the icon to see what happens!

To get help, select How To Play from the Help menu. The game screen clears and displays the game help (see Figure 16.2). If you have resized the playing area, you may need to resize the window to see all the help text. Just select and drag the Ping window border.

Figure 16.2. Getting help.

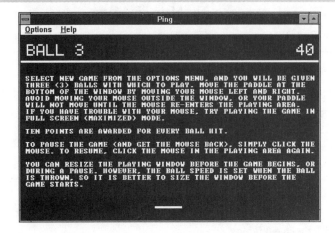

Hints

Okay, so it's obvious that video games have come a long way. Other than keeping your eye on the ball, keep these hints in mind:

➡ If you are having trouble hitting the ball, try this: always keep the paddle directly under the ball no matter where the ball is. Minimize the game screen, and watch the icon to see how this works.

➡ You might prefer to play the game on a full screen. This can be difficult, however, because the lack of window borders makes it hard to tell when the ball is going to bounce on the sides.

➡ Avoid sizing the playing area too narrow—unless you want a challenge. The ball changes direction frequently when it hits the sides often.

➡ Likewise, a short playing area may not give you enough time to get to the ball.

Programming

The makefile for Ping contains the files listed in Table 16.1.

Table 16.1. Ping source files.

Filename	Description
PGABOUT.FRM	The About box form
PGMAIN.FRM	The Main Ping form
PGGLOBAL.BAS	Global constants, variables, and procedures

NOTE

All these files listed in Table 16.1 are included on this book's disk. See Appendix A for installation instructions.

Figure 16.3 and Listing 16.1 show the PGABOUT form and source code. This form is the game's About box.

Figure 16.3. The PGABOUT form.

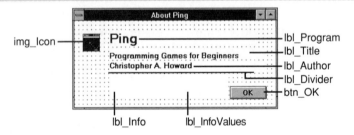

Listing 16.1. The PGABOUT form source code.

```
VERSION 2.00
Begin Form frm_AboutBox
   BorderStyle     =   3   'Fixed Double
   Caption         =   "About Ping"
   ClipControls    =   0   'False
   FontBold        =   -1  'True
   FontItalic      =   0   'False
   FontName        =   "System"
   FontSize        =   9.75
   FontStrikethru  =   0   'False
   FontUnderline   =   0   'False
   Height          =   2775
   Icon            =   0
   Left            =   1590
   MaxButton       =   0   'False
```

```
MinButton       =    0    'False
ScaleHeight     =    2370
ScaleWidth      =    5640
Top             =    1260
Width           =    5760
Begin CommandButton btn_OK
   Caption         =    "OK"
   FontBold        =    -1   'True
   FontItalic      =    0    'False
   FontName        =    "System"
   FontSize        =    9.75
   FontStrikethru  =    0    'False
   FontUnderline   =    0    'False
   Height          =    360
   Left            =    4350
   TabIndex        =    5
   Top             =    1800
   Width           =    1035
End
Begin Image img_Icon
   Height          =    480
   Left            =    240
   Picture         =    PGABOUT.FRX:0000 'PG.ICO
   Top             =    360
   Width           =    480
End
Begin Line lin_Divider
   BorderWidth     =    2
   X1              =    975
   X2              =    5010
   Y1              =    1425
   Y2              =    1425
End
Begin Label lbl_Program
   Caption         =    "Ping"
   FontBold        =    -1   'True
   FontItalic      =    0    'False
   FontName        =    "MS Sans Serif"
   FontSize        =    18
   FontStrikethru  =    0    'False
   FontUnderline   =    0    'False
   Height          =    450
   Left            =    990
   TabIndex        =    1
   Top             =    270
   Width           =    4065
End
Begin Label lbl_Title
   Caption         =    "Programming Games for Beginners"
   FontBold        =    -1   'True
   FontItalic      =    0    'False
```

continues

Listing 16.1. continued

```
    FontName         =     "MS Sans Serif"
    FontSize         =     9.75
    FontStrikethru   =     0     'False
    FontUnderline    =     0     'False
    Height           =     240
    Left             =     990
    TabIndex         =     2
    Top              =     840
    Width            =     4305
End
Begin Label lbl_Author
    Caption          =     "Christopher A. Howard"
    FontBold         =     -1    'True
    FontItalic       =     0     'False
    FontName         =     "MS Sans Serif"
    FontSize         =     9.75
    FontStrikethru   =     0     'False
    FontUnderline    =     0     'False
    Height           =     240
    Left             =     990
    TabIndex         =     3
    Top              =     1110
    Width            =     4365
End
Begin Label lbl_Info
    Height           =     600
    Left             =     1005
    TabIndex         =     4
    Top              =     1545
    Width            =     1875
End
Begin Label lbl_InfoValues
    Height           =     600
    Left             =     2880
    TabIndex         =     0
    Top              =     1545
    Width            =     1410
End
End
Option Explicit

' Windows API functions used
Declare Function GetFreeSpace Lib "Kernel" (ByVal wFlags%) As Long
Declare Function GetWinFlags Lib "Kernel" () As Long

' Windows constants used
Const WF_STANDARD = &H10
```

```
Const WF_ENHANCED = &H20
Const WF_80x87 = &H400

Sub btn_OK_Click ()

  ' We are done
  Unload Me

End Sub

Sub Form_Load ()

  Dim WinFlags&
  Dim Mode$, Processor$, CRLF$

  ' Center the AboutBox on the screen
  Move (Screen.Width - Width) \ 2, (Screen.Height - Height) \ 2

  ' Make it easier for strings
  CRLF$ = Chr$(13) + Chr$(10)

  ' Get current Windows configuration
  WinFlags& = GetWinFlags()

  ' Determine mode
  If (WinFlags& And WF_ENHANCED) Then
    Mode$ = "386 Enhanced Mode"
  Else
    Mode$ = "Standard Mode"
  End If

  ' Free memory
  lbl_Info.Caption = Mode$ + CRLF$ + "Free Memory:" + CRLF$ + "Math Co-
➥processor:"

  ' 80x87 math chip
  If (WinFlags& And WF_80x87) Then
    Processor$ = "Present"
  Else
    Processor$ = "None"
  End If

  ' Free space
  lbl_InfoValues.Caption = CRLF$ + Format$(GetFreeSpace(0) \ 1024) + " KB"
➥+ CRLF$ + Processor$

End Sub
```

Figure 16.4 and Listing 16.2 show the PGMAIN form and source code. This is the main form for the Ping game.

Figure 16.4. The PGMAIN form.

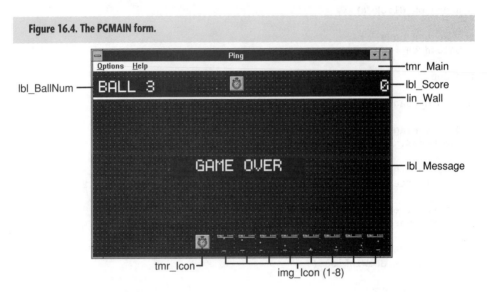

Listing 16.2. The PGMAIN form source code.

```
VERSION 2.00
Begin Form frm_Ping
    BackColor       =   &H00000000&
    Caption         =   "Ping"
    FillColor       =   &H00FFFFFF&
    FillStyle       =   0   'Solid
    FontBold        =   -1  'True
    FontItalic      =   0   'False
    FontName        =   "Terminal"
    FontSize        =   9
    FontStrikethru  =   0   'False
    FontUnderline   =   0   'False
    ForeColor       =   &H00FFFFFF&
    Height          =   5730
    Icon            =   PGMAIN.FRX:0000 'PG.ICO
    KeyPreview      =   -1  'True
    Left            =   1185
    LinkTopic       =   "Form1"
    ScaleHeight     =   336
    ScaleMode       =   3   'Pixel
    ScaleWidth      =   556
    Top             =   1320
    Width           =   8460
    Begin Timer tmr_Icon
       Left             =   192
       Top              =   296
    End
```

```
Begin Timer tmr_Main
   Left            =      256
   Top             =      8
End
Begin Image img_Icon
   Enabled         =      0       'False
   Height          =      480
   Index           =      8
   Left            =      7680
   Picture         =      PGMAIN.FRX:0302 'PG8.ICO
   Top             =      4440
   Visible         =      0       'False
   Width           =      480
End
Begin Image img_Icon
   Enabled         =      0       'False
   Height          =      480
   Index           =      7
   Left            =      7080
   Picture         =      PGMAIN.FRX:0604 'PG7.ICO
   Top             =      4440
   Visible         =      0       'False
   Width           =      480
End
Begin Image img_Icon
   Enabled         =      0       'False
   Height          =      480
   Index           =      6
   Left            =      6480
   Picture         =      PGMAIN.FRX:0906 'PG6.ICO
   Top             =      4440
   Visible         =      0       'False
   Width           =      480
End
Begin Image img_Icon
   Enabled         =      0       'False
   Height          =      480
   Index           =      5
   Left            =      5880
   Picture         =      PGMAIN.FRX:0C08 'PG5.ICO
   Top             =      4440
   Visible         =      0       'False
   Width           =      480
End
Begin Image img_Icon
   Enabled         =      0       'False
   Height          =      480
   Index           =      4
   Left            =      5280
   Picture         =      PGMAIN.FRX:0F0A 'PG4.ICO
   Top             =      4440
```

continues

Listing 16.2. continued

```
        Visible        =    0    'False
        Width          =    480
     End
     Begin Image img_Icon
        Enabled        =    0    'False
        Height         =    480
        Index          =    3
        Left           =    4680
        Picture        =    PGMAIN.FRX:120C 'PG3.ICO
        Top            =    4440
        Visible        =    0    'False
        Width          =    480
     End
     Begin Image img_Icon
        Enabled        =    0    'False
        Height         =    480
        Index          =    2
        Left           =    4080
        Picture        =    PGMAIN.FRX:150E 'PG2.ICO
        Top            =    4440
        Visible        =    0    'False
        Width          =    480
     End
     Begin Image img_Icon
        Enabled        =    0    'False
        Height         =    480
        Index          =    1
        Left           =    3480
        Picture        =    PGMAIN.FRX:1810 'PG1.ICO
        Top            =    4440
        Visible        =    0    'False
        Width          =    480
     End
     Begin Line lin_Wall
        BorderColor    =    &H00FFFFFF&
        BorderWidth    =    4
        X1             =    0
        X2             =    552
        Y1             =    48
        Y2             =    48
     End
     Begin Label lbl_Message
        Alignment      =    2 'Center
        BackColor      =    &H00000000&
        Caption        =    "GAME OVER"
        FontBold       =    -1 'True
        FontItalic     =    0  'False
        FontName       =    "Terminal"
        FontSize       =    18
        FontStrikethru =    0  'False
```

```
         FontUnderline   =   0    'False
         ForeColor       =   &H00FFFFFF&
         Height          =   495
         Left            =   2280
         TabIndex        =   2
         Top             =   2400
         Width           =   3615
      End
      Begin Label lbl_BallNum
         BackColor       =   &H00000000&
         Caption         =   "BALL 3"
         FontBold        =   -1   'True
         FontItalic      =   0    'False
         FontName        =   "Terminal"
         FontSize        =   18
         FontStrikethru  =   0    'False
         FontUnderline   =   0    'False
         ForeColor       =   &H00FFFFFF&
         Height          =   375
         Left            =   120
         TabIndex        =   1
         Top             =   240
         Width           =   2655
      End
      Begin Label lbl_Score
         Alignment       =   1    'Right Justify
         BackColor       =   &H00000000&
         Caption         =   "0"
         FontBold        =   -1   'True
         FontItalic      =   0    'False
         FontName        =   "Terminal"
         FontSize        =   18
         FontStrikethru  =   0    'False
         FontUnderline   =   0    'False
         ForeColor       =   &H00FFFFFF&
         Height          =   375
         Left            =   5640
         TabIndex        =   0
         Top             =   240
         Width           =   2655
      End
      Begin Menu mnu_Options
         Caption         =   "&Options"
         Begin Menu mnu_NewGame
            Caption      =   "&New Game"
         End
         Begin Menu mnu_Pause
            Caption      =   "&Pause"
         End
         Begin Menu mnu_ExitSep
            Caption      =   "-"
         End
```

continues

Listing 16.2. continued

```
      Begin Menu mnu_Exit
         Caption           =    "E&xit"
      End
   End
   Begin Menu mnu_Help
      Caption           =    "&Help"
      Begin Menu mnu_HowToPlay
         Caption           =    "&How to Play ..."
      End
      Begin Menu mnu_AboutSep
         Caption           =    "-"
      End
      Begin Menu mnu_About
         Caption           =    "&About Ping ..."
      End
   End
End

Option Explicit

'
' This procedure updates the player status (score, etc).
'
Sub DisplayStatus ()

  ' Display the number of lives left
  lbl_BallNum.Caption = "BALL" + Str$(BallNum%)

  ' Display the score
  lbl_Score.Caption = Str$(Score%)

End Sub

'
' This procedure ends the game.
'
Sub EndGame ()

  ' Stop the timer
  tmr_Main.Interval = 0

  ' Hide the ball
  HideBall

  ' Display "Game Over" message
  lbl_Message.Caption = "GAME OVER"
  lbl_Message.Visible = True

  ' Restore the mouse
  FreeMouse
```

```
  ' Game is over
  GameOver% = True

End Sub

Sub Form_Click ()

  ' Toggle the pause state
  If (Not GameOver%) Then
    mnu_Pause_Click
  Else
    Cls
  End If

End Sub

Sub Form_Load ()

  ' Center on the screen
  Move (screen.Width - Width) \ 2, (screen.Height - Height) \ 2

  ' Start with game over
  GameOver% = True

  ' Show About box
  frm_AboutBox.Show 1

End Sub

Sub Form_MouseMove (Button As Integer, Shift As Integer, x As Single, y As
➡Single)

  ' Hide the paddle
  HidePaddle

  ' Update the paddle position
  PadX% = x - (PadW% \ 2)

  ' Show the paddle
  ShowPaddle

End Sub

Sub Form_Resize ()

  ' Are we minimizing?
  If (WindowState = 1) Then
    ' Make sure game is paused, when minimizing
    If (mnu_Pause.Checked = False) Then
      ' Pause the game
      mnu_Pause_Click
    End If
```

continues

Listing 16.2. continued

```
        ' Begin changing the icon
      tmr_Icon.Interval = ICONINC
    Else
        ' Maximizing or Normal, so stop the icon timer
      tmr_Icon.Interval = 0
        ' Resize the screen
      ResizeScreen
        ' Draw the ball
      If (Not GameOver%) Then
        ShowBall
      End If
    End If
  End If

End Sub

'
' This function frees the mouse from our paddle.
'
Sub FreeMouse ()

    ' Clear the clipping region
    ClipCursorClear 0

    ' Show the mouse again
    ShowCursor True

End Sub

'
' This function grabs the mouse, so we can use just the paddle.
'
Sub GrabMouse ()

    Dim pt As APIPOINT
    Dim rect As APIRECT

    ' Get the upper-left corner of our screen area
    pt.x% = 0
    pt.y% = 0
    ClientToScreen hWnd, pt
    ' And store
    rect.x1% = pt.x%
    rect.Y1% = pt.y%

    ' Get the lower-right corner
    pt.x% = ScaleWidth
    pt.y% = ScaleHeight
    ClientToScreen hWnd, pt
    ' And store
    rect.X2% = pt.x%
    rect.y2% = pt.y%
```

```
  ' Restrict the mouse to our window
  ClipCursorRect rect

  ' Hide the mouse
  ShowCursor False

End Sub

'
' This procedure hides (erases) the ball.
'
Sub HideBall ()

  ' Erase the ball
  FillColor = BackColor
  Circle (BallX%, BallY%), BallR%, BackColor

End Sub

'
' This procedure hides (erases) the paddle.
'
Sub HidePaddle ()

  ' Erase the paddle
  Line (PadX%, PadY%)-Step(PadW%, PadD%), BackColor, BF

End Sub

'
' This procedure initializes all the game variables at the beginning
' of a new game.
'
Sub InitNewGame ()

  ' Get a new sequence of numbers
  Randomize

  ' Are we currently in a game?
  If (Not GameOver%) Then
    ' Yes, so end it
    EndGame
    ' And if it was paused, clear the menu item
    mnu_Pause.Checked = False
  End If

  ' Game is no longer over
  GameOver% = False

  ' Remove "Game Over" message
  lbl_Message.Visible = False
```

continues

Listing 16.2. continued

```
' Reset score
Score% = 0

' And the ball number
BallNum% = 1

' Reset the ball
ResetBall

' Make sure status is updated
DisplayStatus

' Delay (for effect, and for "Game Over" to disappear)
Delay 1

' Start the timer
tmr_Main.Interval = TIMERINC

' Grab the mouse to our paddle
GrabMouse

End Sub

Sub mnu_About_Click ()

  ' Show the About box
  frm_AboutBox.Show 1

End Sub

Sub mnu_Exit_Click ()

  ' Exit, so just unload the form
  Unload Me

End Sub

Sub mnu_HowToPlay_Click ()

  ' If we are in a game, pause it
  If (Not mnu_Pause.Checked) Then
    mnu_Pause_Click
  End If

  ' Hide the message
  lbl_Message.Visible = False

  ' Clear the screen, and wait
  Cls
  Delay 1
```

```
' Show the help
CurrentX = 0
CurrentY = WallY% + 20
Print " SELECT NEW GAME FROM THE OPTIONS MENU, AND YOU WILL BE GIVEN"
Print " THREE (3) BALLS WITH WHICH TO PLAY. MOVE THE PADDLE AT THE"
Print " BOTTOM OF THE WINDOW BY MOVING YOUR MOUSE LEFT AND RIGHT."
Print " AVOID MOVING YOUR MOUSE OUTSIDE THE WINDOW, OR YOUR PADDLE"
Print " WILL NOT MOVE UNTIL THE MOUSE RE-ENTERS THE PLAYING AREA."
Print " IF YOU HAVE TROUBLE WITH YOUR MOUSE, TRY PLAYING THE GAME IN"
Print " FULL SCREEN (MAXIMIZED) MODE."
Print
Print " TEN POINTS ARE AWARDED FOR EVERY BALL HIT."
Print
Print " TO PAUSE THE GAME (AND GET THE MOUSE BACK), SIMPLY CLICK THE"
Print " MOUSE. TO RESUME, CLICK THE MOUSE IN THE PLAYING AREA AGAIN."
Print
Print " YOU CAN RESIZE THE PLAYING WINDOW BEFORE THE GAME BEGINS, OR"
Print " DURING A PAUSE. HOWEVER, THE BALL SPEED IS SET WHEN THE BALL"
Print " IS THROWN, SO IT IS BETTER TO SIZE THE WINDOW BEFORE THE"
Print " GAME STARTS."

End Sub

Sub mnu_NewGame_Click ()

  ' Make sure the ball is hidden
  HideBall

  ' Start a new game
  InitNewGame

  ' If game is paused, unpause it
  If (mnu_Pause.Checked) Then
    mnu_Pause_Click
  End If

End Sub

Sub mnu_Pause_Click ()

  ' Is the game already over?
  If (Not GameOver%) Then

    ' Is the game already paused?
    If (mnu_Pause.Checked = True) Then
      ' Remove pause message
      lbl_Message.Visible = False
      ' Clear the screen (removes any help)
      Cls
      ' Restart the timer
      tmr_Main.Interval = TIMERINC
```

continues

Listing 16.2. continued

```
          ' Grab the mouse
          GrabMouse
       Else
          ' Suspend the timer
          tmr_Main.Interval = 0
          ' Free the mouse
          FreeMouse
          ' Display pause message
          lbl_Message.Caption = "PAUSED"
          lbl_Message.Visible = True
       End If

       ' Toggle the pause state
       mnu_Pause.Checked = Not mnu_Pause.Checked

    End If

End Sub

'
' This procedure moves the ball and updates its position.
'
Sub MoveBall ()

    ' Hide the ball
    HideBall

    ' Update the ball position
    BallX% = BallX% + XInc%
    BallY% = BallY% + YInc%

    ' Bounce against left wall?
    If (BallX% <= BallR%) Then
      BallX% = BallR%
      XInc% = -XInc%
      Beep
    End If

    ' Bounce against right wall?
    If (BallX% >= (ScaleWidth - BallR%)) Then
      BallX% = ScaleWidth - BallR%
      XInc% = -XInc%
      Beep
    End If

    ' Bounce against top?
    If (BallY% <= (WallY% + BallH% + 1)) Then
      BallY% = WallY% + BallH% + 1
      YInc% = -YInc%
      Beep
    End If
```

```
' Make sure the player hasn't missed already
If (Not Missed%) Then
  ' Bounce against paddle?
  If (BallY% >= (PadY% - BallH% - 1)) Then
    ' Did the paddle miss it?
    If ((BallX% + BallR% < PadX%) Or (BallX% - BallR% > (PadX% +
    ➥PADWIDTH)))
Then
      ' Player missed, so mark it for later
      Missed% = True
      ' Refresh paddle, in case the ball overlapped it
      ShowPaddle
    Else
      ' Paddle hit
      BallY% = PadY% - BallH% - 1
      YInc% = -YInc%
      Beep
      ' Bump score
      Score% = Score% + SCOREINC
    End If
  End If
Else
  ' They already missed, so refresh paddle
  ShowPaddle
  ' Is ball off screen yet?
  If (BallY% > ScaleHeight) Then
    ' Any balls left?
    If (BallNum% < MAXBALLS) Then
      ' Give them another ball
      BallNum% = BallNum% + 1
      ' And reset the ball
      ResetBall
    Else
      ' No balls, so game is over
      EndGame
    End If
  End If
End If

  ' Show the ball
  ShowBall

End Sub

'
' This procedure resets the ball at the beginning of a session.
'
Sub ResetBall ()

  ' Clear any help, etc.
  Cls
```

continues

Listing 16.2. continued

```
' Wait
Delay 1

' Display message
lbl_Message.Caption = "GET READY"
lbl_Message.Visible = True

' Place ball randomly at top of screen, down a ways
BallX% = GetRandom%(Int(ScaleWidth))
BallY% = WallY% + (4 * BallH%)

' Pick a trajectory (1% to 2% of width, 2% of height)
XInc% = (((GetRandom%(2) + 1) * ScaleWidth) \ 100)
YInc% = (2 * ScaleHeight) \ 100

' Player hasn't missed (yet!)
Missed% = False

' Delay for awhile more
Delay 1

' Hide message
lbl_Message.Visible = False

' Give the user even more time to get ready
Delay 1

End Sub

'
' This procedure sets up the scaling for the current screen size.
'
Sub ResizeScreen ()

    ' Clear old objects
    Cls

    ' Position top wall for bounce
    lin_Wall.X2 = ScaleWidth
    WallY% = lin_Wall.Y1 + lin_Wall.BorderWidth + 1

    ' Move score to right edge
    lbl_Score.Left = ScaleWidth - lbl_Score.Width - 10

    ' Center message
    lbl_Message.Left = (ScaleWidth - lbl_Message.Width) \ 2
    lbl_Message.Top = (ScaleHeight - lbl_Message.Height) \ 2

    ' Hide the paddle
    HidePaddle
```

```
 ' Width is 10% of screen width, and 1% of height
 PadW% = ScaleWidth / 10
 PadD% = ScaleHeight / 100
 ' Don't let depth get too big or too small
 If (PadD% < 2) Then
   PadD% = 2
 Else
   If (PadD% > PADDEPTH) Then
     PadD% = PADDEPTH
   End If
 End If
 ' Or width
 If (PadW% > PADWIDTH) Then
   PadW% = PADWIDTH
 End If
 ' Center it, and put it at the bottom
 PadX% = (ScaleWidth - PADWIDTH) \ 2
 PadY% = ScaleHeight - PADDLEY
 ' Show the results
 ShowPaddle

 ' Hide the ball
 HideBall
 ' Center it
 BallX% = ScaleWidth \ 2
 BallY% = ScaleHeight \ 2
 ' Size is paddle depth
 BallR% = (PadD% \ 2) + 1
 BallH% = BallR%
 ' Show it
 If (Not GameOver%) Then
   ShowBall
 End If

End Sub

'
' This procedure shows (draws) the ball.
'
Sub ShowBall ()

 ' Draw the ball
 FillColor = ForeColor
 Circle (BallX%, BallY%), BallR%, ForeColor

End Sub

'
' This procedure shows (draws) the paddle.
'
Sub ShowPaddle ()
```

continues

Listing 16.2. continued

```
    ' Draw the paddle
    Line (PadX%, PadY%)-Step(PadW%, PadD%), ForeColor, BF

End Sub

Sub tmr_Icon_Timer ()

  ' Update the icon number
  IconNum% = IconNum% + 1
  If (IconNum% > MAXICON) Then
    IconNum% = 1
  End If

  ' Display it
  frm_Ping.Icon = img_Icon(IconNum%).Picture

End Sub

Sub tmr_Main_Timer ()

  ' Move the ball
  MoveBall

  ' Display status info
  DisplayStatus

End Sub
```

Listing 16.3 shows the PGGLOBAL.BAS source code. This file contains the global constants and variables for Ping.

Listing 16.3. The PGGLOBAL.BAS source code.

```
Option Explicit

' Paddle size
Global Const PADWIDTH = 50
Global Const PADDEPTH = 5

' Wall size
Global Const WALLDEPTH = 5

' Maximum number of balls
Global Const MAXBALLS = 3

' Paddle information
Global Const PADDLEY = 25
```

```
' Timers
Global Const TIMERINC = 40
Global Const ICONINC = 250

' Score
Global Const SCOREINC = 10

' Number of icons
Global Const MAXICON = 8

' Player score
Global Score%

' Current ball number
Global BallNum%

' Player missed flag
Global Missed%

' Ball statistics
Global BallX%, BallY%
Global BallR%, BallH%
Global XInc%, YInc%

' Paddle statistics
Global PadX%, PadY%, PadW%, PadD%

' Top wall
Global WallY%

' Icon
Global IconNum%

' Game over flag
Global GameOver%

' Point type
Type APIPOINT
  x As Integer
  y As Integer
End Type

' Rectangle type
Type APIRECT
  x1 As Integer
  y1 As Integer
  x2 As Integer
  y2 As Integer
End Type
```

continues

Listing 16.3. continued

```
' Windows Functions
Declare Sub ClientToScreen Lib "User" (ByVal hWnd%, Pt As APIPOINT)
Declare Sub ShowCursor Lib "User" (ByVal bShow%)
Declare Sub ClipCursorRect Lib "User" Alias "ClipCursor" (Rect As APIRECT)
Declare Sub ClipCursorClear Lib "User" Alias "ClipCursor" (ByVal Rect&)

'

' This procedure delays the given number of seconds,
' which can be fractional.
'

Sub Delay (secs!)

  Dim Start!

  ' Get the current seconds since midnight
  Start! = Timer

  ' Wait for seconds to elapse
  While (Timer < (Start! + secs!))
    ' Let other things run while we wait
    DoEvents
  Wend

End Sub

'

' This function returns a random number between 0 and range%-1, inclusive.
'

Function GetRandom% (range%)

  ' In the Visual Basic manual, the generic formula is:
  ' Int((upperbound-lowerbound+1)*Rnd+lowerbound)
  GetRandom% = Int(range% * Rnd)

End Function
```

Form Overview

Unlike some of this book's other games, Ping includes only two forms—one of those is the standard About box; the other is the main Ping form. The following is a brief discussion about the forms and their controls. Consult the form figures for additional information.

About Box

The PGABOUT form is my standard About box form. I set the label to Ping and the image to PG.ICO. For a full description of this form, see Chapter 10, "Apples & Oranges."

Global

The PGGLOBAL basic file contains the global variable and constant definitions. It also contains the global procedures Delay and GetRandom.

The Main Form

The PGMAIN form is the main form for the game.

There are three labels: lbl_BallNum, lbl_Score, and lbl_Message. As their names imply, these labels display the current ball number, the current score, and any message (such as GET READY and GAME OVER).

There are two timer controls: tmr_Main and tmr_Icon. The main timer controls the ball movement, and the icon timer controls the icon animation when Ping's screen is minimized. The img_Icon control array contains the images for the animated icon.

Finally, the lin_Wall object forms the top wall that the ball bounces against.

Programming Overview

The Ping program is simple in theory, but it does include several new game concepts. It differs from this book's other board and card games, because it's more dynamic. It demonstrates Visual Basic's drawing functions, object and icon animation, coordinate scaling, and collision detection.

Creating the Images

This game requires no images—the ball and paddle are drawn dynamically. I created the icons for the main program and animation in IconWorks.

There aren't any tricks in creating the artwork for animation frames quickly (even for small icons). I wanted the animation to loop without an obvious break, so I had to get the ball spacing right. I began by drawing eight ball positions on a single icon. This helped me visualize the trajectory and select the ball positions appropriately.

After I had created this single icon, I saved it into a temporary icon file. Creating the individual icons consisted of loading the temporary icon, erasing the seven balls I didn't need, and drawing the paddle underneath the remaining ball. This resulted in the eight icons shown on the form.

Program Flow

When the game runs, the program flows as follows:

➡ When the main form is loaded, it is centered and the About box is displayed. The game is declared over by setting the GameOver% flag.

➡ The player begins a new game by selecting New Game from the Options menu. The mnu_NewGame_Click routine initializes a new game by calling InitNewGame.

➡ The InitNewGame procedure randomizes the number generator and ends any current game. It starts a new game by resetting the GameOver% flag, setting the score to zero, and resetting the ball with ResetBall. The status (ball count and score) is displayed, the main timer set, and the mouse is captured to the paddle. Whew!

➡ The game is now controlled by the tmr_Main_Timer and Form_MouseMove routines. The timer updates the ball with the MoveBall function, and the mouse movements control the paddle.

➡ MoveBall hides the ball, moves the position, and checks to see whether the ball hits the left, right, or top wall—each side changes the ball direction. If the ball is at the bottom of the window, it must be hit by the paddle. A missed ball leads to a new ball with ResetBall. If no balls remain, EndGame is called.

➡ During the game, you can pause by selecting Pause from the Options menu or by clicking the left mouse button. mnu_Pause_Click (called by Form_Click) pauses the game by stopping the timer and freeing the mouse. It also unpauses the game by starting the timer again.

➡ When the player resizes the screen during the game, the resizing is handled by Form_Resize. When the game is completely minimized or restored, the game logic is affected. If minimized, the game pauses and the icon timer begins. The icon timer cycles through the img_Icon control array for the icon animation. When the game is restored, the icon timer is disabled.

➡ Play continues until the player misses three balls—at which point the EndGame routine is called. EndGame stops the main timer, displays the GAME OVER message, and sets the GameOver% flag.

You can view the game rules and the About box by selecting the Help menu options. These options display frm_AboutBox and call the mnu_HowToPlay function.

Techniques Used

The Ping game includes several new game concepts that I outline in the following sections.

Object Animation

I used the Visual Basic Line and Circle drawing commands to draw the paddle and the ball. The HidePaddle function draws the paddle using the background color of the form—which effectively erases the paddle. The ShowPaddle function uses the foreground color to draw, making the paddle appear. The HideBall and ShowBall functions work in the same manner.

The HidePaddle and ShowPaddle functions are very short. I could have used the Line and Circle commands directly, but using functions has several advantages. When designing the game, I wasn't sure which animation method would produce the best results. Having specific functions enabled me to change the animation algorithms in one place—without having to hunt through the code for drawing commands. These functions also make the code more readable.

At first, I tried using the XOR animation technique (which I covered in Chapter 4, "Animation"). This led to some problems, however. The technique works fine for moving the ball and paddle. A problem occurs, however, when another window is moved over the Ping window. Remember that with XOR animation, you draw the object to make it appear, and draw it again to make it disappear. When the window is moved away from Ping (or Ping is brought to the front), the HideBall function draws with XOR to hide the ball—but there isn't a ball to hide. I hadn't drawn the ball, because the other window was in the way. With no ball to hide, the ball gets displayed instead of hidden! The XOR animation method expects the previous object to be there—otherwise, it doesn't work. Confused? Modify HideBall and ShowBall so they use XOR animation, and experiment with it yourself.

With the hide and show functions, you can easily move objects. The ball movement is tied to a timer, so it moves a given amount every so many milliseconds. The ball changes direction when it collides with a wall or the paddle (see the following explanation about collision detection). The timer calls the MoveBall function, which handles everything. The paddle is tied to the mouse, so right and left mouse movements move the paddle. Getting the mouse pointer out of the way is another trick (see the explanation about Mouse Capture).

Another important point concerns the frm_Ping AutoRedraw property. When set to True, it causes all drawings to be written both to the screen and to a graphics bitmap in memory. The memory bitmap repaints the form when necessary. Visual Basic refers to this as *persistent graphics,* because the graphics don't have to be completely redrawn when the window is repainted—they persist. This is a nice feature for some applications, but not for Ping. The ball is moved very often, and it takes too long for the memory bitmap to be updated each time. The ball and paddle animation would slow to a crawl. Set the AutoRedraw property to True, and see how slow the movements are.

Icon Animation

Another form of animation illustrated in Ping is Icon Animation. The hardest part of animating an icon (or any form of bitmap animation) is creating the icon images. I explained this earlier in the chapter (see the "Creating the Images" section and Chapter 4, "Animation").

When you have images, you need a timer (tmr_Icon). It's important that you start with the timer interval at zero, because you'll want the icon animated only when the game is minimized. How can you detect when the game is minimized? In the Form_Resize function, check the WindowState property:

```
' Are we minimizing?
If (WindowState = 1) Then
  ' Make sure game is paused, when minimizing
  If (mnu_Pause.Checked = False) Then
    ' Pause the game
    mnu_Pause_Click
  End If
  ' Begin changing the icon
  tmr_Icon.Interval = ICONINC
Else
  ' Maximizing or Normal, so stop the icon timer
  tmr_Icon.Interval = 0
  ' Resize the screen
  ResizeScreen
  ' Draw the ball
  If (Not GameOver%) Then
    ShowBall
  End If
End If
```

The tmr_Icon_Timer function gets control every timer interval. Animating the icon becomes a matter of cycling through the icon array, img_Icon:

```
' Update the icon number
IconNum% = IconNum% + 1
If (IconNum% > MAXICON) Then
  IconNum% = 1
End If

' Display it
frm_Ping.Icon = img_Icon(IconNum%).Picture
```

Notice (in the preceding code) how the icon timer stops when the game is maximized again.

A Mouse Trap

The mouse movement is monitored with the `Form_MouseMove` function, which moves the paddle. Unfortunately, the actual mouse cursor is still visible (which is distracting). However, a function in Windows, called `ShowCursor` (declared in `PGGLOBAL.BAS`) solves this problem:

```
Declare Sub ShowCursor Lib "User" (ByVal bShow%)
```

The `ShowCursor` function enables you to show or hide the mouse cursor whenever you want. This solves one problem and causes another.

> Be careful with the `ShowCursor` function! If you use the Visual Basic End menu option or Stop icon when the cursor is hidden, it will remain hidden. In fact, you'll have to quit Windows to get the cursor back. Mouse Hide and Show commands must be paired together. In Ping, make sure you end or pause the game before using Visual Basic menu commands.

When the mouse is hidden, the pointer can easily be moved outside the game window. When that happens, the Ping game stops receiving mouse movement messages—and the paddle stops moving. You can imagine how frustrating that would be for the player. You need to restrict the mouse to within the window. This can be accomplished with one Windows API function:

```
Declare Sub ClipCursorRect Lib "User" Alias "ClipCursor" (Rect As APIRECT)
Declare Sub ClipCursorClear Lib "User" Alias "ClipCursor" (ByVal Rect&)
```

You're thinking, "I thought he said one function." That function is `ClipCursor`. I declared two variations of it, because you have to pass a null pointer (zero) in order to restore the cursor area. Null pointers are easy to do in C but difficult in Basic—hence the two versions of the same function. Declaring two versions makes the code more readable anyway.

The rectangular region required by `ClipCursorRect` consists of the physical screen pixel coordinates. To get that region, you need one more Windows function:

```
Declare Sub ClientToScreen Lib "User" (ByVal hWnd%, Pt As APIPOINT)
```

The `ClientToScreen` function converts a client (window) coordinate to a physical screen coordinate. The `GrabMouse` function gets the window coordinates for the upper-left and lower-right corners, then calls `ClipCursorRect`. When the mouse is restricted to moving within the window, you can hide it without worrying about the pointer leaving the game window (and freezing the game paddle). `FreeMouse` calls `ClipCursorClear` to remove the movement restriction and redesign the mouse pointer. Neat, huh?

Coordinate Scaling

The main Ping form (`frm_Ping`) uses a `ScaleMode` of 3 (Pixel). This ensures that the `ScaleHeight` and `ScaleWidth` properties represent true pixel values. This is important when detecting when the ball hits the sides, the top, or the paddle.

I attempted to use a `ScaleMode` of 0 (User) at one point during the game development. My reasoning was that I could set the `ScaleHeight` and `ScaleWidth` properties to constant values (such as 500 by 300). I could scale the window to any size and not affect the code. This worked, but it wreaked havoc with the collision detection.

As the ball moved across the window, its physical radius (in pixels) varied, depending on its location. I had to know the exact ball radius to detect a collision, and because the ball radius varied, my calculations were inaccurate. This inaccuracy allowed the ball to occasionally overlap the top wall and paddle. The overlap appeared as "bites" on the wall and paddle (caused when the ball was erased).

It took me awhile to understand what was happening. Finally, I commented out the `HideBall` routine and played the game for a few seconds. When I pressed the PrtScr key, the current screen copied to the Windows clipboard. I pasted the screen to Paintbrush and zoomed in. Sure enough—the ball size varied as it moved.

Thankfully, using pixel coordinates solves the varying ball size problem.

Collision Detection

The collision detection in Ping is simplified. The `MoveBall` routine handles all the detection. The ball position is incremented and checked against the wall values. To hit the left wall, the ball edge must be negative (left of zero). To hit the right wall, the edge must be greater than `ScaleWidth`. In either case, the ball X increment is negated. So, the ball starts traveling in the opposite direction. For the top wall, the idea is the same. If the ball is past the top wall Y position, the Y direction changes.

The collision with the paddle becomes more complicated. When the ball is beyond the paddle Y position, `MoveBall` checks to see whether the ball is between the paddle's left and right edges. If so, the ball gets hit and its direction changes. If not, it's registered as a miss. For effect, the ball travels off the screen when it's missed.

> I disuss more about collision detection in Chapter 4, "Animation," and in Chapter 17, "Bricks."

Sound

This game doesn't have a lot of sound, but it has an appropriate ping! Every time the ball hits a wall or the paddle, the Beep function is called. Normally, this causes the PC speaker to beep. However, you can use the Windows Control Panel Sound feature (in Windows Setup) to assign a new sound. I assigned Default Beep to DING.WAV, because I have a Sound Blaster on my system which gives a much nicer ping sound. Alternatively, you can use the SndPlaySound function described in Chapter 5, "Sound Generation," to explicitly play the DING.WAV file.

There are many sound packages available for Windows that enable you to set almost any kind of sound to Windows events. If you have one of them, play around with some different Default Beep sounds. Some of them can be pretty interesting!

Data Organization

The global variables include the score (Score%), the current ball number (BallNum%), and the player missed flag (Missed%). The ball statistics (BallX%, BallY%, BallR%, BallH%, XInc%, and YInc%) keep track of the ball position, size, and increment. Likewise, the paddle statistics (PadX%, PadY%, PadW%, and PadD%) keep track of the paddle. Rounding it out, the final variables are the wall position (WallY%), the current icon animation frame number (IconNum%), and the game over flag (GameOver%).

Constants are also used, when appropriate, to define widths and depths of objects, minimums and maximums, and standard increments.

Summary

I have covered the following important programming points:

➡ You can draw and animate simple objects using the Visual Basic drawing commands. You can use the AutoRedraw property to make drawings persist, but this can slow down animation considerably.

➡ Icons can be animated easily—you'll need artwork and a timer. You can detect a minimized window (in the Form_Resize procedure) by examining the WindowState property.

➡ With the help of Windows API, the mouse can be hidden and restricted to your window.

➡ Pixel coordinate scaling is probably best for most dynamic games, but other coordinate scaling (such as User) can also be useful.

➡ Collision detection doesn't have to be complicated. And it really doesn't get much harder, as you'll see in Chapter 17, "Bricks."

➡ Sound output is performed by the Beep function and customized with the Windows Control Panel.

Suggestions for Improvement

The following suggestions are ideas for enhancing Ping.

➡ Change the ball direction. The farther the ball hits from the middle of the paddle, the more you can angle the ball outward. Adding this feature would allow the player to influence the ball direction.

➡ Add a menu option that controls the maximum speed of the ball. You can do this with the ResetBall routine.

➡ Add a menu option for turning the sound on or off.

➡ Allow cursor keys to control the paddle.

➡ Animate the About box icon like the main form icon.

➡ Give the player more balls for every 1000 points (or something similar).

➡ Add some "bricks" to the game. Read Chapter 17, "Bricks," where I explain just that!

What's Ahead

Ping is a nice start, but it could be jazzed up a little. In the next chapter, I explain how to build on the Ping game by adding some bricks. I also describe how to perform more advanced collision detection. If you have a few quarters left, bring them to the next chapter.

Bricks

Bricks is a computer game similar to the arcade games Pong and Break-Out. In this chapter, I describe how to play Bricks, offer some hints, and cover the game's programming. I also provide a full description of the techniques used. You will learn about

- ➡ Modifying an existing game into a new game

- ➡ Using the Visual Basic drawing functions

- ➡ Animation (moving objects)

- ➡ Calling the Windows API

- ➡ Hiding, showing, and restricting the mouse cursor

- ➡ Coordinate scaling

- ➡ Collision detection

Background

Bricks is my variation of Break-Out. Break-Out was an attempt to make the game of Pong more interesting. Rows of "bricks" are added to the top of the game arena, giving the ball something more to bounce against. The bricks are also colorful, and when the ball hits a brick, it is destroyed. Many variations of this game have appeared over the years, such as the popular game Arkanoid.

Gameplay

Bricks is a one-player game. The object is to keep hitting a moving ball with your paddle and to destroy all the bricks at the top of the game screen. The ball bounces off the walls and the bricks, and when you hit a brick, the brick is destroyed. When all of the bricks have been hit, you advance to the next level—where you'll find more bricks! When you miss, the ball stops (although you get three balls a game).

Running Bricks

To begin playing Bricks, select the Bricks icon from the program group you installed. See Appendix A for installation instructions. The file BRICKS.EXE contains the game. When you run the game, you'll see the About box first. Click OK, and Bricks appears.

Playing a Game

From the Options menu, select New Game. A GET READY message flashes on the screen, and the first ball is served. Move the mouse right and left to move the game paddle. You get 10 points every time you hit the ball. You also get 10 points for every blue brick you hit, 20 points for each green brick, and 30 points for each red brick. Figure 17.1 shows a game in progress.

Figure 17.1. Playing a game of Bricks.

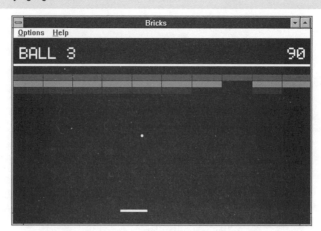

Every time you clear all the bricks, you get a 1,000 point bonus and a new set of bricks.

To pause the game, click the left mouse button. The ball freezes in position, and the mouse cursor appears. A PAUSED message shows on-screen.

You get three balls, and the game continues until you miss three times. You can change the size of the playing area by sizing the Bricks window (just grab a corner of the window and drag it with the mouse). It's best to resize before you begin a new game, but you can adjust the size during a pause. You might want to play the game on a full screen (maximize the window).

To get help, select How To Play from the Help menu. The game screen clears and displays the game help (see Figure 17.2). If you have resized the playing area to a smaller size, you may need to resize the window to see all the help text.

Figure 17.2. Getting help.

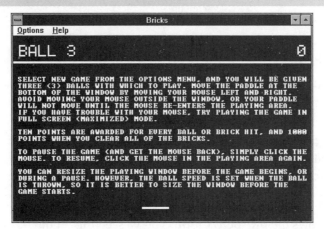

Hints

Other than keeping your eye on the ball, keep these hints in mind (most are the same as in the Ping game):

➡ If you are having trouble hitting the ball, try this: always keep the paddle directly under the ball no matter where the ball is. To see how this works, minimize the Ping game and watch the animated icon.

➡ You may prefer playing the game on a full screen. However, this can be difficult, because the lack of window borders makes it hard to tell when the ball is going to bounce on the sides.

➡ Avoid sizing the playing area too narrow—unless you want a challenge. The ball changes direction frequently when it hits the sides often.

➡ Also, a short playing area may not give you enough time to get to the ball!

➡ You can destroy a lot of bricks if you clear a path through the bricks and get the ball behind a row. You don't have a lot of control over making this happen, but it's something to hope for!

Programming

The makefile for Bricks contains the files listed in Table 12.1.

Table 17.1. Bricks source files.

Filename	Description
BRABOUT.FRM	The About box form
BRMAIN.FRM	The Main Bricks form
BRGLOBAL.BAS	Global constants, variables, and procedures

All these files are included in this book's disk. See Appendix A for installation instructions.

Figure 17.3 shows the BRABOUT form. You've seen this About box form often.

Figure 17.3. The BRABOUT form.

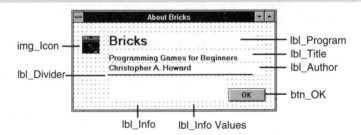

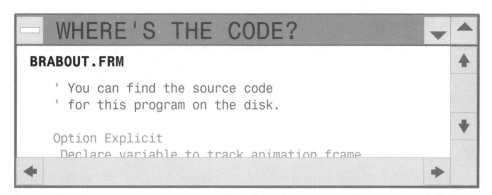

Figure 17.4 shows the BRMAIN form. This is the main game screen for the Bricks game.

Figure 17.4. The BRMAIN form.

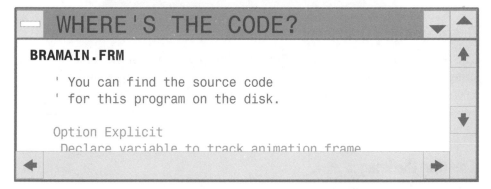

Form Overview

Like Ping, Bricks has only two forms—one is the standard About box—the other is the Main Bricks form. The following is a brief discussion of the forms and their controls. The forms closely match the Ping forms, so if you studied those, you might want to skip this overview. Consult the previous form figures for additional information.

About Box

The BRABOUT form is the standard About box form. I set the label to Bricks and the image to BR.ICO. For a full description of the form, see Chapter 10, "Apples & Oranges."

Global

The BRGLOBAL basic file contains the global variable and constant definitions. It also contains the global procedures Delay and GetRandom.

The Main Form

The BRMAIN form is the main form for the game, as its name implies. There are several controls on the main form.

There are three labels: lbl_BallNum, lbl_Score, and lbl_Message. As their names imply, they display the current ball number, the current score, and any message (such as GET READY and GAME OVER).

There is one timer control: tmr_Main (there is no icon timer, like there is in Ping). This main timer controls the ball movement, collision detection, and more.

Finally, the lin_Wall object forms the top wall that the ball bounces against.

Programming Overview

The Bricks program is similar to Ping, so it includes many of the same programming concepts. I touch briefly on those concepts here. The biggest addition, however, is the collision detection involved with the ball and the bricks—so if you read Chapter 16, "Ping," you may want to skip ahead to the section about collision detection.

Creating the Images

This game doesn't require images—the ball, paddle, and bricks are drawn dynamically. I created the icons for the main program in IconWorks.

Program Flow

When the game runs, the program flows as follows:

▶ When the main form is loaded, it is centered and the About box is displayed. The bricks are reset (redrawn), and the game is declared over with the GameOver% flag.

▶ The player begins by selecting New Game from the Options menu. The mnu_NewGame_Click routine initializes a new game by calling InitNewGame.

▶ The InitNewGame procedure randomizes the number generator and ends any current game. It starts a new game by resetting the GameOver% flag, setting the score to zero, and resetting the bricks and the ball with ResetBricks and ResetBall. The status is displayed (balls remaining and score), the main timer set, and the mouse captured to the paddle.

▶ Now, the game is controlled by the tmr_Main_Timer and Form_MouseMove routines. The timer updates the ball with the MoveBall function, and the mouse movements control the paddle.

▶ MoveBall hides the ball, moves the position, and then checks to see whether the ball hits the left, right, or top wall—each change the ball direction. MoveBall also checks for brick hits with the TestBricks function. When the ball is at the bottom of the window, it must be hit by the paddle. If missed, and any balls are left, ResetBall initiates a new ball. If no balls remain, EndGame is called.

▶ During the game, the player can pause by selecting Pause from the Options menu. He or she also can click either mouse button. The mnu_Pause_Click routine (called by Form_Click) pauses the game by stopping the timer and freeing the mouse. It also unpauses the game by starting the timer again.

▶ You can resize the game area during the game using Form_Resize. The game logic is affected when the game is completely minimized or restored, however. When the screen is minimized, the game is paused, and when the screen is restored, the player must unpause the game to continue playing.

▶ Play continues until the player misses three balls. Then, the EndGame routine is called. EndGame stops the main timer, displays the GAME OVER message, and sets the GameOver% flag.

You can view the game rules and the About box by selecting menu options. These options display frm_AboutBox and call the mnu_HowToPlay function.

Techniques Used

The Bricks game includes several game concepts that I cover in the following sections.

Object Animation

The Visual Basic `Line` and `Circle` drawing commands are used to draw the paddle and the ball (as they are in Ping). The `Line` command is also used to draw the bricks. Remember that the `Line` command enables you to draw a filled box when you use the `BF` (Box Fill) parameter.

A Mouse Trap

The mouse is trapped (as in Ping) when Windows API calls `ShowCursor` and `ClipCursor`. See Chapter 16, "Ping," for a complete description.

Coordinate Scaling

The main Bricks form (`frm_Bricks`) uses a `ScaleMode` of 3 (Pixel). This ensures that the `ScaleHeight` and `ScaleWidth` properties represent true pixel values. This is important when detecting whether the ball hits a side wall, the bricks, or the paddle.

Collision Detection

The collision detection in Bricks is more robust than it is in Ping. I test for collision against the walls in the same manner, but having bricks adds a degree of complication.

I admit that I thought it was going to be a piece of cake to add bricks to the Ping game framework. Although Bricks is very similar to Ping, I included the Ping game framework because of the brick collision detection and logic.

Collision detection determines whether two objects overlap. In Bricks, it looks for the overlap of the ball with a brick. To simplify matters, the ball is treated as a square and serves as a rectangular region (comparable with a brick). The function `Overlap%` (which is the function carrying out the collision detection algorithm) does the work for you.

It's a common mistake to write a collision detection function so that it tests whether any part of a rectangular region lies within the other region. This involves many conditionals and gets kind of messy. The elegant (and faster) solution is to determine whether the regions lie completely outside of each other—if they don't, they have to overlap. There is a subtle difference between the testing (inside or outside), but it is an important one. The test to determine the overlapping regions can be performed in one IF statement.

Detecting the collision was easy, so I thought adding the bricks to the game would be easy. I was wrong.

Which Way Do I Go?

The ball can hit the brick on four different sides (unlike the walls and the paddle which are hit on one side). The ball also travels two directions for each side. So, there are eight conditions to handle (see Figure 17.5).

Figure 17.5. Bouncing off a brick.

Fortunately, these eight conditions can be combined and simplified. When the ball collides with the brick (any side), the direction simply changes. The TestBricks code handles all of the conditions. First, TestBricks looks at whether the ball is moving left or right. After that, the function tests whether the ball is moving up or down. Finally, TestBricks decides what action to take. The logic from the TestBricks code is as follows:

```
' Overlaps, so determine new direction
Select Case ix%
  Case -1
    ' Going left--did it hit right side?
    If (Col% <> BRICKCOLS) Then
      ' Brick is not last in row, so make sure no brick to right
      If (((x% + BallR%) > (Col% * BrickW%)) And (Not Brick%(Row%, Col% +
      ➥1))) Then
        ' Yes
        XInc% = -XInc%
      Else
        'No
        YInc% = -YInc%
      End If
    Else
      ' Can't hit from right, since rightmost brick
      YInc% = -YInc%
    End If
```

continues

```
Case 1
  ' Going right--did it hit left side?
  If (Col% <> 1) Then
    ' Brick is not first, so make sure no brick to left
    If (((x% - BallR%) < ((Col% - 1) * BrickW%)) And (Not Brick%(Row%,
➥Col% - 1))) Then
      ' Yes
      XInc% = -XInc%
    Else
      ' No
      YInc% = -YInc%
    End If
  Else
    ' Can't hit from left, since leftmost brick
    YInc% = -YInc%
  End If
End Select
```

To make sure the ball hits the brick without skipping past a corner, the MoveBall function steps the ball one pixel at a time when it is near a brick. It continues from its last move to its new destination.

Hitting All the Bricks

While I was writing the game, I worried that the ball would not hit all the bricks. I pictured the player sitting there, hitting the ball over and over, and waiting for it to hit the last couple of bricks. Amazingly, this never happens (at least not in all the games I've played). In fact, I've rarely had to hit the ball more than a few times, even with one brick left.

There are several reasons why all bricks are cleared. The ball bounces off of the various bricks in the game, which continually changes the ball's path. As the ball travels along the new path, it will encounter more bricks. The bricks are also wide enough that the ball eventually collides with them. Finally, the trajectory of the ball carries it through two to four brick positions every time the ball heads toward the top wall and back.

The smaller the brick, the more likely the chance the ball has of missing it. A solution is to give the user the ability to change the ball direction. See the Suggestions for Improvement at the end of the chapter.

Sound

There isn't a lot of sound in this game. As in Ping, the Beep function is used. You might want to add sound support (as shown in Chapter 4, "Sound Generation") so that each row of bricks has a different tone.

Data Organization

The global variables include the score (Score%), the current ball number (BallNum%), and the player missed flag (Missed%). The ball statistics (BallX%, BallY%, BallR%, BallH%, XInc%, and YInc%) keep track of the ball position, size, and increment. Likewise, the paddle statistics (PadX%, PadY%, PadW%, and PadD%) keep track of the paddle. The other variables are the wall position (WallY%), and the game over flag (GameOver%).

From Ping, I added the Brick statistics (BrickW% and BrickD%) and the brick array Brick%(BRICKROWS, BRICKCOLS). The brick array records whether a brick is visible or not.

Constants also are used (when appropriate) to define widths and depths of objects, minimums and maximums, and standard increments.

Summary

I have covered the following important programming points:

◆ You can draw and animate simple objects with the Visual Basic drawing commands.

◆ With the help of Windows API, the mouse can be hidden and restricted to your window.

◆ Pixel coordinate scaling is fine for most dynamic games, but other coordinate scaling (such as User) can be useful.

◆ Collision detection doesn't have to be complicated. The Overlap% function detects whether two rectangular objects overlap (collide). Figuring out what to do after detecting a collision is usually harder than doing the actual collision test itself!

◆ Sound output can be performed by the Beep function and customized with the Windows Control Panel.

Suggestions for Improvement

The following suggestions are ideas for enhancing Bricks:

◆ Make the direction of the ball depend on where the ball hits the paddle. The farther the ball hits from the middle of the paddle, the more it angles outward. This would let the player influence the ball direction.

◆ Add a Catch feature, enabling the player to catch the ball (by holding the right mouse button down, perhaps). The ball could stick to the paddle, and the user could let it go as well.

➡ Add a menu option (using the ResetBall routine) that controls the maximum speed of the ball.

➡ Add a menu option for turning the sound on or off.

➡ Allow the cursor keys to control the paddle.

➡ Animate the Bricks icon like the Ping game.

➡ Animate the bricks themselves! Make them change colors, shapes, or positions.

➡ Give the player more balls for every 1,000 points (or something similar).

➡ Add another row of bricks for every new level (or every so many levels).

➡ Add a kid level, making the size of the ball much larger. (My kids love it.) Doing so involves changing the BallR% and BallH% variables (assign them a larger number, like 10).

➡ Add a High Score option.

What's Ahead

I've now covered two of the first commercial arcade games, which I have named Ping and Bricks. Our last game is ahead—complete with joystick support, wave files (lasers and explosions), animation, and sprites. Put your space suit on and meet me on deck 18...er, Chapter 18...for a true arcade adventure!

Space Miner

Space Miner is a one-player computer game similar to arcade games (such as Galaga). In this chapter, I describe how to play Space Miner, offer some hints, and cover the game's programming. I also provide a full description of the techniques used. You will learn about

- ➡ Animating sprites
- ➡ Animating icons
- ➡ Creating infinitely scrolling images
- ➡ Playing MIDI sound files
- ➡ Playing Wave sound files
- ➡ Marking time
- ➡ Calling the Windows API
- ➡ Detecting collisions
- ➡ Using the joystick
- ➡ Reading and writing to WIN.INI

Background

Space Miner isn't a variation of any one specific arcade game. It represents the graphical arcade games such as Galaga and even Pac-Man. Many objects are animated and move around the screen simultaneously. If you have a sound card (or at least the PC Speaker Wave file driver), you'll be able to hear background music, laser blasts, and explosions too!

Gameplay

Space Miner is a one-player game in which you maneuver a mining ship through space. Your mission is to gather (mine) ore, which is in abundant supply in the Mega-Ore system. Unfortunately, an evil regime has declared the ore its own— even though your family has mined it for generations. You boldly ignore the regime's claim and mine the ore anyway. In the process, you must avoid alien drones and their deadly lasers and try to meet your ore quota. Luckily, you're equipped with ammunition, even though it's limited.

Running Space Miner

To begin playing Space Miner, select the Space Miner icon from the program group you installed. See Appendix A for installation instructions. The file MINER.EXE contains the game. When you run the game, you'll see the About box first. Click OK, and Space Miner appears.

Because of the intense use of graphics, Space Miner requires a 386 (or higher) computer running at 33MHz or more. You can play the game on slower systems, but the game's speed might not be acceptable. The use of an accelerator card or fast display driver also will improve the game speed. If you are low on memory, close any other applications while you play Space Miner.

Playing a Game

From the Options menu, select Joystick (if you have one). This enables you to use the joystick while playing Space Miner. If you don't have a joystick, use the keyboard cursor keys (left, right, up, and down arrows). Now, select New Game. If you have a Musical Instrument Digital Interface (MIDI) compatible sound card, you should hear background music playing.

You might have to run the MIDI Mapper application from the Windows Control Panel to set up your MIDI board. I have a Sound Blaster, and I had to select the "Adlib General" mapping before I could hear anything.

Next, the scrolling space scene appears in the Space Miner window. To mine the ore randomly moving throughout the sector, your ship has a small ore vacuum.

Simply move your ship over the ore, and your vacuum will collect it. If sound is enabled, you will hear the vacuum when the ore is collected.

To fire a torpedo, press the Shift or Ctrl keyboard keys, or button #1 on your joystick. Several torpedoes can be fired and active at the same time. A sound confirms the launch. Figure 18.1 illustrates a game in progress.

Figure 18.1. Playing a game of Space Miner.

Alien drones attempt to line up with your ship and fire at you. Several aliens can attack at one time. They break off the attack if they pass your ship. You can shoot the alien ships with your torpedoes; when hit, the alien ships explode. They also explode when they touch your ship—destroying you in the process as well. These are drone ships, so they don't mind colliding with you.

You get three extra ships to complete your mission. To leave the sector and complete your mission, you must gather your quota of ore. As you pick up each piece, it will be subtracted from your quota. When you gather your full quota of ore, you can leave the sector. You will see (and hear) a message when you can leave—which you do by flying your ship past the top edge of the screen.

You receive points for each piece of ore collected, and for every alien drone destroyed. Your high score is saved.

To pause the game, select the Pause menu item on the Options menu. You can begin a new game by selecting New Game, or end the current one by selecting End Game. The Music option allows you to turn the MIDI background music on and off, and Sound Effects turns the Wave file sound effects on and off.

To get help, select Rules from the Help menu. The Rules form will appear, listing some general instructions (see Figure 18.2).

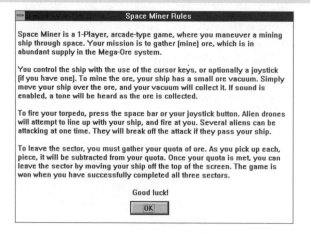

Figure 18.2. Getting help.

Hints

Space Miner is a fun game to play. Keep these hints in mind while playing to get the most out of the game:

➡️ Your main mission is to collect ore, so concentrate on that. It's easy to get caught up in playing shoot-'em-up with the alien drones.

➡️ Sometimes, it's better to run away from the aliens than to get cornered. Remember, they will break off their attack when they get past you. Move your ship up and away from an attacking alien drone.

➡️ Don't waste your first shot. If you shoot too hastily, your torpedo may not reload in time for you to make another shot.

➡️ It's fun to shoot the alien drones, but don't waste all of your ammo—you'll need it! When you run out of ammunition, you stay out of ammunition (until your next ship, if you get one).

➡️ If you do collect all your quota, fire some torpedos ahead of you as you leave the sector. This helps protect you from unseen aliens.

➡️ Space Miner is best played with a joystick. If you are using the keyboard, keep in mind that firing your torpedo will stop your momentum. Re-press the cursor key to keep your speed up after a torpedo launch.

Programming

The makefile for Space Miner contains the files listed in Table 18.1.

Table 18.1. Space Miner source files.

Filename	Description
SMABOUT.FRM	The About box form
SMMAIN.FRM	The Main Space Miner form
SMRULES.FRM	The Rules form
SMWINLOS.FRM	The Winning or Losing form
SMGLOBAL.BAS	Global constants, variables, and procedures

All these files are included in this book's disk. See Appendix A for installation instructions.

Figure 18.3 shows the SMABOUT form. This is the last About box you'll see for this book.

Figure 18.3. The SMABOUT form.

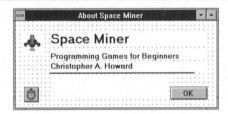

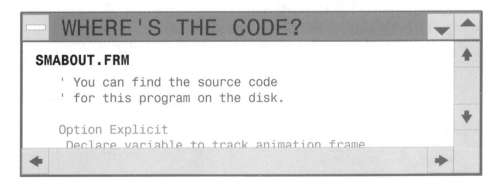

SMABOUT.FRM

```
' You can find the source code
' for this program on the disk.

Option Explicit
Declare variable to track animation frame
```

Figure 18.4 shows the important portions of the SMMAIN form (some controls extend further off-screen, but all controls are at least partially visible). This is the main game screen for the Space Miner game. Listing 18.1 gives a partial listing of the SMMAIN source code. The HandleOre routine illustrates how the sprite objects are animated, and the tmr_Main_Timer routine shows the main timer loop controlling the game.

Figure 18.4. The SMMAIN form.

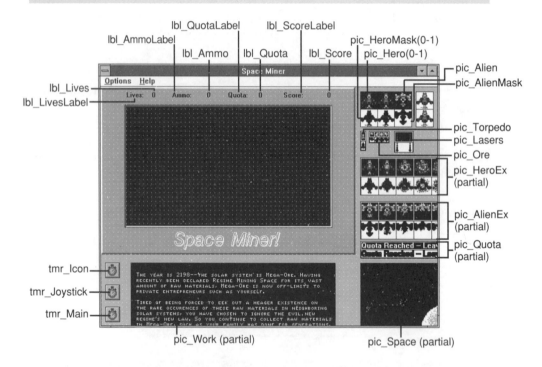

Listing 18.1. Partial listing of the SMMAIN form source code.

```
Sub HandleOre ()

    Dim i%, MarkTime&
    Dim rc%

    ' Mark the time (for speed)
    MarkTime& = GameTimer&

    ' Search through all ore
    For i% = 0 To MAXORE - 1

        ' Is this ore available?
```

```
If (Ore(i%).Active% = False) Then

  ' Yes, so see if reincarnation time has elapsed
  If (MarkTime& >= Ore(i%).RTime&) Then

    ' Place randomly
    Ore(i%).X% = GetRandom%(VIEWWIDTH)

    ' Start it at top, or bottom?
    ➥If (GetRandom%(2) = 0) Then
      ' Top of screen, moving down
      Ore(i%).Y% = 0
      ' At a speed of 1 to MAXOREINC
      Ore(i%).Yinc% = GetRandom%(MAXOREINC) + 1
    Else
      ' Bottom of screen, moving up
      Ore(i%).Y% = VIEWDEPTH
      ' At a speed of -MAXORINC to -1
      Ore(i%).Yinc% = GetRandom%(MAXOREINC) - MAXOREINC
    End If

    ' Choose a horizontal speed, from -MAX/2 to +MAX/2
    Ore(i%).Xinc% = GetRandom%(MAXOREINC) - (MAXOREINC \ 2)

    ' Get an ore image
    Ore(i%).Frame% = GetRandom%(OREIMAGES) + 1

    ' All set, so activate it
    Ore(i%).Active% = True

  End If

Else

  ' Check if the hero can pick ore up
  If (Overlap%(Hero.X%, Hero.Y%, HEROWIDTH, HERODEPTH,
  ➥Ore(i%).X%, Ore(i%).Y%, OREWIDTH, OREDEPTH)) Then
    ' Yes, but can he and does he need it?
    If ((Hero.Exploding = 0) And (Hero.Quota% > 0)) Then
      ' He needs it!
      Hero.Quota% = Hero.Quota% - 1
      Hero.Score& = Hero.Score& + ORESCORE
      DisplayStatus
      ' Give some audio feedback
      If (mnu_Sound.Checked) Then
        rc% = sndPlaySound%("SMVACUUM.WAV", SND_ASYNC
        ➥+ SND_NOSTOP + SND_NODEFAULT)
      End If
      ' Take the ore away
      Ore(i%).Active% = False
    End If
  End If
```

continues

Listing 18.1. continued

```
' Is the ore still active? (The hero might overlap the ore,
' but he may have reached his quota already)
If (Ore(i%).Active) Then

  ' We need to move it
  Ore(i%).Y% = Ore(i%).Y% + Ore(i%).Yinc%
  Ore(i%).X% = Ore(i%).X% + Ore(i%).Xinc%

  ' Has it moved outside the viewport horizontally?
  If (((Ore(i%).X% + OREWIDTH) < 0) Or
➡(Ore(i%).X% > VIEWWIDTH)) Then
    ' Yes
    Ore(i%).Active% = False
  Else
    ' Has it moved off vertically?
    If (((Ore(i%).Y% + OREDEPTH) < 0) Or
    ➡(Ore(i%).Y% > VIEWDEPTH)) Then
      ' Yes
      Ore(i%).Active% = False
    Else
      ' No, so display it
      Call DisplaySpriteFrame(pic_Ore, Ore(i%).Frame,
      ➡Ore(i%).X, Ore(i%).Y, OREWIDTH, OREDEPTH)
    End If
  End If
End If

  ' If ore has been deactivated, set it up for next
  ' reincarnation
  If (Ore(i%).Active% = False) Then
    Ore(i%).RTime& = GameTimer& + GetRandom%(MAXOREWAIT)
  End If

  End If

Next i%

End Sub

Sub tmr_Main_Timer ()

Dim rc%

' Display the space background in the work area
DisplaySpace

' Handle the Ore
HandleOre
```

```
      ' Handle any active shots
      HandleHeroShots
      HandleAlienShots

      ' Handle the Hero
      HandleHero

      ' Handle the Aliens
      HandleAliens

      ' Display the Hero's ship
      DisplayHero

      ' Copy the work area to the display window
      DisplayWork

      ' Count this frame
      FrameNum% = FrameNum% + 1
      If (FrameNum% = MAXFRAMES) Then
        FrameNum% = 0
      End If

      ' Keep our own internal timer
      GameTimer& = GameTimer& + tmr_Main.Interval

End Sub
```

Figure 18.5 shows the SMRULES form. This form displays the rules when the user selects Rules from the Help menu.

Figure 18.5. The SMRULES form.

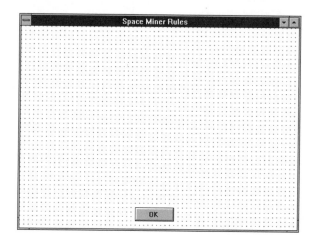

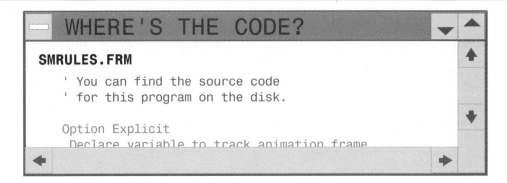

WHERE'S THE CODE?

SMRULES.FRM

```
' You can find the source code
' for this program on the disk.

Option Explicit
Declare variable to track animation frame
```

Figure 18.6 shows the SMWINLOS form. This form is displayed when the game is over, and it shows whether the user wins or loses.

Figure 18.6. The SMWINLOS form.

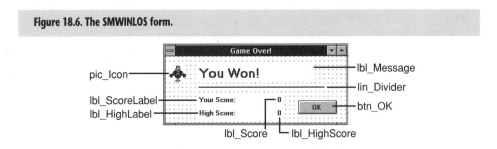

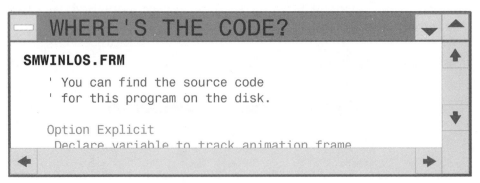

WHERE'S THE CODE?

SMWINLOS.FRM

```
' You can find the source code
' for this program on the disk.

Option Explicit
Declare variable to track animation frame
```

The SMGLOBAL file contains the global constant and variable definitions for the Space Miner game.

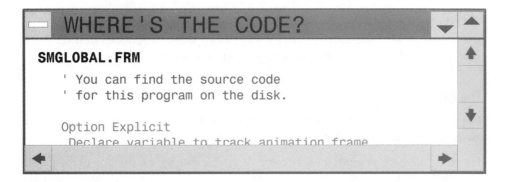

Form Overview

Space Miner contains several forms, but the most comprehensive one is the main game form, SMMAIN.FRM. The following is a brief discussion of the forms and their controls. Consult the form figures for additional information.

About Box

The SMABOUT form is the standard About box form. I set the label to Space Miner and the image to SM.ICO. For a full description of the form, see Chapter 10, "Apples & Oranges."

Rules

The SMRULES form displays the A&O rules when the player selects Rules from the Help menu. The form consists of blank space for the rule text, and a single OK button (which unloads the form). The form is centered when it's loaded, and the rule text is displayed when the window is painted.

Win or Lose

The SMWINLOS form displays whether the player wins or loses the game. It's also displayed when a player runs out of lives or wins the game by leaving the sector. This form retrieves the previous high score. If the player loses, the form displays some animation (the ship icon explodes!).

Global

The SMGLOBAL basic file contains the global variable and constant definitions. It also contains the global procedures Delay and GetRandom.

The Main Form

The SMMAIN form is the main form for the game, as its name implies. There are many controls on the main form—mainly picture controls.

The status labels represent the few controls visible during the playing of the game. The labels lbl_LivesLabel, lbl_AmmoLabel, lbl_ScoreLabel, and lbl_QuotaLabel are the labels for the status bar. The lbl_Lives, lbl_Ammo, lbl_Quota, and lbl_Score labels display the status values. All other controls are timer, image, and picture controls.

The game has three timers: tmr_Icon, tmr_Main, and tmr_Joystick. tmr_Icon controls the icon animation while the game is minimized, and it checks the status of the background music. tmr_Main is the main game timer, which serves as the main game loop for updating the sprites. Finally, tmr_Joystick reads the joystick, keeping the joystick position and button information current.

Because of the large number of graphics images, the images are stored outside the view of the main form window. To ensure the images are current and available, their AutoRedraw properties are set to True. There are numerous images, so I won't list them all here (refer to Figure 18.4).

Programming Overview

The Space Miner game is somewhat similar to Ping and Bricks, because the main game loop is timer-controlled. Unlike those games, however, Space Miner makes heavy use of bit-mapped images and animation. The game also includes joystick support and both MIDI and Wave sound file playback. This section covers the programming techniques used to develop Space Miner.

Creating the Images

Space Miner contains the most diverse number of images of any of the games (BlackJack and Draw Poker contain a deck of cards, but the cards are all similar). All of the sprites and images were created using Paintbrush for Windows and IconWorks.

Sprite is a term used to describe an object that moves dynamically. A sprite also has a defined shape, so you can see the background around it (it's not just a rectangular area). The space ships are examples of the many sprites used in Space Miner. If the ships weren't sprites, you would see a box around each ship (like you see when you use a picture control). This would not be as realistic.

Creating sprite images is a little different than creating ordinary images, so this bears some explaining. For this game, I drew a box as large as the sprite that I wanted to create. Then, I filled the inside with a color other than a color I used for my sprite. This served to indicate my transparent color—similar to using IconWorks.

Next, I drew the sprite in the box. For most of the sprites, I outlined the sprite image in black. This keeps a line around the sprite as it moves against the background. Otherwise, the sprite would blend into the background. The easiest way to visualize this is by using a sprite of all one color—such as red. If you move a red sprite against an all red background, the sprite would be invisible! A black border solves this problem.

With the sprite drawn, I made two copies of the box using the Paintbrush Cut tool. In one of the copies, I changed all the purple pixels (the color used for the transparent color) to black. Don't worry if you can't see your black border anymore—it's still there. This first image is the sprite image. In the second box, I changed all the purple pixels to white, and every pixel of any other color to black. The second image forms the sprite mask.

> An icon is basically a sprite that doesn't move. The .ICO file contains both the image and the mask.

NOTE

Now that the image and mask are created, you can save the sprite to a BMP file. If there are several frames (like for the ship explosions), you can create the sprite images and masks side by side—and store them as one BMP file. Make sure that you keep the sprite boxes the same size and the same distance apart. This makes using the sprites easier. Displaying the sprite is fairly straightforward. I'll discuss that later. For more information on sprites, see Chapter 4, "Animation."

Program Flow

When the game runs, the program flows as follows:

→ When the main form is loaded, it is centered and the About box is displayed. The game is declared over with the `GameOver%` flag.

→ The player begins by selecting New Game from the Options menu. The `mnu_NewGame_Click` routine initializes a new game by calling `InitNewGame`.

➤ The `InitNewGame` procedure initializes the game timer `GameTimer&` (an internal count of the number of milliseconds elapsed since the start of the game). The `Hero`, `Alien`, and `Ore` sprite structures are all initialized. The game status information is then updated by calling `DisplayStatus`, and the main timer `tmr_Main` is enabled. If background music is requested, it is played by calling the `PlayMusic` routine.

➤ Now, the game is controlled by the `tmr_Main_Timer` loop. All the animation is performed in the work buffer `pic_Work`. The space image is displayed by `DisplaySpace`, and any active shots are handled by `HandleHeroShots` and `HandleAlienShots`. The sprites are handled by `HandleHero`, `HandleAliens`, and `HandleOre`; the hero's ship is displayed by `DisplayHero`; and the entire frame is displayed to the player by the `DisplayWork` routine. A frame count is toggled for the sprite animation, and the internal timer count `GameTimer&` is updated.

➤ The shot routines search through all active shots and look for collisions. If a shot hits, the alien or hero is exploded by calling `ExplodeAlien` or `ExplodeHero`. The explode routines increment the `Exploding%` count. This variable causes the display functions to use the exploding sprite images when displaying the alien or hero sprites later. Otherwise, the shot position is updated and redisplayed.

➤ The sprite handling functions keep the hero sprite on the screen, as well as update the positions of the aliens and the ore. The functions also reincarnate new aliens and ore when necessary. The `HandleHero` routine checks for a win when the quota has been reached. The sprites are displayed by the `DisplayHero` and `DisplayAlien` routines. The `DisplayHero` routine handles reincarnating the hero after an explosion, and if there are no more lives left, the game ends.

➤ The `Form_KeyDown` routine provides the keyboard input for the hero ship movement. The `tmr_Joystick` routine reads the joystick position and updates the hero—if the user has enabled joystick input.

➤ During the game, the player can pause by selecting Pause from the Options menu. The `mnu_Pause_Click` routine pauses the game by stopping the timer and any music. It also unpauses the game by starting the timer again and playing the music.

➤ Play continues until the player loses three ships or beats the game. Play also ends when the player selects End Game from the Options menu.

You can view the game rules and the About box by selecting the Help menu options. These options display `frm_AboutBox` and call the `mnu_Rules` function.

Techniques Used

The Space Miner game includes several game concepts that I cover in the following sections.

Background Music

This is the only game that provides background MIDI music. This feature requires a Sound Card—the PC Speaker driver will only work for wave files (sound effects).

It's difficult to create a MIDI file (unlike wave files, which are simple). Usually, you need a piano keyboard and a MIDI interface, because the computer keyboard isn't designed to compose music! Some good composition programs are out there, one of which is called "Cakewalk."

Originally, I used a file that contained a few minutes of the theme from *Star Trek: The Wrath of Khan*. The problem is that most MIDI files you find are renditions of popular songs or movie themes. These are copyrighted, so you'll need permission from the author/composer to use the music in your game.

Rather than license the theme from Star Trek (probably an expensive prospect!), I composed a couple of minutes of music myself. I spent an evening with a friend, who has a MIDI setup. The result is what you'll hear in the background of Space Miner. I found the experience interesting, so I encourage you to experiment with MIDI as well. Be careful about what songs you use, if you don't write them yourself!

> To change the Space Miner background music, copy your own MIDI file to the directory containing the Space Miner program (MINER.EXE), and name the file SMMUSIC.MID. When you play Space Miner, your music will play instead.

As I illustrated in Chapter 5, "Sound Generation," MIDI files can be played in the background by using the `mciSendString` routine. Here, I illustrate one important technique: looping.

I wanted continuous background music, but the MIDI sequencer can't loop. My solution was to poll the sequencer status mode every five seconds (using the icon timer tmr_Icon, which isn't used during gameplay). This is done with the MODE option of the STATUS command, which I used as follows:

```
Dim rc%, rcm&
Dim mciStatus$, mciStatLen%

' Is the music playing?
If (MusicPlaying% = True) Then
  ' Yes, so check the status
  mciStatLen% = 15
  mciStatus$ = String$(mciStatLen% + 1, " ")
  rcm& = mciSendString&("STATUS SQ MODE", mciStatus$, mciStatLen%, 0)
  Debug.Print "mciStatus$: ["; rcm&; "], "; mciStatus$
  If (UCase$(Left$(mciStatus$, 7)) = "STOPPED") Then
    ' Play the MIDI file from the beginning
    Debug.Print "Detected Stop! Playing again ..."
    rcm& = mciSendString&("PLAY SQ FROM 0", "", 0, 0)
  End If
End If
```

This is the first time you've seen the return buffer used in mciSendString. The sequencer returns the status, which will be one of the strings "not ready," "paused," "playing," "seeking," or "stopped." When I detect the "stopped" status, I simply start playing from the beginning of the file again.

CAUTION

> You have to be careful here. The string buffer must be initialized to the size required, plus one character. Otherwise, a memory overwrite will occur and your program will crash!

If you run Space Miner from within the Visual Basic environment, the sequencer status will be displayed in the Debug window every five seconds.

Sound Effects

I cover sound effects and playing wave files in Chapter 5, "Sound Generation," but I have a few more items to note.

First, creating the sound effects is always a challenge. In fact, I consider this the hard part of adding sound to a game. When you have the sound effect in a file, playing it is easy. One call to sndPlaySound is all it takes.

I created the ore vacuum noises and missile *whoosh* using the Windows Sound Recorder. I just recorded myself making these sound effects (luckily it was two a.m.

and no one was listening!). I did the same thing for the quota reached message at the end of the game. I got the explosion and laser sounds from a friend. I thought about recording a video game, but my friend had already created the sounds.

I wanted something unique for the alien explosions. I drew the alien explosion images to look like an electrical disintegration, so I needed an electrical crackling sound. I got some tin foil, and recorded the sound of crinkling the tin foil into a ball. That wasn't enough, though, so I mixed in the explosion sound at a lower volume level. I used Windows Sound Recorder for these sounds too.

After I had the sounds, the `sndPlaySound` function was all I needed to play them back. I used the `SND_ASYNC` flag to play the effect in the background. I also used the `SND_NODEFAULT` flag to inhibit the PC Speaker beep (in the event the user doesn't have a sound card). I ran into a slight aesthetic problem, though.

Whenever a new sound is played, it interrupts the currently playing sound. This is usually okay, but in some cases it's undesirable. For example, an explosion should take precedent over the ore vacuum. Otherwise, the explosion sound starts for an alien, and gets cut off prematurely when an ore piece hits the hero's vacuum. To solve this problem, use the `SND_NOSTOP` flag, which ensures the current sound isn't overridden by a requested one. I added this to the flags of the ore `sndPlaySound` function, so that the ore sound only gets played if no other sound is playing. This looks like

```
' Play the vacuum sound
rc% = sndPlaySound%("SMVACUUM.WAV", SND_ASYNC + SND_NOSTOP
➥+ SND_NODEFAULT)
```

This allows the explosions to keep playing even though some ore is collected. Use the `SND_NOSTOP` flag to create priorities for sound in your game.

Joystick Support

Space Miner optionally supports a joystick. The routine is similar to the one used by Joystick example in Chapter 2, "Handling Input."

When I was just getting started with Space Miner, I had enough code to have the hero's ship displayed. I hooked up the joystick routine, and the ship was able to move all around the viewport. It wasn't that realistic, though, because the ship moved around in the same manner as the blue dot in the Joystick example. For Space Miner, I really didn't want absolute ship positioning.

My solution was to treat the joystick movement as more of a direction indicator. If the joystick position is in the first 30 percent of its range, the joystick is pointing left. If the joystick is in the last 30 percent of its range (in other words, greater than 70 percent), it is pointing right. This is done as follows:

```
' Calculate 10% of the joystick movement range
jthresh& = JoyMaxX& / 10
' If the joystick is at < 30% or > 70%, move
If (JoyX& < (3 * jthresh&)) Then
  ' Move left
  Hero.Xinc = Hero.Xinc - HEROINC
ElseIf (JoyX& > (7 * jthresh&)) Then
  ' Move right
  Hero.Xinc = Hero.Xinc + HEROINC
End If
```

The same logic applies for the Y direction. If the joystick is held in a particular direction, the movement increment is steadily increased. The HandleHero routine makes sure that the increment stays within range. HandleHero also adds some resistance to the movement, so the ship doesn't continue to drift when the joystick is returned to the center:

```
' Add some resistance to the X momentum
If (Hero.Xinc% > 0) Then
  Hero.Xinc% = Hero.Xinc% - HEROINC
ElseIf (Hero.Xinc% < 0) Then
  Hero.Xinc% = Hero.Xinc% + HEROINC
End If
```

Because the joystick timer occurs more frequently than the main timer, the X increment continues to increase faster than the HandleHero routine can take it away. However, if the joystick is in the center, the preceding code slows the ship down to a stop. The same code is used to add resistance to the Y direction as well.

> **NOTE**
>
> There is no resistence to movement in space. Although this statement is true, I've found that games with true space movement are very difficult to play. Players have a tendency to overcompensate, and the ship never stabilizes. Take out the compensation code above, and try it for yourself!

Infinite Space

The scrolling space background adds the illusion of movement to Space Miner. It also appears to go on forever. The space image is very long, but it is certainly not infinite.

To give the illusion of infinite space, you have to prepare the image properly. When you create the space image (or any image you wish to scroll), match the top end of the picture with the bottom. This is your seam, and you don't want it to be visible. Don't start to draw a picture of a world or some other object at the bottom of the image, where you'll run out of room. It is easier to leave the top and bottom areas simple—like blank space. Otherwise, you'll have to finish what you've drawn at the bottom of the image by completing it at the top!

If you are having trouble visualizing this, try creating a cylinder out of a piece of paper. Tape the top edge of the paper to the bottom. The paper represents your image, and the taped area is your seam. Sketch your drawing on the paper cylinder and cut the tape. Now, use the paper sketch as your guide when creating the image in Paintbrush.

After the image is created, you can animate it. In Space Miner, the `DisplaySpace` routine handles this. Basically, the routine displays the next section of space from the space image `pic_Space`. When a seam appears, `DisplaySpace` uses the bottom of the image for the top half of the display, and the top of the image for the bottom of the display. This simple process provides the illusion of infinite space!

Sprites Using Icons

I created the hero ship and alien ship sprites (and their masks) with IconWorks. These icons are then placed into Picture controls.

The Windows API function `BitBlt%` is required for displaying sprites. As I illustrated in Chapter 4, "Animation," the mask must be ANDed with the destination image, followed by the ORing of the sprite image. This removes the box around the sprite.

> Remember that you have to use Picture controls, and not Image controls, for your sprites. The `BitBlt%` function requires the `hDC` property, only found on Picture controls.

To animate the flames of the hero's ship, I created two icons. When the hero sprite is displayed, one of the two icons is selected. The two icons are alternately displayed, and the result is animated flames.

Multiple Sprite Frames

I used icons for the hero and alien ships, because I wanted to illustrate the use of icons for animation in a game. I could have also stored the images in a single bitmap (BMP file), with a Picture control. I used this method for the ore images, the missile and laser images, and the ship explosions.

If I would have used icons for each of the animated frames, Space Miner would have a lot of picture controls. This would take up memory and isn't necessary. In fact, it's simpler and easier to store all the frames for an animated sprite (including its mask) in a single bitmap.

If you look at the `pic_HeroEx` control (refer back to Figure 18.4), you'll see all the animated frames for the hero's ship explosion. This is a single BMP file, which I created using Paintbrush. I surrounded each frame in a box; each box is the same size. The masks for each sprite are located directly below the appropriate image.

Displaying a frame from this image is very easy, because each box is the same size and same distance apart. The `DisplaySpriteFrame` function accomplishes this:

```
Sub DisplaySpriteFrame (pic_Sprite As Control, Frame%, ByVal X%, ByVal Y%,
➡ByVal W%, ByVal D%)

  Dim rc%
  Dim sx%, sy%, mx%, my%

  ' Figure out where the sprite is
  ' (remember to account for sprite borders)
  sx% = (Frame% - 1) * (W% + 1) + 1
  sy% = 1

  ' The mask is directly below it
  mx% = sx%
  my% = sy% + D% + 2

  ' Mask the sprite area
  rc% = BitBlt%(pic_Work.hDC, X%, Y%, W%, D%, pic_Sprite.hDC,
➡mx%, my%, SRCAND)

  ' Now place the sprite
  rc% = BitBlt%(pic_Work.hDC, X%, Y%, W%, D%, pic_Sprite.hDC,
➡sx%, sy%, SRCPAINT)

End Sub
```

This generic routine handles all the sprite bitmaps in Space Miner. All the function needs is the picture control name of the sprite, the frame number you want to display, the position at which you want it displayed, and the width and depth of the individual sprite frames.

When an alien or a missile strikes the hero's ship, the `pic_HeroEx` sprite images are played in sequence (frame 1 through frame 8). The effect is an exploding ship!

The Work Frame Area

All the animation for Space Miner is performed in the work frame area, `pic_Work`. Why? Because this removes any problem with flickering. If all the animation was performed directly on the Space Miner form window, the sprites would flicker and flash. Remember the swimming fish from the Animation example (in Chapter 4, "Animation")? If not, run the Animation example program and watch the fish sprite without the Flickerless box checked.

It's worth examining the display steps performed while animating the work buffer. Specifically, the steps are as follows:

➡ The next region of the space image is copied to the work area. This overwrites all the previous sprites and images and gives a clean slate on which to work.

➡ All the ore images are displayed. This forms the next layer of images, because the ore must always be underneath the ships and missiles.

➡ Any hero or alien shots are displayed next. I wanted the missiles and torpedoes to be located underneath the ships, especially when they are first fired.

➡ The alien drone ships are displayed next.

➡ The hero is displayed last. The hero is always displayed on top of everything else.

➡ Lastly, the entire work area is copied to the display screen. This gives the illusion that all images were updated simultaneously. It also displays the area without flickering the sprites.

Animation involves quite a process, but the effects are great. This is the same process used for DOS video games, although the work area is usually a hidden video page.

By using the frame work area, you don't have to save the background underneath all of those sprites—because the background is kept in the space image. The background is also moving (the constantly scrolling space), so saving the sprite backgrounds would not be helpful.

Collision Detection

I used the same `Overlap%` function in Space Miner as I did in Bricks. I used simple collision detection, even though most of the sprites are irregularly shaped. I made this decision because of speed limitations.

Ideally, it would be nice to compare the masks of the sprites to detect an exact collision (see the "Complex Collision Detection" section in Chapter 4, "Animation"). This would be much too time-consuming, however, and Space Miner is already strapped for time. The displaying of all of the images and sprites is very time-intensive.

It's hard to tell that the collision detection regions are really rectangular.

Marking Time

Space Miner keeps track of the time in milliseconds by accounting for each interval in `tmr_Main`. This is done by the following:

```
' Keep our own internal timer
GameTimer& = GameTimer& + tmr_Main.Interval
```

This is useful for several reasons. First, you can read the value of `GameTimer&` quickly. If you have to call the `Timer` function every time you want to know how much time has elapsed, the game would slow down appreciably. Second, the `Timer` function only reports the time elapsed in seconds. This delay is usually too long for game playing. I wanted to allow the hero to fire his torpedo more than once a second! The `GameTimer&` value represents total milliseconds.

One use of the game timer is to delay between hero and alien shots. When the hero fires a torpedo, the time is marked. The hero can't fire another until the correct amount of time has elapsed (`HEROWAITSHOT`). The same method works for the aliens.

The game timer also is used for determining when new aliens and new ore appear. A random time is selected in the future. For aliens, this looks like

```
' Set time up for next alien reincarnation
Alien(a%).RTime& = GameTimer& + GetRandom%(MAXALIENWAIT)
```

The `HandleAliens` routine detects whether the time has elapsed by testing the reincarnation time value, as in

```
' Is it time to reincarnate the alien?
if (MarkTime& >= Alien(a%).RTime&) then ...
```

Once reincarnated, the alien appears on the screen. The alien is either destroyed by the hero, or it drifts past the screen window. Either way, it's destined for another reincarnation.

Saving the High Score

As illustrated in the "Configuration Files" section in Chapter 6, "File I/O," Space Miner stores the high score in the Windows Initialization file, WIN.INI. This is accomplished through the Windows API functions `WriteProfileString` and `GetProfileInt`.

I do want to note that the score can end up to be larger than an integer (65,535). For this reason, Space Miner stores the score by dividing by 100. This allows scores to be as much as 6,553,500! However, anything less than 100 will be truncated. In Space Miner, however, all score increments are 100 or more.

Debugging

In Chapter 9, "Debugging," I discuss some debugging techniques. One technique is to play, play, play! That wasn't a problem for me, because I enjoy playing this game. Sometimes, though, you don't want to play the whole game every time to test something.

I built several *cheat keys* into Space Miner. If you don't want to know what they are, avert your eyes! Pressing the letter L increases the number of lives you have, A increases your ammo by 10, and Q decreases your quota. Of course, I know you'll only use these keys for debugging purposes!

There are two additional keys that take more drastic action than those listed previously. W immediately takes you to a winning situation (Quota = 0). Pressing X will take all of your lives and explode the ship—you lose. Both of these keys helped me debug the ending scenarios. If you've never won the game, press W to see what it's like!

Data Organization

Because of the sprite structures (such as HEROTYPE, ALIENTYPE, ORETYPE, and SHOTTYPE), there are very few global variables in Space Miner. These structures define the Hero variable, and the HeroShot, Alien, AlienShot, and Ore arrays.

The SpaceY% variable keeps track of the current space position, and FrameNum% is the global animation frame count used to alternate between the sprite images. IconNum% and IconDir% handle the icon animation. MusicPlaying% keeps track of whether the background music is currently playing, and QuotaTime& keeps track of how long it has been since the last Quota Reached announcement appeared. The joystick variables joyX&, joyY&, joyMaxX&, and joyMaxY& monitor the joystick position and maximums.

Lastly, the GameTimer& variable counts the elapsed game time (in milliseconds), and the GameOver% and GameWon% flags indicate whether the game is over and won.

Space Miner uses constants for almost everything. Constants define the width and depth of sprites, minimums and maximums, wait times, movement increments, and much more. I can't emphasize enough how important they are.

Summary

I have covered the following important programming points:

→ Background music is a great addition to a game. A game without background music can seem like a movie without sound. However, MIDI music is difficult to create—especially if you are not a music major. Background music can be looped by monitoring the sequencer with the STATUS MODE command.

→ Creating sound effects can be fun, and using them in your game is very easy. Use the SND_ASYNC flag to play sound in the background. Use the SND_NOSTOP flag to control whether new sounds interrupt currently playing sounds.

→ The joystick is easy to program and use. The joystick can be used to position objects at absolute positions, or you can take a percentage of the movement as an indication of direction. You might avoid using true space movement, which can make the game difficult to play.

→ An image can be scrolled indefinitely, to give the illusion of infinite space. The hard part is creating the image so the seam doesn't show.

→ Sprites can be created by using the IconWorks program. The sprite image and mask can be stored in separate Picture controls and then accessed by the Windows API BitBlt% function.

→ Instead of using Picture controls for every sprite and mask, you can use a single bitmap for sprite frames. This bitmap can be placed into a single picture control, and also accessed by the BitBlt% function. A simple function can be written to access any sprite frame quickly, such as the Space Miner DisplaySpriteFrame function.

→ Many sprites can be animated simultaneously by using an off-screen work area. This work area can then be copied to the display in one operation, which updates all the sprite positions. This also eliminates any possible sprite flickering.

→ Collision detection doesn't have to be complicated. The use of rectangular regions makes the collision detection process fast, without any appreciable decrease in game play.

→ Elapsed time can be monitored by using the timer interval property. This value can be used for timing intervals that are less than one second.

→ The high score can be kept in the Windows WIN.INI file. The integer range restricts the value to less than 65,535, but that can be sidestepped by dividing the score by 10 or 100.

➡ Cheat keys can be built into the program to test game features that don't occur often. Cheat keys also can save time, especially when you debug routines at the end of the game.

➡ Structures can be used to organize data. Use constants to make data more readable and code more maintainable.

Suggestions for Improvement

The following suggestions are ideas for enhancing Space Miner:

➡ Add more sectors. Load a new space image into pic_Space using the LoadPicture function. Each new sector level could be more difficult by limiting the ore, increasing the ore quota, using more aliens, restricting the distance of the hero's torpedo, or increasing the range of the alien lasers.

➡ Add police. These could enter from below and come after you if they see you taking any ore. Make them slow enough, though, that you can get underneath them to destroy them.

➡ Add smart bombs. Give the hero a limited number of bombs, released by a keyboard key (like the Spacebar) or button # 2 of the joystick. A smart bomb would destroy all aliens and police currently on the screen. You could award a smart bomb based on the amount of ore gathered.

➡ Add hyperspace. Hyperspace would make the hero's ship disappear and reappear at random locations. This would be most useful in tight spots, such as when the drones and police are closing in. The disadvantage is, of course, that the new place could be even worse. You can restrict the placement so the hero never appears on top of another object. But the hero could appear right in front or below somebody!

➡ Add shields. Shields would allow the hero to protect the ship from alien and police fire, and some collisions. Shield strength would start at a certain level and decrease when hit by bullets or ships. The amount decreased would depend on the type of hit. The shields could regenerate slowly (based on elapsed time), or only be restored at the beginning of each life or sector.

➡ Add larger ore. This ore could be too big for the hero's ship to collect directly, and would actually cause the ship to explode if it collides with a large piece. The hero could bust the ore up with a torpedo and then collect the smaller fragments. Other ships, such as the alien drones and police, also could explode if they collide with the ore. They could be programmed to shoot the larger ore.

➡   Add bonus objects. The bonus objects could float by the screen, similar to the ore. These could appear infrequently and would be brightly colored. The objects, if collected, would be worth more ammo, or be more valuable (worth 10 ore pieces—like gold ore). Other bonuses could provide an extra life or a higher score. If the bonus object is collected, add a special sound effect.

What's Ahead

Space Miner is the last game I cover in this book. In the next section, Part III, "Marketing Your Games," I cover issues regarding the protection of your game. I also cover ways to get your game distributed. Yes, you can actually make money writing games!

Marketing
Your Games

PART

Protecting Your Work

When you write a game, it's only natural to want it protected. Software can be copied easily, and many users aren't aware that it's illegal to do so. In this chapter, I cover some ways you can protect your work, through the legal system and through software programming methods.

Copyright Protection

You own a copyright for your software the moment you write it. As a copyright holder, you have all the exclusive rights defined by the Copyright Act. These include the right to reproduce copies, the right to make changes or additions (derivative works), and the right to distribute your program.

Nonetheless, there are two more things you should do to ensure full protection by the copyright law. First, you should include a proper copyright notice on your software. This notifies your users of your copyright claim. Second, you should register the copyright to your software with the U.S. Copyright Office. This allows you to enforce your copyright, should the need arise.

The Copyright Notice

Although it isn't necessary, the copyright notice is the easiest and cheapest way to deter infringement. By notifying your users of your copyright,

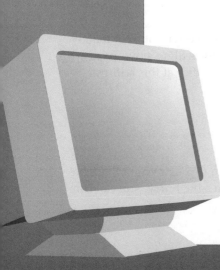

it will be hard for a user to argue that their infringement was innocent—clearing the way for stiffer penalties.

The copyright notice must contain three basic elements:

1. The copyright symbol ©, the word "Copyright," or the abbreviation "Copr."

2. The year of first publication of the software

3. The copyright owner's name in the work

You also can use the symbol "(c)" as a substitute for the symbol "©"— although it's best to include the word "Copyright" along with it. Examples of proper copyrights include:

➡ Copyright 1993 Christopher A. Howard

➡ © 1993 Genus Microprogramming, Inc.

➡ Copyright (c) ACME, Inc.

Put the notice where the user of your software will see it. Place it in your source code, object code, program header, on your disk labels, at the front of your manuals and documentation, and anywhere else which seems fitting.

> This book contains a copyright notice—can you find it? The disk label also has a copyright notice for the games and files on the disk. You can even place a copyright notice in the About box of each game.

Registering

Along with the copyright notice, you should register your copyright. Fortunately, this is a simple and straightforward process, which involves filing a two-page application with the Copyright Office. You can contact the office at this address:

> *Publications Section*
> *Copyright Office*
> *Library of Congress*
> *Washington, DC 20559*

You'll need to request Application Form TX and Circular 61, "Copyright Registration for Computer Programs." Both are free. If you're in a big hurry, you can contact the Copyright Office Forms Hotline at (202) 707-9100.

When you fill out the form, you'll have to send it in with a partial printout of your program and a small fee (around $20). Be sure to read Circular 61 thoroughly, because Form TX might not be the best form to use for some applications.

Getting Help

The previous information is a general discussion of copyright notices and registration. After reading Circular 61, you might want to obtain the advice of an attorney. Use the information in this book as a starting point for your copyright education.

Copy Protection

Unfortunately, owning the copyright is not enough to prevent people from copying it. Years ago, many commercial programs were copy protected—and rightfully so. Computer software was a relatively new concept to many users, and it wasn't clear that copying it and giving it to friends was against the law. There were not many precedents, the public was uneducated, and copying software was easy. Software publishers decided to protect themselves by copy protecting their programs.

This usually involved a scheme in which the original program disk (sometimes called the *key disk*) had to be inserted into a floppy drive before the program could be run. The most popular example of this involved Lotus 1-2-3. Obviously, inserting a key disk each time was quite a hassle for the vast majority of users who owned legal copies of the software. Eventually, even Lotus abandoned this form of copy protection.

Most commercial publishers discontinued copy protection for various reasons. First, it was a nuisance to their paying customers. From a customer service standpoint, publishers were penalizing 99 percent of their users for the 1 percent who illegally copied programs. Second, the users who copied the software probably wouldn't have paid $495 for it anyway, so there wasn't a significant amount of lost revenue. Lastly, the public became more aware of copyright laws. Groups, such as the SPA (Software Publishers Association), communicated the do's and do not's of software usage.

However, a large number of game programs continue to use copy protection. The popularity of games makes them an easy target for copying. The game audience also consists of a large number of children, who are not as aware of copyright issues. However, the price of most games is low enough—you would think people wouldn't bother copying!

So what can you do about it? The following section offers suggestions to discourage the copying of your game—and to keep honest people honest.

The Copyright Notice

As already stated, the copyright notice is enough for most people. It's a legal indication that your program shouldn't be copied without your permission. Your game can display the About box when the game is first played, because that's where the copyright notice is. The user has to click the OK button to clear the box, which should acknowledge that they've seen the box's information.

Recording the User's Name

When you install Visual Basic, the installation program asks for your name and your company's name. This information is displayed when you first start Visual Basic (with a comment about copyrights), and whenever you display the About box (see Figure 19.1).

Figure 19.1. Visual Basic records your name.

A good argument is that a person is less likely to give a copy of the program (with his or her name on it) to a friend!

Hidden Files

An old trick is to create a hidden file on the disk on which the game is installed. This file isn't visible when a directory command is given, but the game knows it's there. When the game runs, you can look for the file. If someone has copied the game, the hidden file won't be on disk.

The disadvantage of this scheme is that the legitimate users might have difficulty removing the game from their hard disk. They can delete all the files, but not the hidden one. When they try to remove the game directory, they won't be able to—because the hidden file still exists. This results in a call to your technical support department.

Manuals and Code Wheels

Some popular forms of copy protection in the game industry are *code wheels* and manual *lookups*. With the code wheel approach, the program displays a series of items, such as pictures. You must match the pictures on the code wheel to whatever shows up in the code wheel window. The idea is that you must have the code wheel to play the game.

The manual lookup works the same way. The game might ask you to complete a sentence from page 15, paragraph 2, sentence 3. Without the manual, you won't know what to type. Other games have bits of trivia on each page. The game asks a question, and you have to type an answer. A third method involves the user selecting a correct pattern or picture from a list. Still others make the copy protection part of the game, where you have to look up a magic incantation from the manual (or something along those lines). This makes the copy protection seem much less intrusive.

The Hack Attack

Some people copy a game just to play it. Others copy a game to make a profit. It's sad but true; however, some people change your copyright notice, put their own name on it, and rerelease it as their own. Using a copyright notice and registering your copyright are two steps to protect yourself, but you have to catch the rascals first. The best thing to do is to make it hard for someone to *hack* (rip off) your game.

A Graphical Copyright

A good place to put your copyright notice is inside a graphics image. Strings are easy to find and change in an EXE, but a bitmap isn't.

Encrypted Strings

Consider *encrypting* some or all of your strings. Shifting each character a fixed amount (one or more) makes those strings hard to find in a program. Here's what a copyright string looks like after it's encrypted:

```
Dpqzsjhiu!2::4!Disjtupqifs!B/!Ipxbse
```

Can you figure out what I used? It looks like gobbledegook to me. Hint: you already know it's a copyright notice! A simple scheme as this makes it hard to find important information, especially if the program file is large.

If you are interested in encrypting strings or parts of your program in a serious way, look for the book *Top Secret Data Encryption Techniques,* also from Sams Publishing.

CRC Check

A *Cyclical Redundancy Check* (CRC) is a method for checking the bytes of a file or memory area to see if they've changed from the original file. If the copyright notice or other parts of the game have been changed, the program has been hacked (at the very least, it isn't the same as when you wrote it!).

Summary

Protecting your work is important. Use a copyright notice and register your copyright with the Copyright Office. Take extra steps to make it harder for people to copy or hack your game. Any extra effort on your part can't hurt.

What's Ahead

If you've written your game and protected it, how do you distribute it? I answer that question in the next chapter, "Distributing Your Game." Find out why you might actually want people to copy your game—over and over again!

Distributing Your Game

You've written your game, created the setup program and help files, and placed your copyright notices in the appropriate places—now what do you do? You have to get your game distributed somehow. In this chapter, I discuss ways of getting your game published and places for you to get more information. And so you don't have to just take my word for it, I also interview another Visual Basic programmer who has just recently made the transition from fun to profit—by releasing his game as Shareware.

Maybe you started out writing your game just for fun. Games are a great way of learning about programming. If you've worked on your game and have continued to enhance it, perhaps the game is at the point that you start thinking, "Hey, this is a game I would pay money for!" But if you're like most game authors, you have a real job (or a day job, if you spend your nights programming!).

As such, you don't have the time, money, or resources to start a game company—so what do you do? Don't despair—make it Shareware!

Shareware

Shareware is a method of distribution that enables a user to try the software before buying. A computer user simply downloads a copy of

your game (using a modem) and tries it out. If the player likes the program, he or she sends you some money! Ideally, anyway. Before you start seeing dollar signs before your eyes, look at the whole picture.

Putting It Together

Writing a game for your own pleasure is one thing, but putting a package together for another user is quite another. You'll need to distribute

- The main game executable (EXE)
- The Visual Basic Runtime Library (VBRUN300.DLL)
- Any control libraries (such as MSCOMM.VBX)
- Wave files (*.WAV)
- A Setup program
- Help files (*.HLP), and any other documentation files
- A READ.ME file, for any program changes and general game comments
- Registration information (such as where to send the money, and how much—very important!)
- Any other files you want to include

This is quite a list. After you have created a disk with these files, you'll want to compress it into a single file. This keeps everything together and makes uploading and downloading quicker (saving potential customers both time and money). A commonly used compression program is PKZIP (which also happens to be Shareware), which is available on Bulletin Board Systems (BBSs) and online services everywhere. You won't need to include PKZIP with your game, because most modem users already have it. If you do use PKZIP, however, you should register it for your own use!

Setting Up Shop

I recommend spending a few dollars on your new venture. You'll want to do the following:

- Pick a company name. In the United States, go to your local courthouse and get a Doing Business As (DBA). This reserves your company name locally for a period of time and lets the government know that you are, for instance, "John Doe doing business as ACME Games."

➡️ Get a post office box. This is the quickest and easiest way to get a business address for your company. It also simplifies things if you change your personal address.

➡️ Open a business checking account. Use this account to keep track of your business expenses (and future profits!). Use your company name (the one you picked out for your checks) and your P.O. box as the address. This keeps things simple for taxes, too.

➡️ Get a second phone line. Ask the phone company for a separate bill, so you can pay it through your business account. A second line usually isn't a big expense, and it lets you answer the phone using your business name. If you can, install an answering machine—so you can get messages while you're at your day job.

➡️ Purchase stationery with your company letterhead, envelopes, and business cards. You don't have to spend money on a logo or artwork yet. Use a local printing company and get the minimum order. The printing company should have samples of other packages they've done, and they might design your letterhead. Use your letterhead for all your business correspondences.

I consider this the minimum for starting your own business—which is what you'll be doing when you release your game.

You as Publisher

The Shareware system is definitely cost effective. It's not expensive to publish your game, and with the potential for revenue, doesn't it sound good? You might be wondering, "How do I get started?"

The easiest way to start with the Shareware system is to upload your game to your local BBS. Many BBSs have lists of other BBS numbers in your area and across the country—you may want to upload your game to them also. Another good location to place your game is on CompuServe or some of the other large online services, such as Prodigy and America Online.

After you upload the game, someone else downloads it. If a user likes your game, you might get paid—or you might not. The player also might upload the game to some favorite BBSs for other users to enjoy. The worst case is for another player to do nothing; the best case is for a user to pay you *and* upload it to many BBSs across the country.

This starts a domino effect. You upload your game to a couple of BBSs. Consequently, several users download it and play it. Each of those users uploads it to a few more BBSs. At each bulletin board, more users download the game, and in turn upload it to more BBSs. After a period of time, your game spreads across the country and, most likely, the world! You'll have a worldwide market potential, and you haven't paid a thing.

Theoretically, registrations will start to appear in your mailbox after some period of time. There is no guarantee, however, that anyone will send you anything.

Giving It Away

You may be thinking, "If I give my game away, why would anyone pay me for it?" Good question. Many people won't pay you for it, but some might. The Shareware system is based on the honor principle—if users like your game, and continue to play it, they should feel inclined to pay for it. There are ways of encouraging payment, though, some of which are

➤ Use a Nag Screen. Usually, this screen appears at the beginning of a program and reminds the player that this is an unregistered, Shareware game (and that they haven't paid for it yet). After a few seconds, the screen goes away (see Figure 20.1). You can place this screen at the end of the program, too, but it's less effective there.

➤ Offer more features. The registered version might have more features (such as the ability to save your game), more levels, more hints, actual documentation, or anything else to entice the user to send in the registration fee.

➤ Cripple the game. A crippled game only allows you to play for a certain amount of time, or it may contain only one level or a partial level. Removing the ability to save the current level is another way of crippling the game, which forces the user to start over at the beginning each time they play. If possible, avoid crippling the game and instead, offer more features. This fosters good will between you and the potential buyer, and more people might download, play, and upload your game if it's complete. More people playing means more people paying!

➤ Offer your latest version. Inform the user of a possible later version of the game. Old versions of your game may stick around on BBSs for quite awhile, but most users want the "latest and greatest."

➤ Don't be afraid to ask for payment. Make it easy for the player to pay the registration fee by prominently displaying your address. Also, include a registration form for the player to print out and send in.

Figure 20.1. A Nag Screen.

Those are just a few suggestions. A lot more is involved in marketing Shareware, and you can get into it as little or as much as you want. In addition, you can contact a Shareware association.

Shareware Associations

You can become a member of a several Shareware organizations. I'll discuss two: ASP and STAR.

The ASP

The Association for Shareware Professionals (ASP) is probably the oldest Shareware organization—and perhaps the largest. Its purpose is to promote the Shareware concept, and it offers many guidelines for Shareware programs.

To contact the ASP, type **GO ASPFORUM** to access their forum on CompuServe. You can download the file PUBAPP.EXE, which is a self-extracting archive (it expands to several files). Included in this file is an ASP application, a list of author requirements, and a list of registration incentives.

An excellent reference guide for potential Shareware publishers is available on CompuServe in the ASPFORUM, Lib 4. The file, GUIDE.EXE, expands to a 60-page document which contains good ideas for developing and marketing Shareware.

If you want to contact the ASP directly, use the following information:

Executive Director
Association of Shareware Professionals
545 Grover Road
Muskegon MI 49442-9427
USA

CompuServe: 72050,1433
  Phone: (616) 788-5131
  FAX: (616) 788-2765

If you don't have a CompuServe ID, try looking for the previous files (PUBAPP.EXE and GUIDE.EXE) on local BBSs in your area. You can also contact your local user group.

STAR

The Shareware Trade Association and Resources (STAR) is a new organization (formed in the last year or two). The major difference between STAR and ASP is that STAR does not regulate marketing methods or the actions of its members. Both groups work to educate people about the Shareware marketing method, and to promote the Shareware industry.

To find out more about STAR, join section 11 of the UK Shareware forum on CompuServe (GO UKSHARE). You also can find a local bulletin board echoing Ilink and join the Shareware Issues Forum. Contact STAR at

STAR
c/o Diana Gruber
P.O. Box 13408
Las Vegas, NV 89112
(702) 735-1980

An Interview with a Shareware Author

Scott A. Murray is a Visual Basic programmer and President of Nisus Development & Technology. He has released a game called *Missile Master* (see Figure 20.2) using the Shareware distribution method.

Figure 20.2. Missile Master.

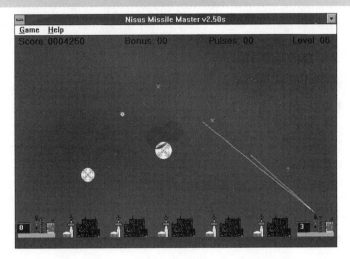

The following is a conversation I had with Scott about his game and his experiences with Shareware.

Chris: Tell me a little about yourself.

Scott: I'm 27, I've been programming since I was about 14, and I currently work for a large company in Ontario, Canada (during the day, anyway). At night I work on games and other utilities using Visual Basic and Windows for my company, Nisus Development & Technology (namely, Me!).

Chris: Why did you write Missile Master?

Scott: I wrote Missile Master partly on a dare from a co-worker, and mostly for myself—it was my favorite arcade game.

Chris: Why did you choose to use Visual Basic?

Scott: I chose Visual Basic, because I think it is a great Windows development environment. It's easy to get something up and running, and I've heard of the ordeals of writing Windows applications in C. With Visual Basic, you still have access to the Windows API, so you're not hampered in any way. My only complaint is that it may be too slow for some kinds of arcade games. I recommend a 386/33 for Missile Master, although I've had people play it with slower systems.

Chris: How long did it take you to develop Missile Master?

Scott: I had the shell of the game up and running in an afternoon. I would say my first version took me about a week and a half. The current version took me another month to write, part time. I guess if you call working 6:00 P.M. to 2:00 A.M. part time!

Chris: How many lines of code is the game?

Scott: I would say approximately 800-900 lines of actual Basic code, which is a little embarrassing.

Chris: Well, that may be misleading. I think that number is a testament of the features that Visual Basic provides. Plus, you have to count the time spent designing the forms, setting the control properties, developing the artwork, recording the sound files, the setup program, and the Windows help file. All of that adds up to a lot of work.

Scott: That's true; you're right.

Chris: Speaking of artwork and sound files, what tools did you use to develop your game?

Scott: I used Windows Paintbrush, and a Shareware program called Paintshop Pro. For the sound files, I used the Windows Sound Recorder, and a sound editing utility called Wave for Windows, I think. I created the artwork myself, and most of the sound files.

Chris: The sound files add a lot to the program. I've tried playing the game both ways, and the sound adds a great deal to the enjoyment of the game. What about the online help, how did you create that?

Scott: I used Microsoft Word 2.0 and created an RTF (Rich Text Format) file. I then compiled it with the Microsoft Help Compiler. The whole process was not that easy—someone should automate the system.

Chris: OK, so now you've written the game, and you decided to release it. What did you do?

Scott: This was my first Shareware game, so the whole thing was new to me. One mistake I made was that I uploaded a beta copy (a test version) to a local BBS here in Canada. I say "mistake" because I uploaded it without any registration information or request for payment. I underestimated the amount of distribution the game would receive in such a short time—I've even seen the beta version on two CD-ROM disks! The first money I ever made from the game was from a user who sent me a letter and $10, even though the beta version didn't ask for anything.

Chris: What did you do next?

Scott: I released the Shareware version in late November of 1992. I uploaded it to a large BBS here in Canada, and I also placed it on CompuServe, in the GAMERS forum.

Chris: That was all?

Scott: Yes.

Chris: This is the question that everyone wants to know—does Shareware work? It's been about six months since you released the game. How is it doing?

Scott: That's a question I always had, too, before I released the game. Unfortunately, no one ever wanted to share any real numbers. It took about three weeks before I received anything in the mail. I sell the game for $15 U.S., and to date I've had about 125 registrations. All in all, I've taken in almost $1,900. Considering that I hadn't planned on making anything, I'm happy with the results.

Chris: I would say that's pretty good. This is the original concept behind Shareware—release the program and let the userbase grow by itself. What percentage of the people do you think register?

Scott: That's hard to say. One nice feature of CompuServe is that it gives you a download count. Over 1,000 people have downloaded the game from CompuServe alone. Perhaps that gives you some idea.

Chris: Where are your registrations coming from? Are they mostly Canadian, from the United States, or are they international?

Scott: I've had about five or six from Canada. The majority are from the U.S., but many are international, too. I've had registrations from Switzerland, Germany, Saudi Arabia, Italy, and several other countries.

Chris: What incentives do you provide to get people to register?

Scott: I have a Nag Screen at the beginning of the program, which stays up for about five seconds. I try to make it humorous, though, so that it isn't so annoying. I also put up a message after they beat level 25—which means they have probably played the game quite a bit.

Chris: That's one of the things I really like about your game: the humor. You use it right from the beginning, and continue to use it in your help files, and even in the sound effects.

Scott: I think a game should be enjoyable, and humor is just another way to add to the experience.

Chris: What do they get once they register?

Scott: I send them the latest version, with a serial number and their name set right into the game. I put it on a disk with a professional looking label, and a note that thanks them for registering. I also include some comments about what I'm working on next, since I get asked that a lot. The registered version has unlimited levels, and unlimited missiles. A lot of the people have said that they look forward to having unlimited missiles!

Chris: Do you belong to any of the Shareware organizations?

Scott: No, not at this time. They're probably beneficial, but it is an extra step that you have to go through. Right now, I just enjoy working for myself and not worrying about any guidelines. I'm not saying that's what everyone should do—check them out and decide for yourself. I may join at some later date.

Chris: Your game was an Editor's Choice in Shareware Magazine—how did that come about?

Scott: By accident, really. The editor of the magazine, Mike Callahan, is a well-known Shareware promoter (who goes by the name "Dr. File Finder"). He called me on the phone one day and said the magazine was picking Missile Master as an Editor's Choice.

It turns out that he receives hundreds of unsolicited Shareware programs each month, and here he downloaded Missile Master himself and selected it as Editor's Choice!

Chris: I guess when a program is good it can sell itself! Now that you've done it for awhile, how do you feel about the Shareware distribution method?

Scott: It works for me. Some people warned me that there would be no registrations for some time, and I've heard some horror stories of people not receiving anything. I like finding registrations in my P.O. box, which are coming in at about five to six a week now. I really enjoy reading the comments.

Chris: What are your plans for the future?

Scott: I'm working on a utility program at the moment, that I will release as Shareware. I also have some ideas for more games, which will also be distributed as Shareware.

Chris: Do you have any advice for future Shareware authors?

Scott: Make sure you allow for postage and handling. At first, I didn't include any charge for shipping. The disk mailers were costing me a dollar, the disks were a dollar, and shipping was about a dollar. That amounted to 20 percent of my registration fee! Now I charge a few dollars for postage and handling.

Besides that, be sure and promote the Shareware concept. Register the Shareware programs that you use—they must be worth it or you wouldn't be using them. If you release your game as Shareware, be sure to send something back to the user in return for registering. Writing "Thanks" on the back of the check is not enough.

> You can find Missile Master on CompuServe in the Gamer's forum (type **GO GAMERS**), in Library #7 (Action/Arcade Games). The file to download is MM262S.ZIP, or search for the keyword **MISSILE**. If you don't have a CompuServe ID, check for Missile Master on your local bulletin board systems.

Going Commercial

If you think your game is the next Tetris, you might not want to release it as Shareware. Going commercial can be tough, though. Unless you have the money to start your own business, you'll have to find a game publisher.

You can find the names of current game publishers at local computer software stores by looking on the game boxes. Companies like Electronic Arts, Broderbund, and Sierra are large game publishers. Call them and ask for their submissions guidelines. You never know!

Summary

There's a lot more to distributing your game than just throwing it onto a BBS. You must pull all of the files together, create setup programs and help files, and provide registration. Take the time to set up your business. After that, use the Shareware system for releasing your game—and hopefully for making money. You can gather more information on Shareware by contacting a Shareware organization, such as ASP or STAR.

The End

The end of this book is the beginning for you. I hope that you found the information in this book to be valuable. If you have any comments regarding the book, or you write a game or release it as Shareware, tell me about it through my CompuServe account: 75100,17. Good luck!

Installation

This appendix describes how to install and run the games so that you can begin playing them as soon as possible. Installation of the games is automated by the disk installation program.

What's on the Disk

The software provided on this book's disk can be divided into several categories. To help you decide what portions to install, see the following descriptions of what is on the game disk.

Games

You should install the executable games. You don't need Visual Basic to play the games, but you do need Microsoft Windows 3.1. The games require about 2 megabytes of disk space.

Source

I include source code for each game, which consists of the necessary makefiles, forms, images, and basic files. The source is well-commented and an excellent learning tool. Although some of the source code is given in the book, having it on disk makes it easier for you to examine or modify the games. Installing the source requires another 2.5 megabytes of disk space.

Installation

Installation of the games is automated by the disk installation program. The games are compressed, so you must run the install program to load the games to your hard disk. To install the games, perform the following steps:

➡️ Run Microsoft Windows (usually by typing **WIN** at the DOS prompt).

➡️ In the Program Manager, choose the Run command from the File menu.

➡️ In the Run dialog box, type the letter of the floppy drive containing the game disk; follow it with a colon, a backslash, and the word INSTALL. For example, if the game disk is in drive A, you would type **A:\INSTALL**.

➡️ Press Enter, or click the OK button.

➡️ The installation program guides you through the rest of the installation.

> You can run the installation program again later if you want to install parts of the disk that you're skipping now.

Installing the Drivers

Joysticks and sound go hand-in-hand with games and game playing. By default, however, Windows does not come with a joystick driver. And, if you aren't lucky enough to have a sound card (such as a Sound Blaster), you won't be able to play wave (WAV) files, either. Fortunately, Microsoft has released a joystick driver and a PC Speaker driver to the public domain. They are included with this book. This section helps you get them installed and running on your system.

Installing the Joystick Driver

To install the Joystick Driver and make it available for the joystick and Space Miner programs, perform the following steps:

➡️ Run the Windows Control Panel and select the DRIVERS CONTROL program. Select the Add... button, and choose the Unlisted or Updated Driver selection.

➡️ Specify the directory that contains this book's games. The listbox should contain the JOYSTICK.DRV file—select it.

➡️ After you have answered the joystick setup questions, the joystick driver will be listed along with your other installed drivers.

⮞ Exit Windows.

⮞ Copy the JOYSTICK.CPL file to your Windows SYSTEM directory, and restart Windows.

⮞ Select Calibrate ... to calibrate your joystick. You will be asked to move the joystick to each of the four corners, which will properly establish the X, Y, and Z variable ranges.

⮞ Select Test to test your joystick after you have calibrated it. This program is similar to the joystick test program described in this chapter. If you can move the cursor around the edges of the box, and the cursor is centered when your joystick is centered, the calibration is correct.

⮞ Run the Windows Control Panel again. The Joystick Calibration application appears (the icon is a joystick). Double-click the joystick to run the program.

The joystick driver should be calibrated each time you begin a new Windows session (or before you use the driver with an application).

Installing the PC Speaker Driver

To install the PC Speaker Driver and make it available for the Sounds and Space Miner programs, perform the following steps:

⮞ Run the Windows Control Panel and the Drivers configuration program. Select the Add... button and choose the Unlisted or Updated Driver selection.

⮞ Specify the directory in which you installed the book games. The listbox should now contain the SPEAKER.DRV file—select it.

⮞ After you have answered the speaker setup questions, the speaker driver is listed with your other installed drivers.

⮞ Restart Windows.

Now, the speaker driver is available to programs playing wave files, such as the SOUNDS program at the end of this chapter.

Playing the Games

Once the installation program is finished (and you elect to install the game executables), you can run any of the games by double-clicking one of the game icons. All of the games are placed in a new program group named "Programming Games." Read the description and instructions for each game in the book, or use the game help option.

Alternatively, if you install the game source, you can load the game into Visual Basic and select the Start command or button.

Modifying the Games

Playing the games is only a small part of what this book is about. Once you are familiar with how the games are played, you might want to modify the games. You are encouraged to do so. Have the peace of mind that if you run into trouble, you will still have the game listing in the book and the original game on the game disk. If you need ideas, see the end of each game section for suggestions on improving the game. You can make the games easier, more challenging, or simply different.

To modify a game, load the appropriate makefile by using the Open Project option of the Visual Basic File menu. This loads the code and forms for your perusal. The source filenames and meanings are given in Table A.1.

Table A.1. Source filenames and their meanings.

Name	Meaning
*.MAK	Project (make) file
*.BAS	Global modules (definitions)
*.FRM	Forms
*.BMP	Images
*.ICO	Icons

Remember that the image and icon files are imbedded into the game form when they are first loaded; to edit them, you'll need the original files. You can edit image (BMP) files with the Windows Paintbrush accessory program, and the icon (ICO) files with the Visual Basic IconWorks example program.

Windows API

This appendix provides a reference for all of the Windows API (Application Programming Interface) function calls used in this book. These functions are stored in the Windows DLLs (Dynamic Link Libraries). Your Visual Basic manual dedicates an entire chapter to declaring and calling a DLL procedure, so be sure to read it over.

BitBlt

The BitBlt function (short for Bit Block Transfer, and usually pronounced *Bit Blit*) copies a rectangular bitmap block of pixels from one location to another. This function is used for animating sprites and images.

Declaration

```
Declare Function BitBlt% Lib "GDI" (ByVal hDestDC%, ByVal dx%,
➡ByVal dy%, ByVal nWidth%, ByVal nHeight%, ByVal hSrcDC%,
➡ByVal sx%, ByVal sy%, ByVal dwRop&)
```

Parameter	Description
hDestDC%	hDC property of the destination form or picture control
dx%, dy%	Upper-left coordinate of the destination region
nWidth%, nHeight%	Width and height of the image region being copied (transferred)
hSrcDC%	hDC property of the source form or picture control
sx%, sy%	Upper-left coordinate of the source region
dwRop&	Raster operation (logical operation) to use during the transfer. Usually one of
	SRCCOPY (&H00CC0020) ' Dest = Src
	SRCAND (&H008800C6) ' Dest = Src AND Dest
	SRCPAINT (&H00EE0086) ' Dest = Src OR Dest
	SRCINVERT (&H00660046).' Dest = Src XOR Dest

The BitBlt function returns True (nonzero) if successful, and zero otherwise.

Usage

The BitBlt function is used by the following programs and games:

Animation (ANIM.MAK), Puzzler (PUZZLER.MAK), Slider (SLIDER.MAK), and Space Miner (MINER.MAK).

ClientToScreen

The ClientToScreen subroutine converts the coordinates of a point on a form to screen coordinates. This is useful when you need to know the exact location of a point on the screen, rather than a point coordinate relative to the upper-left coordinate of the form.

Declaration

```
Declare Sub ClientToScreen Lib "User" (ByVal hWnd%, Pt As APIPOINT)
```

Parameter	Description
hWnd%	hWnd property of the form

Pt As APIPOINT	A point structure containing the coordinates of the form point location. This structure has the following format:
	
	`Type APIPOINT`
	`  x As Integer`
	`  y As Integer`
	`End Type`

The ClientToScreen routine replaces the coordinates in the APIPOINT structure with the equivalent screen coordinates. The screen coordinates are relative to the upper-left corner of the screen.

Usage

The ClientToScreen routine is used by the following programs and games:

Bricks (BRICKS.MAK) and Ping (PING.MAK).

ClipCursorClear

The ClipCursorClear routine is an alternate declaration for the ClipCursorRect function. This function clears cursor clipping, which frees the mouse cursor (pointer) so that it can move freely about the entire screen.

Declaration

`Declare Sub ClipCursorClear Lib "User" Alias "ClipCursor" (ByVal Rect&)`

Parameter	Description
Rect&	This is a placeholder for the rectangle structure. Always pass 0 to clear the cursor clipping.

The ClipCursorClear function does not return anything.

Usage

The ClipCursorClear routine is used by the following programs and games:

Bricks (BRICKS.MAK) and Ping (PING.MAK).

See Also

ClipCursorRect

ClipCursorRect

The ClipCursorRect routine clips (restricts) the mouse cursor (pointer) to the inside of the specified rectangle. To stop cursor clipping, call the ClipCursorClear routine.

Declaration

Declare Sub ClipCursorRect Lib "User" Alias "ClipCursor"(Rect As APIRECT)

Parameter	Description

Rect As APIRECT	A rectangular structure used to pass the screen coordinates of the confining rectangle. This structure has the following format:
	
	Type APIRECT
	  x1 As Integer
	  y1 As Integer
	  x2 As Integer
	  y2 As Integer
	End Type

The ClipCursorRect function does not return anything.

Usage

The ClipCursorRect routine is used by the following programs and games:

Bricks (BRICKS.MAK) and Ping (PING.MAK).

See Also

ClipCursorRect, ClientToScreen

GetProfileInt

The GetProfileInt function gets the integer value of an entry within a specified area of the Windows initialization file WIN.INI.

Declaration

```
Declare Function GetProfileInt% Lib "Kernel" (ByVal AppName$,
➥ByVal KeyName$, ByVal DefaultVal%)
```

Parameter	Description
AppName$	Title of the section (application name) containing the entry to retrieve
KeyName$	Name of the Entry (key name) whose value is to be retrieved
DefaultVal%	Default value to return if the entry cannot be found

The GetProfileInt function returns the integer value of the string following the key name entry. It will return the default value if the key name is not found. If the key name found is not an integer, zero is returned.

Usage

The GetProfileInt function is used by the following programs and games:

Space Miner (MINER.MAK).

See Also

WriteProfileString

GetSystemMetrics

The GetSystemMetrics function retrieves the system metrics, which are the widths and heights of the various elements displayed by Windows.

Declaration

```
Declare Function GetSystemMetrics% Lib "USER" (ByVal nIndex%)
```

Parameter	Description
nIndex%	Index representing the system measurement to be retrieved. All measurements are given in pixels. There are numerous index values, but the ones used in the programs in this book are the caption height SM_CYCAPTION (4) and the menu height SM_CYMENU (15).

The GetSystemMetrics function returns the requested system metric if the function is successful. The values returned will depend on the type of screen and may vary from system to system.

Usage

The GetSystemMetrics function is used by the following programs and games:

Puzzler (PUZZLER.MAK)

joyGetDevCaps

The joyGetDevCaps function queries a joystick device to determine its capabilities. The most important of the capabilities are the maximum horizontal and vertical unit values.

Declaration

```
Declare Function joyGetDevCaps% Lib "MMSystem" (ByVal JoyId%,
➡JCaps As JOYCAPS, ByVal CapSize%)
```

Parameter	Description
JoyId%	Identifies the joystick device to be queried, which is one of JOYSTICKID1 (0), or JOYSTICKID2 (1)
JCaps As JOYCAPS	Specifies a joystick capabilities' structure to be filled in. This structure looks like

```
'Type JOYCAPS
    Mid As Integer           ' Manufacturer ID
    Pid As Integer           ' Product ID
    Pname As String * 32     ' Product name
    Xmin As Integer          ' Min and max
    Xmax As Integer          '  positions
    Ymin As Integer
    Ymax As Integer
    Zmin As Integer
    Zmax As Integer
    NumButtons As Integer ' # of buttons
    PeriodMin As Integer   ' Min msg period
    PeriodMax As Integer   ' Max msg period
End Type
```

CapSize%	JOYCAPS structure size, which is defined as JOYCAPSIZE (54).

The joyGetDevCaps function returns JOYERR_NOERROR (0) if successful. Otherwise, it returns an error code.

Usage

The joyGetDeviceCaps function is used by the following programs and games:

Joystick (JOYSTICK.MAK) and Space Miner (MINER.MAK).

See Also

joyGetPos

joyGetPos

The joyGetPos function queries for the position and button activity of the joystick device.

Declaration

```
Declare Function joyGetPos% Lib "MMSystem" (ByVal JoyId%,
➡JPos As JOYPOS)
```

Parameter	Description
JoyId%	Identifies the joystick device to be queried, which is one of JOYSTICKID1 (0), or JOYSTICKID2 (1)
JPos As JOYPOS	Specifies a joystick position information structure to be filled in. This structure looks like

```
Type JOYPOS
  X As Integer              ' X, Y, & Z values
  Y As Integer
  Z As Integer
  Buttons As Integer        ' Button states
End Type
```

The Buttons field contains the current button status, which you can test against JOY_BUTTON1 (&H1) or JOY_BUTTON2 (&H2). If successful, the joyGetPos function returns JOYERR_NOERROR (0). Otherwise, it returns an error code.

Usage

The joyGetPos function is used by the following programs and games:

Joystick (JOYSTICK.MAK) and Space Miner (MINER.MAK).

mciSendString&

The mciSendString& function sends a command string to an MCI (Media Control Interface) device. In this book, the SEQUENCER device is used to play MIDI (Musical Instrument Digital Interface) music.

Declaration

```
Declare Function mciSendString& Lib "MMSystem" (ByVal SendString$,
➡ByVal ReturnString$, ByVal ReturnLength%, ByVal Callback%)
```

Parameter	Description
SendString$	Specifies an MCI command string. The commands used in this book are OPEN , PLAY, STOP, and CLOSE.
ReturnString&	Specifies a string for return information
ReturnLength%	Length of return string ReturnString&
Callback%	A handle to a window to call back. This parameter cannot be used by Visual Basic, so it must be zero (0).

The mciSendString& function returns zero if the function was successful. Otherwise, it returns error information.

Usage

The mciSendString& function is used by the following programs and games:

Sounds (SOUNDS.MAK) and Space Miner (MINER.MAK).

See Also

MessageBeep, sndPlaySound

MessageBeep

The MessageBeep routine plays a wave file sound matching a given system alert level. The sound for each alert level is listed in the [sounds] section of the WIN.INI file. The sounds can be changed by editing WIN.INI, or by using the Windows Control Panel.

Declaration

```
Declare Sub MessageBeep Lib "User" (ByVal BeepType%)
```

Parameter	Description
BeepType%	Specifies the beep type (alert level) to play, which is one of:

MB_DEFBEEP	(-1) 'PC Speaker Beep
MB_ICONASTERISK	(64)
MB_ICONEXCLAMATION	(48)
MB_ICONHAND	(16)
MB_ICONQUESTION	(32)
MB_OK	(0)

The MessageBeep routine first tries to play the alert sound, and if it can't, it tries to play the system default sound. As a last resort, it will produce a standard beep sound by using the PC Speaker.

Usage

The MessageBeep routine is used by the following programs and games:

Sounds (SOUNDS.MAK).

See Also

mciSendString, sndPlaySound

ShowCursor

The ShowCursor routine shows or hides the mouse cursor (pointer).

Declaration

Declare Sub ShowCursor Lib "User" (ByVal bShow%)

Parameter	Description
bShow%	Boolean flag indicating whether to show the mouse pointer (True), or hide it (False).

A cursor show-level count is kept internally, so that if the cursor is hidden twice, it has to be shown twice for the cursor to appear again. This is useful when a routine hides the mouse cursor, and then calls a routine that also hides the cursor. The ShowCursor function returns the current show-level count, if successful.

Usage

The ShowCursor function is used by the following programs and games:

Bricks (BRICKS.MAK) and Ping (PING.MAK).

sndPlaySound

The sndPlaySound function plays a wave file specified by a filename, or an entry in the [sounds] section of WIN.INI.

Declaration

```
Declare Function sndPlaySound% Lib "MMSystem" (ByVal WaveFile$, ByVal
➡Flags%)
```

Parameter	Description
WaveFile$	The name of the sound to play
Flag%	Specifies the sound flags, which are one or more of the following: SND_SYNC (0) ' Play synchronously SND_ASYNC (1) ' Play asynchronously SND_NODEFAULT (2) ' No default sound SND_LOOP (8) ' Loop indefinitely SND_NOSTOP (16) ' No stop of current

Most of the time, the SND_ASYNC flag is used to play music in the background. The SND_NODEFAULT flag avoids playing the default sound or the PC speaker beep, if the wave file sound cannot be found. The SND_NOSTOP flag causes the function to return without playing the requested sound if a sound is currently playing. The sndPlaySound function returns True if the sound is played; otherwise it returns False.

Usage

The sndPlaySound function is used by the following programs and games:

Sounds (SOUNDS.MAK) and Space Miner (MINER.MAK).

See Also

MessageBeep, mciSendString

WriteProfileString

The WriteProfileString routine writes a string into the specified section of the Windows Initialization file, WIN.INI.

Declaration

```
Declare Sub WriteProfileString Lib "Kernel" (ByVal AppName$,
➡ByVal KeyName$, ByVal KeyStr$)
```

Parameter	Description
AppName$	Title of the section (application name) containing the entry to write
KeyName$	Name of the Entry (key name) whose value is to be associated with the key string
KeyStr$	Key string to be written to the file. If this string is NULL (""), the KeyName$ field is deleted.

The format of the section is as follows:

```
[AppName$]
KeyName$ = KeyStr$
```

If the section does not exist, it will be created. If it already exists, the previous key string is overwritten. The WriteProfileString function returns a nonzero value if successful, and zero otherwise.

Usage

The WriteProfileString function is used by the following programs and games:

Space Miner (MINER.MAK).

See Also

GetProfileInt

INDEX

LoadPicture function, 83-84

M

manual lookups, 419

mapping texture, 95

masks for sprites, 37-39

MaximumMove function, 192

MB_DEFBEEP constant, 66

MB_ICONASTERISK constant, 66

MB_ICONEXCLAMATION constant, 66

MB_ICONHAND constant, 66

MB_ICONQUESTION constant, 66

MCI (Media Control Interface), 69-70

MIDI Sequencer, 70-71

mciSendString function, 69

mciSendString& function, 444

MessageBeep function, 66-67, 444-445

methods

Drag and Drop, 33-35, 42

Move, 33, 42, 291

MIDI (Musical Instrument Digital Interface), 69-70

Sequencer, 70-71

sound cards, Space Miner, 401-402

MINER.EXE file, 388

Missile Master (Scott A. Murray), 426-431

mnu_Load_Click routine, 337

mnu_NewGame_Click function, 290, 381, 399

mnu_Pause_Click routine, 381, 400

mnu_Rules function, 291, 337, 401

mnu_Scramble_Click routine, 337

morphing, 96

mouse

Bricks, 382

Ping, 371-372

pointers

Apples & Oranges, 171

controls, 11

Flip, 189

screens, 12

Slider, 291

types, 10-11

procedures, 9-10

Windows API functions, 12-13

MouseDown procedure, 10

MouseMove procedure, 10

MousePointer property, 189

MouseUp procedure, 10

Move method, 33, 42, 291

MoveBall routine, 372

moving controls, 32-33

multiplayer games, 96-97

Murray, Scott A. (Missile Master), 426-431

music, 69-71

Musical Instrument Digital Interface, *see* MIDI

Add to Your Sams Library Today with the Best Books for Programming, Operating Systems, and New Technologies

The easiest way to order is to pick up the phone and call

1-800-428-5331

between 9:00 a.m. and 5:00 p.m. EST.

For faster service please have your credit card available.

ISBN	Quantity	Description of Item	Unit Cost	Total Cost
0-672-30378-7		Teach Yourself Visual Basic 3.0 in 21 Days	$29.95	
0-672-30259-4		Do-It-Yourself Visual Basic for Windows, 2E	$24.95	
0-672-30145-8		Visual Basic for Windows Developer's Guide (Book/Disk)	$34.95	
0-672-30100-8		Extending Visual Basic for Windows (Book/Disk)	$39.95	
0-672-30138-5		Secrets of the Visual Basic for Windows Master's (Book/Disk)	$39.95	
0-672-30309-4		Programming Sound for DOS and Windows (Book/Disk)	$39.95	
0-672-30288-8		DOS Secrets Unleashed (Book/Disk)	$39.95	
0-672-30269-1		Absolute Beginner's Guide to Programming	$19.95	
0-672-30326-4		Absolute Beginner's Guide to Networking	$19.95	
0-672-30341-8		Absolute Beginner's Guide to C	$16.95	
0-672-27366-7		Memory Management for All of Us	$29.95	
0-672-30190-3		Windows Resource and Memory Management	$29.95	
0-672-30249-7		Multimedia Madness! (Book/Disk/CD-ROM)	$44.95	
0-672-30248-9		Fractal Vision (Book/Disk)	$39.95	
0-672-30040-0		Teach Yourself C in 21 Days	$24.95	
0-672-30324-8		Teach Yourself QBasic in 21 Days	$24.95	

❏ 3 ½" Disk

❏ 5 ¼" Disk

Shipping and Handling: See information below.	
TOTAL	

Shipping and Handling: $4.00 for the first book, and $1.75 for each additional book. Floppy disk: add $1.75 for shipping and handling. If you need to have it NOW, we can ship the product to you in 24 hours for an additional charge of approximately $18.00, and you will receive your item overnight or in two days. Overseas shipping and handling adds $2.00 per book and $8.00 for up to three disks. Prices subject to change. Call for availability and pricing information on latest editions.

11711 N. College Avenue, Suite 140, Carmel, Indiana 46032

1-800-428-5331 — Orders   1-800-835-3202 — FAX   1-800-858-7674 — Customer Service

Book ISBN 0-672-30313-2

.at's on the Disk

➡ All the games discussed in the book. You don't need to be a programmer or own Visual Basic to play the games.

➡ All the code from the programs discussed in this book.

➡ Beautiful, professionally drawn card images you can use in your own games.

Installing the Floppy Disk

The software included with this book is stored in a compressed form. You must run the installation program on the floppy disk to install the software to your hard drive. To install the files, you'll need at least 4.2M of free space on your hard drive.

1. From Windows File Manager or Program Manager, choose **File Run** from the menu.

2. Type **<drive>INSTALL** and press Enter. *<drive>* is the letter of the drive that contains the installation disk. For example, if the disk is in drive B:, type **B:\INSTALL** and press Enter.

3. You will be asked to choose a Full Install or Custom Install. The Custom Install enables you to install just the source code or executables. Choose Full Install, unless you are low on hard disk space.

Follow the on-screen instructions in the install program. The files will be installed to a directory named \PGB, unless you changed this name during the install program.

When the installation is complete, the file README.TXT is displayed for you to read. This file contains important information on the files and programs that were installed.